THE MAGIC
BEHIND
THE VOICES

THE MAGIC BEHIND THE VOICES

A WHO'S WHO OF CARTOON VOICE ACTORS

TIM LAWSON
AND ALISA PERSONS

UNIVERSITY PRESS OF MISSISSIPPI / JACKSON

www.upress.state.ms.us

The University Press of Mississippi is a member of the
Association of American University Presses.

All photographs courtesy of Tim Lawson
unless otherwise noted

12 11 10 09 08 07 06 05 04   4 3 2 1

Library of Congress Cataloging-in-Publication Data

Lawson, Tim, 1961–
  The magic behind the voices : a who's who of cartoon voice actors / Tim Lawson
and Alisa Persons.
    p. cm.
  Includes filmographies.
  Includes bibliographical references and index.
  ISBN 1-57806-695-6 (alk. paper) — ISBN 1-57806-696-4 (pbk. : alk. paper)
    1. Voice actors and actresses—United States—Biography—Dictionaries. 2. Animated
films—United States. 3. Animated television programs—United States. I. Persons,
Alisa, 1964– II. Title.
  PN2285.L38 2004
  791.4302′8′092273—dc22   2004006488

British Library Cataloging-in-Publication Data available

CONTENTS

PREFACE

CARTOONS HAVE NO LIFE-SPAN. THEY LIVE FOREVER.

—JOE BARBERA

I grew up as part of the Hanna-Barbera generation. Although I was partial to *The Jetsons*, Wally Gator, Lippy the Lion, *Jonny Quest*, and *The New Scooby-Doo* movies (How can you not be enthralled by the prospect of Scooby and the gang solving a mystery with Mama Cass?), my all-time favorite cartoon was *The Flintstones*. I must have seen every episode at least thirty times, never tiring of the Hatrocks, Mr. Slate, the Way Outs, or Joe Rockhead. Even though most fans despised the episodes with the Great Gazoo, who showed up in season six, I loved them. You can imagine my excitement when, in 1972, my parents took me to Custer, South Dakota, to visit Flintstone Village, a tourist attraction (or "trap" as my father called it) which was a replica of the town of Bedrock. There were stone houses, a stone bank, and a stone theater, which showed *The Flintstones* exclusively. The best part of it all was the fact that they had Fred's and Barney's cars, which were street legal (on any given day, you could see them motoring around Custer). Little did I know at the time that my fascination with the inhabitants of Bedrock would lead to the book you now hold in your hands.

In 1984, I happened to catch an episode of *The Flintstones*, and, having seen it many times before, I found myself not so much watching the show as listening to it. I became engrossed in the performance of Alan Reed and thought, "I know the voice is perfect for Fred Flintstone, but is it perfect for Alan Reed?" How did Reed look? I figured it would be easy to find the answers to my questions by heading out to my local library (at the time, there was no luxury of surfing the Internet). I was surprised to find that not only was there nothing available on Reed, there was nothing available on any voice-over artists, save for the stray tidbit about Mel Blanc.

I decided that if I was curious about my favorite voice actors, others would be interested as well. That is when I decided to take on this project. I had no idea where to begin until I found a book about animated shows in general. The book had nothing on the actors themselves, but it did have one valuable piece of information—the credits! That is when I first became aware of a man named Daws Butler. Butler's name was associated with almost every cartoon Hanna-Barbera made, as well as dozens of cartoons from just about every other studio. Since Reed had died in 1977, Butler was the logical person with whom to start.

I called the Screen Actors Guild to see if I could get a contact for Butler. The conversation went something like this:

TIM: Hello, I'm trying to locate Mr. Daws Butler.
S.A.G.: Checking. . . . Sorry, we have no listing for a Doug Butler.
TIM: No, it's *Daws* Butler. He does the voices for Yogi Bear, Huckleberry Hound, Snagglepuss, and dozens of other characters.
S.A.G.: Oh, well, no wonder I can't find him. We don't consider voice people to be actors.

I was speechless. How could the Screen Actors Guild not consider these great talents to be actors? I was discouraged, but I decided to give it one last try. On impulse (I was young and very naïve) I packed up my car and drove 2,400 miles to Los Angeles to see if I could get this project off the ground.

I remembered seeing Jay Ward Studios with its giant statue of Rocky and Bullwinkle on Sunset Boulevard on a trip to Los Angeles with my parents in 1977, so I used that as a starting point. I arrived and nervously walked to the entrance of the small, brown building and knocked on the front door. A very nice gentleman answered and asked me to come in. To my surprise, the man turned out to be Bill Hurtz, who directed many of the *Bullwinkle* episodes. The director asked me to excuse the mess and gave me a tour of the building, which looked like a rundown workshop with cereal boxes and bits of animation lying around on antiquated light tables. He then informed me that my timing couldn't have been better, as the studio was closing for good in one week. He was in the process of finishing up some animation for a Capt'n Crunch commercial, but took time out to listen to my idea for a book about voice-over actors and agreed that it was a project that was a long time coming.

I was extremely grateful that I hadn't missed my window of opportunity by showing up a week later, because walking through the door of Jay Ward Studios was like walking into a gold mine. (Incidentally, the last time I saw Jay Ward Studios, in the mid-1990s, although the Bullwinkle cast's hand-prints and autographs still graced the cement under the Bullwinkle statue, the building was, in an act of blasphemy, occupied by a psychic and Tarot card reader. I could almost hear narrator William Conrad punning, "Tune in next time for 'I Get a Psychic Out of You,' or 'Tarots the Neighborhood.'") After patiently listening to everything I had to say, Mr. Hurtz quietly walked to his desk, pulled out his Rolodex, and proceeded to give me the home phone numbers of the greatest voice-over artists in the history of animation. I walked out the door with the private numbers of Daws Butler, June Foray, and Paul Frees.

But what started out so easily in 1984 soon became fraught with obstacles too convoluted to discuss here. The project languished on the shelf until 1990, after I met my co-author, Alisa Persons, while in college. Alisa, a fellow film student at Columbia College who was working in the Animation Department at the time, liked the idea of the book and took on the task of co-author. Dozens of interviews and more stops and starts later, the finished product lies before you. What was originally intended to be an entertaining collection of voice-actor biographies also addresses an area in animation history which has not been definitively examined—how cartoons are created from the point of view of the voice artists.

Like the accounts of animators in previously published memoirs, the recollections of the featured artists are subject to memory and their individual experiences. Consequently, no one individual's accounts may entirely match another's or what has necessarily been reported in other sources. Some of the comments might be considered controversial and are meant solely as a reflection of the individual's opinions and experiences. Although many of the people I have interviewed over the years are no longer with us, their spirit lives on through their work and I hope we have done justice to their memory and to the actors who continue to entertain the world for decades to come.

—**TIM LAWSON**
March 2003

ACKNOWLEDGMENTS

Firstly, a big thank-you to our editor, Craig Gill, as well as Alison Sullenberger, Anne Stascavage, Walter Biggins, and all of the staff at the University Press of Mississippi and our copyeditor, Karen Johnson, for your patience and consideration.

Also, a very heartfelt thank-you to all of the people in the animation industry who have actively supported this project over the many, many years it has been in production and who have kindly invited the authors to speak with them and observe them at work. Among those who deserve special recognition are director Bill Hurtz of Jay Ward Studios, Mr. and Mrs. Jay Ward, Alex Lovy, the extraordinary staff at Hanna-Barbera, Joe Barbera, Maggie Roberts, and, especially, Gordon Hunt, who allowed Tim to meet the original cast and sit between Daws Butler and Janet Waldo at a 1984 taping of *The Jetsons*. We also appreciate the time and consideration of voice directors Susan Blu, Ginny McSwain, Andrea Romano, and Kris Zimmerman, who were very generous with their time.

Of course, one of the biggest thank-yous goes to Daws Butler for being such a generous person—not only allowing the first interview for the project, but bestowing his blessing on it. Similarly, kudos to his number one protégé, Nancy Cartwright, for her extreme generosity and for giving us one of the most unforgettable moments of our lives by graciously allowing us ringside seats to watch a part of the production for a classic episode of *The Simpsons*. Among the voice actors, a very special thank-you goes to Kath Soucie, Maurice LaMarche, and Rob Paulsen, who were very kind in connecting us with some of their contemporaries. To all the voice actors, although we can only portray a very small slice of your lives, we have done our best to do justice to your stories in the limitations of this format.

To the families of the voices who have since been silenced, thank-you for taking the time to share personal stories—especially, thanks to Dino Andrade, Thor Arngrim, Myrtis and Charles Butler; Fred Frees, George O'Hanlon Jr., Laurie O'Hanlon, Nancy O'Hanlon, Charles Howerton, Jeanette McFadden, and Virginia Mercer.

Among the especially helpful agents are Marcia Hurwitz, Don Pitts, Larry Robbins, Sandy Schnarr, Arlene Thornton, and Cory Weisman, who were instrumental in making some of the necessary connections.

With regard to the technical aspects, we would also like to acknowledge Steve Levin, who assisted in proofreading, Paul Lisnik, Keir Walton, Dick Moore of AFTRA, Ron Harvey of the Everett Collection, Claudia Smith of King Features, Steven Worth of John Kricfalusi's studio, Mark Evanier, Fred Grandinetti, Jerry Beck, Joe Bevilacqua, Doreen Mulman (who currently maintains the web sites of several voice actors, including those of Mary Kay Bergman, Charlie Adler, and Frank Welker), and Patrick Owsley. Thank-you to Tim Hollis, who made the referral to our editor (Mr. Hollis is author of *Hi There, Boy and Girls!* also available through the University Press of Mississippi). A special thank-you to Rick Goldschmidt, author of *The Enchanted World of Rankin/Bass*, who provided contacts, photos, and invaluable information (www.rankinbass.com). Also, we would like to thank the following people for their encouragement and moral support: Jim Seavey, Randall Terrock, Dann Fox, Jill Ahlgren, and Jeff Korpi.

On a personal level, Alisa owes more than a debt of gratitude to her family, especially (diligent proofreader) Alimae and Richard Persons, for their immeasurable financial and moral support. Alisa also appreciates the emotional support lent by Allen, Amy, Ashley, Alex, Michael, Akemi, Katrina, and Justin Persons! An additional thank-you goes to the relevant staff at Columbia College, especially the talented and amazing Stan Hughes, Gordon Sheehan, Barry Young, and at the University of Wisconsin, Superior, Dianna Hunter, William Morgan, Tim Cleary, Brent Notbohm (co-editor of *Steven Spielberg: Interviews*, Conversations with Filmmakers Series, also from the University Press of Mississippi), and Thomas Notton.

Tim would like to acknowledge the memory of his mother, Rita Lawson, who always put the needs of her nine children before her own, and his brother, John Lawson, who had a thirst for knowledge, a kind heart, and showed by example what it is to be a good person. Tim would also like to thank Richard and Alimae Persons for their kind generosity and support during the crucial developmental years of this project. Thank-you to my brothers, Ron, Roger, Bill, Joe, and Bernie, and my sisters, Ann Reuter and Mary Troye. Lastly, I would like to thank my wife, Christine, whose love and support I could not do without.

INTRODUCTION

Since the beginning of animation, of the hundreds of people who traditionally worked on cartoons, usually it was only the executives or the directors who were given screen credit, leaving the general public none the wiser. Although it has been noted that a good vocal performance can save a mediocre cartoon or even elevate a good cartoon to a great one, especially when the animation is very limited, there are many reasons why producers were motivated from the very start to keep the voice actors anonymous.

In spite of the fact that animation is now often discussed as an art form, it has always been a business first, with none of the animators or voice artists among the most recognized. It has been suggested that keeping the voice talent anonymous ensured that other studios could not target actors to hire them away; however, the producer may also have wanted to ensure that the public could not associate the part with a specific person, as it could give the actor leverage to ask for more money. The earliest case in point might be the early Fleischer brothers' *Popeye* cartoons of the late 1930s. According to Leslie Cabarga, the author of *The Fleischer Story*, actor William Costello performed the title voice until "success went to his head" and he was judged "too difficult" to work with. Consequently, when *Popeye* animator and writer Jack Mercer was hired away from the drawing board to continue the role for the next five decades, he did not receive screen recognition until the animated character made a cameo appearance in the 1980 Robert Altman live-action film. In fact, this dynamic is still very much in evidence even for an entity that has met with as much commercial success as *The Simpsons*. During the 1998 pay dispute between the Fox network and the voice actors, after nine years of work on the most successful comedy running, the cast was reportedly threatened by network executives that should they not reach an agreement, adequate replacements for the voice talent could be found at "any college campus."

Not long after the animation industry began in earnest, labor struggles began among the production staff; recognition, of course, was an issue that lagged behind better wages and working conditions. Actors' unions had existed from the late nineteenth century when the American Federation of Labor issued a charter to the Associated Actors and Artistes of America to represent the performers of the time; stage actors and vaudevillians had divergent interests and they split into Actor's Equity and the American Guild of Variety. With the invention of radio and film, the separation continued with the Screen Actors Guild created to handle film actors while radio performers were then represented by AFRA—the American Federation of Radio Artists.

Who better among the voice-over artists to take on the establishment than "Bluto," i.e., animation and radio veteran Jackson Beck? Beck, who was a charter member of AFRA, went on to become one of the founders of the American Federated Television and Radio Artists when television representation was incorporated into AFRA in 1952. The holder of AFTRA card number two (after the organizer, Broadway actor George Heller), Beck served in various executive capacities within the union, including that of president in the 1970s. Over seven decades later, the union that Beck helped found remains a powerful organization, not just for animation actors but for all represented recording and broadcasting artists.

Not surprisingly, it was the man who is still the most recognizable name in cartoon voice acting who actively challenged the culture of anonymity for animation actors. In 1942, Mel Blanc and his wife, Estelle, tried unsuccessfully to negotiate a raise from notoriously tight-fisted Warner Bros. executive Leon Schlesinger. In his 1988 autobiography, *That's Not All Folks*, Blanc quoted Schlesinger as replying to the request with "What do you want more money for, Mel? You'll only have to pay more taxes." Blanc, who was not naïve enough to be duped by that strategy, had a sudden inspiration and struck a bargain that cost the studio no more money but paid off for him in more ways than he could have imagined. After the Warner Bros. shorts were graced with the screen credit "Voice Characterizations by Mel Blanc," he was inundated with more offers of work than he could handle, which, he concluded, more than made up for any raise the studio could have offered.

Although it set a precedent for voice artists in general, it was also detrimental to the other Warner's actors as the blanket credit gave the false impression that Blanc did all the voices for the classic Warner's shorts—which, of course, is denying all the remarkable performances of icons like June Foray, Daws Butler, Arthur Q. Bryan, and others. In fact, Walter Lantz granted Daws Butler credit for the *Chilly Willy* theatrical shorts and June Foray credit for her work in the *Woody Woodpecker* cartoons, but, aside from that, Blanc was virtually the only voice actor credited for more than a decade in film or television until Hanna-Barbera recognized Daws Butler and Don Messick for their television work in the late 1950s. That Blanc's name is still more readily recognizable to the general public than even the most successful and versatile contemporary voice artist working today may be as much due to this one genius stroke of self-promotion as to his undeniably colossal talent.

Although very much behind the scenes, voice actors have also been responsible for the evolution of some of the more technical aspects of the industry. When sound began to be incorporated in animation after the success of *The Jazz Singer*, Walt Disney himself was widely credited as the first animation voice-over artist for his portrayal of Mickey Mouse in the 1928 short *Steamboat Willie*. Although the film is commonly referred to as the first sound cartoon, there were many other studios experimenting with sound tracks recorded on various mediums. Donald Crafton, author of the book *Before Mickey*, states, "That Disney was far ahead of all other animation producers in making sound cartoons is a myth. Regardless of quality, by November 1928 both [Amadee] Van Beuren and [Charles] Mintz had announced that they had converted to all-sound production for *Aesop's Fables* and *Oswald*, although these were actually postsynchronized silent films. The Fleischer's Paramount 'Song Cartoons' began in December." Former Fleischer animator Shamus Culhane, in his book *Talking Animals and Other People*, confirms that the Fleischers were involved with sound long before Disney: "Fleischer had been dabbling in sound long before *Steamboat Willie*. Back in 1924, Max and Dave Fleischer had produced the very first sound cartoon, *Oh Mabel*." However, Culhane concludes that their efforts to master the new technology were too early and "the picture was ignored as a curiosity, not a commercial breakthrough."

Although, starting with the 1928 short, Disney had developed soundtracks parallel to the development of the picture, Jackson Beck claims that he and his *Popeye* co-stars demanded changes which may have prompted the contemporary method of animation production in which the dialogue is recorded first before the lip-sync is drawn. In the 1930s, the Fleischer's approach was to create animation "post synchronized," that is, before the soundtrack was recorded. The animator would then have to anticipate exactly how and when the mouth movements of the character would look and draw on the characters' "lip flaps," or lip movements, which the voice actor was expected to match when recording the dialogue for the scene.

Often this method did not work very well—an example of which is when the actor may have to say a word of dialogue with a "B" sound and the artist may have inadvertently drawn an "O." It was for this reason that characters in the early Fleischer *Popeye* cartoons do a lot of improvising. Star Jack Mercer had been especially noted for his witty ad-libs, but he was motivated to do them simply to find something to cover for extra mouth movements! Beck claims that he, Mercer, and (Olive Oyl) Mae Questel finally complained to Fleischer executives about the unnecessary difficulty involved in "post sync" dialogue and, therefore, helped institute the change that revamped their methods, if not the entire animation industry.

Another important element which voice actors brought to the medium was an expertise in the development of vocal characterizations for which they were trained in the heyday of radio. Before shock jocks, album-oriented rock, and call-in shows dominated the airwaves, radio programming of the 1930s and '40s consisted of popular live variety, comedy, soap operas, and other dramatic programs. It was through the many hours of acting on the popular programs of the time that Beck, Blanc, and so many of their peers learned to make their performances come to life—using only words to paint elaborate pictures and create strong characters in the listeners' minds. Obviously, this kind of skill was easily translatable and a welcome asset to the voice actor's job in the field of animation.

Like many of the early radio programs, many early cartoons were conceived primarily to entertain adults and often contained adult subject matter. (Right from the inception of animation, there were even some documented reports of at least one pornographic film that the animators—who, as a lot, were hardly tea-totalers or saints—drew for their own entertainment). The "theatricals," or animated shorts, they produced to run before films contained subject matter that could and often did include very adult themes. (Some of Fleischer's *Betty Boop* shorts, in particular, were noted for some very explicit sexual references and graphic images.) According to Fleischer scholar Leslie Cabarga, animation voice actors like Little Ann Little, who provided one of the first voices for Betty Boop, also created a vaudeville-type show to entertain mature audiences while touring with the character. Of course, as a reflection of the culture of the times, mainstream animation has at times not only been for mature audiences, but, especially from a current viewpoint, is now frequently banned for its content. The most famous of these, seen through a modern viewpoint, are unequivocally racist (Bob Clampett's *Coal Black and de Sebben Dwarfs*, Walter Lantz's *Scrub Me Momma with a Boogie Beat*), explicitly violent (suicides were not an uncommon way to end some of the Warner Bros. shorts), and often featured unflattering ethnic characterizations, evident especially during World War II in the context of wartime propaganda (*Bugs Bunny Nips the Nips, You're a Sap, Mr. Jap, Der Fuehrers Face*, etc.).

It was not until the onset of television that cartoons began to take on an entrenched kid-oriented connotation and the quality gradually declined into such a state that voice actors may have been grateful for a little anonymity. To fill programming slots for early television of the 1930s and '40s, broadcasters first used 16-mm Disney theatrical prints to supply most of the animated schedule. Aside from the occasional attempts at animation using crude paper cut-outs or magnets (Magnitoons), the major players were not interested in the expense of creating original animated programming for the "children's market," which, at the time, was considered only marginally profitable. Although ventriloquist and future voice artist Paul Winchell was among television's earliest on-air personalities, broadcasting on WABD (now WNYW) to a handful of sets in the New York area, no original made-for-television cartoons appeared until 1949 when Jay Ward created *Crusader Rabbit*. Given that the network sponsors' revenue was not very high for the children's time slot, *Crusader*'s star, the first documented television voice artist, Lucille Bliss, made a grand total of five dollars per show.

It was not until the 1950s that the animated television voice-over market was created when the demand for television animation grew. The medium then began to attract the major studios, which were seeking to use their rival to promote their theatrical products. Although Warner Bros., Paramount, and Terrytoons also sold theatrical cartoons repackaged for television, Disney was the first to form an alliance with then newcomer network ABC (which, in turn, even agreed to help fund the construction of Disneyland), and the studio's original work for television allowed Disney to keep his animators busy in the downtime between features in a time when theatrical shorts were on the wane.

Seeking cost-effective programming to fill the early Saturday morning time slot that the networks had promised the advertisers would attract children, corporate sponsors and network executives finally saw the need to produce their own cartoons, but the very limited budgets necessarily meant more limited animation. They turned to new studios like DePatie-Freleng and Hanna-Barbera, which, as the film studios gradually closed, hired the animators for television. The call from the television studios also went out for voice actors, and small-screen recording studios ultimately became the mainstay of cinema's legendary artists like Blanc, Butler, and June Foray.

But, Hanna-Barbera founders Bill Hanna and Joe Barbera, who had been let go from MGM when executives there decided there was "no future in cartoons," well understood the demands of the business side. They were successful in their 1957 introduction of *Ruff and Reddy*, a show whose limited production budget was three thousand dollars per show, but, unlike other animated programming such as *Tom Terrific* or the stylized *Gerald McBoing Boing*, was promoted as having an adult appeal. With its bare-bones animation style, it has been noted that the program's watchability and appeal depended heavily on the cornerstones of their vocal talent—Daws Butler and Don Messick. After that, Hanna-Barbera followed with shows with more adult-oriented fare, shows like *Huckleberry Hound*, *Quick Draw McGraw*, and *Yogi Bear*. Whatever the criticisms of Hanna-Barbera are, it has been lauded for creating the television animation industry (they were behind more cartoons than anyone else with a record 8,500 thirty-minute shows when they stopped production). With *Ruff and Reddy* they proved that there was a market for an adult television cartoon audience—a feat that was subsequently confirmed by the success of their primetime cartoons *Jonny Quest*, *The Flintstones*, and *The Jetsons*.

It was in the following decade that the voice actors noticed that the quality of animation had begun to decline. Despite the notable exceptions of *Roger Ramjet, Milton the Monster,* and especially *Rocky and Bullwinkle*, television animation in general gradually became eviscerated by censorship and commercialization. Theatrical and *Rocky and Bullwinkle* producer and voice-over artist Bill Scott attributed initial problems to increased production costs, which meant that quality suffered as the projects were first shipped out of the country—initially to Mexico and Japan—for production. In addition, the American studios now had to compete with "Japanimation" (what is currently termed "anime") in the form of *Astroboy, Gigantor,* and, of course, *Speed Racer*. Author Gary Grossman in *Saturday Morning TV* quoted Scott as commenting that, at the lowest point, "all the networks really wanted was 'x' number of yards of film. They'd show it on Saturday morning and they didn't care much about the quality or what it was going to do to the medium."

Grossman credits a former fan of the animated theatrical shorts, ABC programming executive Fred Silverman, with revitalizing Saturday morning animation when he arrived in 1965. Silverman was well respected in the industry for his programming creations—which included superheroes like Batman, Superman, Space Ghost, and those who were not so "super" like Scooby Doo (whom Silverman named as a homage to Frank Sinatra, referring to the "Scoobie Doobie Doo" scat line from "Strangers in the Night").

However, the violent content in the superhero cartoons meant that animation studios soon had another factor to contend with as the television industry in the late 1960s experienced an unprecedented wave of "political correctness." Violence, even in the form of "cartoon action," was now suspect after the country reeled over the assassinations of Dr. Martin Luther King and Senator Kennedy. In 1968, the Kerner commission report—the National Commission on the Causes and Prevention of Violence—concurred with several diverse groups who were concerned with the level of excessive violence in children's television. Networks then bowed to the studies, public opinion, and the newly empowered pressure groups and began to heavily censor the content of animated programming.

While it may be argued that the groups were successful in instituting several reforms in the interest of younger viewers, several voice actors working at the time were dismayed to watch their work suffer under network censorship so oppressive that even relatively innocuous "action" and dialogue were frowned upon. In the 1970s, the ABC network went so far as to state in their production guidelines that all buildings that were destroyed in the course of the story had to be rebuilt by the end of the cartoon. Michael Bell, a veteran of several action-oriented cartoons, who portrayed Lex Luthor on the Ruby-Spears production of *Superman* in the 1970s, recalled that, during that time, the most revered of all American superheroes was not allowed to break through windows to conduct a heroic rescue because he would then be guilty of property damage!

The dialogue also came under unprecedented scrutiny. Actress Marilyn Schreffler, who played Olive Oyl on the 1980s version of *Popeye*, commented on the difficulty long-time Popeye voice and story man Jack Mercer had on writing for CBS when the physical slapstick and personal insults that had pretty much constituted the *Popeye* theatrical cartoons were now taboo. She was shocked and dismayed at the fact that the censors would not allow innocuous phrases such as "Frankly, my dear, I don't give a dime," which is, of course, a takeoff on the last line of *Gone with the Wind*, and the reference to a film made over forty years before would have certainly gone over the heads of the younger set.

If animation's "Golden Age" is widely acknowledged to have happened in the films of the 1930s and '40s, by the time the commercialized '80s arrived, it was firmly entrenched in what animator auteur John Krisfaluci irreverently, but accurately, termed "the Dung Age." Former Fleischer and Disney animator Shamus Culhane was probably the most explicit in his comments in the epilogue of his 1986 book, *Animals and Other Talking People:* "The same Philistines who have generously larded our adult television shows with commercial spots for vaginal douches, pile cures, and earnest little men paddling kayaks in toilet bowls laid a heavy hand on the animation medium. . . . The frustration, the emotional and spiritual deprivation inherent in these working conditions is enormous. When there is no more rage, when there is a weary acceptance of the situation (which I find in many of my colleagues), it is a sign that the creative urge had been beaten into submission, leaving only the technical expertise. The artist has become a robot, a controllable part of a vast moneymaking machine."

This development has been attributed (in *Television and America's Children: A Crisis of Neglect*, among other sources) to the laissez-faire attitude of the Reagan administration. Despite decades of discussion on the content of ostensibly children's programming, Mark Fowler, the FCC chairman under Ronald Reagan, decreed that unregulated "market forces" alone would determine programming and "ensure the survival of the First Amendment." Accordingly, the marketplace decided that it was appropriate to allow cereal makers, toy producers, and videogame firms to fund animated programs, and there was a proliferation of shows—*He-Man, G.I. Joe, Transformers, My Little Pony*—that were conceived and funded by toy companies like Mattel and Hasbro solely as half-hour long commercials for their products.

The decades-long slide of quality may have been part of the reason that, at the time, a palpable stigma developed for actors who would work on such a troubled art form. Despite the continued brilliance and versatility of voice artists like Blanc, Butler, Foray, Frank Welker, and Don Messick, on-camera actors shunned cartoon work as it tended to imply that their careers were on a downward trend, and those who did often considered it a last resort just to make a living. Many voice actors and animators alike have commented that for much of the 1980s, there were only fleeting moments of job satisfaction and many were doing no more than collecting paychecks. (Billy West cracked that "the real artists drove cabs or something for ten years.") While the medium's quality suffered greatly under the rampant commercialism, the quantity of available work was plentiful. But even the actors reportedly also became victims of the marketing department. The most often repeated urban legend is that a voice actor once complained mid-season that her part was shrinking, only to be told that it was because "your doll is not selling."

To some extent, there are some in the industry who, up until very recently, considered animation still to be the "poor stepchild" to live-action, as evidenced by the credits or lack thereof. There have been more recent projects where the identity of the celebrity voice is obvious, or even widely publicized, but is not credited at the end of the film. (One example is Bruce Willis, Demi Moore, and David Letterman, who contributed to 1999 *Beavis and Butthead Do America* sans credits—discounting the Lettermanesque pseudonym "Earl Hofert"—although Willis did allow himself to be billed as a headliner for 2003 Wild Thornberrys/Rugrats crossover film, *Rugrats Go Wild*). When the voice actors do receive a credit, it is remarkable the many ways some of the most prominent names have been routinely misspelled. While it may be simple to see how Rob Paulsen could ultimately appear as Paulson, it is more difficult to explain how Maurice LaMarche could be listed as the phonetic spelling of "LaMarsh" or how Kath Soucie becomes "Cathy Souce" or any variation thereof.

Thankfully, animation, especially television animation, underwent a complete renaissance during the 1990s. It has been noted, with more than a little irony, that it was the Reagan administration's decision to allow the deregulation of cable which made the airing of adult-oriented shows such as *Ren & Stimpy, Beavis and Butthead*, and *South Park* even possible. Taken with the release of sophisticated feature films, the former stigma of creating animation has been fading as the current crop of creative forces—behind both the microphone and the drawing board—create cartoons that they personally enjoy. For the past decade, the medium has gradually built an unprecedented popularity and now nets billions of dollars a year largely due to this wave of creative and capable talent. Beginning arguably with the unexpected success of Don Bluth's *American Tail* in the 1980s, there have been efforts at recapturing the all-ages quality and magic of the animated feature films. While Disney always claimed that his features were made for adults, many recent efforts are now consistently attracting "A-list" celebrities who have even been known to ask their agents to secure feature roles and even guest spots on popular animated television series.

Since the resurgence, animation voice actors are now enjoying an increasing respect and growing notoriety allotted to their jobs, but the influx of celebrities has also meant that it is harder to compete for their living wages, if not the choicest parts. Celebrities have even cut into the voice actor's bread-and-butter jobs—such as commercial narration. This is because many on-camera actors have only recently realized how lucrative the pay is for the comparatively minimal time and effort spent recording voice-overs. In addition, studio executives often want a "name" with marquee value to promote their projects, and one should never discount the importance of ego gratification given producers who can then say that they worked with a bona-fide "star." All of which has become a double-edged sword for those who do voice-acting as a vocation.

After high profile successes such as *Shrek* and *Toy Story*, the then co-head of the ICM's animation department was quoted as saying that animation "is the hottest gig in show biz right now" and that when ICM has new actor clients, "they always want to get to know the animation department." But, despite the intense competition with hundreds of people often auditioning for a single part in the main voice-over production centers of Los Angeles and Canada, an ever-increasing number of people vie to enter the voice-over business. Although a guide to aspiring voice actors on how to get into the business has been the subject of entire books and is too lengthy to address in a few pages, some of the veteran animation voice actors, as among them Dick Beals (Gumby), Walter Tetley (Sherman from *Rocky and Bullwinkle*), and Janet Waldo (Judy Jetson), began their professional careers at a early age and/or got their start in the Golden Age of radio drama when the medium had just begun. There was an entire group of radio performers, including Mel Blanc, who found that as the medium was in decline, their skill of fashioning vocal characterizations was readily transferable to cartoons. While voice actors are still created in radio, now more as DJs such as Casey Kasem (*Scooby-Doo*), Neil Ross (*Transformers*), Townsend Coleman (of *The Teenage Mutant Ninja Turtles* and *The Tick*) and Billy West (*Ren & Stimpy* and *Futurama*), who graduated from a stint with Howard Stern to animation immortality, many are also former nightclub and stand-up comedy performers. Among the nightclub stand-outs are the renowned Daws Butler and multi-voiced Paul Frees. The more modern variation—the stand-up comedian—brought Frank Welker (known as much for his unique creature voices as cartoons) and relative newcomers John DiMaggio (Bender, the wise-cracking alcoholic robot from *Futurama*) and, of course, Tom Kenny, who has lent his talent to Nickelodeon's hits *Rocko's Modern Life*, *CatDog*, and the sensational success *SpongeBob Squarepants*.

Prominent voice actor Nancy Cartwright states about her profession, "It's about attitude, delivery, interpretation, making something your own, and acting, really. My first suggestion is to decide, 'Do I have the passion it takes to actually be competitive in this industry?' " (www.nancycartwright.com). For those who are convinced they have that kind of determination, there are resources available to beginners, such as books, tapes, and workshops that are produced by people who actually work in the field (e.g., voice director Susan Blu's book, *Word of Mouth,* and, what is being touted as a Daws Butler workshop by proxy, *Daws Butler's Scenes for Actors and Voices,* edited by Ben Ohmart and Joe Bevilacqua, and even general audition tips from illustrious Hanna-Barbera casting director turned sitcom director Gordon Hunt in his publication *How to Audition for TV, Movies, Commercials, Plays, and Musicals*). Needless to say, the common refrain is that the reputable workshops are often run by those who actually work and hire within the industry—established voice actors and voice directors, who include Charlie Adler, Lucille Bliss, Michael Bell, Bob Bergen, Susan Blu, Gregg Berger, Jennifer Darling, Pat Fraley, Joanie Gerber, and Stu Rosen, to name a few.

Although this book is intended to document the work of voice artists and celebrate the spirit of their art, personal stories, and professional accomplishments, there is also practical inspiration to be gleaned in their experiences and their approach to attaining success in their field. As a further word of encouragement for would-be up-and-comers, many voice actors are not Hollywood natives; and having show business connections before migrating to the Los Angeles area, although helpful, has not been a prerequisite. Unquestionably, the animation landscape would be considerably different today if, at the lowest point of his career in 1935, Mel Blanc had accepted the secure office job in Portland instead of having the persistence to endure a solid year of rejection by Warner Bros. before he was even allowed to audition.

If there is any common ground in the tightly knit community of animation's established voice actors, it is evident that they have an abundance of talent, a willingness to constantly develop that talent, and the tenacity and persistence to audition as frequently as, if not more than, their peers in on-camera acting. During the course of the interviews, the sentiment that was most often repeated was that despite the competitive nature of their field, the established voice actors consider themselves "family," and if they are not selected, they root for their friends to get the part. As Susan Blu noted in *Word of Mouth,* "As you move up in the ever-widening circle of voice-over professionals, you will have the pleasure of meeting some of the most generous and giving people in the whole world.... They are the first to celebrate your successes, and will gladly share their experience and tips with you. Secure in the knowledge of their own excellence, they have no need to distance themselves from 'the competition,' whom they regard as friends and colleagues in the business."

Voice actors even have a unique way to give back to the community in the form of Famous Fone Friends, a novel charity started by "on-set" teacher Linda Stone. The perfect venue for the voice performer, the charity asks actors of high-profile characters to brighten the day of seriously ill or injured children by discussing their interests in the voice of their favorite cartoon character.

Whether it is the nostalgic and amusing remembrances of the past from Adriana Caselotti, the star of Disney's first feature-length cartoon, *Snow White,* or what could be a future trend of animation soundtrack recording in the form of Hal Rayle and Maggie Roswell's Denver studio, which allows them to work remotely, connected to the rest of the country by phone and data transmission lines, this series is focused on the small but mostly anonymous group who have helped create the most enduring cartoon characters of all time. What is not emphasized in this book is "celebrity coverage," not just due to lack of space, but also because they have already attracted a large amount of media coverage. Of course, this is not to discount the contribution that Bill Cosby made as the creative force behind the acclaimed *Fat Albert,* including many of the character voices, or more recent high-profile turns such as former *Seinfeld* star Jason Alexander, who sputtered and blustered his way through the cult-favorite *Duckman,* and Katey Segal, who expertly voiced Leela as part of the superb ensemble cast of *Futurama.* So, this is intended to recognize, instead, the unseen half of cartoon celebrities who may not otherwise be given the celebrity treatment.

As was stated previously, when the project started, due to the lack of on-screen credit and reference materials, there was not much reliable information about animation voice actors. Therefore, often the best source was the actors themselves. Although each actor was asked about the accuracy of the credits that were compiled, sometimes they did not remember if they had done a particular voice. There were very few actors who actually kept track of all of their work—for many, it was one of many jobs they had been hired for at the time. Also, before residuals were granted to the actors, many performed for shows under a "buyout," i.e., they would be paid a flat rate for recording an entire series of shows in a matter of days. Therefore, there were no subsequent residual checks sent to them for later documentation. The credits, therefore, are a compilation of various published sources, such as Jeff Lenburg's *Encyclopedia of Animated Cartoons* as a starting point, then Hal Erickson's excellent *Television Cartoon Shows* and Graham Webb's *The Animated Film Encyclopedia,* supplemented by information supplied directly from individual studios, electronic resources such as imdb.com and the Big Cartoon Database (bcdb.com), in addition to credits taped directly from the various programs as they were broadcast and the individual actor's recollections and personal documentation where available.

In the process, it was apparent that it could not also be discounted that there are some credits which will not be identifiable. While some of the untraceable credits belong to actors who may have been one-part wonders, some are due to a frowned-upon practice of union actors performing under a pseudonym to work on non-union productions. (This is especially the case in anime, for which the English dubbing is often a low wage, non-union proposition.) Working on a non-union production can be a sticky point with steadfast union members especially, as some of the more prominent voice artists have had to negotiate fiercely with the studios for some fairly basic wage and other concessions. While some who have admitted to working on non-union productions expressed regret, citing financial necessity, there are outspoken union members, like actor and voice director Charlie Adler, who are concerned that those who do it habitually can "undermine" union membership so that "producers can get the creme de la creme for free."

Beyond that, the final choices for inclusion were severely limited by space consideration. We apologize in advance for this, especially to Jack Angel, Dick Beals, Jeff Bennett, Julie Bennett, Lucille Bliss, Brad Bolke, Corey Burton, Christine Cavanaugh, Cam Clarke, the family of Linda Gary, Joanie Gerber, Jess Harnell, Charles Howerton, Larry Mann, Mona Marshall, Alan Melvin, Alan Oppenheimer, Gary Owens, Patty Paris, Tony Pope, Thurl Ravenscroft, Mike Road, Neil Ross, Maggie Roswell, the family of Marilyn Shereffler, Susan Silo, Arnold Stang, Cree Summer, B. J. Ward, Lennie Weinrib, Doug Young, and others who graciously allowed themselves to be interviewed but are not included because of space limitations. Also, there is the occasional obvious omission because of an inability to reach the actor through their representative and because certain performers enjoy their anonymity to the extent that they did not want to share their personal details. Hopefully, there will be a chance to include them in a future follow-up.

Finally, we have made an effort to refer the reader who wants further information about the artist to any of the artist's published materials that may be available and/or to an official web site. It should go without saying that all web-site addresses and electronic references are up-to-date as of this writing, but may not be accessible in the future.

But, no matter what technology may bring, since the earliest days of sound cartoons, there has been a symbiotic relationship between the animation and the soundtrack. Although animators on the level of Chuck Jones once dismissed Saturday morning cartoons with the requisite limited animation as "a radio play," the animators cannot do without the voice actors and the actors cannot finish the cartoons without the artists. Accordingly, if there is a last word about the importance of voice-over artists, it may belong to Neil Ross, who explains that (especially in cartoons with limited animation) without the sound track, it becomes apparent that a cartoon is nothing but a series of drawings.

To quote Ross, "I often tell people—maybe I'm prejudiced because I work in that end of the business and I don't want to denigrate any of the animators, but I think the soundtrack carries 60 to 70 percent of the show, if not more. I invite people to try an experiment. Put on a good Saturday morning show, watch it for a while, then turn the sound off. The whole thing will crumble before your eyes and you'll realize these are little drawings I'm looking at. Now, turn the sound back up and turn your back on the television and you will still have a good show. You may not [always] know what is going on, because it's not like radio where [someone states the action]. They can show you that. But, as far as the energy, the excitement: it's all there without the picture."

THE MAGIC
BEHIND
THE VOICES

VOICE ACTORS

CHARLIE ADLER

Successful and acclaimed actor, writer, and voice director Charlie Adler concedes that his first encounter with the Hollywood animation voice-over scene was not exactly love at first sight. In the mid-1980s, after a national stage tour of *Torch Song Trilogy*, in which he replaced Harvey Fierstein (for whom he is a natural sound-alike), The New York actor had settled on the West Coast to live his dream of getting a TV series, thinking,

"They are just going to love me in California!" Although he laughs that it "wasn't the case," Adler was hired for *The Redd Foxx Show* only to find that he hated the dullness and the downtime associated with a live-action shoot. He reflects, "It's funny how you spend your whole life going, 'God, I just want to be in a TV show and have a parking space.' Then I got it and it was just so not what I wanted to do."

In an interview with Will Ryan for *Animation World Magazine*, Adler recalled it was at that point animation literally "grabbed" him. Upon visiting his agent's Los Angeles office, he quickly realized that the voice-over business was different from that in New York. Adler laughed about the incident later, but at the time he was "pissed off" that not only did L.A. voice-overs require separate representation from on-camera work, but they also wanted audition tapes. He replied indignantly, "I don't need a tape in New York—I just work." Pushing his way into the voice-over department, he said that Arlene Thornton and Ginny McSwain (his future agents) had "no interest" in him, but he was told to come back in a week to record an audition tape. He did return, not sure what to do, but drew upon his improvisational skills and "threw together" a tape on the spot. However, so mortified was he at his misbehavior that he did so hiding under a hat and sunglasses—with his back to the control room. "I just absolutely would not be looked at. I was so embarrassed."

Adler must have given a brava performance because since then his almost immediate success as a voice-over artist had to have made up for any initial awkwardness. Within two weeks of his audition, he was hired for *The Smurfs*, which snowballed into more than a decade of work, including all of the leading roles in Cartoon Network's *Cow and Chicken*, Ickis in Nickelodeon's *Aaahh!!! Real Monsters*, Ed and Bev Bighead from *Rocko's Modern Life*, and, of course, the original Buster Bunny in the Steven Spielberg production *Tiny Toons*.

Although Adler has reportedly performed more than one hundred regular characters in over eighty animated television series, features, and specials and his voice is heard an average of twenty times a day all over the world, Adler claims to be "clueless" as to how many voices he has created, stressing that the emphasis is not on "doing a voice" as much as determining the many elements used to create a character. He deadpans, "I really think a lot of this is just the channeling of mental illness"; then he explains that he never approaches his characters as just doing voices per se. "I think if you do, you're dead in the water. . . . If you look at it as a different person and a whole character, as you would in any acting job, then you have many more options. . . . Even if a core voice may be similar to another character, there's so many things that are different—the personality, the rhythm, the sensibility, the delivery, the energy underneath it."

Adler began developing his acting skills in his formative years. Originally from Paterson, New Jersey, he began to "pick-up" on dialects when the family moved to a Boston suburb where he acquired a "very heavy" Kennedyesque accent. His family then relocated to New York, and, embarrassed about sounding like a Kennedy, he affected a "Bowery Boys" accent to fit in. He credits the necessity of developing his acting skills not only to "keep from getting in incredible trouble" but also as the result of his teachers nurturing him and channeling his energy into creative pursuits. By sixteen, he was working professionally in the theater, then added commercial work to his experience.

Like many children of the 1960s, television was his first love and the first eleven years of his life were that of a TV junkie. A fan of old movies and the Three Stooges, Adler confesses, "I was madly in love with Irene Ryan and *The Beverly Hillbillies* . . . [and] my cousins and I would just do Irene Ryan and hoot!" Aside from *Rocky and Bullwinkle* and some of the classic Warner Bros. cartoons, he did not watch much animation. He still does not, especially now that his time is at a premium, but adds, "I love my work when I'm there . . . and I get very involved." After doing his talents, he is eager to see the end result of the collaborative, hoping to be thrilled rather than disappointed. "I love to see what the artists have done with it. I love to see what the music has done and I love to see what they kept of the writing and how it all weaves together."

Adler became one of the "weavers" in the mid-1990s when his name began appearing in the voice directing credits. Voice directing is a job that he enjoys, not just because of the status, but because it allows him to stretch his limitations. He told *Animation World Magazine* in 2002 that "you start to lose your mind if you buy into the boxes that you're put in. So, very luckily for me, even the stuff I'm directing has a lot of diversity which is great for me." Among his voice directing credits are *The Rugrats Movie* and *The Wild Thornberrys*, experiences in which he has had the opportunity to meet some of his real-life heroes. He cites animal behaviorist and activist Dr. Jane Goodall, who guest-starred on a *Wild Thornberrys* episode, as an example, calling her one of the people who are "so inspirational and so remarkable and so exemplary in the life that they have created."

If Adler has any activist tendencies, they might very well concern the preservation of artistic freedom. Saying that "the role of artists is to mirror society and to teach" and being among the many who note that the artist's freedom of expression is being eroded by the state and pressure groups, he believes we have subsequently been "politically corrected to the point of becoming humorless and so homogenized . . . instead of accepting, recognizing, and enjoying differences." Calling animation "a medium of satire," Adler is concerned that the perceived messages may become "so over-thought that just having fun is no longer OK." Adding that animation is a microcosm of efforts at extreme political correctness in other areas, he is concerned that personal expression is endangered when "everybody gets to vote on what we do." Although he hopes this will change, for him the overriding irony is that, despite the well-intentioned efforts at decorum, "we've become more factionalized and more afraid and less open and less willing to exchange ideas."

In addition to pressure from special interest groups, Adler related a hopefully isolated anecdote which he believed illustrated that there are additional restrictions already imposed by censorship from within the system. At a party for one of his cartoons, Adler said he spent a telling evening seated next to a woman, from Network Standards and Practices, whom he believes exemplifies the "watchdog" group mentality. "She was talking to me in these very strange terms where anybody who came over to the table to say 'Hi' to me—when they left, she would make some sort of sexual reference, equating their behavior as a sexual overture . . . but everything she said was of a sexual nature."

Adler said that after some time, he turned to the woman and stated, " 'I just figured you out. You have no business being Standards and Practices because the truth is you probably haven't gotten laid in ten years! And you are so sexually dysfunctional and so obsessed with sex that you assume that everything that somebody says is of a sexual nature and thereby making you completely ill-equipped to do this job! You need help! And you're making decisions for other people?!' Well, this is how I see these groups. I see these groups as people who are either very, very afraid or very, very limited in their thinking or very, very repressed."

Although, at times, his New Yorker edge may be a little exaggerated for effect, he acknowledges that there are those, including some of the more "laid-back" members of the animation industry, who do not "get" him. Stating that the feeling is "fairly mutual," he says, "There are certain personalities that I find very objectionable that I would prefer not to work for as they would probably prefer not to work with me [but] that's what makes the world go around. . . . This is my motto: 'If you please everybody, you're doing it wrong.' And I think that's anything! . . . I think if you please everybody, you're either betraying yourself or you're betraying them. . . . So you're bound to piss people off—God knows I have. And God knows the people that I've pissed off have pissed off me and pissed off other people beyond me. It's not everybody gels, and you know what, so what?"

Although he calls himself the "luckiest man in the world" for being given the opportunity to work with such incredibly creative people, he does not know if he will continue to do voice-overs. His plans, beyond "getting up tomorrow," are to continue to open doors in different areas, cultivating diverse interests including travel, art (his paintings have been displayed on Artnet.com), and holistic medicine such as naturopathy. The proud owner of two shelter rescues ("Gus," a briard mix, and pit bull cross "Roddy"), he was quoted in *Animation World Magazine* as saying, if given the chance to do it all over again, "I would probably have an animal shelter. I probably would spend my life being politically active and being ridiculous about what I committed myself to do. I would paint. I would sculpt. I would write and I don't think I'd ever act again as long as I lived."

Whatever remains on the horizon for Adler—updates should be on his official website, www.mkbmemorial.com—he relents that whatever the many drawbacks of the entertainment business, it has also offered rewards. While he may not have enjoyed his short stay on *The Redd Foxx Show*, he says that he still has good friends from that period, including Pam Segall Adlon, who won an Emmy in 2002 for her turn as Bobby Hill on Fox's *King of the Hill*. Despite his initial introduction, he was eventually able to charm his current agent, Marcia Hurwitz, as well as the "amazing, gifted" voice director Ginny McSwain, whom he regards as his "dearest friend in life." Thanks to his friends, his talent, and his accomplishments, he may have, at least, lived his original dream.

CREDITS

2 Stupid Dogs/Super Secret Squirrel (1993) TV Series
Aaahh!!! Real Monsters (1994) TV Series .... Ickis/Fickis/Thorny
ABC Weekend Specials (1977) TV Series .... Additional Voices
Adventures of Raggedy Ann and Andy, The (1988) TV Series .... Grouchy Bear
Aladdin (1992) .... Additional Voices
Aladdin (1993) TV Series .... Mechanikles
Aladdin's Arabian Adventures: Creatures of Invention (1998) .... Mechanikles
Bears Who Saved Christmas, The (1994) TV .... Christopher Bear
Bonkers (1993) TV Series .... Mr. Doodles/Additional Voices
BraveStarr (1987) TV Series .... Deputy Fuzz/Tex Hex
BraveStarr: The Movie (1988) .... Deputy Fuzz/Tex Hex
Capitol Critters (1992) TV Series .... Jammet
Captain Planet and the Planeteers (1990) TV Series .... Additional Voices
Cartoon Cartoon Fridays (2000) TV Series .... Chicken/Cow/Red Guy/I.R. Baboon
Channel Umptee-3 (1997) TV Series

Charlotte's Web 2: Wilbur's Great Adventure (2003) . . . . Lurvy

Chipmunk Adventure, The (1987) . . . . Additional Voices

Cool World (1992) . . . . Nails

Cow and Chicken (1997) TV Series . . . . Cow/Chicken/Red Guy/I.R. Baboon

Cro (1993) TV Series . . . . "Boss" Dire Wolf/Mojo Mammoth/Earl's Brother/Baby Mammoth

Darkwing Duck (1991) TV Series . . . . Additional Voices

Dino-Riders (1988) TV Series . . . . Hammerhead

Droopy: Master Detective (1993) TV Series . . . . Screwball Squirrel

DuckTales: The Movie—Treasure of the Lost Lamp (1990) . . . . Additional Voices

Earthworm Jim (1995) TV Series . . . . Professor Monkey-for-a-Head

Eek! The Cat (1992) TV Series . . . . Spat/Bill/Biff/Granny/J.B./Jasper/Prof. Wiggly/Dr. Steggy/
Additional Voices

Extreme Ghostbusters (1997) TV Series . . . . Additional Voices

Family Dog (1993) TV Series . . . . Additional Voices

First Thirteenth Annual Fancy Anvil Awards Show Program Special Live in Stereo, The (2002)
TV . . . . Big Red Guy

Flintstone Kids, The (1986) TV Series . . . . Captain Caveman Jr./Additional Voices

Further Adventures of SuperTed, The (1993) TV Series . . . . Additional Voices

G.I. Joe (1983) TV Series . . . . Low-Light/E6 Cooper G. MacBride

G.I. Joe: The Movie (1987) . . . . Low Light/E6 Cooper G. MacBride

Glo Friends, The (1986) TV Series

Glo Friends Save Christmas, The (1986)

Good, the Bad, and Huckleberry Hound, The (1988) . . . . Pinky Dalton/Pig/TV Announcer from Bit-2
News/Additional Voices

Gramps (1992) TV . . . . Alien Dad/Alien Grandpa/Terrified Man/Wimpy Alien

Gravedale High (1990) TV Series

Hillbilly Blue (1995) . . . . Man #2/Mortiche/Waiter

Hollyrock-a-Bye Baby (1993) TV . . . . Rocky

Home to Rent (1997) TV Series . . . . Candy

Hulk Hogan's Rock'n' Wrestling (1985) . . . . Rowdy Roddy Piper

I Am Weasel (1999) TV Series . . . . I.R. Baboon/Red Guy/Cow/Chicken/Additional Voices

It's a Wonderful Tiny Toons Christmas Special (1992) TV . . . . Buster Bunny

Jakers! The Adventures of Piggly Winks (2003) TV Series . . . . Da Winks/Mr. Hornsby

Jem! (1985) TV Series . . . . Eric Raymond/Tech Rat/Additional Voices

Jungle Cubs (1996) TV Series . . . . Ned

Karate Kid, The (1989) TV Series

Little Clowns of Happy Town, The (1987) TV Series . . . . Additional Voices

Little Mermaid, The (1989) . . . . Additional Voices

Little Troll Prince, The (1995) Video . . . . Stav

Little Wizards, The (1987) TV Series

Marsupilami (1993) TV Series . . . . Groom/Stuie

Midnight Patrol, The (1990) TV Series

Mighty Ducks (1996) TV Series . . . . Dr. Droid/Otto Maton/Additional Voices

Mighty Mouse, the New Adventures (1987) TV Series . . . . Bat-Bat (Bruce Vein)/Additional Voices

Monster Bed (1989) TV

My Little Pony: Escape from Catrina (1985) . . . . Spike

My Little Pony: The Movie (1986) . . . . Spike/Woodland Creature

My Little Pony and Friends (1986) TV Series . . . . Spike

No Smoking! (1995) . . . . Cow and Chicken

Once upon a Forest (1993) . . . . Waggs

Paddington Bear (1981) TV Series . . . . Paddington Bear
Pound Puppies (1987) TV Series . . . . Flak/Nathan
Prince and the Pauper, The (1990) . . . . Weasel #2/Weasel #3/Pig Driver/Peasant/Man in Street
Problem Child (1993) TV Series
Project G.e.e.K.e.R. (1996) TV Series . . . . Dr. Maston/Jake Dragonn
Prostars (1991) TV Series
Pup Named Scooby-Doo, A (1988) TV Series . . . . Additional Voices (1988–1991)
Rainbow Brite and the Star Stealer (1985) . . . . Popo
Rockin' with Judy Jetson (1988) TV . . . . Quark/Zappy
Rock'n' Wrestling (1985) TV Series . . . . Rowdy Roddy Piper (animated segments)
Rocko's Modern Life (1993) TV Series . . . . Ed Bighead/Bev Bighead/Mr. Fathead/Gladys the Big
   Hippo Lady/George Wolfe/Grandpa Wolfe/Mr. Dupette (1993–1996)
Rugrats: All Growed Up, The (2001) TV . . . . B-Movie Mad Scientist
Rugrats in Paris: The Movie—Rugrats II (2000) . . . . Inspector
Rugrats Movie, The (1998) . . . . United Express Driver
Rusty: A Dog's Tale (1997) . . . . Agent the Snake
Santo Bugito (1995) TV Series . . . . Eaton/Miguel/Bug #1 (1996)
Schnookums and Meat Funny Cartoon Show (1993) TV Series . . . . Chafe
Scooby-Doo in Arabian Nights (1994) TV
Secret Files of the Spy Dogs, The (1998) TV Series . . . . Additional Voices
Siegfried and Roy: Masters of the Impossible (1996) . . . . Loki/Additional Voices
Sky Commanders (1987) TV Series . . . . Kreeg
Slimer! And the Real Ghostbusters (1988) TV Series . . . . Rafael/Slimer
Smurfs, The (1981) TV Series . . . . Natural "Nat" Smurf (1984–1990)
Sonic the Hedgehog (1993) TV Series . . . . Snively Robotnik
Space Goofs (1997) TV Series
Spawn (1997/II) TV Series . . . . Additional Voices
Super Dave (1987) TV Series . . . . Additional Voices
Super Sunday (1985) TV Series
Swat Kats: The Radical Squadron (1993) TV Series . . . . Chance Furlong/T-Bone/Murray/Creeplings/
   Zed/Taylor/Talon/Lem/Ninjas/Additional Voices
Tale Spin (1990) TV Series . . . . Mad Dog/Additional Voices
Tick, The (1994) TV Series . . . . Sarcastro
Tiny Toon Adventures (1990) TV Series . . . . Buster J.Bunny (1990)/Other Various Voices
Tiny Toon Adventures: How I Spent My Vacation (1992) . . . . Buster Bunny
Tiny Toons Spring Break (1994) TV . . . . Buster Bunny
'Tis the Season to be Smurfy (1984) . . . . Nat/Thief
Tom and Jerry Kids Show (1990) TV Series . . . . Additional Voices
Toonsylvania (1998) TV Series
Transformers (1984) TV Series . . . . Silverbolt/Triggerhappy—Duros/Vorath/Dirk Manus/
   Additional Voices
Wacky Adventures of Ronald McDonald: Scared Silly, The (1998) . . . . Hamburglar/McNugget #3/
   McSplorer
Wake Rattle and Roll (Monster Tails) (1990) TV Series
What a Mess (1995) TV Series
Wild West COWBOYs of Moo Mesa (1992) TV Series
Wizard of Oz, The (1990) TV Series . . . . Cowardly Lion
Yo, Yogi! (1991) TV Series
Yogi the Easter Bear (1994) TV . . . . Additional Voices

DAYTON ALLEN

Long before Robin Williams or Jim Carrey made their marks upon the world of entertainment, there was another rubber-faced, frenetic comedian whose versatility in voice-overs and improvisation helped define the era of children's television in the medium's embryonic stage.

Dayton Allen will probably be remembered most for the roles he played on the groundbreaking children's show *Howdy Doody* in the 1940s and

'50s, but cartoon fanatics remember Allen not only as the voices of the smart-mouthed, trouble-making magpies Heckle and Jeckle and the slow-witted crime fighter Deputy Dawg in the Terrytoons shorts of the 1960s, but also as *Milton the Monster*'s eccentric Professor Weirdo.

Allen, a consummate joker who lived life as though he were perpetually on stage at a comedy club, often mixed fact with fiction when discussing his past. An interview with Allen was often peppered with strings of one-liners and half-truths. Sometimes he claimed to be born in Dayton, Ohio. Other times he claimed that he had no idea where he was born. According to Allen, "My mother, at the time, didn't know where she was and the doctor wouldn't tell her because, after he took a look at me, he thought he might be accused of being an accessory to a crime." In reality, Dayton Allen Bolke made his first appearance on September 24, 1919, in New York City.

In 1936, at the age of sixteen, Allen had what was probably one of the strangest day jobs of all time. He took to the road in a Model A Ford, traveling to different prisons and state institutions, such as the Pilgrim State Hospital in Long Island, New York, and Riker's Island Prison, entertaining the inmates and patients by showing 16-mm movies. Allen recalls, "There was an Indian who came along with me and we would run movies, and he would do a song and dance." Allen also supplemented his income by doing impersonations in amateur shows at the RKO and Loews theaters, earning ten to fifteen dollars, which he split with two singers who had their own act.

In 1939, Allen got a break when New York radio station WINS hired him to do his own radio show. "I was the first disc jockey in New York. I spun records and did a lot of voices. People thought there were several people on the show. I used to write my own material, and from there, I went right into unemployment." Although the radio show was short-lived, Allen gained valuable experience creating characters and performing live on the air.

Hoping to recreate the success of his stint at WINS, Allen began making the rounds, trying to break into a radio series. However, steady work was not easy to come by. "It was virtually impossible to get in. It was a clique. They would throw you a bone here and there doing a stand-in, but I went around like that for about five years." Luckily for Allen, a new form of entertainment was on the horizon. In 1948, the Dumont television network hired Allen to work on a children's puppet show entitled *The Oky Doky Ranch*. Not only did Allen provide the voice for Oky Doky, he was expected to operate the puppet as well. Allen quickly found that he was no puppet master, "I hadn't even done a puppet, and they put me on something that weighed about 800 pounds. It wasn't that much fun." Not one to shy away from a challenge,

Allen took on the cumbersome marionette. The job turned out to be a blessing in disguise.

Allen was only with the show for a few months when the new television division of NBC lured him away to voice and operate puppets for their children's program, *The Howdy Doody Show*. Allen proved to be an integral part of the show. Not only did he master the art of puppetry, bringing life to such characters as the ever-cantankerous Phineas T. Bluster, his brother Don Jose Bluster, the Inspector, and Buffalo Bob's ambiguous pet Flubudub (who possessed the body parts of seven different animals), he also performed several on-camera characters such as Ugly Sam, the wrestler, Sir Archibald, the explorer, Lanky Lou, the cowhand, and Pierre, the chef. But according to Stephen Davis, author of the *Howdy Doody* book *Say Kids, What Time Is It?* Allen also brought a third aspect to the show—chaos.

Davis paints a disturbing picture of various cast members, with Allen portrayed as a disruptive, foul-mouthed, lewd exhibitionist who would, and did, expose himself in the elevator or on the set. According to Davis, Allen exposed himself to a female floor manager in full view of the cast and crew. As to the allegations, Allen's co-worker, puppeteer Rhoda Mann, the woman who literally pulled the strings for Howdy Doody, unequivocally denies Allen's supposed misbehavior: "Nonsense. Who was the floor manager that he supposedly exposed himself to? There's so much misinformation in that book. I don't understand why these authors don't check their information. He was very funny in the elevators. If he was in the elevator, and I walked in and said, 'Hi, Dayton,' he would pretend he didn't know me, and he'd say, 'Who is that strange person?' And he'd do a whole number on you. He'd kiss women or pat them on the behind, but he never exposed himself."

Allen also denies the charges, "No, I'd never do that. They would have fired me right away. . . . In those days you couldn't do anything without worrying about getting fired. You weren't allowed to do any dirty stuff then. Everybody was afraid for their jobs." Regardless of the situation, Allen was a professional who breathed a life into the characters that were never quite the same when he left the series in 1953.

With *The Howdy Doody Show* behind him, Allen took a job on the first interactive television series called *Winky Dink and You*, in which he worked with veteran cartoon voice-over actress Mae Questel (best known as the voices of Betty Boop and Olive Oyl in the Max Fleischer cartoons). Allen, in his first animated role, voiced Woofer, Winky Dink's dog, and played Mr. Bungle, the live-action landlord who was the sidekick to host Jack Barry. (Barry, who was the series co-creator, was also a television game show pioneer, responsible for such shows as *The Joker's Wild*.) The first interactive television show in history, *Winky Dink* consisted of live-action sketches interspersed with primitive animated segments in which the kids at home could help Winky Dink out of seemingly impossible situations by drawing escape routes directly onto the television by using a plastic screen. The show ran on CBS for four years.

Concurrent with his stints on television, Allen earned extra income by writing comedy for a woman named Elsa Maxwell—a Louella Parsons–style columnist. "I got seventy-five dollars per week, even though I didn't figure I was worth that much. I wrote comedy bits for a lot of acts, acts that never went anywhere, but they were the ones who had the money to pay." Though work was steady, Allen got what he considered to be his biggest break in 1958 when he co-starred with Steve Allen. "I got the most notice from doing *The Steve Allen Show* because he was the biggest personality on the air at the time. In fact, most people who got to be big in television started on his show. He had a knack for picking out people who were great." (Steve Allen returns the compliment in his autobiography, *Hi-Ho, Steverino*, in which he names Dayton Allen as having so much natural talent as a comedian that he was one of a small group of performers that were "funny just standing there.") Allen is quick to point out, however, that his employment with Steve Allen was not a case of nepotism. He quipped, "As far as my relationship to Steve: we are related, but not to each other."

Allen had a running character on Steve Allen's show called the "Why Not?" Man, which he developed from an ad-lib in rehearsal. "A friend of mine had been called to do the show, and his brother was dying, and they needed a replacement to do an impersonation of him. When I got up there, I decided I didn't want to do an impersonation. I tried to do something original and I ended up doing this Why Not guy. I was working with Pat Harrington, and I was playing a senator. Pat's line was, 'Senator, would you tell us what you know about Alaska?' I just said, 'Whyyyyy Not?!' Everybody broke up and the thing caught on."

In later shows, the Why Not Man would deliver famous non-sequiturs that Allen claimed "confused eminent psychiatrists for years." One such quote went, "If you shoot a rhinoceros nine or ten or eleven times with some kind of a bullet, and he isn't really dead yet, he seems to sense, through instinct, that he's hurt." Or, "Always stay at least three car lengths in back of the car you're driving in." The character was so popular that *The Steve Allen Show* received letters from people all over the country reporting that boats and dogs were now being named after the character. "There was even a town in Georgia called Why Not. They sent me pictures of all these dopey things." Allen eventually syndicated the quotes for radio in a series of five-minute comedies, and in 1960 released a compilation of the material in a book which could only be entitled *Why Not?*

From *The Steve Allen Show*, Allen jumped to another popular children's show. Allen's old friend Bob Keeshan, who had played Clarabell the Clown on *The Howdy Doody Show*, had started his own series called *Captain Kangaroo*. *Captain Kangaroo* was an immediate hit across the nation, and when he needed talent to voice cartoon segments on the show, Allen got the call. The 1962 *The Adventures of Lariat Sam*, produced by Terrytoons specifically for the series, featured the title character and his faithful horse Tippy-Toes. Allen voiced all of the characters in the show and, having previously worked for Terrytoons in 1960 as the voice of Deputy Dawg, was a favorite of the producers at the studio, who hired him for subsequent cartoons, including the 1965 *The Astronut Show*, aside from their long-running series *Heckle and Jeckle*.

In 1965, Allen moved on to work for Hal Seegar Productions on their cartoon series *The Milton the Monster Show*. Allen played Professor Weirdo, the mad scientist who, by adding too much tenderness to the mix while creating a monster, ends up with Milton, a creature with a southern accent, more resembling Gomer Pyle than Frankenstein. The series had several segments, each of which featured Allen's characterizations—Chester Penguin in the Penny Penguin segments, Stuffy Derma and Bradley Brinkley in the Stuffy Derma segments, and Flukey Luke in the Flukey Luke segments.

Contrary to previous publications, Allen denied providing the voice for Fearless Fly (a superman parody in which a common housefly, Hyram, transforms into a crime-fighting super fly.) A representative from Hal Seegar Productions noted that although Allen did play characters in the segments, Robert McFadden had always voiced Fearless Fly. While the scripts, co-written by *Popeye* voice actor and scriptwriter Jack Mercer, were lauded for being fresh and witty, it was Allen who was instrumental in making Mercer's words spark.

Milton lasted until 1967, but by the late 1960s Allen had started to move away from show business; following in his father's footsteps to become a real estate agent. Although he had not given up acting completely, he was displeased by the turn television was taking. "After Steve Allen went off the air, there was an era that came in where the business was being run by twelve-year-old retarded chimps. Where do you go from Steve Allen? Steve had more talent in his pinkie than the whole business put together." Allen perhaps figured if you can't beat the chimps, you might as well join them. In 1970, he joined the cast of the offbeat series *Lancelot Link, Secret Chimp*.

Lancelot Link was a *Get Smart*-like spy spoof starring an all-chimp cast. Allen provided the voice for Lance, an agent of A.P.E. (Agency to Prevent

Evil) who set out to foil the agents of the evil organization C.H.U.M.P. (Criminal Headquarters for Underworld Master Plan). In-between episodes, the series featured a song by the group the Psychedelic Evolution Revolution, an all-chimp hippie band that was deemed "groovy" enough to release an actual album. Although the show lasted only twenty-six episodes, the series remains a cult classic.

By the mid-1970s Allen again left the business to work with his brother, former *Tennessee Tuxedo* star (Chumley the Walrus) Bradley Bolke, selling real estate in New York. Although Allen re-emerged to appear in two movies in the 1980s, Francis Ford Coppola's *The Cotton Club* (1984) and *Appointment with Fear* (1987), he has since retired and lives in Hollywood, Florida, with his wife, Elvi. In keeping with his reputation as a perpetual comedian, Allen poked fun at the subject of retirement and beyond, joking that Florida "is as good a place as any if you're going to go."

CREDITS

Adventures of Lariat Sam (1962) TV Series . . . . Lariat Sam/Tippy-Toes
Adventures of Oky Doky, The (1948) TV Series . . . . Oky Doky
All This and Rabbit Stew (1950)
Astronut, The (1963) . . . . Astronut
Astronut Show, The (1965) TV Series . . . . Astronut
Balloon Snatcher (1969)
Baron Von Go-Go (1967) . . . . James Hound
Big Chief No Treaty (1962) . . . . Deputy Dawg
Bopin' Hood (1961) . . . . The Cat
Brother from Outer Space (1964)
Bugged by a Bug (1967) . . . . James Hound
Cane and Able (1961) . . . . The Cat
CBS Cartoon Theater . . . . Heckle/Jeckle
Cool Cat Blues (1962) . . . . The Cat
Crackpot King, The (1946) . . . . Crazy Cat King
Deputy Dawg (1959) TV Series . . . . Deputy Dawg/Gandy Goose/Tycoon the Sheriff/Vincent Van Gopher
Dr. Ha Ha (1966) . . . . James Hound
Dr. Rhinestone's Theory (1967) . . . . James Hound
Dreamnapping (1966) . . . . James Hound
Famous Skyscraper, The (1966) . . . . James Hound
Fancy Plants (1967) . . . . James Hound
Frozen Sparklers (1967) . . . . James Hound
Gems from Gemini (1966)
Going Ape (1965) . . . . Astronut
Haunted House Cleaning (1966) . . . . Astronut
Heat's Off, The (1967) . . . . James Hound

Heckle and Jeckle Show, The (1956) TV Series . . . . Heckle/Jeckle (1966)

Hector Heathcote Show, The (1963) TV Series . . . . Cleo the Giraffe/Sidney the Elephant/
   Stanley the Lion

Helpful Genie, The (1951)

Hide and Go Sidney (1960) . . . . Cleo the Giraffe

Home Life (1962) . . . . Sidney/Stanley/Cleo

Invincible vs. Invisible (1965) TV

It's for the Birds (1967) . . . . James Hound

Lancelot Link/Secret Chimp (1970) TV Series . . . . Lancelot Link

Martian Moochers (1970)

McDougal's Rest Farm (1947) . . . . Heckle/Jeckle

Messed up Moviemakers (1966) . . . . Heckle/Jeckle

Miceniks (1960)

Milton the Monster Show, The (1965) TV Series . . . . Professor Weirdo/Stuffy Durma/
   Bradley Brinkley/Flukey Luke/Chester Penguin (1965–1968)

Molecular Mixup (1964) . . . . Astronut

Monster Maker, The (1966) . . . . James Hound

Mr. Winlucky (1967) . . . . James Hound

No Space Like Home (1971) . . . . Astronut

Nobody's Ghoul (1962) . . . . Deputy Dawg

Oil thru the Day (1964)

Old Man and the Flower (1962)

One Weak Vacation (1963)

Opera Caper, The (1967)

Oscar's Birthday Present (1971) . . . . Astronut

Oscar's Thinking Cap (1971) . . . . Astronut

Out Again in Again (1948) . . . . Heckle/Jeckle

Outer Galaxy Gazette (1964) . . . . Astronut

Outer Space Visitor (1969)

Phantom Skyscraper (1966) . . . . James Hound

Puppet Playhouse (1947) TV Series

Rain Drain, The (1966) . . . . James Hound

Rebel Trouble (1962) . . . . Deputy Dawg

Red Tractor, The (1964)

Robots in Toyland (1965) . . . . Astronut

Search for Misery (1964)

Short Term Sheriff (1964)

Sky Is the Limit, The (1965)

Space Pet (1969) . . . . Astronut

Split-Level Treehouse (1963) . . . . Cleo the Giraffe

Top Cat (1960) . . . . The Cat

Traffic Trouble (1967) . . . . James Hound

Trash Program (1963)

Twinkle, Twinkle Little Telstar (1965) . . . . . Astronut

Voodoo Spell, A (1967) . . . . James Hound

Weather Magic (1965) . . . . Astronut

Where There's Smoke (1962) . . . . Deputy Dawg

Which Is Witch? (1967) . . . . James Hound

Winky-Dink and You (1953) TV Series . . . . Mr. Bungle/Woofer

WAYNE ALLWINE

In the beginning—at least of the Disney corporate empire—was Mickey Mouse. Although Walt Disney made two Mickey Mouse silent cartoons— 1928's *Plane Crazy,* inspired by Charles Lindbergh's trip across the Atlantic, and *Gallopin' Gaucho*—it was with 1928's Depression-era sound cartoon *Steamboat Willie* that Disney would have his first commercial success. Although the company he founded has had many multi-million-dollar features and projects since then, it is still known as the "house the mouse built" due to the momentum created by its first animated achievement. And, of course, the third incarnation of the mouse, Wayne Allwine, owes his job to one of animation's first voice-over artists—Walt Disney himself.

It is difficult to believe Disney's simple drawing—long turned corporate signature icon—that Allwine now gives voice to has surpassed its seventy-fifth year of life in the popular culture. According to Disney's wife Lilly, the optimistic, determined little character so closely resembled her husband's disposition that she pronounced them "sympatico." Of course, the original bubbly falsetto also belonged to his creator, who performed the part from the early shorts to features like 1940's *Fantasia* to the voice-over for the *Mickey Mouse Club* animated segments—gradually reliquishing the role as smoking compromised his voice and his already hectic schedule was further burdened by his work on the flagship theme park, Disneyland. Taking over as the voice of Disney's alter-ego was sound-effects technician Jimmy Macdonald in mid-production of 1947's *Fun and Fancy Free*.

Meanwhile, Wayne Allwine was just seven years old in 1950 when he knew that he wanted to work for the fairy-tale studio. This was a dream he realized when, at nineteen, he was hired as a gofer in the mailroom for Disney studios in Burbank. However, with his experience in acoustic folk and rock groups, Allwine was soon recruited into the music department by Bob Jackman, who himself was the voice of Goofy for several shorts. After only eight years, Allwine was then promoted to be Macdonald's protégé as "Chief Sound Effects Person," for which he was hired to learn the production crafts of "playback" (the preparation and on-set supervision of the audio tracks to which actors and singers would lip-sync during the filming of musical numbers), "tempo timing" (determining the proper beat or "click tempo" for an animated or live-action score), and post-production work as a "Foley artist" (recreating and augmenting sound effects for film and television projects after the completion of filming).

However, a promotion of a different kind was in order the day Allwine inadvertently got his start in voice-over: in his first role he was unexpectedly cast as the most famed cartoon character of all time. Asked to fill in for a no-show actor, he suddenly found himself auditioning to take the reins from his good friend and mentor Macdonald, who at seventy-seven was approaching retirement. Although Allwine once met Disney in passing at the studio when he worked in the mailroom, he drew upon his memory as a young fan of the *Mickey Mouse Club* of what Disney's Mickey had sounded like years before. He then won the part with an impromptu try: "I just went down and read the lines and that was it." Even though Ed Ropolo, one of the original producers of the Mickey Mouse club was assessing his performance, Allwine was not all that nervous about trying for the part; after all, he already had a job there.

Allwine, who believes that it was not only his ability to do character work, but that his acting and singing ability were also factors in his hiring, then made his debut as a voice actor on the new *Mickey Mouse Club* in 1977. He credits his ability to do the high-pitched falsetto to the inheritance of his father's unique vocal talent. "Throughout my life, my father's favorite hobby was to sing with different barbershop quartets. He used to describe himself as having a 'freak voice' and it was an unusual voice in that he could sing all the way from his low baritone range up to his first tenor notes with no 'crack' in his voice. . . . Thanks Dad."

There could be no setting more apropos for a fairy-tale romance than the fairy-tale kingdom: in 1991, the voice of Mickey Mouse married the voice of Minnie Mouse in real life. That is, in 1986 at a recording session for the Disney TV project *Totally Minnie*, Allwine had met the actress newly hired to be Minnie, Russi Taylor. (The voice of Huey, Dewey, and Louie, Emmy-award winning Taylor is now also famous for her "side job" as Martin Prince among other characters on *The Simpsons*.) Meeting on various sound stages, the pair who were each facing painful divorces, turned to each other for a sympathetic ear. Over the next five years, the friendship blossomed into a serious romance, then marriage. Not wanting "the wedding of Mickey and Minnie" to be a huge publicity event, Allwine recalls, "First we went to Roy Disney [Walt's nephew and the then Vice Chairman of the Board] and told him what was going on. He said he wasn't surprised but was delighted."

Although Allwine concedes that his years as Mickey may have left him type-cast as a voice-actor, he can only describe himself as "blessed." He explains, "Like Walt Disney and Jimmy Macdonald before me, I'm just a reg-ular guy who's been lucky enough to make my way through life using only my God-given talents. When I add to this the love of my life, my wife Russi, the living 'treasures' that are my children, all of the loving friendships I've enjoyed over the years—the losses, the surprises, the music, the laughter, the tremendous joy I've found in creativity—I cannot find enough words to tell you of the daily joy I find in the sheer 'wonderfulness' of my life."

For his career as a soundman, Allwine has worked on prominent features like *Three Men and a Baby* and has been recognized with a prime-time Emmy for Sound Editing for Steven Spielberg's *Amazing Stories*, along with two Golden Reels for *Stories* and Disney's *The Great Mouse Detective*. Since 1986,

Allwine has been Disney's official voice of Mickey—providing the voice for the theme parks, merchandising, CD-ROMs, not to mention all English-language production and has even recorded character dialogue in various other languages, including Spanish, French, Chinese, Japanese, and Russian. Among his voice-over work are two Academy Award–nominated Mickey Mouse short featurettes—*Mickey's Christmas Carol* and *Runaway Brain*. With achievements such as those, certainly Disney would agree that Wayne Allwine has kept the spirit of his alter ego alive, as well as deftly upheld the tradition of the flagship icon.

CREDITS

Black Cauldron, The (1985) .... Henchman
Disney Sing-along-Songs: Friend like Me (1996) Video.... Mickey Mouse
Disney Sing-along-Songs: The Twelve Days of Christmas (1994) Video.... Mickey Mouse
Disney Sing-along-Songs: Very Merry Christmas Songs (1988) Video.... Mickey Mouse
Fantasia 2000 (1999) .... Mickey Mouse (segment Pomp and Circumstance)
Goofy Movie, A (1995) .... Mickey Mouse
Great Mouse Detective, The (1986) .... Thug Guard
House of Mouse (2001) TV Series.... Mickey Mouse/Additional Voices
Mickey Mouse Works (1999) TV Series.... Mickey Mouse
Mickey's Christmas Carol (1983) .... Bob Cratchit (Mickey Mouse)
Mickey's House of Villains (2002) Video.... Mickey Mouse
Mickey's Magical Christmas: Snowed in at the House of Mouse (2001) Video.... Mickey Mouse
Mickey's Once upon a Christmas (1999) Video.... Mickey Mouse
Mickey's PhilharMagic (2003) .... Mickey Mouse
Mickey's "The Three Musketeers" (2004) Video .... Mickey Mouse
*Muppet*vision 3-D* (1991) .... Mickey Mouse
Muppets at Walt Disney World, The (1990) TV .... Mickey Mouse
Prince and the Pauper, The (1990) .... Mickey Mouse/Prince Mickey
Runaway Brain (1995) .... Mickey Mouse
Sing-along-Songs: Disneyland Fun (1996) Video .... Mickey Mouse
Spirit of Mickey, The (1998) Video .... Mickey Mouse
Walt Disney Story, The (1973) (uncredited) .... Mickey Mouse
Who Framed Roger Rabbit (1988) .... Mickey Mouse

JACKSON BECK

From the early days of radio, Jackson Beck's deep, rich baritone voice could be heard instructing people to "Look, up in the sky" as the narrator on the *Superman* series, and heard as well all over the dial on popular comedies and dramas of the time. In animation, as Popeye's nemesis,

Bluto, he inexplicably fought the spinach-eating sailor time and again for the affections of the woman who has been noted by many to be the most "repulsive" personality in animation history. But, fifty years later, Beck, was still hard at work. As the spokesman on national campaigns for clients as diverse as Little Caesar's pizza and Thompson's Water Seal, Beck proved he had not lost one bit of his energy or vocal prowess.

Born July 23, 1912, the man who would make his mark at the forefront of American broadcasting began his career against the wishes of his actor father, Max Beck. "He didn't want me to become an actor because he knew what kind of a tough business it was, but I persisted anyway." The younger Beck found an odd mentor in the form of a "professional drunk," more specifically, a movie actor named Jack Naughton, who worked mainly playing alcoholics. "He was really marvelous, a great comedy drunk with the collapsible legs and all of that and he said to me, 'You ought to turn pro. You really belong in a theater.' "

However, Beck soon found out that his father had good reason to warn him about the pitfalls of the entertainment business. He was almost immediately swindled when he answered a newspaper ad—"You, too, can be a radio actor!" Beck appeared to audition at the "agency" only to be told, "You're very good, but you need some more instruction." The scam began to unfold when he was then informed that his instruction was to cost him *only* fifty dollars per session. Beck indignantly retorted, "I haven't got fifty cents for Christ's sake! This is the depression."

Beck must have known something was up when, in lieu of the fee, he offered 20 percent of his earnings as payment and got nothing but evasive answers. The "director" then made Beck a counter proposal in the form of a job "teaching" up-and-coming talent. When Beck replied that he had only been on mike once in his life, it was met by, "Well, what the hell, you're smart. You'll be all right." Reluctantly taking the job and teaching "absolutely horrible, off-of-the-street people," his conscience soon got the better of him and in two days he quit.

Beck decided that his next foray into the industry would be a little more systematic. Paging through the phone book, he wrote down the address of every company whose name included "radio" or "audio," any broadcasting concern and advertising agencies from Fifty-seventh Street down to the Battery. "And I hit everything I could, and I swear to God I must have touched every agency in New York." When radio was in its infancy, "You went out and scratched and scraped. You got a break here and there and that was it." His strategy paid off when his contacts became so familiar with him through his weekly visits that they began to hire him on the assumption that he was an experienced professional—unaware he had no experience at all.

Early in his career, part of Beck's bread and butter was performing for Columbia Pictures' condensed radio versions of their new films, which served as a kind of audio "coming attractions" for movies soon to be released in theaters. Hired on the strength of his impersonation skills of the leading actors of the time, Beck recalls that he had little competition in impersonating dramatic leading men like Frederick March or John Payne. "Who the hell goes around impersonating them? But I could do them, so I did them."

His biggest break in radio came when he made friends with a very busy actor named Carl Eastman (the lead on *Life Can Be Beautiful*), who then decided to employ Beck as a "stand-in." A widespread system of stand-ins had been created to cover for actors who were doing two shows in quick succession. In the event that the first show ran long into the second show's rehearsal, Beck would "stand in" for the absent Eastman and perform his part. The actor would then pay him out of his own pocket. "There were a lot of us that did that, so we were making contacts and getting auditions at the same time, and [the directors] could see what the hell you could do and couldn't do. So I began to catch on."

Beck had made his entree into the director's "stable" and was soon getting more work through good word of mouth. "They would pass the word around, and all of a sudden you've got enough work to make a living out of it. That's the way it built in those days." Although the medium was a relatively new proposition, Beck says he was on the ground floor everywhere: "There were twenty-one radio stations in New York, not including the networks, and I was on every one of them, foreign language included. I had the only English-speaking show on a station that was otherwise foreign."

By 1937, the Golden Age of Radio was in full swing and Beck was among the most in demand. But, as he was quoted in *Those Wonderful Terrible Years*, a book which described the advent of the radio and television performers' unions, "For performers it was chaos. Unless you were the star of the show, and they earned thousands, you never knew what your income was going to be." Every station set its own rates: compensation could range from the paltry sum of $11.88 for a daytime serial to $50 for a lead part. "Those figures sound ridiculous today, but if you hustled, you could make two hundred a week. With rent about $140 a month for a three-room apartment, that was pretty good money." However, for actors whose shows were spread out around the city, the tight schedule might mean that generous tips were in order to waiting elevator operators or taxis (or even the occasional ambulance) to get the hurried performers to their next job on time.

However, even with the increase in radio work for performers, it soon became apparent that there was a need for union representation. The radio industry continued to expand, but actors' wages were shrinking as established producers saw no reason to pay more than the cheaper upstart stations. In addition, rehearsals that would often take up to seven hours for a thirty-minute program were considered *gratis*. These grievances and others about the lack of time allowances for meals and about being suddenly "let go with no pay just before air" led in June 1937 to the formation of the radio division of Actor's Equity. Beck attended that first organizational meeting of what would become the American Federation of Radio Artists on a steaming hot New York night and left inspired by Broadway actor George Heller, whom Beck found to be a brilliant and dynamic leader. As Beck was quoted in *Those Wonderful Terrible Years*, "I had built a pretty darned good career with no help from anyone. In that one night, he turned me around to make me what I am today—a union man."

In the turbulent times for freelancers, Beck began to long for a steady paycheck. Although he continued to pursue dramatic parts, he noted that announcers had a permanent place at the stations, so he began to court that post in addition to his regular roles. But, his quest for a regular berth took a sidetrack in 1944, when on a tip from an agent friend he learned that Famous Studios was hiring. He auditioned for the Fleischer brothers as a voice on the *Popeye* animated shorts and landed the role of a character described in the 1932 comic strip as "Bluto the Terrible! Lower than bilge scum, meaner than Satan, and strong as an ox!" Beck had found a new calling in the field of animation.

Beck was not the first Bluto, however; that distinction belonged to William Pennell—then a member of a vocal quartet used by Paramount—who was succeeded by former vaudeville singer Gus Wickie. When Wickie passed away, others tried their hand at the role, including Jack Mercer (the voice of Popeye) and Pinto Colvig (a former circus clown and one of the original Keystone Kops turned voice actor for Disney's Goofy, Pluto, and Grumpy, among others). When Beck was hired, he said he saw his job was simply to not vary too much from Wickie's style as that was the public's expectation. "I just had to carry it on because those were my instructions, and so I carried it on."

The *Popeye* cartoons he, Mercer, and Mae Questel created are still held in high regard. Although many of the viewers of the shorts think that the improvised comments the cast made, especially those by Mercer, lent the series a certain spontaneity and charm, at least in the beginning the improvisations were necessary to cover the fact that the drawings were done before the voice track was recorded. The "post-synchronized" dialogue was no mean feat to record because it was very difficult to match the actor's delivery with the lip movements in the pre-existing drawings. Beck remarks that Mercer was allowed to improvise as he wrote many of the scripts, but the others were not really allowed that latitude. "We could ad-lib now and then, but I don't know how much of it stayed in and how much of it didn't."

Eventually, the voice actors reached their limit of frustration and the recording method had to change. Beck said the confrontation consisted of this: " 'You guys are asking us for five or six hours work on a scene, and then the lips don't match because [the animators] can't see us. So we can't match to what they've drawn, because if they're drawing an 'O,' and the sound comes out a 'B'—it's ridiculous. So, let us do the voices first, and then they know what the hell it is they're drawing. So if it's an 'O,' it's an 'O.' If it's a 'B,' you see the lip move, and it's supposed to be a 'B,' not an 'O.' . . . Do it our way, and you'll find that it goes a lot faster.' So, what used to take us three or four days to do, we did in an hour and a half. The three of us kind of revamped the business."

If he had not changed the industry with that, he certainly did with his continued union involvement; but that also was not without its strife. According to *Those Wonderful Terrible Years*, in the late 1940s, like the rest of the entertainment industry, AFRA was suffering the effects of the widespread anti-Communist movement. Beck says the threat became personal in 1947 when he was met on the street with a warning. Fellow actor and union member Casey Staats told Beck that his friend and *Superman* himself, Bud Collyer, was one of the heads of the "Artist's Committee" who had the power to draw up lists of suspected Communists and blacklist them with the advertisers, effectively ruining their careers. (Although Collyer was later, reportedly, an advocate for hiring at least one such blacklisted actor.) Staats said he was worried about Beck's name appearing on that list; to which Beck retorted, "I'm no Communist; I have never signed anything. And I'm not afraid."

As in his first organizational meeting for AFRA, Beck stood by George Heller as the television union evolved, then merged with existing radio representation. (To exclusively represent the actors in the new medium, a separate Television Authority was created over the objections of the Screen Actors Guild (SAG) and the Screen Extras Guild, who claimed that on-camera actors were under their jurisdiction.) After many hearings and initial wins by SAG, on September 20, 1952, twenty-five thousand actors voted to merge the Television Authority and AFRA into one entity: the American Federation of Television and Radio Artists. Heller, of course, was the first cardholder, with Beck the holder of AFTRA card number two. Beck then began a lifetime of service: a member of the New York local board from 1967 to 1992, he held various vice-presidential positions and was even elected president of the union from 1974 to 1976. If not his work, then the American Federated Television and Radio Union would be a fitting legacy—it is still a powerful force that protects the interests of broadcasting artists today.

By that time, however, Beck, like his co-star Questel, effectively quit doing animation when the Fleischers, who soured on New York after a labor strike, moved their studios to the warmer (and non-union) climates of Miami. Disney had actively siphoned off East Coast animators and many of the other studios headed west. Beck recalls, "Things started to fold around, I guess, at the time that Paramount took *Popeye* back; then everybody left and there weren't too many animators around even then. So if you haven't got an animator, you can't work."

Beck says although he has been asked to come out to Los Angeles for animation work, having steady advertising accounts in New York, he always judged the proposition as too risky. He comments wryly, "Unless I get paid an awful lot of money, they're not going to get me off my ass." Primarily concerned about not inconveniencing his New York clients, his objective in commercial work "is to sell as many carloads of goods as I can get sold, and have the shelves of the supermarkets cleared because I did something. I made people realize that this can of soup is better than that. That's really what I do for a living." However, he added—in 1995, almost thirty years after he stopped doing animation—if "they come back here and do cartoons in New York, I'll be right there at the door."

Although it has been decades since his cartoons have been shown theatrically, the popularity of the *Popeye* series still left him "constantly amazed." He never envisioned that the cartoon would still be as renowned it is today. He has been invited to Chester, Illinois, the birthplace and inspiration of *Popeye* creator E. C. Segar and home of the official *Popeye* fan club (www. popeyethesailor.com), to participate in the annual celebrations. Even while doing voice-overs for NBC's sports programming, "the engineers and all the attendants would constantly be asking about *Popeye*." Not knowing the answers, he would often have to reach for the phone to consult Questel, with whom he remained good friends until her death in 1998.

While Beck does not make a habit of watching animation, he was "blown away" by the restorative treatment the cartoons have been given. Although there has been some controversy among fans about the colorization of black and white cartoons, Beck said that the material looked as "fresh" as if it had been made yesterday. "When I was at this *Popeye* celebration for Famous's seventy-fifth anniversary, they showed a lot of stuff and I was flabber-gasted. . . . It shocked me because it was so modern. . . . The artwork and the concepts on this was so brilliant, I sat there one after the other. . . . It was like being at the modern museum. I was really knocked out."

He lauded Ted Turner's group when he subsequently tuned into Cartoon Network to see more of the same. "They were better than the originals. The color was incredible. . . . I thought they'd saved the voices and redone all of the drawings."

When informed that the 1980s Hanna-Barbera versions were ones of modern manufacture with the heavy censorship that story man and voice artist Mercer was then obligated to endure, Beck comments that he could look at the political correctness in two ways. "I can understand the thing, but I think that some people are overly sensitized and are making a lot of noise, while the rest of those people don't really give a damn." Commenting that the country has survived since its inception without these kinds of restrictions, he recalls that the audiences in his heyday of the 1930s and '40s were not unduly concerned by portrayals of violence or ethnic humor. Although he concedes that "this is a different age and a different time and a different sensitivity," he does not believe in censorship and feels it is more disturbing than any possible offense that might be construed.

As a voice-over artist who has worked in the business longer than any other, Beck has worked with some of the greatest actors in his field. When asked to single out the best of all time, he has a short list of three: Jack Mercer, Mel Blanc, and Daws Butler. Although he never worked with Butler or Blanc on a cartoon, Beck has some fond memories of a one-off nostalgia radio show with Blanc in Boston. There, Beck recreated the Cisco Kid, a role he originated on the radio, while Blanc filled in as his side-kick Poncho. "In the middle of this presentation, Blanc started ad-libbing, and the place broke up . . . and I ad-libbed back at him. . . . We left the show altogether and just kept talking." It was over an hour before it was suggested that they return to the script.

Certainly, Beck has met many successes in his incredibly long and varied career culminating in an honor for his contribution by AFTRA on his nine-tieth birthday in 2002. But perhaps his proudest personal moment happened years before when his father first acknowledged his son's proficiency in his chosen career. Beck said that despite his father's initial reservations, Max Beck was very proud of his son's professional success. The younger Beck was especially touched and flattered on the day his father asked him if they could read the lines together for a radio audition. When they arrived at the studio,

Beck recalled that the director's voice came from the control room: " 'Will one of you do something with your voice? You sound so alike, I can't tell which one is talking.' So, I said, 'Okay, Pop, you stay where you are and I'll go higher.' That's how we did it. He didn't get anywhere with [radio] because he was more interested in theater anyway. So I took over the broadcasting. I did everything in broadcasting you could do." (Sadly, Jackson Beck passed away on July 8, 2004.)

CREDITS

Abusement Park (1947) .... Bluto
Adventures of Superman (1952) TV Series .... Additional Voices
Aero-nutics (1953)
All's Fair at the Fair (1947) .... Bluto
Alpine for You (1951) .... Bluto
Ancient Fistory (1953) .... Bluto
Anvil Chorus Girl, The (1944) .... Bluto
As the Crow Lies (1951) .... Buzzy
Assault and Flattery (1956) .... Bluto
Audrey the Rainmaker (1951)
Baby Huey (1954) .... Fox
Baby Wants a Battle (1953) .... Bluto
Baby Wants Spinach (1950) .... Bluto
Balmy Swami, A (1949) .... Bluto
Bargain Counter Attack (1946)
Barking Dogs Don't Fite (1949) .... Bluto
Batman/Superman Hour, The (1968) TV Series .... Lex Luthor/Perry White
Beaus Will Be Beaus (1955) .... Bluto
Better Bait than Never (1953) .... Buzzy
Bicep Built for Two (1955)
Big Bad Sinbad (1952) .... Sinbad
Boo Moon (1954)
Boo Scout (1951)
Bored of Education (1946)
Boss Is Always Right, The (1960)
Bride and Gloom (1954) .... Bluto
Bullfight (1955)
Cad and Caddy (1947)
Candy Cabaret (1954)
Cane and Able (1961)
Car-azy Drivers (1954) .... Bluto
Cat o' Nine Ails (1948)
Cat-Choo (1951) .... Buzzy
Charade Quiz (1947) TV Series .... Himself/Panelist
Cheese Burglar (1946)
Chew, Chew Baby (1958)
Child Sockology (1953) .... Bluto

Circus Comes to Clown, The (1947)
Clown on the Farm (1952)
Cookin' with Gags (1955) .... Bluto
Cops Is Tops (1955) .... Bluto
Cry Uncle! (1971) .... Narrator
Crystal Brawl, The (1957) .... Bluto
Dawg Gawn (1958)
Deep Boo Sea (1952)
Dizzy Dinosaurs (1952)
Dog Show Off (1948)
Double-Cross-Country Race (1951) .... Bluto
Down to Mirth (1958)
Enchanted Square (1947)
Farm Foolery (1949)
Farmer and the Belle, The (1950) .... Bluto
Fido Beta Kappa (1954)
Fiesta Time (1950)
Finnegan's Flea (1958)
Firemen's Brawl (1953) .... Bluto
Fistic Mystic, The (1946) .... Bluto
Fit to Be Toyed (1959)
Flip Flap (1948)
Floor Flusher (1954) .... Bluto
For Better or Nurse (1945) .... Bluto
Fresh Yeggs (1950)
Friend or Phony (1952) .... Bluto
Fright from Wrong (1956)
Fright to the Finish (1954) .... Bluto
From Dime to Dime (1960)
Funshine State, The (1949)
G.I. Joe (1983) TV Series .... Announcer
Gag and Baggage (1952)
Ghost of Honor (1957)
Ghost of the Town (1944)
Ghost Writers (1958)
Gift of Gag (1955) .... Bluto
Git along Li'l Duckie (1955)
Gobs of Fun (1950)
Grateful Gus (1958)
Greek Mirthology (1954) .... Bluto
Gym Jam (1950) .... Bluto
Hair Today, Gone Tomorrow (1954) .... Buzzy
Haul in One, A (1956) .... Bluto
Hep Cat Symphony (1949)
Hot Air Aces (1949) .... Bluto
House Tricks (1945) .... Bluto
How Green Is My Spinach (1950) .... Bluto
Hysterical History (1953)
I Don't Scare (1956) .... Bluto
I'll Be Skiing Ya (1947) .... Bluto

Island Fling, The (1946) . . . . Bluto
Jingle Jangle Jungle (1950)
Jitterbug Jive (1950) . . . . Bluto
Job for a Gob, A (1955) . . . . Bluto
Jolly the Clown (1957)
Jumping with Toy (1957)
Katnip's Big Day (1959)
King Leonardo and His Short Subjects (1960) TV Series . . . . King Leonardo/Biggy Rat
Kitty Cornered (1955)
Klondike Casanova (1946) . . . . Bluto
Land of Lost Watches (1951)
Land of the Lost Jewels (1950) . . . . Red Lantern
Let's Stalk Spinach (1951) . . . . Bluto
Lifeline (1978) TV Series . . . . Narrator
Little Audrey Riding Hood (1955)
Lone Ranger, The (1966)
Loose in a Caboose (1947)
Lulu at the Zoo (1944)
Lumberjacks and Jill (1949) . . . . Bluto
Lunch with a Punch (1952) . . . . Bluto
Man's Pest Friend (1945)
Matty's Funday Funnies (1959) TV Series . . . . Additional Voices
Mess Production (1945) . . . . Bluto
Mister and Mistletoe (1955) . . . . Bluto
Mite Makes Right, The (1948)
Moving Aweigh (1944) . . . . Bluto
Musical Lulu (1946)
Nearlyweds (1957) . . . . Bluto
New Adventures of Superman, The (1966) TV Series . . . . Narrator
Newshound (1955)
No Ifs, ands, or Butts (1954) . . . . Buzzy
Not Ghoulty (1959)
Nurse to Meet Ya (1955) . . . . Bluto
Olive Oyl for President (1948) . . . . Bluto
Once upon a Rhyme (1950)
One Quack Mind (1951)
Our Funny Finny Friends (1949)
Out to Punch (1956) . . . . Bluto
Parlez Vous Woo (1956) . . . . Bluto
Party Smarty (1951)
Pedro and Lorenzo (1956)
Peep in the Deep (1946) . . . . Bluto
Penny Antics (1955) . . . . Bluto
Philharmonics (1953)
Pilgrim Popeye (1951) . . . . Bluto
Pitchin' Woo at the Zoo (1944) . . . . Bluto
Pop Pie a'la Mode (1945) . . . . Bluto
Pop-a-Long Popeye (1952) . . . . Bluto
Popeye (1956) TV Series . . . . Bluto/Brutus
Popeye and the Pirates (1947) . . . . Bluto
Popeye for President (1956) . . . . Bluto

Popeye Makes a Movie (1950)
Popeye Meets Hercules (1948)
Popeye the Sailor (1960) TV Series . . . . Brutus/Additional Voices
Popeye's Premiere (1949)
Popeye's Twentieth Anniversary (1954) . . . . Bluto
Private Eye Popeye (1954) . . . . Butler
Punch and Judo (1951)
Puppet Love (1944) . . . . Bluto
Quick on the Vigor (1950) . . . . Bluto
Red, White, and Boo (1955)
Right off the Bat (1958)
Robin Hood-Winked (1948) . . . . Bluto
Rocket to Mars (1946) . . . . Bluto
Rodeo Romeo (1946) . . . . Bluto
Royal Four-Flusher, The (1947) . . . . Bluto
Safari So Good (1947) . . . . Bluto
Scout Fellow (1951)
Scout with a Gout, A (1947)
Seapreme Court, The (1947)
Seein' Red, White, 'n' Blue (1943) . . . . Bluto
Service with a Guile (1946) . . . . Bluto
Shape Ahoy (1945) . . . . Bluto
Shaving Muggs (1953) . . . . Bluto
She-Sick Sailors (1944) . . . . Bluto
Shootin' Stars (1960)
Shuteye Popeye (1952) . . . . Bluto
Silly Hillbilly (1949) . . . . Bluto
Sing or Swim (1948)
Ski's the Limit, The (1949)
Sleuth but Sure (1956)
Snap Happy (1945)
Snooze Reel (1951)
Snow Place like Home (1948)
Sock-a-Bye Kitty (1950) . . . . Buzzy
Spinach vs. Hamburgers (1948) . . . . Bluto
Spooky Swabs (1957)
Sporticles (1958)
Spree Lunch (1957) . . . . Bluto
Starting from Hatch (1953)
Stork Raving Mad (1958)
Stupidstitious Cat, The (1947) . . . . Buzzy
Super Lulu (1947)
Superman/Aquaman Hour of Adventure, The (1967) TV Series . . . . Superman Narrator
Surf Bored (1953)
Swab the Duck (1956)
Swimmer Take All (1952) . . . . Bluto
Symphony in Spinach (1948) . . . . Bluto
T.V. Fuddlehead (1959)
Tar with a Star (1949) . . . . Bluto
Taxi-Turvy (1954) . . . . Bluto
Tennessee Tuxedo and His Tales (1963) TV Series . . . . Additional Voices

To Boo or Not to Boo (1951)
Too Weak to Work (1943) . . . . Bluto
Tops in the Big Top (1945) . . . . Bluto
Toreadorable (1953) . . . . Bluto
Tots of Fun (1952) . . . . Bluto
Toys Will Be Toys (1949)
Travelaffs (1958)
Trigger Treat (1960)
Vacation with Play (1951) . . . . Bluto
Wee Man, The (1947)
We're on Our Way to Rio (1944) . . . . Bluto
Wigwam Whoopee (1948) . . . . Indian Chief/Bluto
Wimmin is a Myskery (1940) . . . . Bluto
Winner by a Hare (1953)
Winter Draws On (1948)
Wolf in Sheik's Clothing, A (1948) . . . . Bluto
Wotta Knight (1947)

MARY KAY BERGMAN

Mary Kay Bergman's voice-over credits are as diverse as those of any actor in the business, from the sweetness of Snow White (whom she officially took over in 1989 from Adriana Caselotti, who had done the voice from its inception) and various other down-home, wholesome Disney characters to the depraved world of *South Park*. On the ground-breaking Trey Parker–Matt Stone series, Bergman provided the voices for almost all of the female characters, including Wendy Testaburger, Shelly Marsh, Principal

Victoria, Mayor McDaniels, and all of the main characters' mothers, including Mrs. Cartman, whom Bergman described as a "perfect, sweet, cookie-baking, hermaphrodite crack-whore." Bergman established herself as one of the most versatile voice-over artists of all time.

Born on June 5, 1961, Bergman inherited a love for show business and animation from her parents. Her mother, Patricia, worked at the age of sixteen as a cel painter for legendary animator Max Fleischer on the original *Popeye* cartoons in New York City and later formed a singing duo with her husband, playing lounges in Reno and Las Vegas and various clubs throughout Los Angeles. Upon learning of Patricia's pregnancy, the Bergmans settled down in Los Angeles in order to give their daughter a stable home life. Characterizing her mother's previous work inking and painting cels for Fleischer, Bergman says it was a mechanical task, but it piqued her mother's interest in animation, an interest which she shared with Bergman years later by sitting down and watching cartoons with her on Saturday mornings.

Shows such as *Jonny Quest, The Flintstones,* and *Wait 'til your Father Gets Home,* which Bergman likened to "a precursor to *The Simpsons*," ranked among her favorites. Ironically, it was a trip with her mother to a local movie theater that gave Bergman the inspiration to cross over from the status of mere fan to performer. Her mother took her to a re-released screening of *Snow White and the Seven Dwarfs,* and Bergman was hooked. "I was about six or seven the first time I saw that film, and it made such a complete impression on me that I came home and I started singing the songs. That's what started me." From then on, Bergman started impersonating everyone and everything, from Lily Tomlin on *Laugh In* to her neighbor's barking dogs.

At first, Bergman thought of herself as a bit of an oddball, but seeing a future co-worker on television changed her outlook. "Frank Welker was one of my mentors. I remember seeing him on shows doing impressions and everything. I grew up making noise, and it was really interesting for me to figure out, yeah, there is a niche for all these weird things you do, because it's not really normal to do that. He is an absolutely fantastic talent; and years later, getting the opportunity to work with the man, it's been phenomenal." Like her mentor, Bergman at an early age envisioned herself becoming a film star. "I'm kind of like Frank Welker. We both thought that we were going to end up in movies. That's what we wanted." It was while she was still in high school that Bergman took steps toward making her dream a reality.

At the age of sixteen, Bergman secured her first professional acting job in a television movie called *Return Engagement,* starring Elizabeth Taylor. Bergman's excitement turned to dismay when the movie aired: "I got cut out at the very end of the thing. You see this red hair going by and that's it. My famous scene was on the cutting-room floor." The experience wasn't a total loss, however. The role was enough to get her into the Screen Actors Guild, which was and still is a very difficult union to join.

Upon graduating from Hollywood High School, Bergman immediately enrolled at UCLA as a theater arts major. According to her husband, Dino Andrade, Mary Kay's decision to attend that particular college was due to a case of hero worship. "She adored Carol Burnett. Carol went to UCLA; that was why Mary Kay went." It was while attending the university that Bergman befriended fellow classmate and future *Simpson*'s star Nancy Cartwright. Apart from college coursework, Cartwright also studied voice-over techniques with veteran Hanna-Barbera star Daws Butler, but, according to Bergman, they never discussed the subject of voice-overs. At that point in her life, Bergman did not think of voice-overs as an option.

After spending three years in college, Bergman's life took off in an unexpected direction. "I got a role in a play outside of school, and I thought this is what I've been wanting. I can obviously make it in the real world, so forget school; I'm out of here, because a degree doesn't mean anything when you're an actress." Consequently, Bergman left school on an upbeat note to begin her professional life.

It looked as though Bergman was off to a good start. The acquisition of an agent bolstered her hopes for a promising future, but her experience turned into what she called "the worst agent story in the business," explaining, "I had this lovely lady who was my agent at the time, and she had a small agency in the Valley that she started six months before I joined them. She got me an audition for an exercise program that was going to be on cable, and I got the role. It was going to be a really different kind of exercise program. Basically, they hired us because we all had nice figures, but we were also either dancers, comedians, singers, or impressionists. My talent was impressions, so that's where I fit into the show. I was just tickled. I figured this was going to be my ticket to stardom. I'm actually going to become something big here. Not a week after I got the job, my agent closed the agency and opened a candy store, instead, and that was the end of the show. Everything fell apart. I thought, I'm really not getting anywhere. Maybe I should give up this silly dream of mine about becoming this great star and actually get a real job."

Reluctantly, Bergman's next starring role was that of "receptionist" for the Boy Scouts of America. Although she actually enjoyed the work and the people in the organization were a pleasure to work with, it was a far cry from the glamour of Hollywood. Also, comments she received from the various people coming and going throughout the day only added to her frustration. "All the time I kept hearing, 'Gosh, you have a lovely speaking voice. You should do something with that.'"

What Bergman did was take another receptionist position, this time with an insurance company. There she quickly moved up in the ranks to become an assistant underwriter, which she found extremely boring and stagnating. "When you want to do something in your life that's creative and fun and wonderful, that's not the place to be, to say the least." To break the monotony, Bergman thought about becoming a disc jockey, but she could not even find information about where to take classes. "It was kind of a bad time for me as a person. I wasn't married then, and I had no prospects. Nothing was really going in."

As fate would have it, an invitation to a housewarming party from one of her co-workers at the insurance company was the door that finally opened for Bergman. "I went to the party and one of the people had brought a karaoke machine, which at that time was something hardly anybody had heard of, and I just went nuts." Bergman proceeded to dance and sing. But, it was her Ethel Merman impersonation which caught the eye of a fellow party goer, a voice actor by the name of Perry Hall, who, impressed by Bergman's talent, referred her to a voice-over teacher named Kat Lehman. "I started studying with Kat and I absolutely loved it. I took all of Kat's classes." After the last class, Lehman took Bergman aside and told her she was ready to make a demo tape. Lehman then referred her to another voice-over instructor who not only made the demo, but delivered it to Abrams, Rubaloff, and Lawrence, Bergman's first agency.

Although Bergman still kept her day job at the insurance company, she soon realized that squeezing auditions into a regular work schedule was not working. "I thought to myself, I can go on auditions on my lunch hour, or, I get off at 4:30, so I can be at an audition anytime after a quarter to five. I had to make a decision: stay and be an insurance adjuster or leap out in total faith, hoping that I would actually be able to work." Bergman decided to leap. She loved her new agents and believed that they were willing to work and push for her. She found a part-time job at a department store to supplement her income while she did radio spots here and there.

Being fiercely loyal to her personal agent Libby Westby, when Westby switched agencies to Sutton, Barth, and Vennari, Bergman went with her. It was soon afterwards that she received her big break. Disney was looking for a replacement for Adriana Caselotti, the original voice of Snow White. Caselotti had done the voice since 1938 and was not always available to work.

Les Perkins, the Disney executive in charge of recasting Snow White, was not just looking for a voice; he was looking for a manner and a sweetness that came with the Snow White character. He searched the talent agencies and combed the voice-over classes throughout the city to see if there were any up-and-coming students who were able to do the voice. After a long and tedious search, he decided on Bergman.

Upon learning that she would be Disney's official replacement for Snow White, Bergman felt some trepidation. She said of the part, "It's a very difficult voice, in a very high range. Children respond to it. Adults respond to it. [With] something like that, you want to make sure it's absolutely right, and Les, God bless him, is a perfectionist, and because of that, it also touched me. I'm definitely a perfectionist."

Winning the Snow White audition finally marked the end of Bergman's day jobs. Her first assignment was for a Snow White book on tape, but when it came time to record she had a conflict. Her husband, Dino Andrade, recalled in 2003, "She told her boss she needed the day off for the recording, but he refused, saying that she had a choice: Keep her job or do this 'Disney thing.' She asked the clod to make sure he spelled her name right on her check and walked out the door." Bergman never looked back and from that point forward, any assignments she accepted were show-business related.

Bergman worshipped Walt Disney and delighted in being chosen to be a part of the Disney legacy. She had an understanding with the company that they would use her as Snow White only when Adriana Caselotti was unavailable, but, secretly, Disney executives were positioning her as a replacement for the venerable Caselotti.

When Disney issued a restored version of *Snow White and the Seven Dwarfs* on laser disc, Caselotti was brought in to do voice replacement for a rediscovered scene that had no audio. After listening to her work, studio executives brought in Bergman. Caselotti was oblivious to the fact that she had been replaced until the broadcast of the 1993 Academy Awards when both Bergman and Caselotti realized what was taking place. During the ceremony, an animated Snow White was to present the award for the best animated short subject. Not only was Bergman brought in to record the voice in place of Caselotti, studio executive Jeffrey Katzenberg made a controversial decision. Concerned that kids would be turned off by Snow White's character, judging it too old-fashioned, he ordered a costume change to go with the more updated voice, to modernize Snow White.

Bergman made clear in 1995 that neither she nor Caselotti had anything to do with that. "That was one of the most uncomfortable times in my entire career, and I'm sure Adriana was cringing, and I know she was livid, and I don't blame her. I felt so bad for her because that's not the way it should be. In fact, I consider Adriana the definitive Snow White. She created the most cherished character in animation feature history, period. So, I feel a deep responsibility to keep that character as true to the work of Adriana Caselotti as possible. I consider it a great honor, because to me, it's like being the ultimate understudy." After the ceremony, Disney studios was flooded with hundreds of complaint letters, chastising them for tampering with an American icon. Subsequently, Katzenberg issued written apologies, and, as a courtesy, Bergman never publicly admitted doing the voice of Snow White as long as Adriana Caselotti was alive. Though Bergman enjoyed steady work as Caselotti's "understudy," she had yet to do a voice for an animated television show, but that was about to change, taking her far beyond the confines of Disney.

When actress Meg Ryan signed on to do the 1990 animated series *Captain Planet and the Planeteers*, the consensus was that the series would last thirteen episodes and end. However, when the show became a tremendous hit, Ryan, who had a stellar movie career, opted out. The producers needed a replacement, someone who could match Meg Ryan's "Dr. Blight" perfectly. Once again, it was Bergman to the rescue. "They sent tapes to all the agents, and when it came to my agency it was like, 'Yes. I can do this.' So I submitted the audition tape with everybody else and I got the role. Dr. Blight is a wonderful part because she's so nasty and she loves it. She's sexy and nasty at the same time." It did not take long for the rest of Hollywood to catch on to Bergman's incredible gift for mimicry.

In addition to providing vocal matches for such stars as Jodie Foster, Julia Roberts, Helen Hunt, and Gillian Anderson, Bergman's voice could be heard in every aspect of the media, from radio spots and CD-ROMS to computer games and feature films. Her credits include Disney's Academy Award–nominated *Beauty and the Beast*, in which she played two of the Bimbettes, the closest she had ever come to using her own voice for an animated character. On television, she provided the voice of Mrs. Butterworth for a national advertising campaign and performed on several animated series, including 1992's *The Little Mermaid* and 1995's *The Twisted Tales of Felix the Cat*.

To further sharpen her acting skills, Bergman joined the Groundlings, a Los Angeles–based improvisational troupe best known for spawning such talent as Phil Hartman and Paul Reubens (a.k.a. Pee Wee Herman). Bergman credits the Groundlings with honing her ability to come up with voices on demand—skills that came in handy when auditioning for the Steven Spielberg–produced series *Family Dog*. "They needed a female dog to play the love interest to this little, ugly sort of ratty-looking Chihuahua. It was weird, because on the audition, the man was asking me, 'How would you be sexy? Don't give me a 'woof.' Don't give me an 'arf.' You've got to be real—so how would you be sexy?'" Bergman improvised her best sexy dog, and the audition ended with no indication from the casting director of how she fared. "He was totally cold, stone silent. I went through this whole thing feeling like an idiot and thinking I'm probably doing everything wrong, and I left thinking I blew it." In actuality, the only thing that Bergman did wrong was the way she read the casting director's reaction.

Three weeks after the audition, Bergman received a call notifying her that not only did she get the part of "Katie," but also Steven Spielberg personally picked her tape out of the hundreds that were submitted. The short-lived series about a family seen through the eyes of their dog became one of Bergman's favorites. "The reason was because it was like being part of a repertory company. Literally, we wouldn't know what characters we were going to do that day. So, I would show up and maybe do five or six voices in each episode. I really enjoyed that and I kind of grew with that show." The show also teamed her with her idol, Frank Welker, which was a big thrill for her. "When I saw Frank . . . it was such a cool thing because he was doing some of the other dogs. I told him at that session, 'You are my mentor. I don't know if you knew that,' and he got this big smile. That sure was an exciting thing." Although Bergman had finally realized her dreams, her biggest success was yet to come.

In 1997, Bergman became an integral part of the first television animated series to ever earn a "Mature" rating, *South Park*. Animators Trey Parker and Matt Stone—who were inspired by Monty Python animator Terry Gilliam's cut-out style—had made a couple of shorts featuring the South Park gang, the second of which was commissioned by a Fox executive as a video Christmas card; it counted among its diverse fan base Metallica and George Clooney. But that could not get it on the air until Comedy Central—the only taker—began producing the series in 1996 with a few difficulties. While the creators voiced most of the male character voices, Bergman's husband, Dino Andrade, relates how his wife got involved with the series to do the women. "As I understand it, the very first episode, 'Cartman Gets an Anal Probe,' had been voiced by a different actress, and they were not happy with the actress's performance. They came to re-cast in Los Angeles, and there was another actress who was a rather sizable name who they wanted and she said, 'I can't do these things. I have kids. I can't say this kind of stuff on TV.' So, Mary Kay went in, and she just went gangbusters and gave them tons of ideas that they originally did not have."

Some ideas Bergman contributed to the series included portraying Liane Cartman as a 1950s sit-com–style mother, interjecting the frantic "What, what, what!" whenever Sheila Broflovski got flustered, and adding the lateral lisp to Stan's sister, Shelly Marsh. Andrade continues, "She just saw the mouth brace, and she did it . . . [and] they just gave her the latitude to create those characters." Parker and Stone knew talent when they heard it, and turned to Bergman to voice almost every female character in the show.

South Park was an instant success, but it was also the most offensive animated television series to date, dealing with subject matter that went far beyond the boundaries of good taste. Although the show appealed to Bergman's dark sense of humor, she opted to use the pseudonym "Shannen Cassidy" on the series for two reasons. Dino Andrade explained, "There never had been a company that Mary Kay loved more than Disney. The thing she prized more than anything was doing Snow White. She loved Disney so, and she was a bit concerned that if the Disney company knew that she was in *South Park*, because of the vulgarity in it, that they might, out of worry for political correctness, take the role of Snow White away from her. The second reason was, because . . . nobody believed that the show was really going to last. Everybody thought this is going to be gone in eight or nine episodes. There'll be an uproar and the thing will get yanked." Not only did *South Park* not get "yanked," it did well enough to warrant a feature-length motion picture, 1999's *South Park: Bigger, Longer, Uncut*, in which Bergman performed an unprecedented sixteen voices as well as overdubbing nine separate voices for the Academy Award–nominated song "Blame Canada."

Bergman's career was soaring to new heights. *The Hollywood Reporter* named her one of the top five voice-over artists in the business, and *South Park* was looking to be the most popular animated series since *The Simpsons*. She began to branch out by teaching commercial voice-over classes to up-and-coming young talent, but privately, Bergman began to suffer physically. She dealt with bouts of insomnia, muscle aches, and nausea, which, when diagnosed by a physician, were determined to be brought on by severe stress.

Bergman and Andrade planned an elaborate getaway to Las Vegas in hopes that some time off from performing would alleviate her stress, but the proposed trip never materialized. On November 11, 1999, Bergman, wracked by severe depression, took her own life.

What was diagnosed as severe stress was, in reality, a condition called Generalized Anxiety Disorder, which her husband explains is "a fear-based mental disorder in which the brain chemical imbalance makes it impossible for you and your body to distinguish perceived fears from reality." After her suicide, members of Bergman's family revealed that she had admitted to them that she suffered from a mental disorder, but she did not want her husband to know. "She was in such a great deal of pain and suffering, and she didn't want me to share in that ... She couldn't put me through any pain." Andrade also revealed that "privately she confessed that she was afraid that she was losing her talent, that sessions weren't going well and that soon people would learn that she had lost it and that would be the end of her career. I found no evidence of that, and everything was done to reassure her that this was untrue."

Bergman's demise was steeped in irony. On the morning of her death, she kept an appointment for one last voice-over job, a radio commercial as Snow White for Disney, bringing her professional career full circle. In the 1998 release, she does an uncredited turn in the Robin William's movie *What Dreams May Come*. Williams plays a man who searches through Hell for his wife, who has been condemned to eternal damnation for committing suicide. There is a sequence where Williams has to literally walk across a sea of the faces of the damned while they wail and moan—all of the female voices in that scene belong to Bergman.

One of the biggest thrills in Bergman's life was attending a private screening of Disney's *Beauty and the Beast* (which studio executive Michael Eisner hosted in Walt Disney's original personal-screening room). Because of this, Andrade made the decision that his wife would be laid to rest in a place of great sentimental value. "I buried Mary Kay on a hillside at Forrest Lawn overlooking the Disney studios, where you can see the area where Walt's screening room is—from her gravesite you can see the famous arch of the Disney studios with the Seven Dwarfs."

Andrade wants to emphasize that his wife was not a casualty of the industry—emphasizing that her problems did not stem from "Hollywood excess" or pressure. "She had command of this business. If she had not been ill, she would still have command of this business. Anybody who has been in the business as long as she was knows you cannot accomplish what she did over the long period of time that she did it and not have control. It wasn't like she was an overnight success, or that drugs and alcohol were involved. These were not factors."

Since Bergman's passing, Andrade has been on a crusade for suicide prevention, raising thousands of dollars toward the cause. Her official website, mkbmemorial.com, has been converted to support a mental health outreach program to help people who suffer from Generalized Anxiety Disorder but do not know where to turn. Through this program, the memory of Mary Kay Bergman will live on while helping others.

CREDITS

Annabelle's Wish (1997) . . . . Hens
Balto II: Wolf Quest (2001) . . . . Fox/Wolverine 3
Batman and Mr. Freeze: SubZero (1998) . . . . Barbara Gordon/Batgirl
Beauty and the Beast (1991) . . . . Bimbette
Captain Planet and the Planeteers (1990) TV Series . . . . Dr. Blight (1991–1993)
Christmas in South Park (2000) . . . . Sheila Broslofski/Shelley Marsh/Other Woman
Disney Sing-along-Songs: The Lion King Circle of Life (1994) (archive footage) . . . . Bimbette
Family Dog (1993) TV Series . . . . Sexy Dog/Additional Voices
Fantastic Four, The (1994/I) TV Series . . . . Skrull Princess Annelle/Additional Voices
Fifty-first Annual Primetime Emmy Awards, The (1999) TV (uncredited) . . . . Additional Voices
Funtastic Voyages of Sinbad the Sailor, The (1993) TV Series
Hercules (1997) . . . . Earthquake Lady/Wood Nypmh/Water Nymph/Earth Nymph/Teenage Girls
Hunchback of Notre Dame, The (1996) . . . . Quasimodo's mother
Iron Giant, The (1999) . . . . Additional Voices
Iron Man (1994) TV Series . . . . Princess Annelle/Additional Voices
Jay Jay the Jet Plane (1999) . . . . Jay Jay the Jet Plane/Herky/Savannah/Revvin' Evan
Kitchen Casanova, The (1996) . . . . Doris
Lady and the Tramp II: Scamp's Adventure (2001) . . . . Si (Siamese Cat)
Life and Adventures of Santa Claus, The (2000) . . . . Martha
Little Mermaid, The (1992) TV Series . . . . Arista/Spot/Additional Voices
Mulan (1998) . . . . Female Ancestor/Additional Voices
Roar (1997) TV Series . . . . Additional Voices
Rusty: A Dog's Tale (1997) . . . . Myrtle the Duck
Scooby-Doo and the Alien Invaders (2000) . . . . Daphne Blake
Scooby-Doo and the Witch's Ghost (1999) . . . . Daphne Blake
Scooby-Doo on Zombie Island (1998) . . . . Daphne Blake
Scooby-Doo Project, The (1999) TV . . . . Daphne Blake
Secret Files of the Spy Dogs, The (1998) TV Series . . . . Mitzy/Mitzy's Owner/Timmy/Scribble's Owner
Secrets of the Back to the Future Trilogy, The (1990) TV . . . . Young Girl
Sing Me a Story with Belle (1999) TV Series . . . . Fifi/Hansel/Gretel/Elf/Witch/Additional Voices
South Park (1997) TV Series . . . . (as Shannen Cassidy) Principal Victoria/Liane Cartman/Shelly
  Marsh/Sheila Broflovski/Mrs. McCormick/Nurse Gollum/Wendy Testaberger/Mrs. Crabtree/
  Additional Voices (1997–1999)
South Park: Bigger, Longer, and Uncut (1999) . . . . Liane Cartman/Sheila Broslofski/Sharon Marsh/
  Wendy Testeberger/Clitoris/Additional Voices
South Park Gift Pack 4 (Volumes 10–12) (1998) . . . . Various Female Voices
Toy Story 2 (1999) . . . . Jessie the Yodeling Cowgirl (yodeling voice)
Twisted Adventures of Felix the Cat, The (1995) TV Series . . . . Additional Voices
Zorro (1997) TV Series . . . . Ursula

MEL BLANC

The world-famous alter ego of Bugs Bunny, Porky Pig, Sylvester and
Tweety, Yosemite Sam, Mr. Spacely, and Barney Rubble, among so many
others, was a thoughtful and reserved person whose co-workers sometimes
described as not at all like the joking cut-up from *The Jack Benny Show* or
his stage personality from numerous other TV or radio programs. Melvin
Jerome Blank was born on May 30, 1908, in San Francisco; his family

subsequently moved to a predominantly Jewish neighborhood in Portland, Oregon. That afforded a head start for the future stellar voice-actor as the ethnic diversity of the region encouraged him to develop his natural talent for mimicry and dialects.

He apparently was a better student of music and people than academic subjects. According to his 1988 autobiography, *That's Not All Folks*, an exasperated grammar school teacher changed his life with one cutting remark. She reprimanded him for giving his answer to a class exercise in four different voices: "You'll never amount to anything! You're just like your last name: Blank!" The shame of her censure stayed with him—at sixteen, he began to spell his last name with a "c," until he became an adult and could have it legally changed.

Similar antics continued to get him into trouble at Portland's Lincoln High School. He used the school's echoing hallways to develop what would be Woody Woodpecker's cackling laugh, catching the attention of the principal. As he recalled during a 1978 interview for Chuck Shaden's *Those Were the Days* radio program, "I had laughed down the hall to see if I could hear the echo and I ran down the hall to hear it and I bumped into the principal. . . . He said, 'What were you doing?' And I said 'Just laughing.' And he said, 'I know, but *what were you doing*?' So, I almost got kicked out of school for doing it."

Fortunately, by the time he graduated high school, his talent as a "storyteller, musician, and vocalist" had earned him a job with local radio station KGW—as part of an ensemble for a local variety show called *The Hoot Owls*. As the station only paid a "pittance," Blanc found union-scale work as a tuba player and performed with various bands, playing jazz and big band tunes for all-comers, from dive bars to ballrooms, and occasionally stepping out in front to sing. After a stint in the NBC Trocaderans radio orchestra for San Francisco station KPO, twenty-two-year-old Blanc accepted a position as a musical conductor for Portland's Orpheum Theatre, where he worked with many high caliber vaudeville acts, such as Edgar Bergen and Charlie McCarthy.

Sensing that vaudeville's days were reaching an end with the arrival of "talking pictures," Blanc recognized there might be great opportunity in Hollywood for voice talent. While neither of his parents were in entertainment, his father agreed—recognizing his son's potential "to do something big." With his parents' wholehearted blessing, Blanc was assured that he would always have a place to come back to in the family's clothing business, should he not be able to find work as an actor.

After a year's diversion, from 1931 through 1932, working for a San Francisco NBC radio affiliate, Blanc finally arrived in Hollywood in his Model A car. At the time, the "dream factory" was an absurd oasis of extravagant luxury and wealth in a country that was still mired in the Great Depression. Blanc, who "had a thin waistline and a thinner wallet," could only afford shared lodgings in a small bungalow at the top of steep Hyperion Avenue. He then spent his days unsuccessfully pounding the pavement at affiliates of the two major radio networks of the time—NBC and CBS. The pressure to succeed was made greater by the fact that the depression had now claimed his father's business, and there was nothing to fall back on. But Blanc, shocked at the desperation of Peg Entwhistle, the first unemployed actress to leap to her death from the landmark Hollywood sign, quickly steeled himself against the inevitable rejection by reassuring himself that if he did not make it in Hollywood it was still not the end of the world.

His personal life was a little more successful. In an effort to lift his spirits, Blanc and a friend attended a dance where he met his future wife, Estelle Rosenbaum. After they were married in a Jewish ceremony, the newlyweds were quickly hired away to Portland to create and star in a variety radio program entitled *Cobwebs to Nuts*, a show that relied heavily on improvisation and forced Blanc to expand his repertoire of voices. The greatest challenge to his burgeoning skills came one winter day when a blizzard forced the cancellation of a scheduled talent contest. Faced with the unacceptable prospect of dead air, Blanc held the contest anyway, competing against himself while doing the characterizations of a hillbilly yodeler, a guitarist, a female singer, and a violin soloist. Although he did not claim the prize, perhaps his reward was that the audience was none the wiser.

Despite the success of the show with sponsors, the Blancs often ran short of funds. (In his autobiography, he recalls a particularly discouraging evening when the couple went to buy some caramel corn and found they could not scrounge up the one penny they were short of the nickel price.) The station management's stinginess with his salary caused him for the first time to seriously consider leaving show business for steady money as an insurance salesman. This time, it was his wife who encouraged him to realize his potential and make a second try at Hollywood.

Upon their return, Blanc was delighted to gain national exposure in radio on *The Baker's Broadcast*, starring then-popular comedian Joe Penner. However, Blanc was sobered to the fleeting nature of fame as he watched Penner meet a swift professional, then personal demise, dying of a heart attack at the age of thirty-six. The increasing fickleness of radio audiences, who were now faced with a growing number of entertainment choices, was sufficient persuasion that a more stable career might be found in film. For Blanc, who did not like on-camera work and personally believed he could improve the state of voice acting in animation, the decision to try the cartoon studios made sense. Besides, he had heard they paid well.

The last part certainly proved to be true as Blanc earned eight hundred dollars for what turned out to be a very small part on Disney's *Pinocchio*. Walt Disney hired him for the part of Gideon, the cat, on the strength of his impression of a drunk. "I had worked for sixteen days doing the voice that had the hiccup in it. . . . And, after working sixteen days, they changed and had a different character . . . take the lead. But they still used this cat, and of the sixteen days work, they used one hiccup out of the whole thing." According to Blanc, Walt Disney had become concerned that children might think that the character in the film was a "lush" and so decided to edit it down to a solitary hiccup. At eight hundred dollars, it probably remains film's most expensive hiccup.

Ironically, the next studio on the list was Warner Bros. Although their names would someday be forever intertwined, they initially wanted nothing to do with him. At the time, Warners—which had been siphoning free labor from whatever actors it had in its other films to do voice-overs—was a much harder sell. Blanc found that he couldn't get past one of Leon Schlessinger's gatekeepers, that is, until Fate took some fairly drastic measures. "I had tried to get in there for a year and a half and the guy always said, 'No, I'm sorry, we've got all the voices we need.' And I kept going back and he said, 'No, we still have all the voices we need.' And, I don't like to say this, but the guy *died*. So, I went to the next man in charge. And told him I wanted to audition for him. He said, 'Well, swell, let's hear what you've got?' So, I auditioned for him and he said, 'Would you mind doing it again for the directors?' "

The directors that the new man, Treg Brown, was so nonchalantly introducing him to were a dream team of legendary animators—Isadore "Friz" Freleng, Bob Clampett, and Fred "Tex" Avery (who later went on to become one of MGM's greatest animation directors, as well). If that were not intimidating enough, as Blanc was impressing the directors with the same routine he had done for Disney, Chuck Jones joined the group. Fortunately, they were delighted and spontaneously broke into applause as Blanc finished.

Tex Avery was particularly interested in Blanc's drunk routine, as there was a drunken bull character in one of his upcoming Porky Pig cartoons—*Picador Porky*. But it was Leon Schlessinger who eventually approached Blanc as a replacement for Porky's voice. At the time, the role of Porky was being played by another actor—Joe Dougherty. Dougherty had a real-life stuttering problem and, consequently, missed cues in the recording sessions, which cost the studio money. Blanc's first reaction was to joke along the lines that it may not be exactly kosher to ask a "nice Jewish boy" to do the voice of a pig, but he accepted.

Deciding to research the part as a method actor would, Blanc traveled to a pig farm near San Fernando, to the bewilderment of the farm's owner. Although Freleng had originally wanted Porky to stutter as a means of setting the character apart, Blanc's interpretation was a little different. "I went out to a pig farm and wallowed around with them and found out if pig could talk, he'd talk with a grunt. That's how Porky talks—with a grunt." He thought of Porky's stutter as "more or less of an 'oink, oink, oink.' If you hear a pig, you hear 'oink, oink, oink' and 'bit, bit, bit, bit'—th-th-th-that's all folks! It's actually an 'oink.' I don't think anybody stutters that badly."

By the late 1930s and into the early '40s, Blanc believed that his first major Warner Bros. character was waning as other classic characters began to emerge, especially Blanc's personal favorite—Bugs Bunny. Blanc said he "nearly gagged" when he first read the original script for Bug's introduction in the 1938 short *Porky's Hare Hunt*. "They were going to call him '*Happy Rabbit*.' . . . And I took the name from the man who actually drew the first character. His name was [Ben] "Bugs" Hardaway. . . . I thought, 'Gee, why don't they call it Bugs Bunny?' because it was his bunny. And the name fit the kind of character he was. He was a little buggy. So, Schlessinger said that was a good idea. So, they called him Bugs Bunny."

The voice characterization for Bugs proved difficult as Hardaway was still refining the character. The early, crudely drawn Bugs had protruding buck-teeth, and Blanc's voice reflected that feature as a "pronounced lisp." But by the early 1940s, Bugs's image was updated and the animators referred to him as "a tough little stinker," and along with that came the inspiration for the New York accent. "They wanted a tough little character. So, I thought maybe either someone who came from Brooklyn or the Bronx, which was the toughest talking area in the world. And I thought, 'Why don't I put them both together?'" Along with the accent came his most famous ad-lib. Instead of the written "What's cooking?" Blanc came up with what he thought was a hipper-sounding catch phrase, "What's up, Doc?" Blanc then came to identify with his character so well that he often brainstormed with the director and story men, ad-libbing or changing lines that he felt were out of character.

Many people may not realize that Blanc was not the first voice for Elmer Fudd. Oddly enough, Blanc stated that his one-time mentor Joe Penner's voice was an obscure influence. According to Blanc, Penner was the inspiration for a little-known early Warner's character named "Egghead" (voiced by Cliff Nazarro), which gradually evolved into the character of Fudd. After the 1939 short *Believe It or Else*, radio actor Arthur Q. Bryan (*Fibber McGee and Molly, The Great Guildersleeve*) took over the role. Blanc collaborated with Bryan on many cartoons until Bryan passed away in 1959. Elmer was consequently voiced by Daws Butler, then Hal Smith, until director Friz Freleng insisted that Blanc take over the part. Blanc was initially uncomfortable with the idea, as he viewed imitating someone else's voice as a form of plagiarism—later going so far as to call his own imitators "thieves" and state that if there were a law against it he would "become a very wealthy man by suing them for stealing [his] voice."

Blanc was one of the first voice-over artists to experience a predicament that continues to plague voice artists today. Although the actor is integral to creating a particular characterization, it is hard to claim ownership when the studios may have contractual rights to it. Also, talented newcomers may have no qualms about subsequently imitating an actor's established character. As Blanc reiterated in the Shaden interview, "I don't like to impersonate people. If I can't create a character, then I don't feel that it's my voice and it doesn't belong to me. And I don't like to steal from anybody. In other words, if I did a Cary Grant and didn't say who it was and just did it in the cartoon, I don't think that would be right. Because, after all, it's his voice and he should get the money from it, because it's his property." However, with regard to Elmer Fudd, as Bryan had passed away, Blanc agreed to add it to his repertoire.

Blanc also voiced Freleng's next major character, Yosemite Sam, claiming that Freleng not only conceived the character, but, as he was also of a short stature and quick temper, served as Sam's inspiration. When Blanc was first shown the bushy red-haired cowboy in an oversized ten-gallon hat, he came up with a "mild Western drawl" which was only inadvertently whipped into Sam's voice by a case of road rage. While Blanc was practicing Sam's voice driving down Santa Monica Boulevard, someone cut him off. Blanc immediately retaliated at the top of his lungs and was amused to realize that "loud and raucous" was the right attitude for Sam. However, while recording in the studio, the volume and gruffness left him so hoarse at times that his lines had to be separated to allow him to rest between takes.

There continues to be a wide range of ongoing discussion on the subject of Blanc's vocal techniques. For example, Daffy Duck's lisp has been a source of comment among certain factions who have speculated on his possible orientation. (Incidentally, Bugs also came under scrutiny as a frequent cross-dresser who had a propensity to kiss his male antagonists). Blanc maintained none of his characters were gay. Explaining away Daffy's lisp as being caused by his protracted bill, Blanc interpreted that the feature would hinder his speech, particularly when it came to "s" sounds. It was also one of the few voices (including Porky Pig, Henery Hawk, Speedy Gonzales, and Tweety) which were subject to manipulation using some of the most sophisticated recording techniques long before current advances in post-production technology. According to Blanc, an engineer would record his performance at a slower speed (18–20 percent), then play it back at normal speed to raise the pitch while still retaining the clarity of the performance.

While Blanc's most ubiquitous character has to be Bugs, he gave much consideration to the creation of his entire lineup. He held a particular fondness for Sylvester, the "big sloppy-looking cat" with the "big sloppy voice." He joked that in doing the voice for Sylvester, he warned his co-star to wear a raincoat because by the end of the session, the scripts would be "so covered with saliva that they needed to be wiped clean." The pretext for Sylvester existed in characters from prior radio work—the "Thsufferin' thsuccotash" catchphrase was a line from his character he performed on one of his earlier radio programs, *The Judy Canova Show*. Inspiration for other characters could spring from such diverse sources as French actor Charles Boyer, on whom Blanc based Pepe le Pew. Blanc also gleaned the accent for Speedy Gonzales from a source as unassuming as one of the Mexican construction workers hired to renovate Blanc's house. Even his bit players came in for serious consideration—in Blanc's interpretation, the Tasmanian Devil's "ravenous appetite" meant that he "should growl slobbering, indecipherable gibberish," while Marvin the Martian's wavering voice is meant to convey a "sound-barrier-breaking motion sickness."

Whereas Blanc's name became synonymous with Warners Brothers' characters, he did do some prominent work in the 1960s for Hanna-Barbera. This included Saturday morning fare like Heathcliff, Capt. Caveman, and Speed Buggy. But, most notably, he performed Barney Rubble and Dino the Dinosaur for *The Flintstones* (erroneously attributed in other print sources as "Chips Spam") and Cosmo Spacely, George Jetsons's short-tempered boss on *The Jetsons*. However, on principle, he nearly turned down his foray into television. When Joe Barbera initially described Rubble as a "prehistoric Art Carney," Blanc immediately reiterated that he did not believe in impersonating others. Once Barbera assured him that he did not have to mimic anyone, Blanc then began to work out the character over the telephone, complete with Barney's "silly hiccup of a laugh."

But it was on January 24, 1961, during the time of the tapings of *The Flintstones*, that Blanc cheated death. Characterizing his expensive collection of "fast cars" as the "lone self-indulgence" of a frugal depression survivor, he was driving his exotic Aston Martin on the infamous stretch of Sunset Boulevard so treacherous that it was immortalized in Jan and Dean's song "Deadman's Curve" when he was hit head-on by an eighteen-year-old in an Oldsmobile. Blanc's car collapsed around him and it would be a half an hour before rescuers could free him from the wreckage.

The illustrious actor was reported dead in at least one newspaper, and they were almost right. Left in a coma, Blanc had suffered "numerous internal injuries, compound fractures of both legs, a fractured arm, and a severe concussion." He regained consciousness not as concerned with his broken body as much as any possible damage to his vocal cords and was overjoyed to find that his voice was still intact. Although in a full body cast for months, both Warner Bros. and Hanna-Barbera sent remote recording units to his home after his discharge from the hospital so he could continue working. Joe Barbera called him "a real trooper" when *Flintstones* cast members Alan Reed (Fred Flintstone), Bea Benederet (Betty Rubble), and Jean Vander Pyl (Wilma Flintstone) joined Blanc at his house for the tapings. Despite the fact that Blanc received thousands of get-well letters and visits from many friends, including his former costar and employer Jack Benny, he was grateful to have some work to keep his mind off his recovery.

While Blanc was incapacitated, he said he had plenty of time to reflect upon his career in animation. Obviously, there was plenty of material to mull over as he claimed to recall over some four hundred voices in his repertoire before he lost his concentration. However, despite the artistic rewards of playing a pivotal part in creating numerous cartoon masterpieces, financial compensation always seemed to be in short supply. Freleng was quoted as saying that part of the reason Blanc was called upon to do a constant stream of voices for Warner Bros. was that executive Jack Warner saw an opportunity to save money. As they had the definitive "Man of 1,000 Voices," they would not have to hire two or three people for each cartoon. Of course, when Blanc and his wife tried to negotiate a raise with "notoriously tightfisted" Schlessinger, it seemed that the studio never had enough money. Nevertheless, Warners retained all the rights to the characters, phrases, and Blanc's performances, which would eventually net them untold billions of dollars, reportedly paying him, until the mid-1960s, no more than twenty thousand dollars a year for his part.

Instead, Warners consented to grant fame in lieu of fortune. Blanc was animation's first actor to have his name prominently mentioned in the screen credits. He said in his autobiography that the single line "Voice Characterizations by Mel Blanc" was almost the equivalent to a raise because the notoriety brought offers of work from other studios and radio producers, so much so that he even had to turn down many offers. Despite his newly found fame and the fact that his contribution was an essential part of Warner Bros.' Oscar-winning animation, it was not possible for him to be given an Oscar as an individual, as the Motion Picture Academy Association's policy was only to recognize the cartoon's producer. Although Blanc was always disappointed never to have personally received an Oscar for his work, eventually he received one by proxy. Producer Eddie Selzer, who was awarded all Warner Bros.' cartoon Oscars, ultimately bequeathed one to Blanc for a Sylvester and Tweety cartoon, *Birds Anonymous*.

Certainly, there must have been some consolation in the fact that during Blanc's lifetime, he earned congressional and presidential citations and both he and Bugs Bunny were awarded stars on the Hollywood Walk of Fame. Blanc was also particularly proud of his inclusion into the Smithsonian Museum. But perhaps just as important to him, according to his autobiography (which came out in the year before he died), he wondered if his grammar school teacher who had changed his life with one sentence and speculated that he would never amount to anything knew how he had proved her wrong.

In 1989, after changing an industry and entertaining generations of cartoon viewers, with the promise of entertaining generations to come, at age eighty-one, the best-known animation voice actor passed away—survived by his wife and his son, Noel, whom he had mentored in the field of voice-over techniques and recording. At the time of his death it was estimated that more than 20 million people heard his voices on a daily basis. He left his own best tribute in the form of a last masterpiece of his voice-over work in the classic *Who Framed Roger Rabbit*. In his *USA Today* obituary, he was lauded by *Roger Rabbit* director Robert Zemeckis and producer Steven Spielberg, who eulogized him by saying he "was not simply a one-man band—he was a one-man symphony orchestra of characters." The accolades continued among his former co-stars, with June Foray describing him simply as "a talented delight." Having a sense of humor to the end, Mel Blanc's epitaph that graces his tombstone below a carved Star of David is really the last words he is reported to have professionally recorded, "That's all folks!"

CREDITS

14-Carrot Rabbit (1952) .... Bugs Bunny/Chillicothe (Yosemite) Sam/Louie/Pierre/Military Police
8-Ball Bunny (1950) .... Bugs Bunny
90-Day Wondering (1956)

Abominable Snow Rabbit, The (1961) .... Bugs Bunny/Daffy Duck/Abominable Snowman

Acrobatty Bunny (1946) .... Bugs Bunny/Nero

Adventures of the Road Runner (1962) TV .... Wile E. Coyote

Africa Squeaks (1940) .... Porky Pig

Ah! Sweet Mouse-Story of Life (1965) .... Tom/Jerry

A-Haunting We Will Go (1966) .... Daffy Duck/Speedy Gonzales

Ain't She Tweet (1952) .... Sylvester/Tweety

Ain't That Ducky (1945) (uncredited) .... Daffy Duck/Sobbing Duckling

A-Lad-in His Lamp (1948) .... Bugs Bunny/Mad Man Hassan

Ali-Baba Bound (1940) .... Porky Pig/Suicide Squad/Baby Dumpling/Humpmobile Camel

Ali Baba Bunny (1957) .... Bugs Bunny/Daffy Duck/Hassan/Sultan/Genie

All a Bir-r-r-rd (1950) .... Sylvester/Tweety/Conductor

All Fowled Up (1955) .... Foghorn Leghorn/Henery Hawk/Barnyard Dog

All This and Rabbit Stew (1941) .... Bugs Bunny

Aloha Hooey (1942) (uncredited) .... Sammy Seagull

Along Came Daffy (1947) .... Daffy Duck/Yosemite Sam/Sam's Brother/Duck Decoys

Andy Panda's Pop (1941) (uncredited) .... Acme Roofing Company Man

Angel Puss (1944) .... Lil' Sambo/Angel Puss

Ant Pasted (1953)

Any Bonds Today (1942) .... Bugs Bunny/Porky Pig

Apes of Wrath (1959) .... Bugs Bunny

Aqua Duck (1963) .... Daffy Duck

Assault and Peppered (1965) .... Speedy Gonzales/Daffy Duck

Astroduck, The (1966) .... Daffy Duck/Speedy Gonzales/Realtor

Atom Ant/Secret Squirrel Show, The (1967) TV Series .... Secret Squirrel

Awful Orphan (1949) .... Porky Pig/Charlie Dog

Baby Bottleneck (1946) .... Porky Pig/Daffy Duck/Narrator/Stork/Scotty Dog/Dog Inventor/Various Babies

Baby Buggy Bunny (1954) .... Bugs Bunny/Finster

Bacall to Arms (1946) .... Fat Theater Patron

Back Alley Op-Roar (1948) .... Sylvester

Backwoods Bunny (1959) .... Bugs Bunny

Bad Ol' Putty Tat (1949) .... Sylvester/Tweety

Ballot Box Bunny (1951) .... Bugs Bunny/Yosemite Sam

Banty Raids (1963) .... Foghorn Leghorn/Barnyard Dog/Banty Rooster/Tough Rooster/Giggling Chicken

Barbary-Coast Bunny (1956) .... Bugs Bunny

Bars and Stripes Forever (1939) .... Warden Paws

Bartholomew versus the Wheel (1964) .... Bartholomew/Cat/Egyptians/Egyptian Dog

Baseball Bugs (1946) .... Bugs Bunny/Tea Totaler/Umpire

Bashful Buzzard, The (1945) .... Farmer/Lover in Coach

Baton Bunny (1959) .... Bugs Bunny/Coughing Bum

Beanstalk Bunny (1955) .... Bugs Bunny/Daffy Duck

Bear Feat (1949) .... Additional Voices

Bedevilled Rabbit (1957) .... Bugs Bunny/Tasmanian Devil

Bee-Deviled Bruin, The (1949) .... Vocal effects

Behind the Meat-Ball (1945)

Believe It or Else (1939) .... Buck Dodgers

Bell Hoppy (1954) .... Sylvester

Bewitched Bunny (1954) .... Bugs Bunny/Hansel/Prince Charming

Big House Bunny (1950) .... Bugs Bunny/(Yosemite) Sam Schultz/Warden
Big Snooze, The (1946) .... Bugs Bunny/Hollywood Wolf
Big Top Bunny (1951) .... Bugs Bunny/Bruno the Bear/Colonel Korny
Bill of Hare (1962) .... Bugs Bunny/Tasmanian Devil
Bird Came C.O.D., The (1942) (uncredited) .... Conrad Cat
Bird in a Bonnet, A (1957) .... Sylvester/Tweety
Bird in a Guilty Cage, A (1952) .... Sylvester/Tweety
Birds Anonymous (1957) .... Sylvester/Tweety/B. A. Cat
Birds of a Father (1961) .... Sylvester/Sylvester Jr.
Birdy and the Beast (1944) .... Tweety/Putty Tat
Birth of a Notion (1947) .... Daffy Duck/Leopold/Joe Besser Duck
Bonanza Bunny (1959) .... Bugs Bunny
Bone for a Bone, A (1951) .... Mac
Bone Sweet Bone (1948) .... Curator/Shep
Boobs in the Woods (1950) .... Porky Pig/Daffy Duck
Booby Hatched (1944) (uncredited) .... Robespierre
Booby Traps (1944) .... Private Snafu
Book Revue (1946) .... Daffy Duck/Big Bad Wolf/Coo
Bookworm, The (1939) (uncredited) .... Raven/Racket-Buster
Boston Quackie (1957) .... Daffy Duck/Porky Pig
Bowery Bugs (1949) .... Bugs Bunny
Broken Leghorn, A (1959) .... Foghorn Leghorn
Broom-Stick Bunny (1956) .... Bugs Bunny/Genie
Brother Brat (1944) .... Porky Pig
Buccaneer Bunny (1948) .... Bugs Bunny/Yosemite Sam
Buckaroo Bugs (1944) .... Bugs Bunny/Red Hot Ryder/Villagers
Bugs and Thugs (1954) .... Bugs Bunny/Rocky/Mugsy/Policeman
Bugs' Bonnets (1956) .... Bugs Bunny
Bugs Bunny: All-American Hero (1981) TV .... Bugs Bunny/Clyde Rabbit/Yosemite Sam/Porky
  Pig/Tweety/Sylvester
Bugs Bunny/Looney Tunes Comedy Hour, The (1985) TV Series .... Bugs Bunny/Daffy Duck/Porky
  Pig/Sylvester/Yosemite Sam/Marvin Martian/Tweety/Speedy Gonzales/Road Runner/Wile E.
  Coyote/Charlie the Dog/Others
Bugs Bunny/Road Runner Hour, The (1968) TV Series .... Bugs Bunny/Daffy Duck/Porky Pig/
  Tweety/Sylvester/Yosemite Sam/Pepe le Pew/Foghorn Leghorn/Speedy Gonzales/Road Runner/
  Marvin Martian/Wile E. Coyote
Bugs Bunny/Road Runner Movie, The (1979) .... Bugs Bunny/Daffy Duck/Porky Pig/Marvin the
  Martian/Wile E. Coyote/Pepe le Pew/Dr. I.Q. High/Hassan
Bugs Bunny and the Three Bears (1944) .... Bugs Bunny/Papa Bear
Bugs Bunny and Tweety Show, The (1986) TV Series .... Daffy Duck/Bugs Bunny/Porky Pig/Tweety/
  Sylvester/Foghorn Leghorn/Pepe le Pew/Marvin Martian/Speedy Gonzales/Yosemite Sam/Road
  Runner/Wile E. Coyote/Henery Hawk
Bugs Bunny Gets the Boid (1942) .... Bugs Bunny
Bugs Bunny in Space (1977) TV .... Bugs Bunny/Marvin the Martian/Daffy Duck/Porky Pig
Bugs Bunny Mother's Day Special, The (1979) TV .... Bugs Bunny/Daffy Duck/Stork/Foghorn
  Leghorn/Sylvester
Bugs Bunny Mystery Special, The (1980) TV .... Bugs Bunny/Porky Pig/Elmer Fudd/Yosemite
  Sam/Wile E. Coyote/Sylvester/Tweety/Rocky/Mugsy
Bugs Bunny Nips the Nips (1944) .... Bugs Bunny/Japanese Soldiers/Sumo Wrestler
Bugs Bunny Rides Again (1948) .... Bugs Bunny/Yosemite Sam/Cowboys/Skunk

Bugs Bunny Show, The (1960) TV Series . . . . Bugs Bunny/Daffy Duck/Yosemite Sam/Sylvester/
Tweety/Porky Pig/Wile E. Coyote/Foghorn Leghorn/Tasmanian Devil/Marvin the Martian/
Pepe le Pew/Speedy Gonzales

Bugs Bunny Superstar (1975) . . . . Various Characters

Bugs Bunny's Bustin' out All Over (1980) TV . . . . Bugs Bunny/Elmer Fudd/Grouchy Butterfly/Marvin the Martian/Hugo the Abominable Snowman/Road Runner

Bugs Bunny's Christmas Carol (1979) TV . . . . Bugs Bunny/Yosemite Sam/Porky
Pig/Sylvester/Tweety/Pepe le Pew/Foghorn Leghorn

Bugs Bunny's Easter Special (1977) TV . . . . Bugs Bunny/Daffy Duck/Yosemite
Sam/Tweety/Sylvester/Pepe le Pew/Foghorn Leghorn/Porky Pig

Bugs Bunny's Howl-Oween Special (1978) TV . . . . Bugs Bunny/Daffy Duck/Porky Pig/Sylvester/
Tweety/Dr. Jekyl/Speedy Gonzales/Daffy's Nephew

Bugs Bunny's Looney Christmas Tales (1979) TV . . . . Bugs Bunny/Yosemite Sam/Porky Pig/Foghorn
Leghorn/Pepe le Pew/Tweety/Sylvester/Tasmanian Devil/Light Company Man/Airplane Pilots/
Santa Claus/Elmer Fudd

Bugs Bunny's Mad World of Television (1982) TV . . . . Bugs Bunny/Yosemite Sam/Porky Pig/Daffy
Duck/Pepe le Pew

Bugs Bunny's Thanksgiving Diet (1979) TV . . . . Bugs Bunny/Tasmanian Devil/Porky Pig/Wile E.
Coyote/Sylvester/Tweety

Bugs Bunny's Third Movie: 1001 Rabbit Tales (1982) . . . . Bugs Bunny/Daffy Duck/Porky
Pig/Yosemite Sam/Sylvester/Sylvester Jr./Speedy Gonzales/Tweety/Genie/Hassan/Big Bad
Wolf/Beanstalk Giant/Elvis Gorilla/Stork

Bugs Bunny's Valentine (1979) TV . . . . Bugs Bunny/Elmer Fudd/Cupid/Daffy Duck

Bugs Bunny's Wide World of Sports (1989) TV . . . . Bugs Bunny/Daffy Duck/Foghorn Leghorn

Bugs 'n' Daffy Show, The (1996) TV Series . . . . Various Characters

Bugs vs. Daffy: Battle of the Music Video Stars (1988) TV . . . . Bugs Bunny/Daffy Duck/Porky
Pig/Tweety/Yosemite Sam/Pepe le Pew/Sylvester

Bugsy and Mugsy (1957) . . . . Bugs Bunny/Rocky/Mugsy

Bully for Bugs (1953) . . . . Bugs Bunny

Bunker Hill Bunny (1950) . . . . Bugs Bunny/Yosemite Sam

Bunny and Claude: We Rob Carrot Patches (1968) . . . . Claude/Sheriff

Bunny Hugged (1951) . . . . Bugs Bunny/Announcer

Bushy Hare (1950) . . . . Bugs Bunny

Busy Bakers (1940) (uncredited) . . . . Blind Man

By Word of Mouse (1954) . . . . Sylvester/Hans/Uncle/Aunt/Elevator Operator/Mice Children

Bye Bye Bluebeard (1949) . . . . Porky Pig/Mouse/Bluebeard/Workout Host/News Reporter

Cagey Canary, The (1941) . . . . Canary

Calling Dr. Porky (1940) . . . . Porky Pig/Elephant-Seeing Drunk/Pink Elephant/Dizzy-Spelled Man

Canary Row (1950) . . . . Sylvester/Tweety/Desk Clerk/Monkey

Canned Feud (1951) . . . . Sylvester

Cannery Woe (1961) . . . . Speedy Gonzales/Sylvester

Captain Caveman and the Teen Angels (1971) TV Series . . . . Captain Caveman

Captain Hareblower (1954) . . . . Bugs Bunny/Pirate (Yosemite) Sam/Captain/Crewmen

Carnival of the Animals (1976) . . . . Bugs Bunny/Daffy Duck/Porky Pig

Case of the Missing Hare (1942) . . . . Bugs Bunny, Ala Bama

Case of the Stuttering Pig, The (1937) . . . . Porky Pig

Cat and Dupli-cat (1967) . . . . Tom/Jerry/Rival Cat

Cat Feud (1958) . . . . Marc Anthony/Pussyfoot

Catch as Cats Can (1947) . . . . Sylvester

Cats and Bruises (1965) . . . . Speedy Gonzales/Sylvester

Cats a-Weigh! (1953) . . . . Sylvester/Sylvester Jr.

Cats Bah, The (1954) . . . . Pepe le Pew

Cat's Me-Ouch, The (1965) . . . . Vocal Effects

Cat's Paw (1959) . . . . Sylvester/Sylvester Jr.

Cat's Tale, The (1941)

Cat-Tails for Two (1953) . . . . Speedy Gonzales

Catty Cornered (1953) . . . . Sylvester/Tweety/Rocky/Nick/Newsboy/News Reporter/Police Officer/Photographer/Mayor

Censored (1944) . . . . Private Snafu

Champagne for Caesar (1950) . . . . Caesar

Cheese Chasers (1951) . . . . Hubie

Chewin' Bruin, The (1940) (uncredited) . . . . Porky Pig/Tabaccy-Chewing Hunter

Chicken Jitters (1939) (uncredited) . . . . Porky Pig

Chili Corn Corny (1965) . . . . Daffy Duck/Speedy Gonzales

Chili Weather (1963) . . . . Speedy Gonzales/Sylvester

Chimp and Zee (1968)

China Jones (1959) . . . . Daffy Duck/Porky Pig

Chocolate Chase, The (1980) TV . . . . Daffy Duck/Speedy Gonzales

Chow Hound, The (1944) . . . . Private Snafu

Chow Hound (1951) . . . . Cat/Mouse/Additional Voices

Cinderella Meets Fella (1938) (uncredited) . . . . Cuckoo Clock/Royal Guard/Cinderella (screaming)

Claws for Alarm (1954) . . . . Porky Pig

Claws in the Lease (1963) . . . . Sylvester/Sylvester Jr.

Coal Black and de Sebben Dwarfs (1943) (uncredited) . . . . Dopey Dwarf/Worm/Hitman/Dwarfs

Coming Snafu (1943) . . . . Private Snafu

Compressed Hare (1961) . . . . Bugs Bunny/Wile E. Coyote

Confederate Honey (1940) (uncredited) . . . . Lazy Slave

Confusions of a Nutzy Spy (1943) . . . . Porky Pig/Missing Lynx

Connecticut Rabbit in King Arthur's Court, A (1978) TV . . . . Connecticut Rabbit (Bugs Bunny)/King Arthur (Daffy Duck)/Merlin (Yosemite Sam)/Varlet (Porky Pig)/Sir Elmer of Fudd (Elmer Fudd)

Conrad the Sailor (1942) . . . . Daffy Duck

Corn on the Cop (1965) . . . . Daffy Duck/Porky Pig/Robber/Pirate Trick-or-Treater/Clerk/Police Dispatcher/Officer Flaherty

Corn Plastered (1951) . . . . Farmer

Corny Concerto, A (1943) . . . . Bugs Bunny/Dog/Swans/Daffy Duck

Count Me Out (1938) . . . . Boxing Coach

Coy Decoy, A (1941) . . . . Porky Pig/Daffy Duck/Decoy Duckling

Cracked Ice (1938) (uncredited) . . . . Russian Dogs/Drowning Bird/Drunk Fish/Skating Judge

Cracked Quack (1952) . . . . Daffy Duck/Porky Pig

Crackpot Quail, The (1941) . . . . Quail

Cricket in Times Square, The (1973) TV . . . . Tucker the Mouse

Crockett-Doodle-Do (1960) . . . . Foghorn Leghorn

Crow's Feat (1962) . . . . Elmer Fudd

Crowing Pains (1947) . . . . Foghorn Leghorn/Sylvester/Henery Hawk/Barnyard Dog

Curiosity Shop (1971) TV Series

Curtain Razor (1949) . . . . Porky Pig/Various Characters

D' Fightin' Ones (1961) . . . . Sylvester/Bulldog

Daffy the Commando (1943) . . . . Daffy Duck/Von Vulture/Hitler

Daffy Dilly (1948) . . . . Daffy Duck

Daffy Doc, The (1938) . . . . Daffy Duck/Porky Pig

Daffy Doodles (1946) . . . . Daffy Duck/Porky Pig/Judge/Jury

Daffy Duck and Egghead (1938) . . . . Daffy Duck/Turtle Referee/Nut House Duck

Daffy Duck and Porky Pig Meet the Groovie Goolies (1972) TV . . . . Daffy Duck/Porky Pig/Elmer
    Fudd/Yosemite Sam/Tweety Pie/Wile E. Coyote/Pepe le Pew/Foghorn Leghorn/Sylvester
Daffy Duck and the Dinosaur (1939) . . . . Daffy Duck
Daffy Duck Hunt (1949) . . . . Daffy Duck/Porky Pig/Barnyard Dog
Daffy Duck in Hollywood (1938) . . . . Daffy Duck/I. M. Stupendous/Rooster Actor/Assistant Directors
Daffy Duck Show, The (1978) TV Series . . . . Daffy Duck/Porky Pig/Speedy
    Gonzales/Sylvester/Tweety/Foghorn Leghorn/Pepe le Pew/Yosemite Sam
Daffy Duck Slept Here (1948) . . . . Daffy Duck/Porky Pig/Hotel Clerks/Manager
Daffy Duckaroo, The (1942) . . . . Daffy Duck
Daffy Duck's Movie: Fantastic Island (1983) . . . . Bugs Bunny/Daffy Duck/Porky Pig/Tweety/Sylvester/
    Yosemite Sam/Speedy Gonzales/Taz/Foghorn Leghorn
Daffy Duck's Quackbusters (1988) . . . . Various Characters
Daffy Duck's Thanks-for-Giving (1981) TV . . . . Daffy Duck
Daffy Flies North (1980) TV . . . . Daffy Duck/Duck Flock Leader
Daffy Rents (1966) . . . . Daffy Duck/Speedy Gonzales
Daffy's Diner (1967) . . . . Daffy Duck/Speedy Gonzales/El Supremo/Garbageman
Daffy's Inn Trouble (1961) . . . . Daffy Duck/Porky Pig/Robber
Daffy's Southern Exposure (1942) . . . . Daffy Duck/Fox
Dangerous Dan McFoo (1939) (uncredited) . . . . Character Who Fights Dan McFoo
Deduce, You Say (1956) . . . . Daffy Duck/Dorlock Homes/Porky Pig/Shropshire Slasher
Design for Leaving (1954) . . . . Daffy Duck
Detouring America (1939) (uncredited) . . . . Butterfinger/Cow Puncher/Full-grown Papoose
Devil May Hare (1954) . . . . Bugs Bunny/Tasmanian Devil
Devil's Feud Cake (1963) . . . . Bugs Bunny/Yosemite Sam
Dick Tracy Show, The (1961) TV Series . . . . Go Go Gomez
Dime to Retire (1955) . . . . Daffy Duck/Porky Pig
Dixie Fryer, The (1960) . . . . Foghorn Leghorn
Dog Collared (1951) . . . . Porky Pig/Announcer
Dog Gone People (1960) . . . . Elmer Fudd
Dog Gone South (1950) . . . . Charlie Dog/Colonel
Dog Pounded (1954) . . . . Sylvester/Tweety/Dog Catcher
Dog Tales (1958) . . . . Chihuahua/French Poodle/Doberman/Elvis Dog/Victor Barky/Charlie Dog/
    Cat/St. Bernard/Coach Dog/Laddie/Laddie's Owner
Dog Tired (1942) . . . . Hyena/Lovebird
Doggone Cats (1947) . . . . Sylvester
Don't Axe Me (1958) . . . . Daffy Duck/Barnyard Dog
Don't Give up the Sheep (1953) . . . . Ralph (Sam) Sheepdog/Ralph Wolf/Fred Sheepdog
Double or Mutton (1955) . . . . Ralph Wolf/Sam Sheepdog
Dough for the Do-Do (1949) . . . . Porky Pig
Dough Ray Me-ow (1948) . . . . Louie the Parrot/Heathcliff/Radio Music
Dover Boys at Pimento University or, The Rivals of Roquefort Hall, The (1942) . . . . Dan
    Backslide/Telegraph Boy
Dr. Devil and Mr. Hare (1964) . . . . Bugs Bunny/Tasmanian Devil
Dr. Jerkyl's Hide (1954) . . . . Sylvester/Alfie
Draft Horse, The (1942) (uncredited) . . . . Draft Horse/Recruiting Sergeant/Private
Draftee Daffy (1945) . . . . Daffy Duck/Little Man from the Draft Board
Drip-along Daffy (1951) . . . . Daffy Duck/Porky Pig
Duck! Rabbit, Duck! (1953) . . . . Bugs Bunny/Daffy Duck
Duck Amuck (1953) . . . . Daffy Duck/Bugs Bunny
Duck Dodgers and the Return of the 24½th Century (1980) TV . . . . Daffy Duck/Porky Pig/Marvin
    Martian/Gossamer/Voice on Computer

Duck Dodgers in the 24½th Century (1953) .... Daffy/Duck Dodgers/Porky Pig/Marvin Martian

Duck Soup to Nuts (1944) .... Porky Pig/Daffy Duck

Ducking the Devil (1957) .... Daffy Duck/Tasmanian Devil/Announcer

Ducksters, The (1950) .... Daffy Duck/Porky Pig

Ducktators, The (1942) .... Hitler Duck/Hirohito Duck/Dove of Peace/Jerry Colonna Rabbit/South German Duck

Duel Personality (1966) (uncredited) .... Tom (screaming)/Jerry (laughing)

Dumb Patrol (1964) .... Bugs Bunny/Baron (Yosemite) Sam von Schmam/Porky Pig/French Officer/German Officer

Duxorcist, The (1987) .... Daffy Duck

Eager Beaver, The (1946) .... Beaver Foreman

Early to Bet (1951) .... Cat/Dog/Gambling Bug

Easter Yeggs (1947) .... Bugs Bunny/Easter Rabbit/Bratty Kid

Easy Peckin's (1953) .... Fox/George the Rooster

Eatin' on the Cuff, or The Moth Who Came to Dinner (1942) .... Piano-Playing Narrator/Moth

Egg Scramble, An (1950) .... Porky Pig/Pretty Boy Bagel

EGGcited Rooster, The (1952) .... Foghorn Leghorn/Henery Hawk/Barnyard Dog

Egghead Rides Again (1937) .... Egghead/Laughing Cowboy

Elmer's Candid Camera (1940) .... Rabbit

Elmer's Pet Rabbit (1941) (uncredited) .... Bugs Bunny

Fair Haired Hare, The (1951) .... Bugs Bunny/Yosemite Sam/Judge

Fair Today (1941) (uncredited) .... People and Animal Voices

Falling Hare (1943) .... Bugs Bunny/Gremlin

False Hare (1964) .... Bugs Bunny/Big Bad Wolf/Nephew/Foghorn Leghorn

Farm Frolics (1941) (uncredited) .... Farm Dog/Rosebud/Piggy

Fast Buck Duck (1963) .... Daffy Duck

Fastest with the Mostest (1960) (uncredited) .... Wile E. Coyote

Feather Bluster (1958) .... Foghorn Leghorn/Barnyard Dog

Feather Dusted (1955) .... Foghorn Leghorn

Feather Finger (1966) .... Daffy Duck/Speedy Gonzales/Mayor Katt

Feather in His Hare, A (1948) .... Bugs Bunny/Baby Rabbits

Feline Frame-up (1954) .... Claude Cat/Pet Owner

Fella with the Fiddle, The (1937) (uncredited) .... Fiddling Mouse

Fiesta Fiasco (1967) .... Daffy Duck/Speedy Gonzales

Fifty Years of Bugs Bunny in 3½ Minutes (1989) .... Bugs Bunny/Daffy Duck/Wile E. Coyote

Fighting 69½th, The (1941) (uncredited) .... Black Ant/Red Ant Captain/Black Ant General

Fighting Tools (1943) .... Private Snafu

Film Fan, The (1939) .... Porky Pig/Theater Usher

First Thirteenth Annual Fancy Anvil Awards Show Program Special Live in Stereo, The (2002) TV (uncredited) (archive recordings) .... Bugs Bunny

Fish and Slips (1962) .... Sylvester/Sylvester Jr.

Flintstone Christmas, A (1977) TV .... Barney Rubble

Flintstone Kids, The (1986) .... Barney Rubble/Capt. Caveman/Dino

Flintstones, The (1960) TV Series .... Barney Rubble/Dino (1960, 1963–1966)/Additional Voices

Flintstones, The (1994) (archive recordings) .... Dino

Flintstones: Fred's Final Fling, The (1981) TV .... Barney Rubble/Dino/Monkey #3

Flintstones: Jogging Fever (1981) TV .... Barney Rubble/Dino

Flintstones: Wacky Inventions, The (1994) Video (archive footage) .... Barney Rubble/Dino/ Additional Gadgets/Additional Voices

Flintstones Comedy Hour, The (1972) TV Series .... Barney Rubble

Flintstones in Viva Rock Vegas, The (2000) (archive recordings) .... Puppy Dino

Flintstones Little Big League, The (1979) TV .... Barney Rubble
Flintstones Meet Rockula and Frankenstone, The (1979) TV .... Barney Rubble
Flintstones' New Neighbors, The (1980) TV .... Barney Rubble
Flop Goes the Weasel (1943) .... Baby Chick/Weasel
Foghorn Leghorn, The (1948) .... Foghorn Leghorn/Barnyard Dog/Henery Hawk
Foney Fables (1942) .... The Boy Who Cried Wolf/Two-Headed Giant/Aladdin/Baby/Old Mother
   Hubbard's Dog/The Goose That Laid the Golden Egg
Fool Coverage (1952) .... Daffy Duck/Porky Pig
For Scent-imental Reasons (1949) .... Pepe le Pew/Perfume Shop Owner
Forward March Hare (1953) .... Bugs Bunny/General/Eye Examiner
Fowl Weather (1953) .... Sylvester/Tweety/Hector Bulldog/Rooster
Fox and the Grapes, The (1941) (uncredited) .... Fox/Crow
Fox in a Fix, A (1951) .... Fox/Bulldog
Fox Pop (1942) .... Fox/Crow/Trapper/Dogs
Fox-Terror (1957) .... Foghorn Leghorn/Barnyard Dog/Fox
Foxy by Proxy (1952) .... Bugs Bunny
Fractured Leghorn, A (1950) .... Foghorn Leghorn/Cat
Fred and Barney Meet the Shmoo (1979) TV Series .... Barney Rubble/Dino
Fred and Barney Meet the Thing (1979) TV Series .... Barney Rubble/Dino
Fred Flintstone and Friends (1977) TV Series .... Barney Rubble/Dino
Fred's Final Fling (1980) TV .... Barney Rubble
French Rarebit (1951) .... Bugs Bunny/Louis/Antoine
Fresh Airedale (1945) .... Cat/Prowler/Nightmare Voices/Shep
Fresh Fish (1939) (uncredited) .... Drunk Fish
Fresh Hare (1942) .... Bugs Bunny
Freudy Cat (1964) .... Sylvester/Sylvester Jr.
Fright before Christmas (1979) TV .... Bugs Bunny/Tasmanian Devil
Frigid Hare (1949) .... Bugs Bunny/Eskimo
Friz Freleng's Looney Looney Looney Bugs Bunny Movie (1981) .... Bugs Bunny/Yosemite Sam/Daffy
   Duck/Sylvester/Rocky/Nick
From A to Z-Z-Z-Z (1953)
From Hand to Mouse (1944) .... Mouse/Lion
From Hare to Heir (1960) .... Bugs Bunny/Yosemite Sam
Galaxy Goof-Ups, The (1978) TV Series .... Quack-Up
Gas (1944) .... Private Snafu
Gay Purr-ee (1962)
Get Rich Quick Porky (1937) .... Porky Pig
Gift Wrapped (1952) .... Sylvester/Tweety
Go Away Stowaway (1967) .... Daffy Duck/Speedy Gonzales
Go Fly a Kit (1957) .... Customer
Go Go Amigo (1965) .... Daffy Duck/Speedy Gonzales
Going Home (1944) .... Private Snafu
Goldbrick, The (1943) (uncredited) .... Goldie the Goldbrick/Bird/Japanese Goldbrick
Golden Yeggs (1950) .... Daffy Duck/Porky Pig/Rocky/Nick/Hotel Employee/Chickens
Goldilocks and the Jivin' Bears (1944) (uncredited) .... Telegram Messenger/Short Bear
Goldimouse and the Three Cats (1960) .... Sylvester/Sylvester Jr.
Gold Is Where You Lose It (1944) .... Luke/Stuttering Deadbeat Customer
Gone Batty (1954) .... Baseball Players
Gonzales Tamales (1957) .... Speedy Gonzales/Sylvester
Goo Goo Goliath (1954) .... Additional Voices
Good Egg, The (1939) (uncredited) .... Baby Hook

Good Noose (1962) .... Daffy Duck/Captain/Mr. Tristan/Islander

Goofy Gophers, The (1947) .... Mac/Dog/Bugs Bunny

Gopher Broke (1958) .... Mac

Gopher Goofy (1942) .... Farmer/Gophers

Gorilla My Dreams (1948) .... Bugs Bunny/Gruesome Gorilla/Mrs. Gruesome Gorilla/Tarzan/Gorillas

Great Carrot-Train Robbery, The (1969) .... Claude/Sheriff

Great Piggy Bank Robbery, The (1946) .... Daffy Duck/Duck Twacy/Wolf Man/Rubber Head/Neon Noodle/Pig

Greedy for Tweety (1957) .... Sylvester/Tweety

Greetings Bait (1943) .... Wacky Worm/Jerry Colonna

Grey Hounded Hare, The (1949) .... Bugs Bunny

Gripes (1943) .... Private Snafu

Gruesome Twosome, A (1945) .... Tweety/Durante Cat/Dumb Cat

Hair-Raising Hare (1946) .... Bugs Bunny/Peter Lorre Scientist/Gossamer/Doctor

Half-Fare Hare (1956) .... Bugs Bunny

Ham in a Role, A (1949) .... Mac/Dog

Happy Birthday, Bugs! Fifty Looney Years (1990) TV (archive footage) .... Himself

Hare Brush (1955) .... Bugs Bunny

Hare Conditioned (1945) .... Bugs Bunny/Gildersleeve (one line)

Hare Do (1949) .... Bugs Bunny/Usher

Hare Force (1944) .... Bugs Bunny/Sylvester

Hare Grows in Manhattan, A (1947) .... Bugs Bunny/Spike/Dogs

Hare Lift (1952) .... Bugs Bunny/Yosemite Sam

Hare Remover (1946) .... Bugs Bunny/Rover

Hare Ribbin' (1944) .... Bugs Bunny/Russian Dog (speaking like Elmer Fudd)

Hare Splitter (1948) .... Bugs Bunny/Casbah

Hare Tonic (1945) .... Bugs Bunny

Hare Trigger (1945) .... Bugs Bunny/Yosemite Sam/Train Passengers

Hare Trimmed (1953) .... Bugs Bunny/Yosemite Sam

Hare We Go (1951) .... Bugs Bunny

Hare-Abian Nights (1959) .... Bugs Bunny/Yosemite Sam

Hare-Brained Hypnotist, The (1942) .... Bugs Bunny

Hare-Breadth Hurry (1963) .... Bugs Bunny

Haredevil Hare (1948) .... Bugs Bunny/Marvin the Martian/K-9/Radio Jingle Singer/Control Center Technicians

Hare-Less Wolf (1958) .... Bugs Bunny/Charles M. Wolf

Hare-um Scare-um (1939) (uncredited) .... Hunter/Rabbit/Dog

Hare-Way to the Stars (1958) .... Bugs Bunny/Marvin Martian

Hasty Hare, The (1952) .... Bugs Bunny/Marvin Martian

Haunted Mouse (1965) .... Tom/Jerry

Have You Got Any Castles? (1938)

Hawaiian Aye Aye (1964) .... Sylvester/Tweety

Heathcliff (1980) TV Series .... Heathcliff

Heathcliff: The Movie (1986)

Heathcliff & the Catillac Cats (1984) TV Series .... Heathcliff

Heaven Scent (1956) .... Pepe le Pew

Heckling Hare, The (1941) .... Bugs Bunny

Heir-Conditioned (1955) .... Sylvester

Henhouse Henery (1949) .... Foghorn Leghorn/Henery Hawk/Barnyard Dog

Henpecked Duck, The (1941) .... Porky Pig/Daffy Duck/Baby Duckling

Hep Cat, The (1942) .... Hep Cat/Rosebud
Here Comes the Grump (1969) TV Series .... Blip
Here Today, Gone Tamale (1959) .... Speedy Gonzales/Sylvester
Herr Meets Hare (1945) .... Bugs Bunny/Goering/Hitler
Hey There, It's Yogi Bear (1964) .... Grifter
Hiawatha's Rabbit Hunt (1941) .... Bugs Bunny/Hiawatha
Hick a Slick and a Chick, A (1948)
High and the Flighty, The (1956) .... Foghorn Leghorn/Daffy Duck/Barnyard Dog
High Diving Hare (1949) .... Bugs Bunny/Yosemite Sam
Hillbilly Hare (1950) .... Bugs Bunny/Curt Martin
Hippety Hopper (1949) .... Sylvester/Mouse/Bulldog
His Bitter Half (1950) .... Daffy Duck
His Hare Raising Tale (1951) .... Bugs Bunny
Hiss and Make Up (1943) .... Roscoe
Hitch in Time, A (1955) .... Blip
Hobo Bobo (1947) .... New Yorkers/Baby
Hold the Lion, Please (1942) .... Bugs Bunny/Monkey/Giraffe/Mrs. Bugs Bunny
Hole Idea, The (1955) .... Prof. Calvin Q. Calculus
Holiday for Drumsticks (1949) .... Daffy Duck/Tom Turk
Hollywood Canine Canteen (1946) .... Colonna Dog/Costello Dog/Besser Dog/Service Dog/Sailor
Hollywood Daffy (1946) .... Daffy Duck/Studio Guard/Jack Benny/Jimmy Durante
Hollywood Steps Out (1941) (uncredited) .... Jerry Colonna
Home, Tweet Home (1950) .... Sylvester/Tweety
Home Front, The (1943/I) .... Private Snafu
Homeless Hare (1950) .... Bugs Bunny
Honey's Money (1962) .... Yosemite Sam
Hop, Look, and Listen (1948) .... Sylvester/Bulldog/Mother Kangaroo
Hoppy Daze (1961) .... Sylvester/Gruff Cat/Hippety Hopper
Hoppy-Go-Lucky (1952) .... Sylvester
Horse Hare (1960) .... Bugs Bunny/Yosemite Sam
Horsefly Fleas, A (1948) .... Anthony Flea/Horsefly/Dog/Flea Circus Performers
Hot Cross Bunny (1948) .... Bugs Bunny/Doctor
Hot Spot (1945) .... Private Snafu
Hound for Trouble, A (1951) .... Charlie Dog/Pizzeria Owner
House-Hunting Mice (1948) .... Hubie
How Bugs Bunny Won the West (1978) TV .... Bugs Bunny/Yosemite Sam/Daffy Duck
How's Your Love Life? (1971) .... Blackie
Hungry Wolf, The (1942) .... Wolf
Hurdy-Gurdy Hare (1950) .... Bugs Bunny
Hush My Mouse (1946) .... Filligan
Hyde and Go Tweet (1960) .... Sylvester/Tweety/Mr. Hyde
Hyde and Hare (1955) .... Bugs Bunny/Dr. Jekyll
Hypo-Chondri-Cat, The (1950) .... Hubie/Claude Cat
I Gopher You (1954) .... Mac
I Taw a Putty Tat (1948) .... Sylvester/Tweety
I Was a Teenage Thumb (1963) .... George Ebeneezer Thumb/Ralph K. Merlin/King Arthur
Iceman Ducketh, The (1964) .... Bugs Bunny/Daffy Duck
Impatient Patient, The (1942) .... Daffy Duck/Chloe/Dr. Jerkyl/Intercom/Radio Announcer
In the Aleutians (1945) .... Private Snafu
Infantry Blues, The (1943) .... Private Snafu
Injun Trouble (1938) .... Porky Pig/Sloppy Moe/Trail Boss

Is There a Doctor in the Mouse? (1964) . . . . Tom/Jerry/Sound Effects
Isle of Pingo Pongo, The (1938) (uncredited) . . . . Egghead
Itch in Time, An (1943) (uncredited) . . . . Dog/Cat/A. Flea (screaming)
It's a Great Feeling (1949) . . . . Bugs Bunny
It's an Ill Wind (1939) . . . . Porky Pig
It's Hummer Time (1950) . . . . Cat
It's Murder She Says (1945) . . . . Private Snafu
It's Nice to Have a Mouse around the House (1965) . . . . Speedy Gonzales/Daffy Duck
Jack-Wabbit and the Beanstalk (1943) . . . . Bugs Bunny/Giant/Narrator
Jasper Goes Hunting (1944) . . . . Bugs Bunny
Jeepers Creepers (1939/II) . . . . Porky Pig/Ghost (singing)
Jerry, Jerry, Quite Contrary (1966) . . . . Tom/Jerry
Jet Cage, The (1962) . . . . Sylvester/Tweety/Blackbird
Jetsons, The (1962) TV Series . . . . Cosmo S. Spacely/Additional Voices
Jetsons, The (1985) TV Series . . . . Mr. Spacely
Jetsons: The Movie (1990) . . . . Mr. Spacely
Jetsons Christmas Carol, The (1985) TV . . . . Mr. Spacely/Jacob Marsley
Jetsons Meet the Flintstones, The (1987) TV . . . . Barney Rubble/Dino/Mr. Spacely
Jitterbug Follies (1939) (uncredited) . . . . Count Screwloose
Joe Glow the Firefly (1941) . . . . Joe Glow
Journey Back to Oz (1971) . . . . Crow
Jumpin' Jupiter (1955) . . . . Porky Pig
Jungle Jitters (1938) (uncredited) . . . . Natives
Kiddies Kitty, A (1955) . . . . Sylvester/TV Announcer/Bulldog
Kiss Me Cat (1953) . . . . Marc Anthony/Pussyfoot/Tom/Mouse
Kiss Me Stupid (1964) . . . . Dr. Sheldrake
Kit for Cat (1948) . . . . Sylvester/Kitten/Melvin/Landlord
Kitty Kornered (1946) . . . . Porky Pig/Sylvester/Small Cat/Tiny Cat/Drunk Cat/Goldfish
  Wife/Moose
Knight-Mare Hare (1955) . . . . Bugs Bunny/Sir O of K/Merlin/Donkey Owner
Knights Must Fall (1949) . . . . Bugs Bunny/Sir Pantsalot of Dropseat Manor/Usher
Knighty Knight Bugs (1958) . . . . Bugs Bunny/Yosemite Sam/King Arthur
Knock Knock (1940) (uncredited) . . . . Woody Woodpecker
Kristopher Kolumbus Jr. (1939) . . . . Porky Pig
Lancelot Link/Secret Chimp (1970) TV Series
Last Hungry Cat, The (1961) . . . . Sylvester/Tweety
Lecture on Camouflage, A (1944) . . . . Private Snafu
Leghorn Blows at Midnight, The (1950) . . . . Foghorn Leghorn/Henery Hawk/Barnyard Dog
Leghorn Swoggled (1951) . . . . Foghorn Leghorn/Henery Hawk/Barnyard Dog
Life with Feathers (1945) (uncredited) . . . . Sylvester
Lighter Than Hare (1960) . . . . Bugs Bunny/Yosemite Sam
Lighthouse Mouse (1955) . . . . Sylvester/Lighthouse Owner
Lights Fantastic (1942) . . . . Eye Test Announcer
Lion's Busy, The (1950) . . . . Beaky Buzzard
Lippy the Lion (1971) TV Series . . . . Hardy Har Har
Little Beau Pepé (1952) . . . . Pepe le Pew/Foreign Legion Soldiers
Little Blabbermouse (1940) (uncredited) . . . . Little Blabbermouse
Little Boy Boo (1954) . . . . Foghorn Leghorn
Little Brother Rat (1939) (uncredited) . . . . Owl/Baby Owls
Little Orphan Airedale (1947) . . . . Porky Pig/Charlie Dog/Rags McMutt/City Geek
Little Red Riding Rabbit (1944) . . . . Bugs Bunny

Little Red Rodent Hood (1952) . . . . Sylvester

Long-Haired Hare (1949) . . . . Bugs Bunny/Giovanni Jones

Looney, Looney, Looney Bugs Bunny Movie, The (1981) . . . . Bugs Bunny/King Arthur/Sir Osis of Liver/Sir Loin of Beef/Yosemite Sam/Gerry the Idgit Dragon/Daffy Duck/Sylvester/Tweety Pie/ Porky Pig/Speedy Gonzales/Satan/Treasury Director/Rocky/Mugsy/Judge/Clancy/O'Hara/Cops/ Pepe le Pew/Clarence (B. A. Bird)

Louvre Come Back to Me! (1962) . . . . Pepe le Pew

Lovelorn Leghorn (1951) . . . . Foghorn Leghorn/Barnyard Dog

Lumber Jack-Rabbit (1954) . . . . Bugs Bunny

Lumber Jerks (1955) . . . . Mac

Lyin' Mouse, The (1937) . . . . Cat

Mad as a Mars Hare (1963) . . . . Bugs Bunny/Marvin Martian/Cape Canaveral Controller

Magilla Gorilla (1964) TV Series . . . . Deputy Droop-a-Long

Malibu Beach Party (1940) . . . . Rochester

Man Called Flintstone, The (1966) . . . . Barney Rubble

Martian through Georgia (1962) . . . . Little Martian

Matinee Mouse (1966) (uncredited) . . . . Tom/Jerry

Matty's Funday Funnies (Beanie & Cecil) (1959) TV Series . . . . Additional Voices

Meet John Doughboy (1941) . . . . Porky Pig

Merrie Melodies: Starring Bugs Bunny and Friends (1990) TV Series . . . . Various Characters

Message to Gracias, A (1964) . . . . Speedy Gonzales/Sylvester

Mexicali Shmoes (1959) . . . . Speedy Gonzales

Mexican Boarders (1962) . . . . Speedy Gonzales/Slowpoke Rodriguez/Sylvester

Mexican Cat Dance (1963) . . . . Speedy Gonzales/Sylvester

Mexican Joyride (1947) . . . . Daffy Duck/Bull

Mexican Mousepiece (1966) . . . . Daffy Duck/Speedy Gonzales

Million Hare, The (1963) . . . . Bugs Bunny/Daffy Duck

Mississippi Hare (1949) . . . . Bugs Bunny/Southern Gentleman/Colonel Shuffle/Purser

Mister Magoo (1960) TV Series . . . . Harry/Alice/Chang/Robert the Puppy

Mixed Master (1956)

Moby Duck (1965) . . . . Daffy Duck/Speedy Gonzales

Mother Was a Rooster (1962) . . . . Foghorn Leghorn/Barnyard Dog

Mouse and Garden (1960) . . . . Sylvester

Mouse Divided, A (1953) . . . . Sylvester

Mouse from H.U.N.G.E.R., The (1967) (uncredited) . . . . Tom/Cigar Store Indian

Mouse Mazurka (1949) . . . . Sylvester/Narrator

Mouse Menace (1946) . . . . Porky Pig/Mouse/Robot Cat

Mouse on 57th Street, The (1961) . . . . Little Brown Mouse

Mouse That Jack Built, The (1959) . . . . The Maxwell

Mouse Wreckers (1948) . . . . Hubie

Mouse-Merized Cat, The (1946) . . . . Catsello

Mouse-Placed Kitten (1959) . . . . Clyde/Junior

Mouse-Taken Identity (1957) . . . . Sylvester/Sylvester Jr.

Much Ado about Mousing (1964) . . . . Tom/Jerry/Bulldog/Puppy

Muchos Locos (1966) . . . . Daffy Duck/Speedy Gonzales

Munsters, The (1964) TV Series (uncredited) . . . . Raven (1964–1966)

Muscle Tussle (1953) . . . . Daffy Duck/Hunky Duck

Music Mice-Tro, The (1967) . . . . Daffy Duck/Speedy Gonzales

Mutiny on the Bunny (1950) . . . . Bugs Bunny/Shanghai (Yosemite) Sam/Traumatized Sailor/Mouse

Mutt in a Rut, A (1959) . . . . Rover/Television Announcer

Muzzle Tough (1954) . . . . Sylvester/Tweety/Hector/Dogs

My Bunny Lies over the Sea (1948) . . . . Bugs Bunny/MacRory

My Dream Is Yours (1949) . . . . Bugs Bunny/Tweety

My Favorite Duck (1942) . . . . Daffy Duck/Porky Pig/Eagle/Baby Eagle

My Little Duckaroo (1954) . . . . Daffy Duck

Napoleon Bunny-Part (1956) . . . . Bugs Bunny/Napoleon/Mugsy

Nasty Quacks (1945) . . . . Daffy Duck/Agnes's Father

Naughty Neighbors (1939) . . . . Porky Pig/McCoy Duck

Nelly's Folly (1961)

Neptune's Daughter (1949) . . . . Pancho

New Fred and Barney Show, The (1979) TV Series . . . . Barney Rubble

New Hanna-Barbera Cartoon Series, The (1962) TV Series . . . . Hardy Har Har

Night of the Living Duck, The (1988) . . . . Daffy Duck

Night Watchman, The (1938) . . . . Tough Mice

No Barking (1954) (uncredited) . . . . Tweety

No Buddy Atoll (1945) . . . . Private Snafu

No Parking Hare (1954) . . . . Bugs Bunny

Notes to You (1941) . . . . Porky Pig/Cat

Nothing but the Tooth (1948) . . . . Porky

Now, Hare This (1958) . . . . Bugs Bunny/Big Bad Wolf

Now That Summer Is Gone (1938) (uncredited) . . . . Gambling Squirrel

Nuts and Volts (1964) . . . . Speedy Gonzales/Sylvester

Odor of the Day (1948) . . . . Pepe le Pew/Dog

Odor-able Kitty (1945) . . . . Pepe le Pew/Cat

Of Feline Bondage (1965) . . . . Tom

Of Rice and Hen (1953) . . . . Foghorn Leghorn/Barnyard Dog/Rooster Minister

Often an Orphan (1949) . . . . Porky/Charlie Dog

Oily American, The (1954) . . . . Moe Hican/Butler/Moose

Oily Hare (1952) . . . . Bugs Bunny/Texan

Old Glory (1939) . . . . Porky Pig

Old Grey Hare, The (1944) . . . . Bugs Bunny/God

One Meat Brawl (1947) . . . . Porky Pig/Mandrake/Barnyard Dog/Grover Groundhog (singing)

Operation Rabbit (1952) . . . . Bugs Bunny/Wile E. Coyote

Operation Snafu (1945) . . . . Private Snafu

Orange Blossoms for Violet (1952)

Outpost (1944) . . . . Private Snafu

Pancho's Hideaway (1964) . . . . Speedy Gonzales/Pancho Vanilla

Pantry Panic (1941) . . . . Woody Woodpecker

Pappy's Puppy (1955) . . . . Sylvester

Past Perfumance (1955) . . . . Pepe le Pew

Patient Porky (1940) . . . . Porky Pig/Dr. Chilled Air/Elevator Operator/Rabbit/Bugs Bunny/Oliver
   Owl/Scottish Dog/Program Seller

Payday (1944) . . . . Private Snafu

Paying the Piper (1949) . . . . Porky Pig/Supreme Cat

Peace on Earth (1939) . . . . Grandpa Squirrel

Peck up Your Troubles (1945) . . . . Sylvester

Pent-House Mouse (1963) . . . . Vocal Effects

People Are Bunny (1959) . . . . Bugs Bunny/Daffy Duck/Host

Perils of Penelope Pitstop (1969) TV Series . . . . Bully Brothers/Yak Yak/Chug-a-Boom

Person to Bunny (1960) . . . . Bugs Bunny/Daffy Duck

Pest in the House, A (1947) . . . . Daffy Duck/Drunk/Narrator

Pest That Came to Dinner, The (1948) . . . . Porky Pig/Pierre the Termite/Sureshot

Pests for Guests (1955) . . . . Mac
Peter Potamus and His Magic Flying Balloon (1964) TV Series . . . . Sneezly Seal
Peter Potamus Show, The (1964) TV Series . . . . Sneezly
Phantom Tollbooth, The (1970) . . . . Officer Short Shrift
Picador Porky (1937) . . . . Drunken Bull
Pickled Pink (1965) . . . . Drunk
Pied Piper of Guadalupe, The (1961) . . . . Speedy Gonzales/Sylvester
Pied Piper Porky (1939) . . . . Porky Pig
Piker's Peak (1957) . . . . Bugs Bunny/Yosemite Sam
Pilgrim Porky (1940) . . . . Porky Pig
Pinocchio (1940) (uncredited) . . . . Hiccup sound effect for Gideon
Pizza Tweety-Pie, A (1958) . . . . Sylvester/Tweety/Spaghetti Bird
Pizzicato Pussycat (1955) . . . . Mr. Jones/Males
Plane Daffy (1944) . . . . Daffy Duck/Hitler/Goering/Goebels
Plenty of Money and You (1937) . . . . Ostrich
Plop Goes the Weasel (1953) . . . . Foghorn Leghorn/Barnyard Dog
Polar Pals (1939) (uncredited) . . . . Porky Pig
Political Cartoon, A (1972) . . . . Bugs Bunny
Pop 'Im Pop! (1950) . . . . Sylvester/Sylvester Jr.
Porky and Daffy (1938) . . . . Porky Pig/Daffy Duck/Champ/Pelican Referee
Porky and Gabby (1937) . . . . Porky Pig
Porky and Teabiscuit (1939) . . . . Porky Pig
Porky at the Crocadero (1938) . . . . Porky Pig
Porky Chops (1949) . . . . Porky Pig/Squirrel
Porky in Egypt (1938) . . . . Porky Pig/Camel
Porky in Wackyland (1938) . . . . Porky Pig/Do-Do/Various Wackyland Citizens
Porky Pig Show, The (1964) TV Series . . . . Porky Pig/Daffy Duck/Sylvester/Marvin the
    Martian/Charlie Dog/Bugs Bunny/Tweety/Sylvester Jr./Speedy Gonzales/Foghorn Leghorn/Pepe
    le Pew/Goofy Gopher Mac/Beak Buzzard/Ralph Wolf/Sam Sheepdog
Porky Pig's Feat (1943) . . . . Porky Pig/Daffy Duck/Broken Arms Hotel Manager/Elevator Gam-
    bler/Bugs Bunny
Porky the Fireman (1938) . . . . Porky Pig/Slow Dog
Porky the Giant Killer (1939) . . . . Porky Pig
Porky the Gob (1938) . . . . Porky Pig
Porky's Ant (1941) . . . . Porky Pig
Porky's Badtime Story (1937) . . . . Porky Pig
Porky's Baseball Broadcast (1940) . . . . Porky Pig
Porky's Bear Facts (1941) . . . . Porky Pig/Bear/Cow/Dog/Mouse
Porky's Building (1937) . . . . Porky Pig
Porky's Cafe (1942) . . . . Porky Pig/Conrad Cat/Customer
Porky's Double Trouble (1937) . . . . Porky Pig/Killer
Porky's Duck Hunt (1937) . . . . Porky Pig/Daffy Duck
Porky's Five and Ten (1938) . . . . Porky Pig
Porky's Garden (1937) . . . . Porky Pig
Porky's Hare Hunt (1938) . . . . Porky Pig/Zero/Rabbit
Porky's Hero Agency (1937) . . . . Porky Pig
Porky's Hired Hand (1940) . . . . Porky Pig/Gregory Grunt/Steam-Reduced Fox
Porky's Hotel (1939) . . . . Porky Pig/Gabby Goose/Gouty Goat
Porky's Last Stand (1940) . . . . Porky Pig/Daffy Duck
Porky's Midnight Matinee (1941) . . . . Porky Pig
Porky's Movie Mystery (1939) . . . . Porky Pig/Mr. Motto

Porky's Naughty Nephew (1938) .... Porky Pig
Porky's Party (1938) .... Porky Pig/Black Fury/Penguin
Porky's Pastry Pirates (1942) .... Porky Pig
Porky's Phoney Express (1938) .... Porky Pig
Porky's Picnic (1939) .... Porky Pig
Porky's Pooch (1941) .... Porky Pig/Rover/Sandy
Porky's Poor Fish (1940) .... Porky Pig
Porky's Poppa (1938) .... Porky Pig/Porky's Poppa/Duck
Porky's Preview (1941) .... Porky Pig/Kangaroo/Firefly Usher/Skunk
Porky's Prize Pony (1941) .... Porky Pig
Porky's Railroad (1937) .... Porky Pig
Porky's Snooze Reel (1941) .... Porky Pig
Porky's Spring Planting (1938) .... Porky Pig/Streamline
Porky's Super Service (1937) .... Porky Pig
Porky's Tire Trouble (1939) .... Porky Pig
Portrait of the Artist as a Young Bunny (1980) TV .... Bugs Bunny/Elmer Fudd
Prehistoric Porky (1940) .... Porky Pig/Prehistoric Black Panther/Vulture
Pre-Hysterical Hare (1958) .... Bugs Bunny/Saber-Tooth Rabbit/Narrator/Dinosaurs/Saber-Tooth Tiger
Prince Violent (1961) .... Bugs Bunny/Yosemite Sam
Private Snafu vs. Malaria Mike (1944) .... Private Snafu
Prize Pest, The (1951) .... Porky Pig/Daffy Duck
Punch Trunk (1953) .... Birdbath Owner/Asylum Collector/John/Drunk/Circus Cat/Dr. Robert Bruce Cameron
Puny Express (1950) (uncredited) .... Woody Woodpecker
Putty Tat Trouble (1951) .... Sylvester/Tweety/Sam
Quack Shot (1954) .... Daffy Duck/Large Fish
Quacker Tracker (1967) .... Daffy Duck/Speedy Gonzales
Quackodile Tears (1962) .... Daffy Duck
Rabbit Every Monday (1951) .... Bugs Bunny/Yosemite Sam
Rabbit Fire (1951) .... Bugs Bunny/Daffy Duck/Elephant
Rabbit Hood (1949) .... Bugs Bunny/Sheriff of Nottingham/Little John
Rabbit of Seville (1950) .... Bugs Bunny
Rabbit Punch (1948) .... Bugs Bunny/Ring Announcer
Rabbit Rampage (1955) .... Bugs Bunny
Rabbit Romeo (1957) .... Bugs Bunny
Rabbit Seasoning (1952) .... Bugs Bunny/Daffy Duck
Rabbit Transit (1947) .... Bugs Bunny/Cecil Turtle/Deliverymen
Rabbit's Feat (1960) .... Bugs Bunny/Wile E. Coyote
Rabbit's Kin (1952) .... Bugs Bunny/Shorty
Rabbitson Crusoe (1956) .... Bugs Bunny/Yosemite Sam
Racketeer Rabbit (1946) .... Bugs Bunny/Hugo
Rattled Rooster, The (1948) .... Rooster/Worm/Rattlesnake
Raw! Raw! Rooster! (1956) .... Foghorn Leghorn/Rhode Island Red (dazed)
Ready, Woolen, and Able (1960) .... Ralph Wolf/Sam Sheepdog
Really Scent (1959) .... Pepe le Pew
Rebel Rabbit (1949) .... Bugs Bunny/Bounty Commissioner/Congressman
Rebel without Claws, The (1961) .... Sylvester/Tweety/Southern Colonel/Soldier
Red Riding Hoodwinked (1955) .... Sylvester/Tweety/Big Bad Wolf
Return of Mr. Hook, The (1943) (uncredited) .... Sailors/Sales Clerk/Realtor
Rhapsody Rabbit (1946) .... Bugs Bunny/Coughing Audience Member

Riff Raffy Daffy (1948) .... Daffy Duck/Porky Pig/Gopher/Cuckoo Bird

Road Runner Show, The (1966) TV Series .... Road Runner/Various Characters

Road to Andalay (1964) .... Speedy Gonzales/Sylvester

Roadrunner a Go-Go (1965) .... Wile E. Coyote

Robin Hood Daffy (1958) .... Daffy Duck/Robin Hood/Porky Pig/Friar Tuck

Robinhood Makes Good (1939) (uncredited) .... Fox

Robinson Crusoe Jr. (1941) .... Porky Pig

Robot Rabbit (1953) .... Bugs Bunny

Rocket Squad (1956) .... Daffy Duck/Sgt. Joe Monday/Porky Pig/Detective Shmoe Tuesday/George "Mother" Machree/Chief

Rockin' with Judy Jetson (1988) TV .... Cosmo Spacely

Rodent to Stardom (1967) .... Daffy Duck/Speedy Gonzales

Roger Rabbit and the Secrets of Toon Town (1988) TV .... Himself

Roman Legion-Hare (1955) .... Bugs Bunny/Yosemite Sam/Emperor Nero

Room and Bird (1951) .... Sylvester/Tweety/Desk Clerk

Roughly Squeaking (1946) .... Hubie/Cat/Dog

Rover's Rival (1937) .... Porky Pig/Rover/Pup

Rumors (1943) .... Private Snafu

Russian Rhapsody (1944) .... Adolf Hitler/Gremlin from the Kremlin

Sabrina, the Teenage Witch (1971) TV Series .... Salem Spellman

Sabrina and the Groovy Ghoulies (1970) TV Series .... Salem Spellman

Saddle Silly (1941) .... Pony Express Rider/Dispatcher

Sahara Hare (1955) .... Bugs Bunny/Yosemite Sam/Daffy Duck

Sandy Claws (1954) .... Sylvester/Tweety

Satan's Waitin' (1954) .... Sylvester/Tweety/Devil Dog

Scalawag (1973) .... Barfly the Parrot

Scalp Trouble (1939) .... Daffy Duck/Porky Pig/Jerry Colonna Indian

Scaredy Cat (1948) .... Porky Pig

Scarlet Pumpernickel, The (1950) .... Daffy Duck/Porky Pig/Sylvester/Highwayman/Narrator

Scent of the Matterhorn, A (1961) .... Pepe le Pew/Penelope/Cow/Chickens/Pig/Dog/Frog

Scent-imental over You (1947) .... Pepe le Pew

Scent-imental Romeo (1951) .... Pepe le Pew/Penelope/Zookeeper/Lion/Popcorn Cart Bird/Pigeon Feeder/Poodle

Scooby All-Stars (1979) TV Series .... Captain Caveman/Speed Buggy

Scooby's All-Star Laff-a-Lympics (1977) TV Series .... Captain Caveman/Speed Buggy

Scrap Happy Daffy (1943) .... Daffy Duck/Hitler/Nazi Soldiers/Submarine Captain/Billy Goat/Great-Great-Great-Great-Great-Uncle Dillingham Duck/Minuteman Duck/Pioneer Duck/Admiral Duck/Lincoln Duck/Daffy's Ancestors

Screwdriver, The (1941) .... Woody Woodpecker

Scrub Me Mama with a Boogie Beat (1941) (uncredited) .... Boat Captain/Fighter One/Fighter Two/Mammy Washing Clothes/Various Citizens

Secret Squirrel Show, The (1965) TV Series .... Secret Squirrel

Secrets of the Caribbean (1945) .... Private Snafu

See Ya Later Gladiator (1968) .... Daffy Duck/Speedy Gonzales/Emperor Nero

Señorella and the Glass Huarache (1964)

She Was an Acrobat's Daughter (1937) (uncredited) .... Dole Promise/Who Dehr/Stickoutski

Sheep Ahoy (1954) .... Fred (Sam) Sheepdog/Ralph Sheepdog/George (Ralph) Wolf/Sam Wolf

Sheep in the Deep, A (1962) .... Ralph Wolf/Sam Sheepdog

Shell-Shocked Egg, The (1948)

Shishkabugs (1962) .... Bugs Bunny/Yosemite Sam/King

Shop, Look, & Listen (1940) (uncredited) .... Little Blabbermouse
Show Biz Bugs (1957) .... Bugs Bunny/Daffy Duck
Sinbad Jr. (1965) TV Series .... Salty the Parrott
Skyscraper Caper (1968) .... Daffy Duck/Speedy Gonzales
Slap Happy Pappy (1940) .... Porky Pig
Slap-Hoppy Mouse, The (1956) .... Sylvester/Sylvester Jr.
Sleepy-Time Possum (1951) .... Ma/Pa/Junior Possum
Slick Chick, The (1962) .... Foghorn Leghorn
Slick Hare (1947) .... Bugs Bunny
Slightly Daffy (1944) (uncredited) .... Porky Pig/Daffy Duck
Snafuperman (1944) .... Private Snafu
Snow Business (1953) .... Sylvester/Tweety/Ranger
Snow Excuse (1966) .... Daffy Duck/Speedy Gonzales
Snowbody Loves Me (1964) .... Tom/Jerry
Snowman's Land (1939) .... Head Mountie/Dirty Pierre
Sock a Doodle Do (1952) .... Foghorn Leghorn/Barnyard Dog/Kid Banty
Soup or Sonic (1980) TV .... Road Runner
Sour Puss, The (1940) .... Porky Pig/Cat/Flying Fish
Southern Fried Rabbit (1953) .... Bugs Bunny/Yosemite Sam
Spaced Out Bunny (1980) TV .... Bugs Bunny/Marvin Martian/Hugo/Grouchy Butterfly
Speed Buggy (1973) TV Series .... Speed Buggy
Speedy Ghost to Town (1967) .... Daffy Duck/Speedy Gonzales
Speedy Gonzales (1955) .... Speedy Gonzales/Sylvester
Spies (1943) (uncredited) .... Private Snafu
Spy Swatter, The (1967) .... Daffy Duck/Speedy Gonzales/Mr. Brain (Sam)/Professor/Hugo the Robot
Squeak in the Deep, A (1966) .... Daffy Duck/Speedy Gonzales
Stage Door Cartoon (1944) .... Bugs Bunny/Southern Sheriff
Star Is Bored, A (1956) .... Bugs Bunny/Daffy Duck/Yosemite Sam/Producer
Steal Wool (1957) .... Ralph Wolf/Sam Sheepdog
Stooge for a Mouse (1950) .... Sylvester/Mike Bulldog/Mouse
Stork Naked (1955) .... Daffy Duck/Drunken Stork
Strangled Eggs (1961) .... Foghorn Leghorn/Henery Hawk
Street Cat Named Sylvester, A (1953) .... Sylvester/Tweety/Hector Bulldog
Strife with Father (1950) .... Beaky Buzzard
Stupid Cupid, The (1944) .... Daffy Duck/Elmer Fudd/Rooster/Dog/Cat/Bluebird/Emily
Stupor Duck (1956) .... Daffy Duck/Aardvark Ratnik
Stupor Salesman, The (1948) .... Daffy Duck/Slug McSlug
Super Snooper, The (1952) .... Daffy Duck
Super-Rabbit (1943) (uncredited) .... Bugs Bunny/Cottontail Smith/Narrator/Horse/Texas Rabbit/Observer
Suppressed Duck (1965) .... Daffy Duck/Ranger/Bear
Swallow the Leader (1949) .... Cat
Swing Ding Amigo (1966) .... Daffy Duck/Speedy Gonzales
Swooner Crooner (1944) .... Porky Pig
Sylvester & Tweety, Daffy & Speedy Show, The (1981) TV Series .... Daffy Duck/Speedy Gonzales/Sylvester/Tweety/Hector
Sylvester & Tweety Show, The (1976) TV Series .... Various Characters
Tabasco Road (1957) .... Speedy Gonzales
Tale of Two Kitties, A (1942) .... Catstello/Tweety

Tale of Two Mice, A (1945) .... Catsello
Tales of Washington Irving (1970) TV
Target Snafu (1944) .... Private Snafu
Taste of Catnip, A (1966) .... Daffy Duck/Speedy Gonzales
Tease for Two (1965) .... Daffy Duck/Mac/Tosh/Cosmonaut
That's Warner Bros.! (1995) TV Series .... Various Characters
There Auto Be a Law (1953) .... Timid Motorist/Additional Voices
This Is a Life? (1955) .... Bugs Bunny/Daffy Duck/Yosemite Sam
Thread of Life, The (1960) TV .... Ship
Three Brothers, The (1944) .... Private Snafu
Thugs with Dirty Mugs (1939) (uncredited) .... Tattle-Tale Bank Clerk/Annoyed Mobster/Secret Agent 2⅜/Man in Audience
Thumb Fun (1952) .... Porky Pig/Daffy Duck
Tick Tock Tuckered (1944) .... Porky Pig/Daffy Duck/Boss
Timid Toreador, The (1940) .... Porky Pig/Slapsy Maxie Rosenbull/Announcer/Heckler/Mexicans
To Duck . . . or Not to Duck (1943) .... Daffy Duck/Duck Referee/Laramore/Porky Pig
To Hare Is Human (1956) .... Bugs Bunny/Wile E. Coyote
Tokio Jokio (1943) (uncredited) .... Nipponews Buzzard/Japanese Narrator/Air Raid/Professor Tojo/Red Togoson/Admiral Yamamoto/Lord Hee Haw/Human Torpedo
Tokyo Woes (1945) (uncredited) .... Japanese Announcer/Sad Sack/Singing Bond
Tom and Jerry (1965) TV Series .... Various Characters (1965–1972)
Tom Tom Tomcat (1953) .... Sylvester/Tweety
Tom Turk and Daffy (1944) .... Porky Pig/Daffy Duck
Tom Turkey and His Harmonica Humdingers (1940) .... Tom Turkey
Tom-ic Energy (1965)
Too Hop to Handle (1956) .... Sylvester/Sylvester Jr./Zoo Official/Man in Park
Tortilla Flaps (1958) .... Speedy Gonzales/Crow
Tortoise Beats Hare (1941) .... Bugs Bunny/Cecil Turtle/Chester Turtle/Turtles
Tortoise Wins by a Hare (1943) .... Bugs Bunny/Cecil Turtle/Mrs. Turtle/Narrators/Rabbit Bookee/Rabbit Thugs
Touché and Go (1957) .... Pepe le Pew
Transylvania 6-5000 (1963) (uncredited) .... Bugs Bunny
Trap Happy Porky (1945) .... Porky Pig/Drunk Cat
Tree Cornered Tweety (1956) .... Sylvester/Tweety
Tree for Two (1952) .... Sylvester/Spike
Trial of Mr. Wolf, The (1941) .... Mr. Wolf
Trick or Tweet (1959) .... Sylvester/Tweety
Trip for Tat (1960) .... Sylvester/Tweety
Trollkins (1981) TV Series
Tugboat Granny (1956) .... Sylvester/Tweety
Turn-Tale Wolf, The (1952) .... Big Bad Wolf/Wolf's Son
Tweet and Lovely (1959) .... Sylvester/Tweety
Tweet and Sour (1956) .... Sylvester/Tweety
Tweet Dreams (1959) .... Sylvester/Tweety
Tweet Tweet Tweety (1951) .... Sylvester/Tweety/Ranger
Tweet Zoo (1957) .... Sylvester/Tweety/Zoo Conductor
Tweetie Pie (1947) (uncredited) .... Tweety/Sylvester/Thomas
Tweety and the Beanstalk (1957) .... Sylvester/Tweety/Giant
Tweety's Circus (1955) .... Sylvester/Tweety
Tweety's S.O.S. (1951) .... Sylvester/Tweety/Ship Captain
Two Gophers from Texas (1948) .... Mac

Two Guys from Texas (1948) . . . . Bugs Bunny
Two Scent's Worth (1955) . . . . Pepe le Pew
Two's a Crowd (1950) . . . . John
Unbearable Bear, The (1943) . . . . Burglar/Officer Bear
Unexpected Pest, The (1956) . . . . Sylvester/Man/Mouse
Unmentionables, The (1963) . . . . Elegant Mess (Bugs Bunny)/Rocky/Mugsy/Snitch/Agency Director
Unnatural History (1959)
Unruly Hare, The (1945) . . . . Bugs Bunny/Railroad Workers
Unshrinkable Jerry Mouse, The (1964)
Up-Standing Sitter, The (1948) . . . . Daffy Duck
Upswept Hare (1953) . . . . Bugs Bunny
Vice Squad (1953)
Wabbit Twouble (1941) . . . . Bugs Bunny/Bear
Wabbit Who Came to Supper, The (1942) . . . . Bugs Bunny/Telegram Boy/Delivery Man
Wackiki Wabbit (1943) (uncredited) . . . . Bugs Bunny
Wacky Races (1968) . . . . The Ant Hill Mob
Wacky Wabbit, The (1942) . . . . Bugs Bunny
Wacky Worm, The (1941) (uncredited) . . . . Wacky Worm/Crow
Wagon Heels (1945) . . . . Porky Pig/Injun Joe/Sloppy Moe/Trail Boss
Walky Talky Hawky (1946) . . . . Foghorn Leghorn/Henery Hawk/Barnyard Dog
Wanted: No Master (1939) . . . . (uncredited)
Water, Water Every Hare (1952) . . . . Bugs Bunny/Rudolph (Gossamer)/Mouse
We, the Animals, Squeak! (1941) (uncredited) . . . . Mother Cat (crying)
Weakly Reporter, The (1944) . . . . Men's Voices
Wearing of the Grin, The (1951) . . . . Porky Pig
Weasel Stop (1956) . . . . Foghorn Leghorn
Weasel While You Work (1958) . . . . Foghorn Leghorn/Barnyard Dog/Willy the Weasel
"Weird Al" Yankovic: The Videos (1996) Video (archive recordings) . . . . Barney Rubble/Dino
Well-Worn Daffy (1965) . . . . Daffy Duck/Speedy Gonzales
West of the Pesos (1960) . . . . Speedy Gonzales/Sylvester
Wet Hare (1962) . . . . Bugs Bunny
What Makes Daffy Duck (1948) . . . . Daffy Duck/Fox
What Price Porky (1938) . . . . Porky Pig
What's a Nice Kid like You Doing in a Place Like This? (1966) TV . . . . Talking Caterpillar (Barney Rubble)
What's Cookin' Doc? (1944) . . . . Bugs Bunny/M.C./Hiawatha/Audience Member
What's My Lion? (1961)
What's Opera, Doc? (1957) . . . . Bugs Bunny as Brunhilde/Elmer Fudd as Siegfried (screaming)
What's up Doc? (1950) . . . . Bugs Bunny/Eddie Cantor/Director
What's up Doc? A Salute to Bugs Bunny (1990) TV (archive footage) . . . . Bugs Bunny/Yosemite Sam/Gruesome Gorilla/Himself
Where's Huddles (1970) TV Series . . . . Bubba McCoy
Which Is Witch? (1949) . . . . Bugs Bunny
Who Framed Roger Rabbit (1988) . . . . Daffy Duck/Tweety Pie/Bugs Bunny/Sylvester/Porky Pig
Who Scent You? (1960) . . . . Pepe le Pew/Penelope/Le Capitaine/First Mate/Crewmates
Wholly Smoke (1938) . . . . Porky Pig/Bully
Who's Kitten Who? (1952) . . . . Sylvester
Who's Who in the Zoo (1942) (uncredited) . . . . Porky Pig
Wideo Wabbit (1956) . . . . Bugs Bunny/QTTV Producer/Elmer Fudd (yelping)
Wild, Wild World (1960)
Wild and Woolly Hare (1959) . . . . Bugs Bunny/Yosemite Sam

Wild Chase, The (1965) . . . . Speedy Gonzales

Wild Hare, A (1940) . . . . Bugs Bunny

Wild over You (1953) . . . . Pepe le Pew

Wild Wife (1954) . . . . John/Son/Mailman/Bank Teller/Red Cross Nurse/Casper J. Fragile/Soda Jerk/Pedestrian/Officer

Windblown Hare, The (1949) . . . . Bugs Bunny/Three Little Pigs/Big Bad Wolf

Wind-up Wilma (1981) TV . . . . Barney Rubble/Dino

Wise Quackers (1949) . . . . Daffy Duck

Wise Quacking Duck, The (1943) . . . . Daffy Duck/Mr. Meek

Wise Quacks (1939) . . . . Daffy Duck/Porky Pig/Baby Duckling

Witch's Tangled Hare, A (1959) . . . . Bugs Bunny

Woody Woodpecker (1941) . . . . Woody Woodpecker

Woody Woodpecker and His Friends (1982) Video (uncredited) . . . . Various Voices

Woody Woodpecker Show, The (1957) TV Series . . . . Woody Woodpecker

Woolen under Where (1963) . . . . Ralph Wolf/Sam Sheepdog

Yankee Dood It (1956) . . . . Sylvester

Yankee Doodle Bugs (1954) . . . . Bugs Bunny

Yankee Doodle Daffy (1943) . . . . Daffy Duck/Porky Pig/Sleepy Lagoon (coughing)

Year of the Mouse, The (1965)

Yogi Bear Show, The (1960) TV Series

Yogi's Gang (1973) TV Series . . . . Secret Squirrel

Yogi's Space Race (1978) TV Series . . . . Quack-up

Yolks on You, The (1980) TV . . . . Daffy Duck/Sylvester/Foghorn Leghorn

You Ought to Be in Pictures (1940) . . . . Porky Pig/Daffy Duck/Studio Guard/Stagehand/Animator

You Were Never Duckier (1948) . . . . Daffy Duck/Henery Hawk/Rooster/George K. Chickenhawk

Young Samson and Goliath (1967) TV Series . . . . Goliath

Zip, Zip Hooray! (1965) . . . . Wile E. Coyote

Zip 'n' Snort (1961) . . . . Wile E. Coyote

DAWS BUTLER

During his lifetime, Charles Dawson "Daws" Butler exemplified the standards for professionalism to which all who have followed in his path have aspired. He was an incredibly gifted actor, a prolific writer, a focused teacher, and a devoted husband and father. Although Butler never reached the level of public recognition of his contemporary Mel Blanc, it would be very difficult to find his equal in humility and generosity. With characters ranging from Chilly Willy to Huckleberry Hound, from Yogi Bear to Cap'n Crunch, peers and fans alike agree that Daws Butler was arguably the greatest talent in the history of voice-overs.

He was born in Toledo, Ohio, on November 16, 1916. When he was five, his father moved the family to the small town of Oak Park, Illinois, a city nine miles west of Chicago known primarily for its association with former residents Ernest Hemingway and Frank Lloyd Wright. An only child, Butler was admittedly shy and withdrawn, but he realized at an early age that he had a certain wit, which made him stand out from the rest of his classmates.

Butler's father had related the following story to family friend Bill Hamlin. "In Oak Park, there was an older gentleman who used to routinely pat Butler on the head and say, 'Hello, young man. How old are you?' This continued for weeks, and young Butler came to dread the inevitable meetings. One day, the old gentleman patted Butler on the head and asked, 'How old are you?' to which the five-year-old angrily replied, 'I'm forty-five years old. I'm a midget!'" The ensuing laughter marked the beginning of a long career in the business of making people laugh.

In school, Butler was terrified of the girls, but when surrounded by his male friends he would gradually come out of his shell. "I would do takeoffs on other people, not realizing that I was doing anything out of the ordinary. The guys thought I was funny, and they would laugh. I was okay as long as I was with my male peers." However, when Butler entered high school, not even the presence of his friends could save him from the embarrassment of having to recite in front of the entire class. Frustrated with himself for being so shy, he enrolled in a public-speaking class to bolster his confidence.

Although it helped somewhat, Butler was still looking for new ways to overcome his shyness. He finally hit upon an idea that would eventually change his life. "In Chicago there were a lot of amateur contests going on. It was the rear end of the depression. It was still pretty rough. Show business was doing very badly, so they had amateur contests. On Monday nights in big hotels in downtown Chicago, and in the supper clubs and nightclubs, they would have amateur talent, and they would give an award for the one that got the most applause from the audience. It took quite a bit of courage to go down and sign up for the first one, but I did. I had a few little impressions I was doing around high school: President Roosevelt, who was very big at that time, Charles Laughton, and Joe E. Brown. I even did an imitation of a Ford starting on a cold day. I didn't have much, but I had a little bit of guts and I went and signed up for these things, then lived in fear and trepidation that they'd actually call me to be on."

When the organizers of the talent contests finally did call, Butler found, much to his amazement, that his fear had vanished. "I felt great out there. I did my few little miggly impersonations, gave them a big smile, and found myself winning first prize. They'd put their hands over the heads of the finalists and the one that got the most applause would get three bucks, second place would get two bucks, and one buck would go to the third prize winner. The also-rans, of course, got nothing."

The initial confidence boost of winning his first amateur contest prompted Butler to enter other competitions. He still did not have any real "material," but his goal was not to perfect an act as much as it was to conquer his performance phobia. "I was always frightened before I went on, but the minute I did go on, I felt great. It was sort of a self-imposed therapy. I was trying to prove something—that I could stand up in front of people—which I did. I didn't want to be an actor."

But it wasn't long before Butler's public therapy sessions caught the attention of two young men who wanted desperately to be actors. Will Owets and Jack Lavin had been competing against Butler on the amateur circuit. Both were mimics who specialized in different fields. One impersonated the famous singers of the time, and the other mimicked famous actors. Butler had an element that they lacked; the ability to do physical comedy. This prompted Owets and Lavin to confront Butler and talk him into joining them. "They were adamant about it. They wanted to start an act, and I kept saying, 'No, no, no. I don't want to be in show business. I just did this to prove something to myself.' They would call my parents and say, 'Talk to Daws. Get him to be a member of our group.'" Against his better judgment, Butler agreed, and as he explained, "Once I did get talked into it, I enjoyed it, and I was hooked!" The trio, because they did so many impersonations of famous radio stars of the time, became known as the Three Short Waves.

Before the Three Short Waves embarked on their professional careers, they honed their act by continuing on the amateur circuit. Butler, who was all of seventeen years old at the time, continued to imitate the stars of the day. "I did Charlie McCarthy. You know Edgar Bergen and Charlie McCarthy? I did the dummy and one of my partners did Edgar Bergen." The spectacle of his partner drinking a glass of water while Butler sat on his lap cracking jokes helped propel the actors into the professional spotlight. "We got booked into one of the biggest nightclubs in Chicago and stayed there for about three or four weeks. Four shows a night, every night. We didn't find ourselves an agent, an agent found us. He said he'd like to represent us. He got us to a tailor who dressed us properly so we looked good, and we had music written for the show."

From 1933 to 1935, the Three Short Waves branched out and began touring other cities in the Midwest. Their success then led them to other parts of the country, from the south, Shreveport and Miami, to the east, New York and Philadelphia. Butler knew the value of touring with other gifted actors and took advantage of what they had to offer to hone his natural talent. "We really got around in a couple of years, and I soaked up many, many things that I now consider my timing, just by listening to other actors wiser and more experienced than myself, who gave me tips. A lot of the old-timers would help me out. I'd be doing a joke, and I wouldn't be getting a laugh, and they'd say, 'Hey, kid. You're not timing it right. You're not giving the audience a chance to digest what you just said. You ought to say the first part of that line and then actually count to two, then say the rest of the line, and I bet you get a laugh.' So I would take the two count, and I would read the line, and I would get the laugh."

Butler readily admits that it took more than just listening to other actors' advice; it took a lot of hard work. "Basically, it took me a couple of years to get a handle on my delivery and timing. What really helped was that I was a good student. You've got to be a good student to learn anything. So, while I didn't go to college or study dramatics, or go to a coach or anything like that, I did a lot of observing. I would stand in the wings when the other acts were on, and I would watch what they did, whether they were dancers or singers. If they were doing things that I wasn't going to do, it didn't matter. It was watching their timing and how it applied to what they were doing."

By the end of 1935, the Three Short Waves hit its peak, and they soon went their separate ways. According to Butler, "The act broke up like all acts break up. I guess we had different ambitions or different things we wanted to do. It's hard to pinpoint exactly how, but it just sort of dissolved, and, in effect, I had had my taste. I really wasn't all that crazy about show business. I took to it and learned it and developed technique because that is what I had done with other things. I could draw to a certain extent, and I used to study my drawing. I loved to write, and I used to write a lot of essays and themes for school. I would write material for our act. To me it was like a ploy. It was something I was doing with a couple of years of my life, and I really didn't think beyond that."

At the age of twenty-one, Butler had moved with his parents to Geneva, Illinois, a small town fifty miles west of Chicago. Butler's father was a salesman who sold clamps, vices, and the like to Woolworth's. Butler joined him in business, overseeing a group of forty women who filled small, pull-string canvas bags with jacks and other small toys and trinkets which were sold at

Woolworth's as grab bags for ten cents apiece. With the advent of World War II, Butler left the family business to help with the war effort, inspecting bombs for the military.

Bill Hamlin recalls how Butler could not resist the acting bug during this period, even if it was just in the form of practical jokes. "Daws and I would stop on our way home from work to have a beer. We happened to walk into this restaurant and Daws said, 'You wait here, and come in a little later.' He would go in and sit at the bar, and I'd come in later acting like I was bombed, and I'd stand beside him. I'd start to lean on him, and he'd get mad and push me away. I'd wait until he got his beer, and then knock his glass over. He'd jump up and grab me around the neck, and I'd push him back and hold him at arm's length by holding my hand on the top of his head, and he'd be swinging at me under my arms. By then, the bartender, who knew nothing about what we were actually doing, would come out from around the bar with a baseball bat. Just before he'd hit me, Daws would grab me by the collar of my coat and shove me against the wall, and I'd stand on my tippy toes like he'd hung me on the wall. By then, the bartender would finally get the picture. We would go back to the same place, and every time we'd come in, Daws would peek in the front door and say, 'Stay out, Bill. There's a new group here.'"

As the war raged on overseas, Butler felt that, although inspecting bombs was an important responsibility, he could do more for his country by enlisting in the military. Much to his surprise, he was turned down for active duty because he was an eighth of an inch too short. According to Hamlin, "One day I walked in and Daws was hanging in the doorway with bricks tied to his feet. I said, 'What in the heck are you doing?' he said, 'Doc says I can stretch an eighth of an inch this way.' And, you know, he did! He became a navy man."

Butler spent close to four years in the U.S. Naval Intelligence Service and Navy Reserve. Although he was stationed in the United States for the duration of World War II, he shied away from show business with the exception of the occasional off-base party. "I really didn't develop my talent while I was in the service, but I think that unbeknownst to myself, in my subconscious, what we later called the sub-text, I piled up these things in my mind to use both as a writer and an actor in later years."

One of the most popular characters of Butler's career, one that he stored in his subconscious during this period, was Huckleberry Hound. Though Hanna-Barbera claims that Huckleberry Hound was based on Andy Griffith, the voice was actually based on William Harwood, a North Carolina man who was a veterinarian and next-door neighbor of Butler's future wife, Myrtis.

"Myrtis was from Albemarle, North Carolina. When I was in the navy, I'd hitchhike home on the weekend and this fella would be sitting on the front porch next door. He'd see me come panting just to see Myrtis, and he'd say (in a drawl), 'Hi, Daws! Come on up and sit down. We'll talk a bit.' I'd say, 'Well, maybe a half an hour or an hour.' Anyway, he kind of stuck in my head. I was in the navy then, but I put him in a little separate box. I didn't even realize I was doing it. Then when Huckleberry Hound came along, there he was!"

In 1943, Butler married his sweetheart Myrtis. His future was still uncertain when he was discharged at the war's end in 1945. With his parents, his wife, and new son, David, Butler moved to Hollywood, California. He was probably the only Hollywood resident *ever* who had moved there with no intention of getting into show business. "I had this acting talent and some experience, but it had sort of drifted away from me. There was a GI bill where you could get money if you were in the service and didn't have a job and had to get on your feet." Without a clue as to what he wanted to do for a career, Butler eventually took the advice of his father, who steered him back into performing. "My Dad said, 'Why don't you go to radio school? You'd get paid, you could take care of your family, and what the heck, it might be a way to go.'"

Although Butler's performing had been limited to the stage, he signed up to learn the ropes in radio broadcasting. "I had a couple of good teachers. A lot of times teachers get knocked at these schools, but there were two very good ones, and I learned a lot from them." One encouraged Butler by telling him that he was one of the "most natural readers" he had ever heard. The years of learning material for his nightclub act had prepared Butler for interpreting written lines and instantly coming up with characters.

Within a year, Butler was auditioning for and getting roles on shows such as *Suspense*, *The Whistler*, and *The U.S. Steel Hour*. "I started to work those shows, not as a comedian, but doing original, dramatic parts. I did heavies, plain characters, and straight characters, but they all came from experiences I had had before and my study of people. I was always studying people for different types."

Though Butler had hit his stride in radio, he knew that it would not last. "When I broke into vaudeville, it was on its way out. I did radio for a few years, but I knew it was on its last legs. At least I got to work on some very, very big shows, especially the Columbia Studio, which was put on by CBS National. It went all over the country. It was a prestige show, and you had to be good before you played on it. I played on it about fifteen or twenty times, so it was a great boost to my ego." Although Butler's career up to that point had been in areas of entertainment that were on the wane, he was about to get in on the ground floor of the medium that would change the face of entertainment—television!

Legendary Warner Bros. animation director Bob Clampett had heard Butler perform on radio and contacted him about an idea he had for a live-action television puppet show entitled *Time for Beany*. Clampett was interested in using Butler as the puppeteer and voice for the title character. Butler recalled his first experiences in the relatively new medium. "I hadn't done any television, so I figured, What the heck? So, I went over to talk to Bob Clampett about *Time for Beany*. He had this thing fairly well put together, and he got hold of a writer. I, at that particular point, wasn't up to writing that type of a show. I didn't have the experience, so he had a good writer come in. Beany was a little boy who wore a propeller in his hat. He wanted a little boy voice, and I had been doing little boy voices for radio then." The voice he came up with for Beany (a forerunner to Elroy Jetson) was exactly what Clampett was looking for, and Butler became Beany.

Winning the role in *Time for Beany* marked the beginning of a long-term partnership, not with director Bob Clampett, but with Stan Freberg, the actor hired to play Beany's counterpart, Cecil the Sea Sick Sea Serpent. Butler and Freberg had a big future in store for them, but for the moment they worked their magic in the world of puppets. "It was like a boy and his dog, except it was a boy and his sea serpent, which was kind of neat. We did all the characters. In fact, Stan was about six foot one or so and I was five foot two. He used to bend over, trying to keep his head down below the puppet stage, and I used to have to stretch to get my puppets high enough, so I used to wear combat boots, which would add a few inches to my feet so that we could equalize ourselves. We played every joke in the book. It was like animation with puppets." Every joke in the book would not have worked if not for the compatibility of the show's two stars. As Butler commented in a 1987 PBS documentary, *Daws Butler, Voice Magician*, "I don't think I ever read with anybody that I enjoyed reading with as much as Stan. It's like one mind just switching back and forth. We could read each other."

The low-budget *Time for Beany* became a family affair for the Butlers. In the designing stage for the puppets, Butler' wife, Myrtis, was recruited to create Cecil. Using the leg from a green pair of their son's Dr. Denton footed pajamas, incorporating felt, and using suction cups from a bathroom clothesline for nostrils, Myrtis came up with what was supposed to be a temporary puppet until a better one could be produced. However, when a "professional" Cecil was created, nobody liked it, so they stuck with Myrtis's Cecil.

The suction cups were the basis for a hilarious ad-lib from Butler. On one particular show, Cecil had to break through a brick wall to save Beany and recover a treasure chest. Butler noticed that sometime during the scene Cecil had lost one of his suction cups, to which Butler had Beany exclaim, "We've gained a treasure and lost a nostril." It was these types of ad-libs and the wonderfully creative writing that garnered *Time for Beany* two Emmy awards over its five-year run—and included Albert Einstein among its fans. Butler explained, "It was quite a big show here in California. It was syndicated to thirty or forty other areas around the country, but it was never as big a show anywhere as it was here. It was quite a show. I'm sorry that I never got to see it."

During the five years in which Butler was doing *Time for Beany*, his career began to shift into high gear. Freberg, who had done comedy recordings in the past, recruited Butler to collaborate with him on the writing and recording of *Saint George and the Dragonette* for Capitol Records. The parody of *Dragnet* (backed by the tale of "Little Blue Riding Hood") had the full endorsement of Jack Webb and went on to become the first comedy album in history to sell over a million copies. This album marked the beginning of what would be a long writing association between the two Beany stars, who went on to perform together on *The Stan Freberg Radio Show*, which proved to be one of the last hilarious gasps in the dying medium. It was also during this time period that Butler solidified his place in animation history.

Fred "Tex" Avery had created Daffy Duck and, ironically, had supervised Bob Clampett at Warner Bros. When Avery became supervising director for MGM, he set about making some of the greatest cartoons of all time. Before he could begin, he needed to hire voice talent. That is where Butler came in: "I went out and auditioned at Metro-Goldwyn-Mayer for Tex Avery, who to me is the great genius of animation directors. I called him and asked him if I could come out and audition for him, and he said okay. I went out there and we went into his studio with a microphone, and he sat in another room listening. I must have ad-libbed at least forty different characters as fast as I could, one right after the other, all kinds of dialects and so on. Afterwards, he said, 'Thank you,' and I said 'Thank you,' and I went home. He called me the next day to come in and do a cartoon, which is what got me into the Screen Actors Guild, because you had to have a job before you could get in. That was really my introduction to animation."

Butler and Tex Avery worked well together since they both focused on the same principle, which was timing. Avery timed out his cartoon gags by using a metronome, and this idea of comic timing appealed to Butler, reaffirming his earlier theories on performance methods. In working out character voices, Butler worked on the rhythm of the character's speech, much as Avery developed the rhythm of his gags. "There are rhythms in the way people talk. That's what makes a speech pattern, and there's a lot of music in it, a lot of syncopation. The reason that people are different is because they talk differently, and they talk differently because they think differently."

Butler continues, "Also, rhythm makes the cartoons funny. Something gets set up, set up again, set up again, and the fourth time it pays off, and that's funny. Animators actually time how long it's going to take for a gag to pay off, and they'll count one . . . two . . . three, which is frustration for the audience, making them ask for more. When the animator is ready to give it to them, he gives it to them. And, through their appreciation at being satisfied, they laugh. It's as simple as that. Frustration is a big part of communication: to wonder whether another person likes you or not, to wonder whether you're going to get the job or not, and the delight when you do."

Butler went on to do several cartoons for Avery, co-starring with Bill Thompson in a series of Droopy cartoons and starring in classics such as *Little Rural Riding Hood* and *Magical Maestro*. In the Droopy cartoon *The Three Little Pups* and the short *Billy Boy*, in which a country wolf has a habit of repeating the last word of each sentence he speaks ("Hey, there, Billy Boy, boy, boy, boy, boy.") In these particular cartoons, Butler introduced his William Harwood/Huckleberry Hound voice. There was only one drawback in working for Tex Avery. "I probably did fifteen or twenty cartoons, and they're still bouncing around. I was on them, but I didn't get credit."

In hindsight, the fact that Butler went uncredited at MGM really did not matter. It was while working for Tex Avery that he happened to meet two other MGM animators who needed help on a few of their cartoons. The meeting between Butler, William Hanna, and Joe Barbera changed the face of animation. "I worked for Hanna and Barbera, who were doing *Tom and Jerry* at the time, which didn't require many voices because those characters were mute. But once in a while there would be another character in the cartoon that had a voice, so they would hire me for that." Butler spent a couple of years working on the *Tom and Jerry* Cartoons. "I only did three or four a year, because they took four or five months to animate each one. But I did enough for them to know who I was."

Soon, the viewing public would also get a chance to know who Butler was. While Butler did *Time for Beany*, recordings with Freberg, cartoons for Avery, and voice duty for Hanna and Barbera's MGM *Tom and Jerry* shorts, he also found time to do some memorable work for animation pioneer Walter Lantz. "Walter Lantz was the only animation supervisor who gave me credit on cartoons, which was great, because up until that time Mel Blanc had been the only one who had ever gotten credit." For Walter Lantz Productions, Butler did two of the most popular characters. One was Chilly Willy, a small penguin whose voice was one of the highest pitched that Butler had ever done.

Originally, Chilly Willy was mute, and Butler knew the character from those earlier cartoons, which made it easier for him to come up with a voice. Chilly Willy moved fast, so Butler had him speak very fast. On the other hand, Smedley, Chilly Willy's nemesis, was described by Butler as "a big, dumb dog." Butler did a series of these cartoons for Lantz, as well as many different voices in the *Woody Woodpecker* cartoons. He did all the supporting characters, including the heavies, the announcers, and the narrators and enjoyed the notoriety. "I am indebted to Walter Lantz for giving me credit. That's pretty nice for your ego, and not only that, it makes you valuable to other people who might want to hire you."

In 1954, after a five-year run, *Time for Beany* had finally run its course. All the extracurricular activities within that time frame had also come to an end, with the exception of the occasional voice-over job for Walter Lantz, and Butler found himself looking to a new direction. He had been typecast in Hollywood as a puppeteer, which he never really considered himself to be. By scouring the animation studios, Butler came across an agency that was looking for commercial comedy writers. Rushing home, he completed a week's worth of commercial spots in one night. He took them to the agency the next day, where they were eagerly accepted. Not only did Butler write the spots, but he voiced the characters as well. If he felt he was not right for the part, he would cast a fellow voice-actor he felt filled the role. Butler wrote commercials for products such as Ford Thunderbird and Bosko Chocolate. He spent over a year in his new vocation, but the voices were still beckoning him.

In 1957, MGM decided to close down their animation department, and William Hanna and Joe Barbera found themselves unemployed. Determined to create their own studio, within five months they had started their new operation. Their budget was a mere fraction of what they were used to at MGM, so they were forced to use a style of limited animation, using fewer drawings to keep their costs down. To supplement the watered-down animation, they needed high-quality voice talent. Naturally, they turned to Butler, who, in turn, brought with him another talented actor whom he had used in some of his commercials, Don Messick. Messick and Butler would become for Hanna-Barbera Studios what Mel Blanc was for Warner Bros. Together with William Hanna and Joe Barbera, they would construct a dynasty that would last for decades. What started with a simple cat and dog cartoon called

Ruff and Reddy (Butler providing the voice of Reddy) snowballed into dozens of shows that would dominate network television and ensure Butler that he would never again be without work.

Hanna-Barbera's follow-up to *Ruff and Reddy* put them on the map. Joe Barbera tells the story of pitching *Huckleberry Hound* to the networks. "I went to Chicago to make a pitch for *The Huckleberry Hound Show*. I had never sold a show before because I didn't have to. If we got an idea, we just made it, for over twenty years. All of a sudden, I'm a salesman, and I'm in a room with forty-five people staring at me, and I'm pushing Huckleberry Hound and Yogi Bear and 'the Meeces,' and they bought it. From then on, we used voices for all of our cartoons, and we kept calling on our Rocks of Gibraltar, Butler and Don."

One of the main reasons Joe Barbera went with Butler was his versatility. Barbera remembers the original discussion about a voice for Huckleberry Hound. "There was not one thing you would ask Daws where he would not give you the best that he had in him. I can remember distinctly when I first met him, I said, 'I kind of like this voice, but I think I'm gonna make it kind of a Southern voice because Southern voices are warm and friendly.' Daws said, 'Well, now I can do a Southern voice which is like North Carolina, or I can do a Southern voice that would be like Florida, that would be a cracker kind of voice, or if you want to get a little harder, we could get into Texas,' and, by gosh, he had about twelve different Southerners. That's the way he was. He was thorough and terrific." *The Huckleberry Hound Show* was an instant success. Within the next five years Butler found himself doing a multitude of leading characters, including Yogi Bear, Quick Draw McGraw, Lippy the Lion, Augie Doggie, and Peter Potamus. He even provided the voice of Fred in the pilot of *The Flintstones*, then called "The Flagstones."

Although Butler created some terrific original voices, some characters were based directly on Hollywood character actors. Wally Gator was a take off of Ed Wynn, while Hokey Wolf was a hilarious send-up of Phil Silvers (a voice which can also be found in several episodes of *The Flintstones* and *Fractured Fairytales*). Consciously or unconsciously, Snagglepuss and, later, the Funky Phantom were loose interpretations of Bert Lahr.

But of all the characters he did for Hanna-Barbera, Butler points to two that were his all time favorites. "I did mention Elroy Jetson and Mr. Jinx as being two of my favorite characters. I think I like Elroy for one reason . . . he is based on a little boy. I have never really, I guess, forgotten what it's like to be a little boy, and the way they react, and the way they think. Elroy is open and honest, and there's this sort of sweetness about him. Elroy is pretty straight. You do it in kind of a high voice, but you're thinking like a kid, and that's the way I like it."

Where Elroy was a super-smart product of the space age, Mr. Jinx was on the other end of the spectrum, which is one of the main reasons Butler enjoyed doing the character. "Mr. Jinx I like because he is what I call 'loose.' You can do things I call 'word abuse,' where you use the words in a funny way to make them sound 'Re-Dic-U-Lous.' I'm emphasizing final consonants, and it's very loose, and my jaw is loose, and I feel pretty flaky, and like a pretty sharp guy who really doesn't know too much. Jinx would say things like 'idiot-syncrasy,' instead of 'idiosyncrasy.' 'Idiotsyncrasy' isn't such a bad word. He would say things like 'stupid-stitious.' Well, if you're superstitious, you are kind of stupid-stitious, so they aren't quite as dumb as they sound. I like to work very loose. In commercials, cartoons, or whatever, I would interpolate, that is, I would talk around a line. I wouldn't change the cue at the end of the line for the other actors, but I would interpolate. I would add a word or two that wasn't there, which made the line a little more interesting."

About the same time Butler began working for Hanna-Barbera, he also began to work for another groundbreaking animator, Jay Ward. "One of the highlights of my whole career was doing *Fractured Fairytales* for Jay Ward. We did about eighty of those. On one of those little four- or five-minute cartoons, I would do as many as five characters, as would June Foray and Bill Scott. They were very, very funny and well written. It was just the most wonderful writing that I can imagine. I'm very, very proud of those. The humor was so good in those *Fractured Fairytales*. I remember one line where the king, who was sort of a fuddy duddy, said, 'Oh, Evil Princess, don't change my daughter into a frog! Turn her into a Mercedes so I can enjoy her.' And there was one for the prince with Rapunzel, when he said, 'Rapunzel, Rapunzel, let down your hair. . . . Not one at a time!' It's a pretty funny line. It's hard not to read it well."

Butler continued his work throughout the 1960s and 1970s, providing the voices to what had become staple characters of the Hanna-Barbera (now Warner Bros.) library in various spin-off shows such as *Yogi's Space Race*. He also continued doing commercial work as the voices of Cap'n Crunch for General Mills and Quisp for Quaker Oats. But the 1970s found Butler branching out into yet another profession, that of teacher. Butler believed in young talent and worked very hard with young actors, helping to nurture their craft. Butler viewed talent as a rare gift and would routinely offer "scholarships" to struggling actors whom he felt had promise.

Actor Tony Pope, who went on to lend his voice to such varied projects as Goofy for Disney Studios and the commercially successful 1990s Furby doll, was one of Butler's first students, attending classes from 1974 through 1976. He is one of the many, including Corey Burton, Patty Parris, Brian Cummings, Mona Marshall, and Linda Gary, who called themselves "the Disciples of Daws." Pope recalls, "There was a time after my son was born. My daughter was three and my son was an infant. I was working all day and attending his workshop at night. I called him and said, 'Daws, I'm going to have to miss some workshops. The bills are piling up.' And he said, 'Hey, you just come anyway. You need the work. When you can pay me, you can pay me.' It went on for six or seven months until I started paying him again. Ten dollars! To work with a master!"

Butler had a nose for spotting potential in a person. Putting the entire matter of talent in perspective, he noted, "Without talent, you're out of luck. It cannot be given to you. You can develop what I call a sense of 'enhanced mediocrity.' There are many actors today who have that. They get by, and they drive big cars and live in big houses. But that feeling of true talent is a very glorious, wonderful thing." Giving of himself to his students was payback for all the gifted actors who helped him in his youth. Of those actors, he recalled, "They talk about people in show business being avarice and mean, and spiteful, and out to hurt you, actors not wanting to give you anything, and stars not liking supporting players and wanting it for themselves and so on. But I've found that the truly gifted people are the nice people. They're the ones who seem to recognize the fact that the talent came from somewhere, somewhere out there, from God, and they were blessed. It is a blessing to be given talent, to just have it. Your job is to maintain it and support it and make it better."

One actor to whom Butler gave his whole-hearted support was Nancy Cartwright. Unbeknownst to many students in his classes, Butler mentored Cartwright on the side—giving her private lessons. It was his encouragement that convinced her to come from Ohio to Los Angeles in order to hone her acting skills. With his guidance, she gained the confidence she needed to enter the world of professional actors, eventually claiming her own place in animation history as Bart Simpson.

By the 1980s, animation had changed dramatically. No longer just a handful of directors working with a small group of brilliant voice-over artists, animation was now a big business, with hundreds of people vying for a single role. It seemed as if directors had lost respect for the older voice-over actors. One incident involved Butler and director Wally Burr. As one of Butler's students relates, "Wally Burr was directing Butler, and he wanted Butler to speed up Huckleberry Hound. Butler said, 'You don't understand. The whole thing about Huckleberry Hound is he's got that laconic kind of way of talking. He's never hurried no matter what happens. I don't care what the venue of the show is, the intrinsic thing that makes the character that character is that he's totally unrushed no matter what. It could be the end of the world. That's the gag.' He even wrote Wally a letter about it, explained it to him, and apologized for being 'testy.' Butler was such a gentle, sweet soul. But they had a session where it just didn't go well, and Butler was so frustrated by it because they had so much dialogue they had to get in in a certain time."

In 1985, more than twenty years since the original twenty-four episodes were produced, executives at Hanna-Barbera decided to make forty-one new episodes of *The Jetsons*. The original cast was assembled, but all were made to audition for their roles to make sure they could still do the characters. The honeymoon had ended for the voice-over pioneers. Joe Barbera explained that they were worried about the cast being able to maintain their energy. "The same people cannot come up with the same energy twenty-five or thirty years later. In fact, we had quite a bit of trouble with Daws on the last show we did because of his energy. Daws was walking around with a cane, and we had to keep pushing him to get him to try to get that youthful sound in his voice, and we went along with it." It is impossible to know if Butler lacked energy or, perhaps, just lacked enthusiasm for the material he was being given.

The later *Jetsons* episodes were judged by many to be lackluster stories at best, and Butler worried about the future of animation in general. "The strength of animation is that there is no limit. Anything can be animated. Some things are more believable than others. I think animation opens up more into the future for the creative person to see than anything else, as long as it doesn't get too crazy. There's some animation that's been done in the last few years which gets into the adult province to such an extent that it isn't animation. It's just seamy material and four letter words, and I think it's just letting animation play in a bad neighborhood with bad theatrical children. I don't particularly like it. I think it's a comedown for animation."

In the 1980s, Butler's health began to deteriorate but, ever the professional, he still was intent on doing his best work. Fellow voice actor and co-star Dick Beals remembered in a 1995 interview, "You just couldn't stand yourself if you could have seen him after he had his stroke. They still brought him in to do *The Jetsons*. Daws, because of the stroke he had, his eyes could only pick up the line maybe three quarters of the way across the page. And all of a sudden, he would look at it, but his brain wouldn't click. And poor Gordon Hunt, with all the patience of Job, he would just say, 'Well Daws, why don't you just take it from the middle there and do this or that or this or that.' It was just tremendous the way Gordon handled that, but Daws knew he was taking lines over. He never did a line over. He had it perfect right from the word get go. He showed a lot of intestinal fortitude."

However, on May 19, 1988, Daws Butler died after suffering another stroke. It would be impossible to try to put into words all that Butler meant to his thousands of fans, his students, his friends, his contemporaries, and his family. But he was very eloquent on what meaning his characters held for him: "I had a very close feeling of empathy for all of my characters, what they would and wouldn't say, how they would say it and how they wouldn't say it. They were very important to me. It wasn't just a question of line reading, and that makes the difference. I was very happy with the characters that I had. I was fortunate that there were good writers turning out the material, and I was the interpreter. It was like a musician working under a composer, and I was very, very content with it."

CREDITS

1001 Arabian Nights (1959) .... Omar the Rugmaker/Royal Book-Keeper/Barman
Aesop and Son (1976) TV Series .... Additional Voices
Airlift a la Carte (1971) .... Chilly Willy
All-New Popeye Hour, The (1978) TV Series .... Wimpy
Alphabet Conspiracy, The (1959) TV .... Jabberwocky
Animal Follies (1988) Video .... Yahooey/Reddy/Augie Doggie/Snagglepuss
Backwoods Bunny (1959) (uncredited) .... Pappy Buzzard/Elvis Buzzard
Bailey's Comets (1973) TV Series .... Dooter Roo
Banana Splits Adventure Hour, The (1968) TV Series .... Bingo
Barbary-Coast Bunny (1956) (uncredited) .... Nasty Canasta
Barbeque Brawl (1956)
Beany and Cecil (1962) TV Series .... Beany Boy/Captain Huffenpuff
Bear Hug (1964) .... Loopy De Loop
Bear Knuckles (1964) .... Loopy De Loop
Bear Up! (1963) .... Loopy De Loop
Bearly Able (1962) .... Loopy De Loop
Bee Bopped (1959) .... Windy
Beef for and After (1962) .... Loopy De Loop
Big Mouse Take (1965) .... Loopy De Loop
Big Snooze, The (1957) .... Chilly Willy
Billy Boy (1954) .... Farmer
Bird in a Bonnet (1957) .... Additional Voices
Blackboard Jumble (1957) .... Droopy
Boyhood Daze (1957) (uncredited) .... Headquarters/President
Bugs Bunny and Tweety Show, The (1986) TV Series .... Various Characters
Bugs Bunny Show, The (1960) TV Series .... Various Characters
Bugs Bunny/Road Runner Hour, The (1968) TV Series .... Various Characters

Bullwinkle Show, The (1961) TV Series (uncredited) . . . . Aesop Jr.
Bungle Uncle (1962) . . . . Loopy De Loop
Bunnies Abundant (1962) . . . . Loopy De Loop
Buster's Last Stand (1970)
Bwana Magoo (1959) . . . . Waldo
C.B. Bears, The (1977) TV Series . . . . Hustle/Undercover Elephant
Careless Caretaker (1962) . . . . Smedley
Cat in the Hat, The (1972) TV Series . . . . Fish
Catch Meow (1961) . . . . Loopy De Loop
Cattanooga Cats, The (1969) TV Series . . . . Lambsy Divey
Cheese It, the Cat! (1957) . . . . Ned Morton
Chicken Fracas-See (1963) . . . . Loopy De Loop
Chicken-Hearted Wolf (1963) . . . . Loopy De Loop
Child Sock-Cology (1961) . . . . Loopy De Loop
Chiller Dillers (1968) . . . . Chilly Willy
Chilly and Looney Gooney (1969) . . . . Chilly Willy
Chilly and the Woodchopper (1967) . . . . Chilly Willy
Chilly Chums (1967) . . . . Chilly Willy
Chilly Reception, A (1958) . . . . Chilly Willy
Chilly's Cold War (1970) . . . . Chilly Willy
Chilly's Hide-a-Way (1971) . . . . Chilly Willy
Chilly's Ice Folly (1970) . . . . Chilly Willy
Chump Champ, The (1950) (uncredited) . . . . Master of Ceremonies
Clash and Carry (1961) . . . . Chilly Willy
Common Scents (1962) . . . . Loopy De Loop
Convict Concerto (1954)
CooCoo Nuts (1970)
Count Down Clown (1961) . . . . Loopy De Loop
Counterfeit Cat (1949)
Coy Decoy (1963)
Crazy Mixed-up Pup (1955)
Creepy Time Pal (1960) . . . . Loopy De Loop
Crook Who Cried Wolf (1963) . . . . Loopy De Loop
Crowin' Pains (1962)
Crow's Feat (1965) . . . . Loopy De Loop
Cuckoo Clock, The (1950)
Deep Freeze Squeeze (1964) . . . . Chilly Willy
Deputy Droopy (1955) . . . . Sheriff/Slim
Dixie Fryer, The (1960) (uncredited) . . . . Pappy Buzzard/Elvis Buzzard
Dog House, The (1952)
Dogfather, The (1974) . . . . Louie/Pugg
Do-Good Wolf, The (1960) . . . . Loopy De Loop
Down Beat Bear (1956) (uncredited) . . . . Second Radio Announcer
Drafty, Isn't It? (1957) . . . . Ralph Phillips/Willie N. List
Droopy's Double Trouble (1951) (uncredited) . . . . Mr. Theeves
Drum-Sticked (1963) . . . . Loopy De Loop
Elephantastic (1964) . . . . Loopy De Loop
Everglade Raid (1958)
Explosive Mr. Magoo, The (1958)
Fallible Fable, A (1963) . . . . Loopy De Loop
Fee Fie Foes (1961) . . . . Loopy De Loop

Fish and Chips (1962) . . . . Chilly Willy

Fish Hooked (1960) . . . . Chilly Willy

Fit to Be Tied (1952)

Flagstones, The (The Flintstones' pilot) . . . . Fred Flintstone

Flea Circus, The (1954) (uncredited) . . . . Pepito

Flintstones, The (1960) TV Series (uncredited) . . . . Barney Rubble (alternating) (1960–1962)/Dino
    (1960–1963)/Additional Voices

Flintstones: Wacky Inventions, The (1994) Video (archive footage) . . . . Additional Gadgets/ Addi-
    tional Voices

Flintstones Meet Rockula and Frankenstone, The (1979) TV

Fodder and Son (1957)

Fowled-up Party (1957)

Fractured Friendship (1965) . . . . Chilly Willy

Fred Flintstone and Friends (1977) TV Series

Freeway Fracas (1964)

Funky Phantom (1971) TV Series . . . . Jonathan "Musty" Muddlemore

Gabby's Diner (1961) . . . . Voice of Seminole Sam

Galaxy Goof-Ups, The (1978) TV Series . . . . Yogi Bear/Huckleberry Hound

George of the Jungle (1967) TV Series . . . . Additional Voices

Gift Wrapped (1952)

Give and Tyke (1957) (uncredited) . . . . Spike/Second Dog/Dogcatcher

Go Fly a Kit (1957) (uncredited) . . . . Counter Man

Good, the Bad, and Huckleberry Hound, The (1988) . . . . Huckleberry Hound/Yogi Bear/Quick Draw
    McGraw/Snagglepuss/Baba Luey

Gooney Is Born, A (1970) . . . . Chilly Willy

Gooney's Goofy Landings (1970) . . . . Chilly Willy

Greedy Gabby Gator (1963)

Habit Rabbit (1964) . . . . Loopy De Loop

Habit Troubles (1964) . . . . Loopy De Loop

Half-Baked Alaska (1965) . . . . Chilly Willy

Half-Fare Hare (1956)

Hanna-Barbera Hall of Fame: Yabba Dabba Doo II, The (1979) TV . . . . Himself/Various Character
    Voices

Happy Go Loopy (1961) . . . . Loopy De Loop

Harlem Globetrotters, The (1970) TV Series

Hassle in a Castle (1966)

Heir-Conditioned (1955) . . . . Cat

Help! It's the Hair Bear Bunch (1971) TV Series . . . . Hair Bear

Helter Shelter (1955)

Here, Kiddie, Kiddie (1960) . . . . Loopy De Loop

Hey There, It's Yogi Bear (1964) . . . . Yogi Bear//Dopey Bear/Ranger/TV Announcer

Hic-Cup Pup (1954)

Highway Hecklers (1968) . . . . Chilly Willy

Hold That Rock (1956) . . . . Chilly Willy

Honey-Mousers, The (1956) . . . . Ralph Crumden/Ned Morton

Hook, Line, and Stinker (1969)

Horse Play (1967)

Horse Shoo (1965) . . . . Loopy De Loop

Hot and Cold Penguin (1955) . . . . Chilly Willy

Hot Time on Ice (1967) . . . . Chilly Willy

Houndcats, The (1972) TV Series . . . . Studs

How to Trap a Woodpecker (1971)
Huckleberry Hound Show, The (1958) TV Series .... Huckleberry Hound/Mr. Jinks/Hokey
    Wolf/Yogi/Dixie/Pixie
Hoppity Hooper (1964) TV Series
Houndcats, The (1972) TV Series .... Stutz
Hunger Strife (1960)
I'm Cold (1954) .... Chilly Willy
Indian Corn (1972)
International Woodpecker (1957)
Jerry and the Goldfish (1951) (uncredited) .... Radio Chef François
Jetsons, The (1962) TV Series .... Elroy Jetson/Henry Orbit/W. C. Cogswell
Jetsons Christmas Carol, The (1985) TV .... Elroy Jetson
Jetsons Meet the Flintstones, The (1987) TV .... Elroy Jetson/Cogswell/Henry Orbit
Josie and the Pussycats (1970) TV Series (uncredited) .... Additional Voices
Just a Wolf at Heart (1963) .... Loopy De Loop
Kitty from the City (1971)
Kooky Loopy (1961) .... Loopy De Loop
Lad in Bagdad, A (1968)
Legend of Rockabye Point, The (1955) (uncredited) .... Chilly Willy
Life with Loopy (1960) .... Loopy De Loop
Lighthouse Keeping Blues (1964)
Lippy the Lion (1971) TV Series .... Lippy the Lion
Little Bo Bopped (1959) .... Loopy De Loop
Little Johnny Jet (1953) (uncredited) .... Father Jet
Little Rural Riding Hood (1949) (uncredited) .... City Wolf
Little Skeeter (1969)
Little Televillain (1958) .... Chilly Willy
Little Woody Riding Hood (1962)
Log Jammed (1959)
Loopy de Loop (1969) TV Series .... Loopy de Loop
Loopy's Hare Do (1961) .... Loopy De Loop
Love Comes to Magoo (1958) .... Waldo
Love That Pup (1949)
Mackerel Moocher (1961) .... Chilly Willy
Magical Maestro (1952) (uncredited) .... Mysto the Magician
Magoo Goes Overboard (1957) .... Waldo
Magoo Saves the Bank (1957) .... Waldo
Magoo's Glorious Fourth (1957) .... Waldo
Magoo's Homecoming (1959) .... Waldo
Magoo's Masquerade (1957) .... Waldo
Magoo's Private War (1957) .... Waldo
Magoo's Problem Child (1956) .... Waldo
Magoo's Puddle Jumper (1956) .... Waldo
Magoo's Three-Point Landing (1958) .... Waldo
Magoo's Young Manhood (1958) .... Waldo
Mary Poppins (1964) .... Turtle/Penguin
Matty's Funnies (Beanie & Cecil) (1962) TV Series .... Beany Boy/Captain Huffenpuff/Additional
    Voices
Merlin the Magic Mouse (1967) .... Merlin
Merrie Melodies: Starring Bugs Bunny and Friends (1990) TV Series .... Various Characters
Merry Minstrel Magoo (1959) .... Waldo

Mice Follies (1960) . . . . Ned Morton
Mister Magoo (1960) TV Series . . . . Prezley
Mouse and Garden (1960) (uncredited) . . . . Sam
Mouse for Sale (1955) (uncredited) . . . . Man
Mucho Mouse (1957) (uncredited) . . . . Tom
Mutt in a Rut, A (1959) . . . . Additional Voices
Nautical Nut, The (1967)
New Adventures of Huck Finn, The (1968) TV Series
New Hanna-Barbera Cartoon Series, The (1962) TV Series . . . . Wally Gator/Lippy the Lion
Ninety-Day Wondering (1956)
No Biz like Shoe Biz (1960) . . . . Loopy De Loop
Not in Nottingham (1963) . . . . Loopy De Loop
Off to See the Wizard (1967) TV Series . . . . Scarecrow
One Cab's Family (1952) . . . . Cab Family
One Horse Town (1968)
Operation Cold Feet (1957) . . . . Chilly Willy
Operation Shanghai (1967) . . . . Chilly Willy
Ostrich Egg and I, The (1956)
Out-Foxed (1949)
Papoose on the Loose (1961)
Peachy Cobbler, The (1950) (uncredited) . . . . Narrator
Pecking Holes in Poles (1972)
Pecos Pest (1955)
People Are Bunny (1959) (uncredited) . . . . Art Lamplighter
Person to Bunny (1960) (uncredited) . . . . Elmer Fudd
Pesky Pelican (1963) . . . . Chilly Willy
Pesty Guest (1965) . . . . Chilly Willy
Pet Peeve (1954) (uncredited) . . . . Man
Peter Potamus and His Magic Flying Balloon (1964) TV Series . . . . Peter Potamus/Yahooey
Peter Potamus Show, The (1964) TV Series . . . . Peter Potamus/Yahooey
Phantom Tollbooth, The (1970) . . . . Whether Man/Chroma/Terrible Trivium/Official Senses-Taker/
   Gelatinous Giant
Pixie & Dixie (1958) TV Series . . . . Dixie/Mr. Jinks
Pizza Tweety-Pie, A (1958) (uncredited) . . . . Spaghetti Bird
Plasticman Comedy Adventure Show—Fangface and Fangpuss (1979) TV Series
Polar Fright (1966)
Polar Pests (1958) . . . . Chilly Willy
Popeye's Treasure Hunt (1978) TV Series . . . . Wimpy
Pork Chop Phooey (1965) . . . . Loopy De Loop
Practical Yolk (1966)
Prehistoric Super Salesman (1969)
Project Reject (1969) . . . . Chilly Willy
Punchy de Leon (1950)
Pup on a Picnic (1955)
Quick Draw McGraw (1963) TV Series . . . . Quick Draw McGraw/Baba
   Looie/Snuffles/Snooper/Blabber/Augie Doggie
Raggedy Rug (1964) . . . . Loopy De Loop
Rancid Ransom (1963) . . . . Loopy De Loop
Raw! Raw! Rooster! (1956) (uncredited) . . . . Rhode Island Red
Red Hot Riding Hood (1943) (uncredited) . . . . Wolf (howling)
Reluctant Recruit, The (1971)

Roamin' Roman (1964)

Robin Hoody Woody (1963)

Robinson Crusoe (1959) .... Chilly Willy

Robinson Gruesome (1959) .... Chilly Willy

Rock-a-Bye Gator (1962)

Rocket Racket (1962)

Rocket-bye Baby (1956) (uncredited) .... Narrator/Joe Wilbur/Capt. Schmideo/Lecturer

Rockin with Judy Jetson (1988) TV .... Elroy Jetson

Roman Holidays (1972) TV Series .... Brutus the Lion

Romp in a Swamp

Room and Wrath (1956) .... Chilly Willy

Rough Riding Hood (1966)

Rude Intruder, The (1971) .... Chilly Willy

Ruff and Reddy Show, The (1957) TV Series .... Reddy/Additional Voices

Salmon Loafer (1963) .... Chilly Willy

Salmon Yeggs (1958) .... Windy

Scat Cats (1957) .... Spike

Scooby-Doo/Dynomutt Hour, The (1976) TV Series .... Scooby Dum

Scooby's All-Star Laff-a-Lympics (1977) TV Series .... Augie Doggie/Dirty Dalton/Dixie/Huckleberry
   Hound/Jinks/Quick Draw McGraw/Scooby-Dum/Snagglepuss/Wally Gator/Yogi Bear/Snooper/
   Blabber

Seal on the Loose (1970)

Secret Agent Woody Woodpecker (1967)

Shanghai Woody (1971)

Sheep Stealers Anonymous (1963) .... Loopy De Loop

Sheep Wrecked (1958) .... Wolf

Sh-h-h-h (1955) .... Mr. Twiddle/Doctor/Desk Clerk

Short Snorts on Sports (1948)

Sioux Me (1965)

Ski-Napper (1964) .... Chilly Willy

Sleepy Time Bear (1969) .... Chilly Willy

Sleepy Time Chimes (1971)

Slicked-up Pup (1951)

Slippery Slippers (1962) .... Loopy De Loop

Smarty Cat (1955)

Smitten Kitten (1952)

Snoopy Loopy (1960) .... Loopy De Loop

Snow Place like Home (1966) .... Chilly Willy

South Pole Pals (1966) .... Chilly Willy

Southern-Fried Hospitality (1960)

Space Kidettes, The (1966) TV Series .... Captain Sky Hooked/Static

Speaking of Animals (1941–1949)

St. Moritz Blitz (1961) .... Chilly Willy

Stuporduck (1956) (uncredited) .... Narrator/Newspaper Editor

Super President (1967) TV Series .... Richard Vance

Super Six and Spy Shadow, The (1966) TV Series .... Magnet Man

Swash Buckled (1962) .... Loopy De Loop

Swiss-Mis-Fit (1957) .... Chilly Willy

Sylvester and Tweety Show, The (1976) TV Series .... Various Characters

Tale of a Wolf (1960) .... Loopy De Loop

Talking Dog, The (1956) .... Sam/Conman/Dog

Teeny Weeny Meany (1966) . . . . Chilly Willy
Tenant's Racket, The (1963)
Tepee for Two (1963)
Terror Faces Magoo (1959) . . . . Waldo
That's My Pup (1953)
This Is My Ducky Day (1961) . . . . Loopy De Loop
Three Little Pups, The (1954) . . . . Guard
Three Little Woodpeckers (1965)
Three-Ring Fling (1958) . . . . Windy
Time for Beany (1949) TV Series . . . . Beany/Uncle Captain
To Catch a Woodpecker (1957)
Tom and Jerry (1965) TV Series . . . . Various Characters (1965–1972)
Tomcat Combat (1959)
Tom's Photo Finish (1957) (uncredited) . . . . George
Top Cat (1961) TV Series . . . . Additional Voices
Tree's a Crowd (1958)
Trick or Tweet (1959) (uncredited) . . . . Sam
Tricky Trout (1961) . . . . Chilly Willy
Trouble Bruin (1964) . . . . Loopy De Loop
Truant Student (1959) . . . . Windy
Two-Faced Wolf (1961) . . . . Loopy De Loop
Unbearable Salesman, The (1957)
Under Sea Dogs (1968) . . . . Chilly Willy
Under the Counter Spy (1954)
Vanishing Duck, The (1958) (uncredited) . . . . George
Vicious Viking (1967) . . . . Chilly Willy
Voo-Doo Boo-Boo (1962)
Wacky Races (1968) TV Series . . . . Rock and Gravel Slag/Red Max/Peter Perfect/Rufus Roughcut/
    Sgt. Blast/Big Gruesome
Waggily Tale, A (1958) . . . . Junior
Wally Gator (1962) TV Series . . . . Wally Gator
Whatcha Watchin'? (1963) . . . . Loopy De Loop
What's a Nice Kid like You Doing in a Place like This? (1966) TV . . . . King of Hearts/March Hare
Wideo Wabbit (1956) (uncredited) . . . . Bugs as Groucho/Bugs as Norton
Wild, Wild World (1960)
Wolf Hounded (1959) . . . . Loopy De Loop
Wolf in Sheepdog's Clothing (1963) . . . . Loopy De Loop
Woody and the Beanstalk (1966)
Woody Meets Davy Crewcut (1956)
Woody Woodpecker and His Friends (1982) Video . . . . Various Voices
Woody Woodpecker Show, The (1957) TV Series . . . . Chilly Willy/Gabby Gator/Windy
Woody's Kook-Out (1961)
Woody's Night Mare (1969)
Yankee Dood It (1956)
Yogi and the Invasion of the Space Bears (1988) . . . . Yogi Bear
Yogi Bear and the Magical Flight of the Spruce Goose (1987) . . . . Yogi Bear/Quick Draw McGraw/
    Snagglepuss/Huckleberry Hound/Augie Doggie
Yogi Bear Show, The (1960) TV Series . . . . Yogi Bear (1958–1988)/Additional Voices
Yogi's Ark Lark (1972) TV . . . . Yogi Bear/Baba Looey/Wally Gator/Huckleberry
    Hound/Lambsy/Quick Draw McGraw/Snagglepuss
Yogi's First Christmas (1980) . . . . Yogi Bear/Snagglepuss/Huckleberry Hound/Auggie Doggie

Yogi's Gang (1973) TV Series . . . . Yogi Bear/Quick Draw McGraw/Huckleberry Hound/ Snaggle-
  puss/Augie Dogie/Wally Gator/Peter Potamus
Yogi's Great Escape (1987) . . . . Yogi Bear
Yogi's Treasure Hunt (1978) TV Series . . . . Yogi Bear
Young Samson and Goliath (1967) TV Series
Yukon Have It (1959) . . . . Chilly Willy
Zoo Is Company (1961) . . . . Loopy De Loop

NANCY CARTWRIGHT

Most viewers would never suspect one of the best and most popular comedies of all time begins its life in trailer 746—an anonymous drab brown oblong building on the Fox lot. It is 10:00 A.M. and the cast of *The Simpsons* is crowded around a twenty-foot oak conference table for the first read-through of a new script, while excited observers—staff and a few lucky visitors—line the periphery. Scattered laughter is heard over noisy conversation as they flip through the pages, some highlighting their parts, appropriately enough, in yellow.

The director calls for quiet; then begins the table read by reciting the opening titles. There is a palpable sense of anticipation and concentration in the air. Although the actors have not seen the script before, the cold reading is almost flawless. The new script has the old *Simpsons* magic and no one wants to break the spell by tripping over a line. A consumer-grade microphone hangs through the plastic grill covering the low ceiling and is connected to a boom box to record a crude reference cassette. The director, respectful of the caliber of the assembled talent, interrupts now and then only to interject stage directions.

The attending writers look pleased that the crowd is laughing loudly in all the right places. And, as usual, Bart is getting most of the laughs. "Don't have a cow, man!" retorts Nancy Cartwright, a petite, blond, forty-something woman with brilliant blue eyes. She is thoughtful, unpretentious, and energetic. Most people would never suspect her to be the world's most popular cartoon ten-year-old, Bart Simpson. After the end of the read-through, most of the cast make a quick exit while a few stragglers network by the door. Cartwright lingers in the corner to make calls on behalf of her favorite charity, Famous Fone Friends. The charity asks cartoon voice actors, in character, to call seriously ill children. After she finishes the last call, she states quietly, "A kid has got Bart or Snow White on the line and he totally believes that. It gives me great pleasure to know that if this kid isn't doing so well, at least he's been made very happy by someone he really loves." Though "Bart" jokes his way through these conversations, "Nancy" is a mother of two young children and cannot help but look a little reflective.

Before Cartwright earned cultural icon status, she was just the fourth of six children in a family from small-town Kettering, Ohio. At ten, she was the "anti-Bart." Never rebelling against her parents because her extra-curricular activities left her with little time, she quickly became the star of a prose reading competition. Imitating the camel in her rendition of Rudyard Kipling's "How the Camel Got His Hump," she won her first performance award for humorous interpretation. The award would set her on a path that would eventually culminate in an Emmy. She then competed against the winners for the sixth, seventh, and eight grades and, again, took top honors. "I already knew I had the ability to make people laugh, but this competition was a kind of an indicator of my future. I started pursuing the arena from involvement in children's theater to all the plays in high school. I was the captain of the forensics team. . . . While my brothers were winning little league and soapbox derbies trophies, I'm bringing home this great hardware for first in national districts for Ohio. I did so well that Ohio University recruited me to be on their team for the university circuit; I was offered a scholarship." Once enrolled at Ohio University in Athens, Cartwright's high school success was repeated. However, it was during a break from her studies that her destiny began to take shape.

Cartwright got a "great" summer job at radio station WING in Dayton, Ohio. (Its slogan was "Winging it in Dayton," in honor of the Wright brothers, who were Ohio natives.) She notes, "I filled in for everyone that went on vacation, from reception to accounting, so I essentially learned how the radio business operated. But my boss knew I had this interest in doing voices, so he let me be on the air in the afternoon and I created this little character as a promotional gimmick for the station. The drive-time disc jockey and I did this remote broadcast in which I played "Lily Padd, the Lifeguard." It was only a four-minute bit, but I *absolutely lived for* that four minutes. One day, this publicist [Anne Schwebel] from Warner Bros. records came in to promote some of their albums. To me, Warner Bros. meant Mel Blanc and all the cartoons and I thought maybe she might know somebody who could help me. I got my boss to introduce me to her. She didn't know anything about the animation division, but she gave me her card, saying, "Put it all in a letter and I'll pass your letter on."

Soon afterward, Cartwright received a reply from Hanna-Barbera director Wally Burr. "He wrote me this two-page letter, and the fact that he took the time to do that knocked my socks off! First, he told me that I'm not going to get anywhere in Ohio. Secondly, the fact that I'm a woman is not to my advantage because a lot of the voice-over work is done by men. Of course, this was in the late '70s and animation was not in the condition that it is now. The third thing was to study anything you can that an actor would study because it is not just doing a voice; it really is acting. Finally, that versatility was the name of the game. They will hire you to do three voices and after three they've got to pay you more money, but it's still cheaper that way. Anyway, I took it as an encouraging letter."

Cartwright recalls, "And then I also got this letter from Anne Schwebel at Warner Bros. and in it was Daws Butler's name and his phone number. He's in Beverly Hills, right? I'm from Ohio. I had never heard of an answering machine and sure enough when I called the number there's this outgoing message on the machine, 'This is Percival Pickle, Mr. Butler's butler.' I'm literally pulling the phone away and looking at it, thinking, 'What is this?' So, I hear the beep and I did this clever character back to him, 'This is Nancy Cartwright. I've heard about you and I'd be interested in finding out about your classes. Could you send me a brochure?' Then I left my address."

"I had no idea how organized he was or what the classes were like. I hung up the phone, and, feeling silly for not leaving my phone number on the off chance he'd actually call me, I left another message, totally embarrassed. But later on that evening he called. We had a half-hour conversation. He was just instantly interested in me because I was from Ohio and I made this *huge* reach to him. He said, 'I'll pop a tape and a script in the mail and you record the script and send it back to me.' We instantaneously had this student-mentor relationship. I became his long-distance protégé."

From then on, Cartwright would regularly record scripts for Butler: "I'd send the tape off to him; he'd write me back a letter with another tape and a critique of what I'd just done, but *always, always, always*, it was encouraging. That's the quality of Daws that I appreciated the very most, the way he handled people. He was so gentle and caring. He really wanted to make sure that his students totally understood what they were doing and that they could make the copy their own. That to me was Daws's technique. He really instilled that in me."

Accepting Wally Burr's advice to move to L.A. and Butler's wish that she finish her education, Cartwright decided to transfer to a California college. "I literally pulled out a map of Los Angeles and said, 'Here's Beverly Hills; this is where Daws lives. Here's UCLA (next to Beverly Hills) and here's USC—wwwwayyyy over here.' So that's why I picked UCLA." Though her future seemed promising, the period after the move was a very low point in her life. "My mom had passed away two weeks before I moved out here. Daws knew that and he totally took me under his wing. He was really the only person I knew. I used to catch the #86 bus in Westwood and take it into Beverly Hills for my one hour lesson; then Daws and his wife would take me out to dinner and drop me off back at the UCLA dorm. I was going through a tough time, but I got involved with theater at UCLA, which helped, and on Sundays Daws would meet with me on my demo tape. In three months he took me out to Hanna-Barbera and I got to sit in on my very first recording session. I watched him do "Wimpy" on *Popeye* and I thought, 'Oh, God, I really want to do this!' He introduced me to a bunch of directors and they started calling me right away to audition. Within about a month, I got my first job [1980s], *Richie Rich*. And from that moment on, I worked on all kinds of Saturday morning stuff."

Needing a way to get to Hanna-Barbera from UCLA, Cartwright was forced to purchase a car slightly less grand than the pink Miata she was since able to afford on her *Simpsons* salary. "I got a '68 Opal Cadet. It looked like a smashed potato so I named it 'Spud.' It floored at like forty-five miles per hour, and people would flip me the bird because I was going too slow on the freeway. But it was the only way I could get over to Hanna-Barbera from UCLA."

Nancy's career was quickly outpacing Spud. She dropped out of school for a quarter after she won a role in a Hollywood play. "I was twenty-two at the time, playing a twelve-year-old on stage, and this theatrical agency saw me and signed me. Before they sent me out on my very first interview, I was warned that I would probably have to cold read. Now, because I did voice-overs, I was an expert at cold reading, so that didn't intimidate me at all. Next thing I know I was signed to a contract with ABC for series development and I started balancing work on-camera with voice-overs. I got *Twilight Zone, the Movie*, after that *Flesh and Blood*, and I played the title role in *Marion Rosewhite* for CBS while still working on *Richie Rich, Pound Puppies*, and *Snorks* and all that."

Consistently being one of the fortunate 2 percent of actors who actually make a living by acting, she believes several skills have made her successful at auditions. "I think I'm very good at taking direction, and I've got my own imagination. I've got super-high energy. I think I have a willingness to play. I think there's a spirit of play that you have to take into consideration: if you are not willing to play and have fun with it, it ain't worth it. Some people take it too seriously. I don't use method acting; I've never researched. I'm not say-ing that you can't do research on it, but they usually don't send you the audi-tion and you just show up about fifteen minutes ahead of time. Then they give you one little monologue and the picture of the character. Even for an audition for on-camera, I don't do a lot of research. I do my own work on it, but I don't open up encyclopedias or go to the library for an audition."

Some of her experiences with other directors in her pre-Bart days make her appreciate the staff of *The Simpsons* all the more. "I had one director who would always say, 'Cartwright, that reading is in the toilet.' I never knew what he meant by that. . . . Another was an alarming stickler for realism. He'd say to the guy next to me, 'Listen, I could use some help on this. Hey, Joe, could you actually put your hands on her throat so we could really get that feeling that she is being choked?' "

Without a clue of her destiny, she went to *The Simpsons* casting call at the behest of casting director Bonnie Pietila. "I had originally gone in to audi-tion for Lisa and I just couldn't wrap my wits around it. As I'm sitting out there, I decided the copy was too vague for me, and then I saw Bart. I picked it up, walked into the studio and said, 'I looked at Lisa [now Yeardly Smith] and I can't do that, but let me do this boy for you.' I was hired on the spot."

There are natural overtones of Bart's voice in her voice, and she can effortlessly switch in and out of character in mid-sentence. "There's an unusual, androgynous quality that you even hear in my regular speaking voice. That was always reinforced even as a child. I do many of the boys on the show—Nelson Munce, Ralph Wiggum, Rod Flanders, etc. I feel I've grooved a niche for myself. I've become a person that can create these boys." Although Cartwright has two brothers and a son, she does not draw upon them extensively to create Bart or any of her other characters. "Somehow there's something inside of me that's easy for me to tap into to do a boy. I don't think of it in terms of sex; I just think of it in terms of a person. There's an energy and a speech pattern that a child has that's different than an adult. Then, husky it up a little and make it sound breathier or give it a croaky kind of quality and there's a lot of agreement that that sounds like a boy." Of course, as should be obvious from the constant turnover on Bill Melendez's *Peanuts* specials of the 1970s, Cartwright affirms that if the producers would have hired a ten-year-old boy when the *The Simpsons* first started, "he would have lost his job a long time ago."

Seemingly unaffected by her success and, like most voice actors, not recognized on the street, she is proud of her work on *The Simpsons*. "We are in thirty-seven different countries [now in seventy countries]; not that I'm doing the voices for Japan or Afghanistan, but I helped to create this icon and I'm proud that it has reached the magnitude of greatness that it has. He was very one-dimensional when the show first started. Although he is still the antagonistic little brat that he always has been, he has gotten more dimensional, more qualities to him that are more human-like." She enjoys shows that extrapolate what Bart may be like as an adult, although most depict him as some kind of "total degraded being."

It is fairly obvious that Bart will never be allowed to grow up. Although the episode in which Bart graduates from the fourth grade after "really, really working his little butt off and passing with a D minus" is one of her favorites, Bart will perpetually be ten years old and in Mrs. Crabapple's fourth-grade classroom. As has even been parodied in the context of the show, no matter how outlandish the plotline, within the half hour everything is back to square one. Any significant changes, such as revealing what state Springfield is in other than "a state of mind" or having Maggie really talking, would, in her opinion, "ruin the show."

Cartwright shrugs off the criticism directed at *The Simpsons*, which put the fledgling Fox network on the map and could have been a factor in the failed elder Bush reelection bid. Despite the negative reaction of conservative critics, which culminated in the then president's denouncing of the show at the 1992 Republican National Convention on national television—comparing it unfavorably to *The Waltons*—Cartwright believes that the basic values of both shows are the same. "The moral in each episode is the success of the show. That and the fact that you know that although this family constantly fights and seemingly doesn't get along, deep down inside there is this affinity they have for each other. There is a love between Bart and Lisa and Bart and Homer. It is there, but you have to see the whole show to get that. I love the episode where Michael Jackson was the guest [1992's Stark Raving Dad]. It was Lisa's birthday and I got to sing 'Happy Birthday' to Lisa. You get this wonderful scene where Bart tells Lisa that he loves her. A lot of people who criticize it don't watch the show." As to the former resident of the White House who dared to denounce *The Simpsons* and subsequently became fodder for an entire episode—*Two Bad Neighbors*—she says, "I guarantee he hasn't watched a whole episode. If you watch it, you get it."

As concerned as any parent about the issue of television, she restricted her young children's television viewing during their formative years. "It's not so much the violence and language, but it's really that television is a bit of a hypnosis box. You're not doing anything, you turn into a robot." Although her children are now old enough to know how cartoons are made, she fondly recalls her son's initial struggle to understand. "When Jackson was two, he was playing with a prototype of the talking Bart doll. He was pulling the string and watching it go back into the body. Then he looks up at me and says, 'I don't see you in there, Mom.' That's an enormous concept for even a seven-year-old to get."

Admittedly biased, she rates *The Simpsons* as the most innovative cartoon in the last two decades, although she concedes *Animaniacs*, *Tiny Toons*, and *Ren & Stimpy* are worthy competitors. Fortunately, the vast majority of adult cartoon fans are not so fanatical that they resemble "Comic Book Guy." "The adults that are fascinated by cartoons haven't let that child in them die. To have that viewpoint about the joy of creating and appreciating what others do, it somehow communicates to a part of you that is associated with youthfulness. I think that is good. It makes you live longer."

She seems excited to contemplate what her life would have been like without Bart. "I could have done so many things. You may not appreciate this unless you know about what Scientology is, but I became a Scientologist because I really admire the work that they do in the community and on the planet to eradicate crime and illiteracy and just help people that need help. It's to ensure our future, the immortality of mankind. I think to me that is one of the most admirable jobs you can have. There's a lot of things I could do in show business also. I could be a great PR person. That would have been really fun. And I *do* do that, anyway." (Examples of Cartwright's personal public relations work include her 2000 autobiography entitled *My Life as a 10-Year-Old-Boy* and also an ongoing newsletter, "The Nancy News," which can be found at www.nancycartwright.com.)

Cartwright can still be found on stage and on camera. In the 1990s, she garnered great reviews for a one-woman show she wrote entitled *In Search of Fellini,* an autobiographical record of a trip to Italy in which she tried to meet film director Federico Fellini. She is also currently developing plays and movies for Happy House Productions, a production company she started with her husband, Warren. Although she considers herself an "all-around artist," she believes that voice actors are finally getting the respect formerly reserved exclusively for on-camera talent. "I know that people who did voice-overs at one time were considered the stepchildren of the Screen Actors Guild. We weren't very highly respected. But it's so funny. It's now the part of the industry that everybody wants to do. You can have a bad hair day. Even better than that, you can be on location in Toronto doing some film and still do a voice-over. Just find a studio and have them fax you a script. Put some headsets on, get the producer on the other line and phone it in. I went through two pregnancies doing *The Simpsons.* It is truly the best job on the planet, for me anyway, as Bart. I don't know how *The Simpsons* is going to end. I'd like to think it never will."

Cartwright's pink Miata has since been bought at a celebrity charity auction by boxing legend and grill promoter George Foreman. The whereabouts of "Spud" is unknown.

CREDITS

2 Stupid Dogs (1993) TV Series . . . . Little Red Riding Hood
51st Annual Primetime Emmy Awards, The (1999) TV (uncredited) . . . . Bart Simpson
Aladdin (1993) TV Series . . . . Sprites/Additional Voices
All-New Pound Puppies . . . . Bright Eyes
Alvin and the Chipmunks (1983) TV Series . . . . Additional Voices
Amazing Bunjee Venture, The (1984) TV . . . . Karen Winsborrow/Baby #2
Animaniacs (1993) TV Series . . . . Mindy Sadlier/Additional Voices
Bart Wars, the Simpsons Strike Back (1999) Video . . . . Bart Simpson
Big Guy and Rusty the Boy Robot (1999) TV Series . . . . Additional Voices (1999)
Bonkers (1993) TV Series . . . . Fawn Deer
Canterville Ghost . . . . Ned and Ted
Casper (1996) TV Series
Chipmunk Adventure, The (1987) . . . . Arabian Prince
Critic, The (1994) TV Series . . . . Margo Sherman
CyberWorld (2000) (archive footage) . . . . Bartholomew "Bart" Simpson
Dangerous: The Short Films (1993) Video . . . . Bart Simpson ("Black or White" video)

Dink, the Little Dinosaur (1989) TV Series . . . . Additional Voices

Droopy, Master Detective (1993) TV Series . . . . Additional Voices

Fantastic Max (1988) TV Series . . . . FX

Flesh & Blood (1985) . . . . Kathleen

Futurama (1999) TV Series . . . . Bart Simpson Doll

Galaxy High School (1986) TV Series . . . . Gilda Gossip/'Flat Freddy' Fender

Glofriends, The (1986) TV Series . . . . Fantastic Man/Scoop

God, the Devil, and Bob (2000) TV Series . . . . Megan Allman

Goof Troop (1992) TV Series . . . . Pistol Pete

Goof Troop Christmas, A (1992) TV . . . . Pistol Pete

Heaven Help Us (1985) (uncredited) . . . . Girl at dance

Hercules (1998) TV Series . . . . Mini

Kellys, The (2003) . . . . Chip

Kim Possible (2002) TV Series . . . . Rufus, Ron's naked mole-rat

Land before Time VI: The Secret of Saurus Rock, The (1998) Video . . . . Dana

Little Mermaid, The (1989) . . . . Additional Voices

Little Nemo: Adventures in Slumberland (1992) . . . . Page

Mike, Lu, and Og (1999) TV Series . . . . Lu

Monchichis (1983) TV Series

My Little Pony: The Movie (1986) . . . . Gusty/Bushwoolie #4

My Little Pony and Friends (1986) TV Series . . . . Gusty

Petal to the Metal (1992) . . . . Fawn Deer

Pink Panther, The (1993) TV Series . . . . Additional Voices

Pinky, Elmyra, & the Brain (1998) TV Series . . . . Rudy Mookich

Popeye and Son (1987) TV Series . . . . Woody

Pound Puppies (1986) TV Series . . . . Bright Eyes

Pound Puppies and the Legend of Big Paw . . . . Bright Eyes/Whopper

Precious Victims (1993) TV

Problem Child (1993) TV Series . . . . Betsy/Ross/Junior Healy

Rapsittie Street Kids: Believe in Santa (2002) TV . . . . Todd

Raw Toonage (1992) TV Series . . . . Additional Voices

Richie Rich (1981) TV Series . . . . Gloria

Richie Rich/Scooby-Doo Hour, The (1980) TV Series . . . . Gloria Patterson (Richie's Girlfriend)

Rugrats (2001–present) . . . . Chuckie Finster, the Junk Food Kid

Rugrats Go Wild! (2003) Chuckie Finster

Shirt Tales, The (1982) TV Series . . . . Kip Kangaroo (1983–1985)

Simpsons, The (1991) TV Series . . . . Bartholomew "Bart" Jo-Jo Simpson/Nelson Muntz/Todd Flanders/Ralph Wiggum/Kearney/Additional Voices

Simpsons: America's First Family, The (2000) TV . . . . Herself

Simpsons Christmas Special, The (1989) TV . . . . Bart Simpson/Todd Flanders/Children at the mall/Others

Snorks, The (1984) TV Series . . . . Daffney

Space Ace (1984) TV Series . . . . Kimberly

Super Sunday (1985) TV Series . . . . Additional Voices

Timber Wolf (2001) Video . . . . Earl the Squirrel

Timon and Pumbaa (1995) TV Series . . . . Additional Voices

Toonsylvania (1998) TV Series . . . . Melissa Screetch

Tracey Ullman Show, The (1987) TV Series . . . . Bart Simpson (1987–1989)

Twisted Adventures of Felix the Cat, The (1995) TV Series . . . . Additional Voices

Wakko's Wish (1999) Video . . . . Mindy

ADRIANA CASELOTTI

Adriana Caselotti remembers the day she auditioned for the original role of *Snow White* in 1935. Frank Churchill, the musical director, handed the eighteen-year-old a manuscript of "Someday My Prince Will Come." "He said to me, 'Now, little girl, I'm going to the piano and play a melody for you a couple of times so that maybe you can sing it.' Well, he never made it to the piano. I started singing 'Someday My Prince Will Come,' and he said, 'Oh my God! The kid reads music.' He couldn't believe it. He was sold on me before we even started."

Apparently, Walt Disney couldn't believe his good fortune either. "I was the first person to audition for the role. Frank said that after I left, Walt told him, 'Frank, I think we've found our Snow White on the first try, but I can't believe this can happen, so we're going to try a lot of other people to be sure.'" Disney tested 149 more hopefuls, including actress Deanna Durbin. After a full year of auditions, the young Caselotti thought they had forgotten her when she suddenly got a phone call from the studio informing her that the part was hers.

Caselotti credits winning the role to the fact that she was born into a family of opera singers. "My sister Louise was Maria Callas's singing teacher, and my father taught us all." When Caselotti was seven, they left Connecticut for Italy and Caselotti was placed in a convent while her mother toured with an opera company. When they returned to New York three years later, Caselotti spoke no English. While relearning her native language, she studied opera with her father. She was determined to continue the family tradition but was side-tracked by work in films. Caselotti landed a one-line role in 1937's *The Bride Wore Red*, with Joan Crawford and Franchot Tone. She was doing mostly uncredited bit parts when a Disney talent scout approached her father inquiring if he might have a student with the fortitude to sing for the demanding role of Snow White. Guido Caselotti was quick to nominate his daughter.

Although she had passed the audition, Walt Disney decided he wanted Caselotti to warm up on a short subject. "Walt had me do *The Tortoise and the Hare* before we started recording *Snow White*. I was one of the rabbits sitting on the fence during the race. Afterwards, when we finally started recording *Snow White*, I did my parts all alone. I was never in the studio with the other actors except for the last three or four days. I was with the witch one day and a couple of the dwarves another day, but that's about it. Somehow I had to make believe I had all these dwarves I was talking to. I'd usually get to the studio around nine o'clock in the morning, and there'd be a long, long script with only my lines on it."

Reading with no interplay between herself and the other actors was not the only difficulty she faced in the studio. Her songs were recorded a cappella. "They wanted to have me sing first, to record the orchestra to my voice. This was a difficult thing for me to do. The band leader would move his finger back and forth and softly hum the music so that I would hear the intonation and make believe there was a great big orchestra."

To make matters worse, there was some doubt as to whether *Snow White* would ever be finished. "They had no money. They actually had shut down for quite some time. Walt went to the Bank of America and the man said, 'Unless you can show us what you have done, we can't give you any more.'" Disney, who had the family fortune wrapped up in the film in addition to bank loans, hated the thought of having to screen a half-finished film, but was forced to relent. Caselotti states, "It was only partially done, but the bank said, 'You can't fail.' They gave him another, I think, $500,000. In those days that was a tremendous amount of money. We worked on the film from the middle of 1935 to the end of 1937. I think the whole thing cost two and a half million."

If Disney had no idea of how the first widely distributed animated feature would fare over the "sneering critics" who doubted the possibilities of the medium, Caselotti was clueless to even the scope of the project. Having just finished *The Tortoise and the Hare*, she was led to believe that *Snow White* was an extension of a Disney short subject. "They told me *Snow White* was going to be a little longer than the usual short. I thought it was a ten- to twenty-minute feature. They wouldn't show me the rushes or let me hear the musical recordings. So, it was a shock when I saw the premiere and realized it was a full-length feature."

The surprises continued as Caselotti arrived at the well-publicized star-studded premiere with co-star Harry Stockwell (the voice of Prince Charming) and was not allowed into the theater. While most of the Disney employees were seated in the back of the theater, Caselotti said, "They forgot to leave tickets for us, so when Harry and I got to the door the girl said, 'May I have your tickets please?' I said, 'Tickets? I'm Snow White and this is Prince Charming and we don't need any tickets.' The girl replied, 'I don't care if you're the Wicked Old Witch. You're not gonna get in here.'" Caselotti and Stockwell snuck into the balcony when the ticket-taker turned her back. Caselotti was thrilled to see that many of Hollywood's biggest stars, such as Gary Cooper and (her idol) Marlene Dietrich, had turned out for the event.

Despite the fact that the film made millions for the Disney studio within six months, Caselotti, certainly an instrumental part of the film, was paid about $960. "The studio was very poor. I never did get residuals. After *Snow White* I had no money." The Great Depression was not yet over, and work was hard to come by. But the actress managed to land a small but memorable voice-over role in MGM's *Wizard of Oz*. "You know the part in the Tin Man's song where he sings 'Picture me a balcony?' I'm the one who says 'Wherefore art thou, Romeo?' I was paid a hundred dollars for that." Afterwards, when she asked Walt Disney for more work, he said, "I absolutely cannot use you again, and the simple reason is that your voice is too identifiable." Caselotti believed that Disney's voice echoed throughout Hollywood as the other animation houses apparently took his lead. "When I tried to get a job at other cartoon studios, they would hardly pay attention to me. I ended up working at the Hitching Post Theater in Hollywood for seventy-five cents an hour. I had just gotten married and we were trying very hard to make ends meet."

Ironically, while Snow White got her Prince Charming, Caselotti's heart belonged to a podiatrist who refused to get married. She eventually decided she could not wait and settled for someone else. "He was a very fine man, but I married him because the one I really cared for would not marry me. It lasted for three and a half years, but it did not work out. When we got a divorce, I married his best friend, Norville Mitchell, who was in charge of makeup, wardrobe, and set dressing at CBS television. We had a beautiful marriage for twenty years, after which he died. Then, I called my childhood sweetheart, the podiatrist, and I told him my husband had died. He said, 'Well, that's too bad. Do you want to go out to dinner?' I said, 'But what about your wife?' He said, 'My wife? I've never been married.' So we went out to dinner, and that very night he said, 'Do you want to get married, Adriana?' I said, 'Oh my God, you've got to be kidding me. I'm waiting thirty-five years. You ask me now?' So we got married a few days later."

Subsequently, whenever *Snow White* was re-released, Caselotti would travel the country promoting it. "We had many reissues, and I went on tour for almost all of them. Disney paid me very well every time I went out." The money she earned was used wisely. She overcame whatever fears a child of the Great Depression might have had and invested in the stock market. "I was just lucky, I guess, because I didn't know too much about it. But I made quite a lot of money in the stock market and in real estate."

The feeling of security offered Caselotti an opportunity to branch out creatively. In addition to writing an instructional book called *Do You Like to Sing?* she reached back into her past to delve into her first passion, opera. She soon found, however, that the career she had romanticized was not suited for her. "I starred in *Rigoletto* three times. The first time I had a cold, the second time I was scared to death, and the third time I threw up backstage, and I said, 'The hell with this, I'm going back to Snow White.' "

One of the most frequently asked questions she encountered on tours was whether or not she felt her fairy-tale ingenue was a bad role model for little girls because the implied message is to look for Prince Charming to rescue them from their lives. "A lot of people have asked me that question, and I never know what to answer because it doesn't affect me that way at all.

I think Snow White is a sweet little girl who loves everyone and just wants to know that everyone is happy. That's all she ever wants. You notice that all through the film."

In 1994, Caselotti received an unexpected call. The Disney Company was about to release the movie on the laser disc format, and they needed her to restore her voice for a scene that had been edited out of the initial release. "It was in the original the first time they showed it, but Walt said, 'We have to cut this thing down three minutes.' Afterwards they'd lost it, or somebody took it home as a souvenir, but we had to do it all over again. This time I had to dub my voice to the picture, which was difficult for me. We had to do several re-takes."

She enjoyed the fact that she was not always recognized in public, "because you can live your life without being stopped every minute, though I enjoy when children know that I'm Snow White. I like to sing to them right away. In fact, I carry a little picture with me when I go shopping, and if I see a little girl who's kind of sad, I ask, 'What do you want?' And I know she doesn't know who I am, so I buy her the thing, and I hand her the picture. I sing, 'I'm wishing for the one I love to find me. . . . I'm the voice of Snow White.' Well, my God, the way these kids' faces light up. There's a little tear that gets in their eyes, and they are placing themselves to the time they saw the film. What a pleasure I get from that. I couldn't buy that anywhere for money."

While many actors would have been bitter about being typecast, Caselotti relished the part, on and off screen, for her entire career. She was known to answer the telephone with a cheery "Hello, Snow White speaking!" and dress in the costume to read fairy tales to the neighborhood children. "I am very, very pleased with my life. If it hadn't been for Snow White, I don't think I would have been the happy woman I've been all these years." Caselotti lived in an Alpine-style A-frame house with a huge wishing well in front, which bears a striking resemblance to Snow White's cottage. Although she had long-ago given away all her original dolls and collectibles, the inside was filled with memorabilia that fans had since sent her. She said in 1994, "I think the adults are more kids than kids are. You should see the fan mail I get. Most of the time they're men in their fifties and sixties who tell me that that was the first film they saw. Some of them send me pictures of rooms that they have completely filled with *Snow White* memorabilia." Delighted to sign autographs for anyone who would show up at her door, she said, "What I tell everybody, if I sign something for them, is to sell it, grab the money, and run like hell; but wait 'til I die!"

Refusing to admit to the fans that she was ever ill, Adriana Caselotti left the world a little sadder place when she passed away in January 1997 of cancer.

She was survived by her fourth husband, whom she met after being widowed following seven years of marriage to her childhood sweetheart, the podiatrist. Certainly, she left knowing that she would always be remembered for her most famous role. "I don't think *Snow White* will ever die. In fact, I'm certain that it cannot. I think it is still the greatest film and I think it will remain so. I also think Walt Disney will never die. I know he's bodily gone, but the spirit remains. He is with us at all times."

Caselotti had nothing but the highest respect for Disney, with only one caveat. "I've told very few people this, but Walt used to drive me home; often for the purpose of speaking with me in detail about the role. Every time we were driving home he'd say the same darn thing. 'If you can come up with any ideas for this film, I can pay you very well. I'll give five dollars for each idea.' I'm really not very clever about ideas, but, I thought, if I could get five dollars, wouldn't that be marvelous? So I kept thinking about it and thinking about it. He was working with me on the set a lot. One day he was sitting there on the floor, and I said, 'You know, Walt. I've got an idea. At the end of "Whistle While You Work," why don't you have the birds imitate me? I'd sing and the bird tweets; then, the same thing repeats and I hold the note until the last.' Walt said, 'Listen guys, the kid's got an idea.' He had me do it for them and finally used the idea."

She continued, "Then I had the other one. It was when Snow White runs through the forest and she's desperate because she's so afraid of all these branches that look like big things grabbing her. She's on the ground and she starts to cry; then all of a sudden she sees these little birds. I start to sing and then the bird imitates, 'Tweet, tweet, tweet, tweet, tweet,' and I hit a very high note. Well, this was all my idea, and what happens is the bird gets all of it, but he can't do the high note at the end. The mama bird and the papa bird look at the baby bird and groan with displeasure. Then it goes into (singing) '*With a smile and a song, life is just like a bright sunny day. Your cares fade away. And your heart is young.*' So it all follows through. He used both of those ideas. You want to know something? He forgot to give me the ten bucks. He owes me ten dollars. Maybe when I die, I'll track him down and make him pay me."

Perhaps somewhere a red-faced Walt Disney is finally making good on his debt.

DAN CASTELLANETA

It is odd that Homer Simpson, the cartoon character that is almost univer-
sally considered to be the world's biggest dolt exemplified, seems to have
so deftly caught the admiration of academia. Homer's catchphrase "D'oh!"
was recently inducted into the *Oxford Dictionary of Quotations*. In 1999,
Time magazine declared *The Simpsons* the best television show in history,
while guest stars have included paleontologist Stephen Jay Gould, artist

Jasper Johns, and poet laureate Robert Pinsky. Revered physicist Steven Hawking even bragged to the press about how much he liked his guest-starring stint on the show, especially pleased that he "got to have a beer with Homer."

Obviously, there must be something more to "hidden comic genius" Dan Castellaneta, who is not only Homer Simpson's alter ego, but also the voice of such diverse characters as Krusty the Clown, Barney Gumble, Grandpa Simpson, Mayor Quimby, and Groundskeeper Willie, among others. The shy and soft-spoken Castellaneta is a non-beer-drinking, non-doughnut-eating vegetarian who was once an art education major. But, fortunately for Hawking and the rest of the world, Castellaneta also graduated from Chicago's Second City Players troupe into the Hollywood limelight.

The Oak Park, Illinois, native has described himself as a natural actor, an introverted child who did not feel "safe" unless he had a character to hide behind. But, for a while, it seemed as if his other talents would pull him into a less glamorous occupation. "I really did want to be an actor but I had, at that time, thought I was . . . a pretty good artist and I thought that maybe I should find something that I would like that I could fall back on and Northern Illinois [University] had a very good art department. I probably should have taken something in design, but I was easily discouraged by some person saying, 'Oh, design, it's harder,' which I think is ridiculous because it's hard to be a teacher, if not harder."

Castellaneta was soon able to confirm that with personal experience. When faced with the realities of student-teaching, he quickly reassessed his career choice and decided to return to NIU, this time, to finish a theater minor. After graduation, he did different odd jobs, including ushering at the Shubert Theater in Chicago and sweltering as a laborer in a hot factory for a printing company. He then spent about a year at a venture that sold power transmissions and parts for machinery. While he was at the last day job, he began to learn the acting trade at the Second City Players Workshop until he was ready to make the final cut for the main troupe.

He downplays that achievement, citing a more casual environment in the 1970s, before the comedy troupe was recognized for turning out comic luminaries like John Belushi, Bill Murray, etc. Second City offered five levels of classes, but Castellaneta says students were better off studying with Chicago legend Del Close (who reportedly willed his skull to the Goodman Theater after his death in 2000 to use in future productions of *Hamlet*!) and Don Depolo because they could actually recommend their students as new talent for the main troupe. Of course, there was the off-chance that admission could be granted by theater producers Joyce Sloan or Bernie Sahlins, who might see a waitress/actress; and Castellaneta (imitating Sahlins) says, " 'I like her, she's funny. Put her in the company or put her in the touring company.' It was very informal. Now they're a little more strict about it."

The Second City seemed to hold the key to Castellaneta's future: in the 1980s, it was there that he met his wife, Debra Lacusta; then, an alumni connection became a direct ticket to work for Fox. Castellaneta was performing onstage when *Cheers'* George Wendt came back to do a set with the cast. He liked Castellaneta's performance and recommended him to *Cheers* writer Heidi Perlman, who was also about to pen a new show for Tracy Ullman. When she flew to Chicago with Ullman to scout for talent, they were eager to watch Castellaneta. Although Ullman later said that when they saw his rendition of a blind man who wanted to be a comedian, he brought her closer to tears than laughter, Castellaneta quickly received an invitation to read in Los Angeles and soon after was asked to be a part of the regular cast.

Considering that Castellaneta and the future *Simpsons* crew were on the brink of worldwide stardom, they came together with little fanfare for most of the initial process. Castellaneta and Julie Kavner had a definite edge for casting. Kavner was already a celebrity, even having been in the 1987 Woody Allen film *Radio Days*. Castellaneta's background included voice-over work, primarily radio spots and shows for prominent Chicago stations such as WXRT. Of course, the finances may have played a part in the decision for Fox; as he points out, the actors were already paid to do a variety of characters and voices on *The Tracy Ullman Show*, and to add the cartoon "bumpers" (short segments before and after the commercial breaks) was not going to cost Fox any more in additional salaries.

Castellaneta recalls that his audition was basically a non-event: "Matt [Groening] showed me the picture of the character of Homer and he said, 'What kind of voice can you do for this guy?' And I said, 'How about this. . . .' He went, 'OK, that's good.' Julie [Kavner] talked—her voice was tired that day, so she said, 'Is this all right? I'll just talk low like this . . .' and he went 'Fine.' Matt just went, 'Fine, fine.' "

To listen to Castellaneta's mild speaking voice, which is more reminiscent of Abe Simpson than his son, it is difficult to believe that Castellaneta can generate the wide range of voices needed to populate his share of *The Simpsons'* universe. Castellaneta says his creativity is supplemented by characterizations which are drawn from various sources. "It can be from people you've met. It can be from voices that you copped from other actors—from movie stars, from other television actors. . . . Voice actors are always trading goofy voices." Of course, Homer's intonations "started out [as] Walter Matthau, but there's probably a little Mr. Magoo in him."

As the character of Homer evolved, so did the voice. It was not just for aesthetic reasons, but it needed to fall into a range that was more comfortable for the actor to consistently reproduce. "If you come up with a new voice that you don't usually do, it's not always in a comfortable spot in your larynx. . . . To do it over a duration of time you have to be comfortable with it because you've got to be able to act and do different inflections. . . . Because Homer is all over the map emotionally, more than any of the other characters, he can be like screaming and crying one minute and then all of a sudden, calm down and then laugh. So I had to find a voice that I can do that there wasn't a tight constriction."

Further, Castellaneta can personally claim to have added "D'oh" to the worldwide lexicon. He says he was given an instruction in the script written as a "frustrated grunt," and he thought of the old Laurel and Hardy character actor Jim Findlayson, who had a grunt that sounded like "Doooowww." When Castellaneta used it, Groening approved, but wanted a shorter version. When Castellaneta interpreted that as "D'oh!" they decided to keep it, not even thinking it might become a national catchphrase.

Certainly, another element of the show that has evolved is the adversarial relationship between Bart and Homer. Castellaneta has said he believes it is now a more Laurel and Hardy–type relationship, with Homer less the antagonist than the foil. "I think [that was] because Matt originally conceived the Homer part as just the grumpy father and the tension was coming out of the fact that Bart and Homer were always at odds. . . . But, *The Simpsons* has such a huge rich kind of tapestry in terms of the background and the world surrounding it. There are so many infinite things that can be done that that's not played up so much. . . . They found other avenues— Lisa's pining and angst and Marge is constantly trying to deny things are wrong. Always, Marge is keeping in her feelings and trying to cope with being stifled by Homer."

Despite the criticism of the inter-familial conflict, Castellaneta believes they are no more dysfunctional than the average family. "I think there are families where there are mothers who keep a lid on what their feelings are, and I think there are families with sort-of boorish fathers that don't necessarily have the answer. Certainly, there are kids like Bart. There are kids like Lisa. I don't know if they're an accurate depiction because in cartoons, things are heightened to a certain extent and even to the point that the Simpsons sometimes become absurd."

Over the years, the writers have also made Homer's character shameless to different degrees. "The guys who sit around and write these things, they all think of the dumbest, stupidest things their fathers ever have done. It's all expressed through Homer." While some of the writers have said that they viewed him as a "big dog trapped in human form," Castellaneta told Christopher Goodwin, in a piece for London's *Sunday Times* in 2000, that he sees Homer as a big twelve-year-old with unfettered male libido. That is, "the myth is that, left to their own devices, men would be just like Homer: lazy, sitting in front of the TV, eating whatever's bad for them, having every single vice, gambling, drinking beer, ogling women, and watching Mexican wrestling."

The longevity and popularity of the show, launched in 1989, and its continuing success have amazed him. He knew from the first script that the show was of high quality, but he had previously been part of many short-lived projects that he thought were "sure things." Believing the show might attract no more than a solid cult following, he expected a good run would amount to no more than five years. Since the show is now more than fifteen years old, the most successful animated program in history and poised to be the longest-running comedy ever, it is surprising to hear Castellaneta say that *The Simpsons* came very close to being just another unrealized idea on the proverbial, if not literal, drawing board.

In the late 1980s, despite the initial desperation for original programming, there was still resistance at the fledgling Fox network to the idea of producing an animated program. Castellaneta says, "They were pretty liberal at the time because they had nothing to lose, but they didn't think that anybody would watch an animated show, because their thinking about cartoons was probably as myopic as most people who run the network—anything halfway creative they're afraid of."

Castellaneta says it took the clout of producer-director James L. Brooks— whom he had been an admirer of since Brooks's series *Taxi*—to get *The Simpsons* on the air in prime time. But even the producer of *Broadcast News* and Fox's own success stories, like *Big, Say Anything*, and *The War of the Roses*, still had to fight to get the executives to commit to thirteen shows. Fox initially offered to produce the cartoon as a special, to which Brooks flatly refused. When Fox countered with the offer to do four shows, Castellaneta said Brooks replied, "No, because if it's a hit, it takes so long to do the animation you've got to have at least thirteen ready to go."

Naturally, when the series became an instant sensation, Castellaneta says the network executives seemed just as unhappy. "We couldn't get the second season in fast enough." He remarks, "I can tell you little anecdotes. . . . I don't know if I can attribute it to [producers] Al Jean or Mike Reiss. One of them told me this: when Fox would complain to them about *The Simpsons* and say, 'You guys are taking too long to the get the shows done. We need more shows every season.'. . . At the time we're saying, 'We're doing all we can to get out a great product.' And then somebody said, 'Well, we're not taking as long on these recording sessions as they are on *Capitol Critters!*'"

Regardless of the production standards of the short-lived *Critters* and the other prime-time animated shows that were rushed out to capitalize on *The Simpsons'* early success, part of the deal that Matt Groening made with Fox was almost complete autonomy in the scripts. That artistic freedom trickled down to the actors in the liberty they are given in interpreting their lines. Castellaneta says, "We give them what they want and they go back to pick whatever they want. . . . Since it is on tape, we can change a line here and there and then a lot of writers or the director will request what they need to take as written. But we make suggestions all the time. Harry Shearer is a brilliant writer on his own, in his own right. And I improvise and have done my own material. Julie Kavner has an improvisation background. Everybody pitches in and ad-libs a line here and there. And, on occasion, we will object to a script and say we think this is missing this and that from the character, much, I suppose, like any sitcom show." Castellaneta says that the inspiration they try to draw upon was the ensemble work of the cast of *The Rocky and Bullwinkle Show*; he believes that "the way they did their reads and the way they did things probably influenced *The Simpsons* the most."

Given the amount of effort and talent the cast has brought to the program to make it such a success, it makes Fox's past animosity in contract negotiations all the more puzzling. For *The Simpsons'* first ten years, the cast was making a minuscule percentage of the program's returns. Also, according to Castellaneta, he only received a percentage of the merchandising when his voice (not a sound-alike) was attached. When the cast protested the low salaries, he says the network's refrain was often, "Well, you're just the voice." He counters, "But, the voice is [what] conjures up the character. It gives it the reality . . . the soul, really." But the attitude of the network has been that "we can always replace the voice." And, in a case of very suspicious timing, during the last round of negotiations in 1998, the network staged a "contest" to find the best sound-alikes for the cast, but did, ultimately, settle with most of the cast for a sum that was reportedly well into the six figures.

As for Castellaneta's vocation of voice acting, he says, "I think I was pretty fortunate to get in on it when it started. . . . I've never really thought of myself as a voice-over actor. . . . I'd always thought that was something that I could do while I was looking for other kinds of acting work. Now, I think of it in terms of—not to compare myself to Orson Welles, but I know that in his day, when radio was popular, that actors, while they were doing theater at night, they would do radio in the day . . . to keep things going if they didn't always get stage work right away." Castellaneta laments that movie actors get recognition when they make the crossover to voice-overs, "but nobody recognizes a voice-over actor as an actor. . . . You can be a bad actor and still have a career, but if you are a bad voice-over person you are not going to make it."

It is ironic that a 1997 *New York Times* article compared the otherwise "reticent" actor's ability to handle multiples roles to that of Peter Sellers. Castellaneta considers Sellers his "acting idol" and would like the opportunity to develop his artistic versatility on film. In 1999, Castellaneta co-wrote and starred in the one-man show *Where Did Vincent Van Gogh?* "a comic assemblage of monologues and sketches" which required him to perform a cast of characters. He has applied his talents to writing for *The Simpsons*, cowriting the 2000 episode "Days of Wine and D'oh'ses" with his wife. While he has directed plays, he has yet to try directing voice-over recording sessions or do what, for many, is still considered the ultimate ambition in Hollywood: "I would much like to direct a film. Whether someone gives me the job or I try to gather my own resources and do it myself, write something and direct it myself. Sometimes, I wish I could actually direct some of the voice-over sessions. I think, sometimes, the way some people do voice-over sessions, they sometimes romance the blind readings as opposed to allowing the actors to flow a little with the scene, which is why I like doing *The Simpsons*."

Castellaneta watches the show regularly and claims that if he was not in it, he would still probably be a "*Simpsons'* Geek." He has numerous past episodes he is fond of, including "Homer Gets Hair" and "Lisa's Substitute Teacher." He also lists, among his favorites, "Homer's Religion," in which Homer refuses to go to church. Commenting that although *The Simpsons* has been so criticized for being anti-family and anti-moral, he says of that episode, "I think that was a perfect little parable about religion and the fact is that Homer didn't go to church and then he went around putting down other people's religions . . . and wound up in the end being helped by them. Then Homer goes, 'God, I understand now this is God's vengeance for not going to church.' And Rev. Lovejoy says, 'No, it was God's showing you that he works through everybody—be they Jewish or Christian or (pointing at Apu) *miscellaneous*.' And, of course, Apu is Hindu. [Castellaneta does an insulted Apu] 'There are several million of us, you know.'"

Whatever his future ambitions, the Emmy-winning actor is reassuring that there is little danger of his walking away from the show, "unless the whole structure of civilization changes in the next twenty or thirty years." Even after the first run of the series, syndication, and a feature film announced in 2004, Castellaneta expects the characters to "go on in perpetuity" in whatever form that may take. Nevertheless, the man who helped create Homer Simpson and set the standard for his worldwide translations still, after over a decade of accolades from the biggest names in entertainment and academia, can remain as anonymous as any voice actor. As he told a *Chicago Tribune* columnist in 2001, although he does enjoy the ability to still get lost in a crowd, "it can be frustrating because Homer is an international superstar and I'm just some guy walking down the street."

CREDITS

51st Annual Primetime Emmy Awards, The (1999) TV (uncredited) .... Himself
Aladdin (1993/I) TV Series .... Genie/Icafrak/Additional Voices
Aladdin's Arabian Adventures: Creatures of Invention (1998) Video .... Genie
Aladdin's Arabian Adventures: Fearless Friends (1998) Video .... Genie
Aladdin's Arabian Adventures: Magic Makers (1998) Video .... Genie
Aladdin's Arabian Adventures: Team Genie (1998) Video .... Genie
All Dogs Go to Heaven 2 (1996)
Animaniacs (1993) TV Series .... Dracula/Additional Voices
Back to the Future (1991) TV Series .... Dr. Emmett Lathrop "Doc" Brown
Bart Wars/The Simpsons Strike Back (1999) Video .... Homer J. Simpson
Bobby's World (1990) TV Series .... Additional Voices
Buzz Lightyear of Star Command (2000) TV Series .... Various Voices
Casper (1996) TV Series .... Dr. Harvey/Additional Voices
Cow and Chicken (1997) TV Series .... Earl
Critic, The (1994) TV Series .... Homer Simpson
CyberWorld (2000) (archive footage) .... Homer Simpson/Abraham Abe/Grampa Simpson
Dangerous: The Short Films (1993) Video .... Homer Simpson ("Black or White" video)
Darkwing Duck (1991) TV Series .... Megavolt
Don't Tell Mom the Babysitter's Dead (1991) .... Animated Babysitter
Duck Tales (1987) .... Additional Voices
Earthworm Jim (1995) TV Series .... Earthworm Jim
Eek! The Cat (1992) TV Series .... Mittens/Bill/Hank the Scientist/Additional Voices
Fievel's American Tails (1991) TV Series .... Chula the Tarantula
Futurama (1999) TV Series .... Beelzebot
Gooftroop (1992) TV Series. ... Additional Voices
Hercules (1998) TV Series .... Homer the Reporter
Hey Arnold! (1996) TV Series .... Monkey Man/Grandpa "Steely" Phil/Willie "the Jolly Olly Man"/
    Earl/Dr. Murray Steiglitz/Nick Vermicelli/Additional Voices
Hey Arnold! The Movie (2002) .... Grandpa/Nick Vermicelli
House of Mouse (2001) TV Series .... Genie

Jonny Bravo (1997) TV Series . . . . Harvey

Joseph: King of Dreams (2000) Video . . . . Auctioneer/Horse Trader

Kim Possible (2002) TV Series

Kim Possible: The Secret Files (2003) Video . . . . Drakken's Goons

Little Mermaid (1992) TV Series . . . . Additional Voices

Marsupalami (1993) TV Series . . . . Stewart

New Pink Panther Show . . . . Voo Doo Man/Additional Voices

Olive, the Other Reindeer (1999) TV . . . . Postman

Online Adventures of Ozzie the Elf, The (1997) TV . . . . Comet/Blitzen

Recess: School's Out (2001) . . . . Guard #1

Return of Jafar, The (1994) Video . . . . Blue Genie

Return to Never Land (2002) . . . . Additional Voice

Rugrats in Paris: The Movie—Rugrats II (2000) . . . . Priest

Simpsons, The (1989) TV Series . . . . Homer Jay Simpson/Abraham J. "Grampa" Simpson/Herschel Smoikel Krustofsky/Krusty the Clown/Barney Gumble/Groundskeeper Willie/Mayor Joseph "Diamond Joe" Quimby/Hans Moleman/Melvin Van Horne/Sideshow Mel/ Itchy the Mouse/Kodos/Arnie "Pie in the Sky" Pie/Gil/Additional Voices

Simpsons: America's First Family, The (2000) TV . . . . Himself

Simpsons Christmas Special, The (1989) TV . . . . Homer Simpson/Other Voices

Super Mario Brothers (1993) . . . . Narrator

Tale Spin (1990) TV Series . . . . Additional Voices

Taz-Mania (1991) TV Series . . . . Mister Thickley

Tick, The (1994) TV Series . . . . Charles's Father

Tiny Toons Adventures (1990) TV Series . . . . Jeffries

Tracey Ullman Show, The (1987) TV Series . . . . Homer Simpson

Here's a dozen Gumbys for you!

Art Clokey

ART CLOKEY

He is Gumby, dammit! Well, not exactly—the creator of Gumby, more properly, voices only his horse, Pokey, but Art Clokey is undoubtedly the king of the green clay empire. To Clokey's amusement, there has been much speculation about the origins and meaning of one of the most exotic and ubiquitous claymation figures ever created. While the name is derived from "gumbo," a term for wet southern soil, he laughingly dismisses the more outlandish urban legends about Gumby having Satanic origins or, conversely, being modeled after Krishna or Jesus. Although Clokey does not discourage the notion that Gumby's asymmetrical head may be symbolic of the "bump of wisdom" devout Buddhists have, he has a much more mundane and practical explanation; it was inspired by his father's irrepressible cowlick. "I was fascinated by the picture of my father when he graduated from high school. It looked like my father has a big bump of hair on his head. I asked my mother when I was five years old, 'Why does Daddy have a bump on his head?' It fascinated me and I thought it would fascinate children, so I gave Gumby a bump."

His father not only served as a physical model for Clokey's characters, but also was a great influence on him as an all-around artist and filmmaker. "He wrote all kinds of music, including symphonies, various concertos, and operas and so on. His hobbies were painting and photography and motion picture photography. That's how I got interested. . . . My first foray into animation was special effects. I had a camera that would go sixty-four frames per second, which was slow-motion. I was in a prep school and the headmaster's son and I built an adobe city on the hillside and planted black powder bombs in all the buildings. Then we blew up the city in slow motion!"

Clokey's interest in film continued through to his college years. "I was studying at the USC cinema department, where George Lucas went, and I had a wonderful professor, Slavko Vorkapich. He was the head of the department at the time and he turned my head around as far as the power of film, and so on, with his 'kinesthetic film principles.' I call them 'kinesthetic film forces' because they have an impact on your nervous system. I did a study film called *Gumbasia*. I used miniature clay forms changing shape to jazz music, instead of people and regular sets, because it was a lot cheaper and faster and I could do the same thing. It was a study of how to shoot certain movements and cuts to organize kinesthetic film forces. You can induce these forces in your eye cells down into your autonomic nervous system. It makes the film more exciting and you can feel it. An extreme example is when you have a camera and you go down a roller coaster. He taught us how to organize ordinary filming to do more subtle stimulation so you can make it more exciting all the way through."

In 1955 after college, Clokey took a teaching position at a prep school in Studio City, California, called the Harvard Military Academy. (Clokey jokes, "I tell people I taught at Harvard to impress them.") The academy student body included sons of prominent Hollywood directors and producers. It was while Clokey was tutoring Charles Engel, the son of 20th Century Fox producer Sam Engel, that he received the opportunity of a lifetime. In appreciation for the special attention showed toward his son, Engel, who was also the president of the Motion Picture Producers Association, invited Clokey to come to the studio to view some previews. During the screening, Clokey mentioned *Gumbasia* to Engel, who replied that on the next visit to the studio he should bring his "little film." Clokey recalls, "I brought this little three and a half minute, you might call it a jazz music video, and it so impressed him that he wanted to see it again. While he was waiting for the projectionist to rewind it, he paced back and forth in front of the screen and said, 'Art, we've got to go into business. That's the most exciting film I've ever seen!' Of course, it was due to the kinesthetic film techniques I learned at USC."

Clokey was immediately star struck, having visions of working with celebrities like Sophia Loren. But Engel quickly dispelled his fantasies by explaining that he wanted Clokey to produce quality children's programming for television. In Clokey's words, Engel then became the "Godfather" of Gumby not only by agreeing to finance the pilot, but by subsequently handing the project over to Clokey, while taking nothing for himself.

According to his press release, "History of Gumby," the next day at his home, Clokey began to study the properties of oil-based clay. Clokey states, "Clay being very dense, ordinary seven-inch clay figures were not stable enough to be animated. I finally devised a main character configured like a pyramid: large feet tapering up to a thin head." Clokey originally cut Gumby out of a slab of green clay with a cheese cutter and later melted the clay in a crock pot and poured it into hard plaster molds in which were inserted wire armatures. Clokey continues, "Each animator would be given a tray of several Gumby figures. As Gumby was being animated, the clay would be distorted so much that the animator would replace the figure with a fresh one after four or more seconds of animation."

Through Engle's connections, NBC decided to pick up the series. After a successful test screening on *The Howdy-Doody Show*, a new star was born. NBC began airing the series in 1957 and claymation television history began.

In characteristic laid-back form, Clokey said he chose Gumby's voice by allowing the Screen Actors Guild to compile a short list of voice actors; he then made the final cut himself. He had the most basic of requirements—the ability to enunciate clearly so that the dialogue was still intelligible when the tape was sped up to increase the pitch and, of course, the ability to take direction. Casting was done on a more practical note when Clokey took on the role of Pokey, explaining his inspiration as, "I just wanted to save money." Unfortunately, NBC stockholders were trying to do the same.

Pat Weaver, the then president of NBC (and father of *Alien* star Sigourney Weaver) began to receive complaints that he was spending too much money on new productions. The stockholders forced him to cut three series from the line-up, of which Gumby was one. Clokey actually looked upon the cancellation as a stroke of good luck, as he was then able to buy out all rights to the property and own *Gumby* outright.

Forming his own production company, Clokey then produced 120 *Gumby* episodes, eventually syndicating the series in 102 markets throughout the United States and Canada. The success of the show spawned a popular line of Gumby and Pokey merchandizing, bendable figures.

With the experience of *Gumby* under his belt, Clokey was set to produce a series that more reflected his religious interests. While still producing the program for NBC, Clokey recalls, "I got a telephone call from New York from the Lutheran church headquarters. They had seen *Gumby* in New York City, and they said they would like to discuss with me making a religious film series using the same techniques." In 1956, the church financed the production of *Davey and Goliath*, a stop-motion production about a boy named Davey Hanson (Dick Beals) and his faithful pet dog, Goliath (Hal Smith), who spoke, though only to Davey, with a laconic drawl. The show's successful long-standing presence—it was recognizable enough that it was referenced in a popular soft drink commercial almost five decades later—has been attributed to the fact that if morals were taught, it was done in an appealing way without being overly preachy.

Clokey was delighted to be a part of a program with pro-religious values. As detailed on his website (www.Gumbyworld.com), his interest in religion had once led him to study to become an Episcopal minister. Although, in typical Clokey style, after one year in the seminary, he just simply decided to quit and go to Hollywood as he "didn't want to be confronted with everybody's problems, 'cause I didn't want to deal with all that."

Given his religious inclinations, one might be tempted to conclude that Clokey would be upset by *Saturday Night Live* and other parodies (including a segment on *Mad TV* where Davey constructs a pipe bomb to blow up the local family planning center), but this is not the case. After *SNL* called him for permission and the infamous Gumby sketch aired, Clokey says, "My son didn't approve. He was shocked when he saw Eddie Murphy in the Gumby costume smoking a cigar and swearing. I told him, 'That's an adult program where Gumby can laugh at himself.'" Moreover, as Clokey wrote in 1986, "Gumby is a symbol of the spark of divinity in each of us, the basis of the ultimate value of each person. Eddie Murphy instinctively picked up on this when he asserted, 'I'm Gumby, dammit.'" Clokey concludes, "When people watch Gumby, they get a blissful feeling. Gumby loves you. We love you. That's about all I can say."

Indeed.

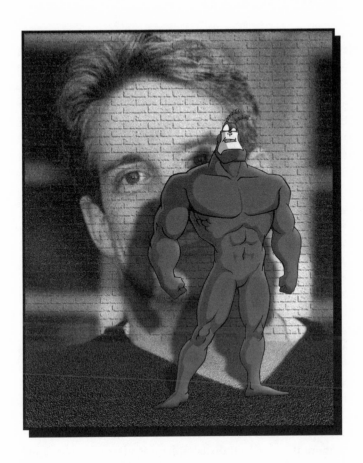

TOWNSEND COLEMAN

Townsend Coleman, whose upbeat voice is heard nightly announcing promos for NBC's late night talk shows and "must-see comedies," spent the better part of the 1990s encountering more than a few strange adventures in animation. As the voice of the slightly off-center superhero "the Tick," Coleman found, one holiday evening during the time of the show's production, that the bizarre aspect of cartoon work did not necessarily end in the studio. In a Burbank toy store to pick up some last-minute Christmas gifts, Coleman happened to spot a thirty-something couple in the crowd, tightly clutching Tick dolls under each arm.

Finding it an irresistible opportunity to surprise his fans, Coleman casually discussed the show for a few minutes before he finally dropped the bombshell and introduced himself, "Well, Hi! I do the voice of the Tick!" To Coleman's embarrassment, they then simply stared back at him as if he were "a Martian." And worse yet, despite Coleman's ever more adamant protests, they absolutely refused to believe him. Now pressed to do the voice just to defend his honor, Coleman worried, "I'm in this crowd of people, and I'm thinking it's the last thing I want to do, and when I do [the Tick] in the studio, he's kind of loud. I did a couple of real short lines, trying to keep it kind of under my breath." Still, the couple remained skeptical, dismissing his best efforts as a "pretty close impression," until he finally had to produce his driver's license as definitive proof of his identity.

Not that their skepticism should have come as a surprise: Coleman had had the same reaction when working on his first animation job, as well. The former Cleveland disc jockey, who was not looking forward to a future as a fifty-year-old still "spinning rock and roll records," simply quit the radio station with no notice, packed up his wife and kids and moved to Los Angeles, having no friends or contacts there. However, he quickly made a powerful acquaintance in the form of a "great" commercial agent—ICM's Jeff Danis, who got him on-camera advertising work and bit parts in film and television. Although Coleman was not one of the very few being handed the "star" parts, no more than six months later, he was pleased to watch his cartoon career take off "all by itself."

At his very first audition, which happened to be for an established program, *Inspector Gadget*, Coleman simply conjured up what he thought might be a good voice and, to his surprise, the executives "roared." He then shared his first session with the star, *Get Smart* legend (and 1963's Tennessee Tuxedo) Don Adams, and voice-over extraordinaires Frank Welker and Maurice LaMarche. Coleman, who had watched *Gadget* in Ohio, scanned the three to try to ascertain which of them could possibly do the booming tones of the villainous Dr. Claw. As they progressed, Coleman saw Claw's lines coming up in the script, but judged none of his present company physically big enough to produce that voice. He recalls, "It comes to his line, and all of a sudden, Welker opens his mouth and out comes this enormous voice, and I just fell off my chair. It was at that point that I realized I was batting in a whole different league."

His next project, NBC's animated version of *Fraggle Rock*, was canceled after only one season (on the whims of programming executive Brandon Tartikoff's daughter). However, that became immaterial because while they still were in production, Coleman was to audition for *Rock* director Stu Rosen for the offbeat and untested concept, *The Teenage Mutant Ninja Turtles*, although the actors were skeptical about the program's chances. "None of us had ever heard of it before. We looked at this thing, and we just thought, 'Oh, man, they're saying that animation is coming back, but this is absurd. This is just so far out there, it's either going to be huge, or it's gonna die a really swift death.' " Regardless, Coleman and castmate Rob Paulsen went to read for it along with "everybody else in town" and the two were promptly booked for the curiosity.

Coleman describes his very first session on the show as a "nightmare fraught with tension." Of the four characters, the executives had named Barry Gordon as Donatello and Rob Paulsen as Raphael, but had not yet decided whether Coleman was to play Michelangelo or Leonardo. Rosen initially asked Coleman to try Michelangelo and then switch parts with Cam Clarke (as Leonardo), but once production began, the casting was set. Coleman remarks that although it might have been interesting to see what they might have done with the parts, "I never got a shot at doing Leonardo, and Cam never got a shot at doing Michelangelo. They just left it, and after that first episode, it was sort of carved in stone."

Once the show premiered, there was no arguing with success, and successful the *Turtles* was, premiering at the top of the ratings both at CBS and in syndication for Group W. At that time, the series had the unique distinction of being the only first-run cartoon to be in production to run concurrently in syndication and on the broadcast network. Still, over the years of its long life, the continued interest in the show did not compel the executives to reward the voice-over cast accordingly; they turned down raises for the cast and even contemplated recasting the series after six years of production. Moreover, Coleman adds that the network treated the show, itself, with a fair degree of indifference, coming close to canceling the program for four years—CBS would "change their mind at the last minute going, 'Yikes, the ratings are still good; let's get some shows!' "

When *The Turtles*—at least for the time being—ended their run in the mid-1990s, Coleman then lent his voice to the Tick. Ben Edlund's big blue comic blowhard of a superhero and his would-be superhero friends spent as much time at the local coffeehouse and dealing with personal problems as they did gallantly defending their community. Edlund, who was a cartoon junkie who loved shows like *Scooby-Doo* and *Space Ghost* from the time he was a child, had developed the mock superhero while playing role-playing games like "Dungeons and Dragons" with other "socially stunted males" who acted as Edlund's captive audience.

Edlund continued to develop a comic book through his years of college at Massachusetts College of Art until he was in sight of his real goal—to pursue a career in TV and film. By the time Edlund was twenty-one, he had been turned down by every network, until 1992 when Sunbow decided to pair him with sometime *Playboy/New Yorker* writer Richard Libmann-Smith to create the program for Fox. To get the title part on one of the hottest animated programs of the time, Coleman went through a huge casting process in which he competed against "everybody in town" for the part—he said his advantage was that he immediately understood the character from the first look at the script.

At the audition, the voice that Coleman heard in his head was an odd amalgam of Gary Owens's Space Ghost with a "younger and more guileless quality," the simpleness of *The Mary Tyler Moore Show's* "Ted Baxter" and the character of Nick Danger from 1970s comedy group Firesign Theater. Then knowing exactly what the Tick should sound like, Coleman boldly burst out the lines to set the tone for the entire series only to hear the executives retort, " '*No, no, no, no, no!* That's all wrong! He's much younger and much more guileless.' "

Stunned, Coleman could only find the voice to reply, "What?! No, that's not at all the way I hear it." After being summarily rejected for the starring role, he read for the sidekick Arthur, supporting characters Die Fliedermaus and Sewer Urchin, and then left, not getting any part on the series at all. While upset and confused because he was convinced that he was "dead-on" for the plum role, Coleman was by then accustomed to creative differences that sometimes occur between the executives and the actor.

In particular, on one of his previous shows, *The Glo Friends,* Coleman recalled playing a character of "Dragonflyer," for which he created a special sound effect. He remarks, "I remember the first time I did that, there were two producers in the room, and one producer just lit up and said, 'Oh, my gosh, that's perfect,' and the other one says, 'That doesn't sound like a dragonfly,' " Meanwhile, Coleman said he was thinking, "This is a cartoon! What do you mean it doesn't sound like a dragonfly?" Coleman remarked, "We hear that kind of thing all the time. [Mimicking,] '*Well, you know, that's not the way a real worm would say it.*' " He then snickered, "Well, you know something? You're right! A REAL WORM DOESN'T TALK!"

Fortunately for Coleman, it was not until *The Tick* had just begun production that executives wanted to start fresh and recast their original choice, who had recorded the first show. As with Coleman's earlier rejection, it was "nothing about the guy's talent; it was just not what they were looking for." This generated another round of auditions, but again, they were not satisfied with any of their options. Coleman said he was then asked to return and, figuring that he had "nothing to lose," again went with his "gut" instinct. This time, the executives seemed to agree with his interpretation.

It was on *The Tick* that Coleman found himself treated to some unexpected perks granted an animation celebrity. One of Fox's biggest shows of the time, it immediately attracted a huge cult following among the non-target audience of teenagers and college students; Coleman's character was then promoted in many forums, not only in the traditional action-figure market—the character even reached a measure of popular icon status when it was featured on a box of Life cereal in 1996. As a personal bonus, Coleman was also delighted to meet and work with some of his favorites remembered from his childhood.

Coleman not only knew *Tick* co-star Cam Clarke as his co-worker on *The Teenage Mutant Ninja Turtles*, but he also had fond memories of him as the nine-year-old "little boy who used to wear knickers" when Clarke was the youngest of the King Family Singers in the mid-1960s. Phil Proctor, of the popular '70s comedy group the Firesign Theater, also guest-starred on a number of episodes of *The Tick*, about which Coleman was extremely excited. "When I was a junior in high school, the big thing in my school was to memorize all of *Nick Danger, Third Eye*, the entire thing from start to finish. . . . That's probably where I really started doing voices. . . . I remember when they hired him for the first time for that episode. . . . This is the weirdest thing for me: here I'm playing the Tick, the lead in this show, and they got Phil Proctor from Firesign Theater playing an incidental dad." Thankfully, by that time Coleman had met other Firesign cast members Phil Austin and Peter Bergman on previous commercial work and had gotten most of the "babbling idiot fan out of his system," or, at least, so he thought.

It was at meeting ex-Monkee Mickey Dolenz, who played the Tick's former accountant sidekick Arthur on the first season, when Coleman began to gush. "For me to be able to work with Mickey Dolenz was—you talk about being a fan boy—I was a way bigger Monkees fan than I was a Beatles fan." Coleman was thrilled to re-record that first episode to replace the previous actor, as he had to share several scenes with Dolenz. "So, it was just me and Mickey in the studio together that first session, and I've got to do everything I can to just bite my tongue and not be a blathering fool."

Coleman described working with the small body of people who make up the animation community as "working with family," remarking that he was especially delighted to have a chance to work with some of the greatest voices in animation. While Coleman was doing incidental voices at Hanna-Barbera, he was introduced to long-time Hanna-Barbera luminary Don Messick. "I remember meeting Don for the first time, going, 'Oh, my God. It's Ranger Smith and Boo Boo Bear!'" Coleman was similarly impressed with his experiences as the lead in 1986's *Teen Wolf*, in which he worked with Warner Bros. icon June Foray. "It was so much fun because here I was, the lead in this show, and June Foray was my grandmother, Donny Most from *Happy Days* was my best friend, and here I was this relatively new kid in town."

Also among Coleman's biggest thrills was the chance to meet Daws Butler. After being hired for his first job on *Inspector Gadget,* his agent had arranged a "general audition" for the informal repertory group at Hanna-Barbera. At the time, he said the studio would hold special auditions twice a year in which the actors were given fifteen minutes to perform their repertoire. "The first five minutes, you would do a script that they prepared for you. The second five minutes would be a script that you prepared, and then the last five minutes, basically, would be anything you wanted to do."

Coleman did his "generals" for voice director Andrea Romano, with his chosen script from the text of Dr. Suess's book, *One Fish, Two Fish, Red Fish, Blue Fish*. "I just did a different character on every page . . . and that just endeared me to her, because that happened to be her all-time favorite book." From there, Coleman started to work steadily at the studio, and he and Romano gradually built a rapport. One day, when discussing his background, he told her that although he was never a cartoon fanatic, per se, the cartoons that he really enjoyed seemed to be the work of Daws Butler.

Hearing that Coleman would "kill to meet Daws someday," Romano then invited him to watch Butler tape an upcoming *Yogi Bear* special. "So, I show up, and I go into the control room, and the recording studio over at Hanna-Barbera is ancient, and it's very small. I sit in there . . . and within about five minutes, this little old man who's like this little gnarled dwarf walks into the studio with the biggest smile on his face, and he crawls up onto this stool. He's got a cane, and he wasn't walking very well. Andrea introduces me to him, and he greets me with this huge smile and this voice that sounds exactly like Huckleberry Hound." While Coleman sat in the control room he was amazed as Butler opened his mouth: out came seven of his best characters, including Huckleberry Hound, Quick Draw McGraw, Yogi Bear, and

Snagglepuss. Coleman concluded, "What an impression he made on everybody he touched."

If the credits for his animation work seem to suddenly end at 1998, it is because the actor has undergone another career transformation. As of this writing, Coleman has primarily settled at NBC working full time as an announcer. Although he has spoken of his time in animation with fondness, he notes that the wonderful excursion into the world of cartoons may never have occurred if he had not happened to make his spontaneous decision to uproot his life in the mid-1980s and arrive in Los Angeles at the time "when the whole animation industry was being reborn." Because of it, Townsend Coleman will forever be a part of the animation landscape, if for nothing else than for his memorable turns as the ostensibly simplest of comic characters—a turtle and a tick.

CREDITS

Amazing Adventures of Inspector Gadget, The (1986) Video . . . . Cpl. Capeman
Animaniacs (1993) TV Series . . . . Katzeneisnerman
Batman & Mr. Freeze: SubZero (1998) Video . . . . Additional Voices
Buster & Chauncey's Silent Night (1998) Video . . . . Additional Voices
Captain Planet and the Planeteers (1990) TV Series . . . . Additional Voices
Cartoon All-Stars to the Rescue (1990) TV . . . . Michaelangelo/Dad
Denver, the Last Dinosaur (1992) TV Series . . . . Additional Voices
Dino-Riders (1988) TV Series . . . . Additional Voices
Don Coyote and Sancho Panda (1990) TV Series . . . . Additional Voicies
Droopy, Master Detective (1993) TV Series . . . . Additional Voices
Fantastic Max (1988) TV Series . . . . Additional Voices
FernGully: The Last Rainforest (1992) . . . . Knotty
Fraggle Rock (1987) TV Series . . . . Gobo/Wrench/Architect
Glofriends (1986) TV Series . . . . Dragonflyer
Glofriends Save Christmas, The (1986) . . . . Dragonflyer
Inspector Gadget (1983) TV Series . . . . Cpl. Capeman
Inspector Gadget: Gadget's Greatest Gadgets (1999) Video . . . . Cpl. Capeman (segments of "The Capeman Cometh" and "Gadget's Gadgets")
Jem! (1985) TV Series . . . . Riot/Rory Llewelyn
Karate Kid, The (1989) TV Series . . . . Additional Voices
Kingdom Chums: Little David's Adventure, The (1986) TV . . . . Eliab/Fox Soldier #2
Legend of Calamity Jane, The (1997) TV Series . . . . Additional Voices
Mighty Ducks the Movie: The First Face-Off (1997) Video . . . . Additional Voices
ProStars (1991) TV Series . . . . Wayne Gretzky
Ring Raiders (1989) TV Series . . . . Yasu Yakamura
Saber Rider and the Star Sheriffs (1986) TV Series
Space Cats (1991) TV Series . . . . Additional Voices

Spider-Man (1994) TV Series . . . . Young Silvermane/Additional Voices

Tale Spin (1990) TV Series . . . . Additional Voices

Teen Wolf (1986) TV Series . . . . Scott Howard/Teen Wolf

Teenage Mutant Ninja Turtles (1987) TV Miniseries . . . . Michaelangelo

Teenage Mutant Ninja Turtles (1987 I/II) TV Series . . . . Michaelangelo/Rat King/Shredder (II)/Usagi
   Yojimbo

Teenage Mutant Ninja Turtles: Planet of the Turtleoids (1991) TV . . . . Michaelangelo

Teenage Mutant Ninja Turtles: The Cufflink Caper (1990) TV . . . . Michaelangelo

Tick, The (1994) TV Series . . . . The Tick

Twisted Adventures of Felix the Cat, The (1995) TV Series . . . . Additional Voices

Where's Waldo? (1991) TV Series . . . . Additional Voices

Widget, the World Watcher (1990) TV Series . . . . Additional Voices

Wildfire (1986) TV Series . . . . Additional Voices

Yogi and the Invasion of the Space . . . . Man/Zorone/Boy

WALLY COX

There's no need to fear, Wally Cox is here! The man who would be Underdog was born in Detroit on December 6, 1924, and spent a relatively quiet Midwestern childhood. But, in the introduction to his 1961 book of childhood remembrances, *My Life as a Small Boy*, Cox said he knew clearly what he wanted to be when he grew up: "I wanted to be a squared-jawed detective who flew airplanes and caught criminals by swinging through the trees, using only his superior musculature, his keen Bowie knife, and his pet lion."

His reality turned out to be just about as glamorous. Like his Clark Kentish cartoon persona of the "humble and lovable" Shoe Shine Boy on the *Underdog* series, Cox's public image was that of a mild-mannered unassuming man behind thick black-rimmed glasses. But, unlike Underdog's transformation into the crime fighter of his childhood fantasies, Cox built on his image to gain fame as "Robinson Peepers," the meek small-town high school teacher who was the title character of the popular 1950s sitcom *Mr. Peepers*.

Prior to becoming a successful actor, Cox worked a variety of odd jobs in New York City—among them shoe weaver, puppeteer apprentice, dance instructor, and silversmith—to support his sister and mother, Eleanor Frances Atkinson (who also wrote mysteries under the name Eleanor Blake). But it was Marlon Brando, his childhood friend from Evanston, Illinois, turned Greenwich Village roommate, who encouraged his show business career. Cox, who, up until then, had only entertained at parties with his monologues about the everyday people he met, became affiliated with the New School theatrical group. Encouraged by Brando, Cox then developed his droll observations into a nightclub act that premiered at the Village Vanguard, where Brando reportedly had to quiet the rowdy audience for his friend's first performance. But in the end Cox charmed the crowd and the show went on to a very successful run in the New York City nightclubs and cafes of the late 1940s.

His small, finely crafted character studies earned him offers of parts in Broadway musicals, films, and television, including guests spots with Perry Como, Ed Sullivan, and Arthur Godfrey. By 1951, he was hosting a New York radio show on WNEW and had the lead as a mild-mannered policeman on an NBC television dramatic production of David Swift's *The Copper*. His continuing popularity warranted that a 1952 sitcom pilot, *Mr. Peepers*, be tailor-made to Cox's mousy public persona.

While Cox was so successful in portraying the gentle character that the program won an Emmy and a Peabody, and Cox, a star on the Hollywood Walk of Fame, in real life, the thrice-married actor was said to be even wilder than his former roommate and lifelong friend. In Patricia Bosworth's biography, *Brando*, Bosworth writes that Cox taught the actor how to ride a motorcycle during the theatrical run of *A Streetcar Named Desire*: "Brando and Cox zoomed around on their motorcycles in identical white T-shirts and jeans;

stubbles of beard on their chins." She quotes *Mr. Peepers* writer Everett Greenbaum as noting about the friendship, " 'What bonded them was their intense curiosity about everything in the universe. Wally spoke four languages and knew about insects, botany, and birds. He understood every page in *Scientific American.* . . . But both men were attracted to the dark side.' "

On that subject, *Underdog* co-star Norma Macmillan (Sweet Polly Purebred) concurred, "We used to joke that he wanted to be Marlon Brando and Marlon Brando wanted to be Wally Cox because Wally was a much more macho straighter person than anybody ever believed. He was quite a hit with the ladies—motorcycles, leather jackets, the works—and very clever, extremely clever."

After a successful career doing secondary roles in numerous films, such as Marilyn Monroe's unfinished *Something's Got to Give,* 1967's *A Guide for the Married Man,* and co-starring with Brando in the 1965 *Morituri,* Cox guest-starred on many classic television series, such as *The Twilight Zone, Beverly Hillbillies,* and *Lost in Space.* However, he may be best remembered as a regular on the original *Hollywood Squares* from 1966 to 1973. There, he often displayed an unscripted wit that was evident in his career as a live performer, writer, and occasional playwright. In a typical exchange, when host Peter Marshall reportedly prompted Cox for Underdog's catch phrase with "What is it that Underdog always says?" Cox was said to dryly quip, "Where are my residuals?"

Cox continued to occupy the upper left square until he passed away at age forty-eight of a heart attack in 1973. His ashes were reportedly scattered in an undisclosed site by Brando, who flew in from his home in Tahiti for the occasion. In his autobiography, *Songs My Mother Taught Me,* Brando began his reminiscence of Cox with this: "In a lifetime of making friends, none was ever closer to me or more important to me than Wally Cox. . . . I'm not sure I will ever forgive Wally for dying. He was more than a friend; he was my brother, closer to me than any human being in my life except my sisters." Of the on-screen commentary at the time of his passing, perhaps Peter Marshall's simple eulogy was the most eloquent, if not concise: "Dear Lord, have no fear, Underdog is there."

JIM CUMMINGS

By many people's standards, Jim Cummings started a little late as an actor. The prolific voice-over artist who has since done more characters than almost anyone else — as well as having the honor of being the voice of this generation's Winnie the Pooh and Tasmanian Devil — did not get started until his mid-forties. But he may owe some of his inspiration to a blessing from "the Master," Mel Blanc. This came about through "Ralph," a friend of his whom he described as a "Broadway Danny Rose" kind of agent: "He was a great guy. He was a quadriplegic veteran from Vietnam, but he would book poodle acts or magicians for your nephew's party or what have you." As Ralph told the story to Cummings, Mel Blanc had offices in his building, and one day Ralph saw Blanc walking down the hall and called out through his open door:

Ralph said, "Oh, Mel, how are you doing?"
"I'm doing great Ralphie, you know."
"Hey, listen. You got a couple of minutes?"
He said, "Sure, what do you need?"
"Well, this buddy of mine just made a tape last month. He's kind of shopping it around to see what happens."
"Oh, put it on, put it on."

Cummings remembers, "He put on my tape and shut his eyes and sat back in the chair. As the tape started rolling, he started to smile and had a big old grin on his face when the tape was over. He got up and shook Ralph's hand and says, 'You tell the kid that I said, 'He's got it! I got to go.' "

"The kid" was especially thrilled as he had been a fan of Blanc's from his time on *The Jack Benny Show*. As a child, Cummings was fascinated watching voice-over artists like Blanc and Paul Winchell perform. "I knew that those were the guys doing the voices and I just thought there is no way they're not having the time of their lives and I know I can do that!" When he was finally old enough to work, the Youngstown, Ohio, native had a nebulous plan to move to California and "do something in the field" but took a slight detour while attending Mardi Gras in 1972. Saying he just "fell in love" with New Orleans, he stayed for eight years, doing "a million different jobs and playing in a million different bands. I even designed and painted Mardi Gras floats for a couple of years and I was a deckhand on a riverboat." It was only after meeting his future wife that they finally made the move to California.

Around the mid-1980s, Cummings struck up a good friendship with a recording engineer who encouraged him to put together a demo, saying, "Geez, all those weird voices of yours, we had better get those on tape." But the completed demo tape just sat there while Cummings was managing a video store in Anaheim Hills, until one of the customers heard it and recommended that it be sent to his friend Don. Don happened to be Don Bluth, the director/animator who was best known for the 1982 feature *The Secret of N.I.M.H.* Although Cummings was not really familiar with Bluth or his work, he sent the tape.

When the tape found the animator in 1983, Bluth was temporarily on hiatus from film projects, designing laser videogames like "Dragon's Lair." Even though he was, for the moment, out of that aspect of the business, he liked the performance and generously offered to pass the tape to anyone who might be able to use him. This is exactly what he did, to Cummings surprise: "because you usually think, 'Well, don't call us; I won't call you.'" Frank Brant and Caroline Hay, producers for the upcoming (1985) *Dumbo's Circus* for the Disney Channel, auditioned Cummings on his day off. He was given the nod— "'OK, we are starting next week. We're going to do two shows a week and they have like 125 or 130 of them.'" With that, Cummings said he became a real-life Disney Cinderella story as he underwent the meteoric rise from working full time as a manager of a video store to working full time as the star of Disney videos.

It seems especially fitting, then, that Mel Blanc approved of Cummings, as the voice actor has taken over some of Blanc's creations for his current repertoire. In continuing an established character, Cummings explains, "The trick is you just have to nail it and you just have to lay your voice print right on top of that and you have to be true to the original character. So the essence of that is just a dead-on impersonation." But, paradoxically, he explains, while the original flavor of the characterization must be maintained, the voice also has to evolve as studios continually strive to keep decades-old characters up to date.

Cummings cites characters like "Pegleg Pete" of *Goof Troop* as an example. "He was in *Steamboat Willie* [the first Mickey Mouse sound cartoon from 1928], so he's really probably tied for first place being the oldest character out there. Louie [from the 1967 *Jungle Book*] is another—they have been updated. They are no longer the same classic characters they were in . . . be it the '30s, '40s, or the '60s. Like in *Goof Troop*, for instance, he's got a family . . . Ol' Pete does, but [in Pete's voice] *he's still good old Pete! He's still a sweetie pie!*"

Cummings remarks that the same is true for the characters he now voices for *Winnie the Pooh* (he has since taken over from his childhood idol Paul Winchell as the voice of Tigger). Pooh was originally voiced by character actor and Disney favorite Sterling Holloway. Cummings claims Pooh's portrayal has been slightly modernized. "Although [he imitates Pooh], *you still have to be Pooh.* There's no getting around that. You have to be true to the original character and all the wide-eyed wonder."

Cummings says in the case of "Taz" (Mel Blanc's Tasmanian Devil) he had to expand the character because there were only five test cartoons made with Blanc. "We did, gosh, sixty-five half-hours and there were like two or three in each. I guess it was over one hundred individual cartoons, so, now, I feel that Taz is more me now than he was Mel, but Mel, still without question, gets all the original credit for creating it."

While much of his varied work experience may not have been applicable to his current vocation, Cummings, who played drums and sang professionally since he was thirteen years old, was able to add his musical talents to the mix and use his singing experience to competitive advantage, "because not all actors sing and not all singers act and not many of them do voices on top of that." Cummings said the combination came together, and that "paid off beautifully" when he was hired to do three songs in 1995's *Pocahontas*, including a duet with himself. In *The Lion King*, he did the singing for "Scar" (Jeremy Irons), in addition to being notable for performing as the lead singer for the California Raisins Claymation Quartet.

Cummings's singing talents were sometimes put to the test with some of his more challenging parts, such as the 1994 episode of *Animaniacs*, entitled "Woodstock Slappy," a parody in which Slappy and Skippy Squirrel went out to the country for "three days of peace, love, and tranquility" only to find a half a million people underneath their tree. Cummings says, "I did a bit as Roger Daltrey. I was Joe Cocker. . . . But Tress [MacNeille, who did Dot Warner], who is the most phenomenal lady, was asked to do a Janis Joplin takeoff and she was a little hoarse that day, so she said, 'Give it to Jimmy. Give it to Jimmy!'" After being assured that they wanted a parody of Joplin, not a song, Cummings gave them the "essence of Janis Joplin" by recreating one of her ear-piercing, drawn-out screaming riffs. "So, I was basically a knockoff of Janis Joplin in the cartoon. I have such a deep voice that I'm not the guy you would call to do any woman's roles, but I kinda pulled that one off."

Hiding his persona behind the many characters he portrays, Cummings's natural speaking voice has been enough to cause some interesting misconceptions about his identity. "At least a hundred times people have said, 'Oh, my God, I thought you are seventy.'" But his favorite misunderstanding took place at a studio when a twenty-something producer was waiting for him to tape a commercial. Ignoring Cummings, she took a phone call and said, "No, he's not here yet. . . . Well, as soon as Jim Cummings gets here, we'll go." And I've been sitting there wondering where *they* were because they weren't in the studio. And I said, "'Well, I'm Jim Cummings.' She goes, 'You're that nice black man on the tape?' I said, 'Well, I didn't realize that I was black!' [To which she replied,] 'I just kind of thought you were.'"

Perhaps Cummings would be a little more recognizable if he had spent more time on-screen, but, like many voice actors, he finds live-action work "a little boring" and slow. Although he did do one television special for comedian Paul Rodriguez years ago, he said he had "a pretty strong taste" of working on live-action projects when he did *Who Framed Roger Rabbit*, "and it was just so much waiting." After waiting in a trailer for "hours and hours," the cast was called to do a few scenes, then was sent back to the trailer to wait some more. Stating that the only time you see him on camera is when *The Entertainment Tonight*–type shows do the occasional feature story on cartoon voice actors, Cummings declares that he likes to be able to be in public without being hounded. "It gets crazy enough. When you go to a party and they find out who you are, 'You're Taz? You're Winnie the Pooh?' Which is great and I have a good time and I'll do tapes for their kids . . . which I enjoy. I always do that."

Now that animation is more sought after among big-name celebrities, its popularity has become a double-edged sword. While there is more animation work than ever before, Cummings laments that so many celebrities "are having a good time playing in the old animation sandbox! . . . I wish they would kind of leave us alone." Albeit, he did have a particularly memorable experience with one celebrity who was a consummate professional not afraid to do what it took to get the job done.

In a particularly amusing story, Carol Channing, whom he describes as "just as sweet as she could be," did a guest-star spot on 1990's *Rescue Rangers* for a parody of "Hello Dolly." "She was wearing a crisply starched blouse. She, herself, is quite animated. She looks like a cartoon character in real life and [doing a perfect Carol Channing] *her arms are just going all over the room and she's doing this and doing that.* And it basically sounded like [static] on the mic . . . and the engineer says 'Gosh, Miss Channing, I'm so sorry, I'm picking up your blouse like mad. I mean, it's almost overpowering your performance.' '*Well, honey, don't you worry about a thing.*' And she stands up and removes her blouse and places it gingerly over on the side and she says, '*This is wonderful! Now! How about now?*' All she was wearing was her stretch pants, sandals, and a brassiere with huge tufts of cotton under the straps that she was using as shoulder pads. . . . I'm sitting right next to Carol Channing for the next three hours and she is wearing her brassiere! [Cummings sighs] What a scene! What a scene!"

Perhaps a little less colorful, but no less famous, are some of Cummings's directors. He was pleased to be hired to play the lead villain on Steven Spielberg's 1996 film, *Balto*. "I'm the only non-famous—or non-facial—guy in the movie *Balto*." He beat out many candidates to replace a movie star, whom he declines to reveal. "But they decided to go with people who kind of did voices . . . because you can't raise an eyebrow and get that Spock feeling. You can't give somebody a dirty look and hear it, so you gotta get [it] in the voice."

Of course, Cummings was even more awe-struck that executive producer Spielberg was also making *Schindler's List* at the time, "and he was preoccupied, to say the least. But, he just wound it right down and was as sweet as could be. A great guy, he was very easy to work for and he loved everything that I did. . . . And the same with John Williams, who conducted me singing a couple of times." After his experience with some of the biggest names in the business, he says, "Those big guys who you would think would possibly be kind of scary and have super-huge egos—they're great."

When asked for his opinion of what will endure of recent animation, Cummings replies that he believes the Disney programs like *Winnie the Pooh, Goof Troop*, and *Tale Spin* are timeless. Although he does say he might be wrong, he is a little concerned about the future relevance of some of the references of "cutting-edge" shows such as *Tiny Toons* and *Animaniacs*, saying that some of the current references may quickly become dated.

Certainly, Cummings never dreamed, in the leaner times when he was peddling encyclopedias door to door or selling pots and pans out of his car, that one day he would be referred to as the "Mel Blanc of Disney." Ultimately, he believes one of the keys to his success in his current, and presumably his last, career venture has been his willingness to take on unglamorous, but complex character roles. When lecturing to those who attend his voice-over seminars, he says his best advice is to "remember that it is acting first. It's an acting job. . . . Everybody knows their brother-in-law who does a perfect John Wayne, but he couldn't act wet if you drown him! So . . . when you go out for plays, *stretch*. Don't be the mailman—be the evil wizard or the maniac. Try and stretch yourself!" Certainly Cummings has followed his own advice not only on stage, but through his life experience.

CREDITS

101 Dalmatians: The Series (1996) TV Series . . . . Mayor Ed Pig/Colonel
2 Stupid Dogs (1993) TV Series . . . . Morocco Mole
2000 MTV Movie Awards (2000) TV . . . . Announcer
Addams Family, The (1992) TV Series . . . . Lurch
Adventures from the Book of Virtues (1996) TV Series . . . . Aristotle
Aladdin (1992) . . . . Razoul the Chief Guard
Aladdin (1993/I) TV Series . . . . Razul/Additional Voices
Aladdin and the King of Thieves (1996) Video . . . . Razoul the Chief Guard/Additional Voices
All Dogs Go to Heaven 2 (1996)
Anastasia (1997) . . . . Rasputin (singing voice)
Animaniacs (1993) TV Series . . . . Narrator/Additional Voices
Antz (1998) . . . . Additional Voices

Atlantis: The Lost Empire (2001) .... Additional Voices
Babe: Pig in the City (1998) .... Pelican
Baby Blues Christmas Special, A (2002) TV .... Hugh Wisowski/Kris
Balto (1995) .... Steele
Batman: The Animated Series (1992) TV Series .... Additional Voices
Beauty and the Beast: The Enchanted Christmas (1997) Video .... Various Voices
Belle's Magical World (1997) Video
Blazing Dragons (1992) TV Series .... Chancellor/King Allfire
Bonkers (1993) TV Series .... Officer Bonkers D. Bobcat/Detective Lucky Piquel
Boo to You Too! Winnie the Pooh (1996) TV .... Winnie the Pooh/Tigger
Book of Pooh, The (2001) TV Series .... Pooh/Tigger
Brave Little Toaster Goes to Mars, The (1998) Video .... Singer
Bugs Bunny's Funky Monkeys (1997) Video
Bump in the Night (1994) TV Series .... Mr. Bumpy/Destructo/Closet Monster Buster
Buzz Lightyear of Star Command (2000) TV Series ... Additional Voices
California Raisins (1989) TV Series
Capitol Critters (1992) TV Series .... Additional Voices
Captain Planet and the Planeteers (1990) TV Series .... Sly Sludge (1990–1993)
Cartoon All-Stars to the Rescue (1990) TV .... Tigger/Winnie the Pooh
CatDog (1998) TV Series .... Cat
CatDog: The Great Parent Mystery (2001) TV .... Cat
Chauncey's Silent Night (1998) Video .... Additional Voices
Chip 'n' Dale Rescue Rangers (1989) TV Series .... Monterey Jack/Fat Cat/Wart/Professor Nimnul/
    Others
Chip 'n' Dale's Rescue Rangers to the Rescue (1989) TV .... Monterey Jack/Fat Cat/Professor Ninmul
Courage the Cowardly Dog (1999) TV Series .... Cajun Fox/Great Fusilli (2000)
Cro (1993) TV Series .... Ogg/Phil
Darkwing Duck (1991) TV Series .... Darkwing Duck/Drake Mallard/Herb Muddlefoot/
    Negaduck/Moliarty (1991–)
Disney Sing-along-Songs: Disneyland Fun (1996) Video .... Winnie the Pooh
Disney's Little Mermaid, The (1992) TV Series .... Additional Voices
Droopy, Master Detective (1993) TV Series .... Additional Voices
Duckman (1994) TV Series .... Additional Voices
Dumbo's Circus (1985) TV Series .... Lionel the Lion
Earthworm Jim (1995) TV Series .... Psy-Crow/Bob the Killer Goldfish
Extremely Goofy Movie, An (2000) Video .... Peter Pete
Flintstones Kids, The (1986) TV Series .... Additional Voices
Foofur (1986) TV Series .... Additional Voices
Freakazoid! (1995) TV Series .... Additional Voices
Garbage Pail Kids Movie, The (1987) .... Greaser Greg
Gargoyles (1994) TV Series .... Dingo/Additional Voices
Goof Troop (1992) TV Series .... Peter "Pete" Pete Sr.
Goof Troop Christmas, A (1992) TV .... Peter Pete
Goofy Movie, A (1995) .... Peter Pete
Gummi Bears, The (1985) TV Series .... Zummi Gummi (1990–)/Chummi
Hercules (1997) .... Nessus the River Centaur/Pot Maker/Tall Thebian/Elderly Thebi
Hercules (1998) TV Series .... Additional Voices
Hillbilly Blue (1995) .... Colonel/Fat Guy/French Chef/Trunker
House of Mouse (2001) TV Series .... Pete/Humphrey the Bear/Censor Monkeys/King Larry/Big
    Bad Wolf/Ed the Hyena/Winnie the Pooh/Kaa/Razoul/Zeke/Additional Voices
Hunchback of Notre Dame, The (1996) .... Various Guards and Gypsies

Hunchback of Notre Dame II, The (2002) Video . . . . Archdeacon

Invasion America (1998) TV Series . . . . Major Lomac

Iron Man (1994) TV Series . . . . War Machine (James R. "Rhodey" Rhodes) (1995)/President Bill Clinton/MODOK

Izzy's Quest for Olympic Gold (1995) TV . . . . Narrator/Anchor #1

Jackie Chan Adventures (2000) TV Series . . . . Hak Foo

Jimmy Neutron: Boy Genius (2001) . . . . Ultra Lord/Mission Control/General

Jungle Book 2, The (2003) . . . . Colonel Hathi

Jungle Cubs (1996) TV Series . . . . Kaa the Snake/Fred/Jed

Karate Kid, The (1989) TV Series . . . . Additional Voices

Kingdom Chums: Little David's Adventure, The (1986) TV . . . . Goliath/Fox Soldier #3

Lady and the Tramp II: Scamp's Adventure (2001) Video . . . . Tony

Land before Time IX: Journey to the Big Water, The (2002) Video . . . . Sierra

Land before Time VII: The Stone of Cold Fire, The (2000) Video . . . . Sierra

Legend of Calamity Jane, The (1997) TV Series . . . . Additional Voices

Legend of Tarzan, The (2001) TV Series . . . . Tantor

Life & Adventures of Santa Claus, The (2000) Video . . . . Old Santa Claus

Lion King, The (1994) (singing voice) . . . . Ed the Hyena/Gopher/Additional Scar Singing Voice Match/Additional Voices

Lion King 1 ½: Hakuna Matata, The (2004) Video . . . . Ed the Hyena

Lion King II: Simba's Pride, The (1998) Video . . . . Additional Voices

Little Mermaid, The (1989) . . . . Additional Voices

Looney Tunes: Reality Check, The (2003) Video . . . Taz

Looney Tunes: Stranger Than Fiction (2003) Video . . . Taz

Marsupilami (1994) TV Series . . . . Maurice/Norman

Mickey Mouse Works (1999) TV Series . . . . Pete/Humphrey the Bear/Zeke/Additional Voices

Mickey's Christmas Carol (1983) . . . . Ghost of Christmas Future (Pete)

Mickey's House of Villains (2002) Video . . . . Big Bad Wolf/Kaa/Ed the Hyena

Mickey's Once upon a Christmas (1999) Video . . . . Pete/Postman

Mickey's The Three Musketeers (2004) Video . . . . Pete

Midnight Patrol, The (1990) TV Series . . . . Additional Voices

Mr. Bogus (1993) TV Series . . . . Teacher

Mummy: The Animated Series, The (2001) TV Series . . . . Imhotep

New Adventures of Winnie the Pooh, The (1988) TV Series . . . . Winnie the Pooh/Tigger (1989–)/ Additional Voices

Nuttiest Nutcracker (1999) Video . . . . Uncle Drosselmeier/Gramps

Oblongs, The (2001) TV Series . . . . Various Voices

Online Adventures of Ozzie the Elf, The (1997) TV . . . . Santa Claus

Ozzy and Drix (2002) TV Series . . . . Police Chief Gluteus

Pagemaster, The (1994) . . . . Long John Silver

Pepper Ann (1997) TV Series . . . . Mr. Carter

Piglet's Big Movie (2003) . . . . Winnie the Pooh/Tigger

Pink Panther, The (1993) TV Series . . . . Additional Voices

Pirates of Darkwater (1991) TV Series . . . . Ioz (II)/Additional Voices

Pocahontas (1995) . . . . Powanton/Wise Man/Additional Voices (singing voice)

Pocahontas II: Journey to a New World (1998) Video . . . . King James

Pokémon (1998) TV Series . . . . Kids WB Pokémon Announcer

Pooh's Grand Adventure: The Search for Christopher Robin (1997) Video . . . . Winnie the Pooh

Powerpuff Girls, The (1998) TV Series . . . . Fuzzy Lumpkins/Additional Voices

Problem Child (1993) TV Series . . . . Additional Voices

Project G.e.e.K.e.R. (1996) TV Series . . . . Moloch/Will Dragonn

Pup Named Scooby-Doo, A (1988) TV Series . . . . Additional Voices (1988–1991)

Raw Toonage (1992) TV Series . . . . Additional Voices

Real Adventures of Jonny Quest, The (1996) TV Series . . . . Additional Voices

Redux Riding Hood (1997) . . . . Thompkins

Return of Jafar, The (1994) Video . . . . Razoul the Chief Guard

Return to Never Land (2002) . . . . Additional Voice

Road Rovers (1996) TV Series . . . . General Parvo

Road to El Dorado, The (2000) . . . . Cortes/Others

Rude Dog and the Dweebs (1989) TV Series . . . . Satch

Rude Dog and the Rovers (1995) TV Series . . . . Satch

Runaway Brain (1995) . . . . Julius

Savage Dragon, The (1996) TV Series . . . . Savage Dragon/Bludgeon

Schnookums and Meat Funny Cartoon Show (1993) TV Series . . . . Dr. Paul Bunion

Scooby-Doo and the Reluctant Werewolf (1989) TV . . . . Frankenstein/Skull Head

Scooby-Doo on Zombie Island (1998) Video . . . . Jacques

Secret Files of the Spy Dogs, The (1998) TV Series . . . . Von Rabie/Scuzzy Duzz/Flea Leader/Bald
Spokesperson/Additional Voices

Shadows of Darkness (1994) . . . . Boris Stovich

Shrek (2001) . . . . Captain of Guards

Siegfried & Roy: Masters of the Impossible (1996) Video . . . . Additional Voices

Sinbad: Legend of the Seven Seas (2003) . . . . Luca/Additional Voices

Skeleton Warriors (1994) TV Series

Small Soldiers (1998) (uncredited) . . . . Ocula

Sonic the Hedgehog (1993) TV Series . . . . Dr. Ivo Robotnik/Julian

Spider-Man (1994) TV Series . . . . Shocker/Additional Voices

Story of Santa Claus, The (1996) TV . . . . Mr. Minch

Superior Duck (1996)

Swat Kats: The Radical Squadron (1993) TV Series . . . . Mayor Manx/Feral's Sergeant/Warden Cyrus
Meece/Morbulus/Charlie/Additional Voices

Tale Spin (1990) TV Series . . . . Don Karnage/Louie/Various Characters

Tarzan (1999) . . . . Additional Voices

Tarzan & Jane (2002) Video . . . . Tantor

Taz-Mania (1991) TV Series . . . . Taz Tasmanian Devil/Tasmanian Wolf/Buddy Boar/Bushwhacker
Bob/Wendel T. Wolf

Teenage Mutant Ninja Turtles (1987/II) TV Series . . . . Leatherhead/Shredder

Tick, The (1994) TV Series . . . . Barry/Other Tick/Thrakkorzog/Mr. Mental/Multiple Santa

Tigger Movie, The (2000) . . . . Tigger/Winnie the Pooh

Timon and Pumbaa (1995) TV Series . . . . Ed the Hyena/Additional Voices

Tiny Toons Adventures (1990) TV Series . . . . Additional Voices

Titan A.E. (2000) . . . . Chowquin

Tom and Jerry: The Magic Ring (2002) Video . . . . Butch

Tom and Jerry Kids (1990) TV Series . . . . Additional Voices

Transformers (1984) TV Series (uncredited) . . . . Afterburner/Rippersnapper

Visionaries: Knights of the Magical Light (1987) TV Series . . . . Witterquick, Bearer of Knowledge

Welcome to Pooh Corner (1983) TV Series . . . . Winnie the Pooh/Owl (1993–1995)

Where's Waldo? (1991) TV Series . . . . Additional Voices

Who Framed Roger Rabbit (1988) . . . . Bullet #2/Andy Devine/Additional Weasels

Widget, the World Watcher (1990) TV Series . . . . MegaBrain

Wild West COWBOYs of Moo Mesa (1992) TV Series . . . . Additional Voices

Winnie the Pooh: A Valentine for You (1998) TV . . . . Winnie the Pooh

Winnie the Pooh: A Very Merry Pooh Year (2002) Video . . . . Winnie the Pooh/Tigger
Winnie the Pooh: Imagine That, Christopher Robin (1999) Video . . . . Winnie the Pooh
Winnie the Pooh: Seasons of Giving (1999) Video . . . . Winnie the Pooh/Tigger
Winnie the Pooh and Christmas Too (1991) TV . . . . Winnie the Pooh
Winnie the Pooh: Franken Pooh (1999) Video . . . . Winnie the Pooh
Winnie the Pooh Friendship: Clever Little Piglet (1999) Video . . . . Winnie the Pooh
Winnie the Pooh Friendship: Pooh Wishes (1999) Video . . . . Winnie the Pooh
Winnie the Pooh Friendship: Tigger-ific Tales (1988) Video . . . . Winnie the Pooh
Winnie the Pooh Learning: Growing Up (1996) Video . . . . Winnie the Pooh
Winnie the Pooh Learning: Helping Others (1997) Video . . . . Winnie the Pooh
Winnie the Pooh Learning: Making Friends (1998) Video . . . . Winnie the Pooh
Winnie the Pooh Learning: Sharing & Caring (1998) Video . . . . Winnie the Pooh
Winnie the Pooh Learning: Working Together (1999) Video . . . . Winnie the Pooh
Winnie the Pooh Playtime: Cowboy Pooh (1997) Video . . . . Winnie the Pooh
Winnie the Pooh Playtime: Detective Tigger (1997) Video . . . . Winnie the Pooh
Winnie the Pooh Playtime: Fun 'n' Games (1998) Video . . . . Winnie the Pooh
Winnie the Pooh Playtime: Happy Pooh Day (1998) Video . . . . Winnie the Pooh
Winnie the Pooh Playtime: Pooh Party (1999) Video . . . . Winnie the Pooh
Winnie the Pooh Spookable Pooh (1999) Video . . . . Winnie the Pooh/Eeyore
Winnie the Pooh Thanksgiving, A (1998) Video . . . . Winnie the Pooh/Tigger (singing)
Winnie the Pooh Un-Valentine's Day (1999) Video . . . . Winnie the Pooh/Eeyore

E. G. DAILY

Extra Good? Extremely Gracious? Easy Going? Perhaps she is all of that and more, but no matter what the "E. G." literally stands for, the exceptionally gifted Daily has consistently juggled three high-profile careers — actress, pop singer, and cartoon voice-over artist. The children of the 1980s may remember her as Dottie, Peewee Herman's long-suffering girlfriend in *Peewee's Big Adventure*, or perhaps they sang along with her songs from the *Scarface* or *Breakfast Club* soundtracks. Over the past decade, while she still acts on camera and has an active recording career, the next generation will probably know her best as "Buttercup" (opposite Cathy Cavadini's "Blossom" and Tara Charendoff-Strong's "Bubbles") of the *Powerpuff Girls* and the spunky *Rugrats* star, Tommy Pickles.

Although the Los Angeles native grew up watching classic Warner Bros. animation, she never intended to be a cartoon voice-over artist—she fell, albeit reluctantly, into the cast of her first animated series. It seemed that the *Rugrats* executives had already cast and recorded Tommy Pickles with another actress, then, and at the last minute, decided to recast the part. Daily's agent urged her to audition, to which she nonchalantly declined, " 'Well, I'll pass today on that one, because I'm busy.' I think I was having carpet installed." After her agent's insistence that it would only take ten minutes, Daily reluctantly agreed to go.

She arrived at the studio anxious to escape, but even though she was the first to audition with several people waiting behind her, once she started, the executives would not let her leave. "They said, 'Just do the first page. . . .' But, when I got in the booth, I read the first page and then they said, 'Oh, can you do another page?' And I read another page and they went, 'Can you read the next page?' And then each page—a new producer or a new executive walked in the room. . . . I ended up reading a bunch of pages and left . . . and my agent called and said, 'Did you realize you booked that job?' "

Daily was surprised that she had, not only because she got the part, but also because she was chosen over the many actors who auditioned in two "massive" searches. While she had done some voice work in the form of a few radio voice-over spots and jingles prior to that, she says it was no problem moving into animation because of her prior acting experience, as well as the vocal manipulation ability she developed as a singer. She has never had to study in formal voice classes, judging that "the combination of being a singer and being an actress . . . was just the perfect combination for the voice-over work."

Daily takes a very intuitive approach to creating her voices, including the one for "sweet, humble, and darling" Tommy, whom she names as her favorite character. "They show me a picture of the character and then the voice comes out of me—just by looking at the picture. And it's usually very obvious to me, when I see a photograph, what kind of voice comes out of that body." To capture children's voices, she studies young children and the physicalities of their speech and speech impediments—noticing how people's mouths move and how they tend to talk. "Everybody has certain characteristics or mannerisms or physicalities that make them sound a certain way, that I take in and use for a lot of my characters."

She does not do a back story because she believes that she is able to endow her characters with "so much depth" just from her life experience and observation of people. "Once I do a voice, it's so clear to me how that person thinks or feels about things. It's so clear to me it's not even a question. . . . I really have a strong feeling that the voice is, like, where a person's soul is. . . . If a person could hide or could wear a mask, or could be under the covers, the voice is where the whole being comes out of. . . . So, for me, the minute I make a voice, the whole person is there already. I don't have to rehash what . . . was so obvious to me. . . . I don't push that—it just is there. I trust it, and it's very instinctive."

While the *Rugrats* may be considered appropriate for general audiences, it does not mean that Daily is interested in projecting a "virginal" image for her other work, as some of her publicity photos on her official web site, www.egdaily.com, will attest. In 1994 she starred in Klasky/Csupo's most controversial series, *Duckman*—based on the underground comic—as the voice of Mambo, and, along with Dana Hill, performed the voices for Duckman's twin-headed son. She has also enjoyed working with adult-oriented animator Ralph Bakshi on "very risqué" projects such as HBO's (1997) *The Spicy Detective*, saying, "I actually enjoyed it because it's stretching out. It's using animation in a way that adults can really enjoy as well." She is not offended by many controversial themes, unless it is "something on violence against animals or kids—I don't have any problem with most things. Animals or kids, don't mess with."

Considering her success as an actress and performer, it may be difficult to imagine that the strikingly attractive Daily once was, as she describes herself, an introverted child who may have just as well chosen to be a veterinarian. "I didn't really know that I was capable of being an actress when I was young, because I was shy and didn't like having to smile, if I didn't want to, and be nice to people, if I didn't want to, and have people watching me. I didn't like that. I didn't like people looking at me."

Describing herself as "very auditory," Daily credits music for drawing her out of her introversion. Naming Tina Turner and Rod Stewart (she was in his video for "Young Turks") among her musical influences, she says, "I was very musical and mostly started off a lot of things with my voice, which kind of just led into acting. And acting sort of broke me a little bit out of my reservedness and my self-consciousness. . . . Now, I feel very free as actor and . . . by breaking free that I'm a good actor and reputable actor. In voice-overs, it really pays to be a good actor." Daily, perhaps with a trace of residual shyness, concludes that doing voice-overs feels "dignified" and "natural" as compared to on-camera work, as she is able to concentrate solely on her performance instead of her appearance.

Having been in various aspects of the entertainment business since she was eight (she made her first television appearance on *Laverne and Shirley* in 1976), Daily says, "In that I started so young, I've had a very consistent career. . . . If I'm not doing a movie, I'm doing a cartoon. If I'm not doing a cartoon, I'm doing an album. If I'm not doing an album, I'm doing another movie. My career has just consistently gone from one thing to another— from one successful movie to one successful cartoon." She is especially grateful for her voice-over career, as it has financed her own record production company, as well as her last album, while still leaving her time to create music and care for her family.

Even though she is busy "making a living from her gifts," she has great admiration for some of her contemporaries who do the same. She is good friends with animation veteran Debbi Derryberry (who voices Nickelodeon's breakout hit character Jimmy Neutron). Although she and Derryberry are competitors for the same parts, they are so close that Derryberry says when they gave birth, "She cut my baby's cord and I cut her baby's cord." Singling out Frank Welker, Jim Cummings, and Rob Paulsen as particularly "brilliant," Daily counts them among the talented people that have proven themselves in the business and looks forward to a long association as one of their peers. "It's a very loyal business; once you've proven yourself in voice-over . . . you've done it. Not like in [on-camera] acting, where if you have a downtime, you're out [and then] you have to reprove yourself."

But on the subject of what her mysterious acronym could possibly stand for, Elizabeth Guttman is exceedingly guarded—saying simply, "It stands for my real first name and my real last name."

CREDITS

Aladdin (1993/I) TV Series . . . . Additional Voices
All Grown Up (2003) TV Series . . . . Tommy Pickles
Alvin and the Chipmunks Meet the Wolfman (2000) Video . . . . Nathan
Babe: Pig in the City (1998) . . . . Babe the Gallant Pig
Baby Blues (2000) TV Series . . . . Zoe MacPherson
Baby Blues Christmas Special, A (2002) TV . . . . Zoey
Beaver Trilogy, The (2001) . . . . (segment "The Orkly Kid")
Beethoven
Bump in the Night (1994) TV Series . . . . Germ Girl
Camp Candy (1989) TV Series
ChalkZone (2000) TV Series . . . . Rudy Tabootie
Country Bears, The (2002) . . . . Beary Barrington (singing voice)
Duckman (1994) TV Series . . . . Mambo
Eek! The Cat (1992) TV Series . . . . Wendy Elizabeth

Game Over (2004) TV Series .... Billy Smashenburn/Zenna
Gargoyles: The Goliath Chronicles (1996) TV Series .... Alex
Gen 13 (1998) .... Freefall/Roxy Spaulding
Goofy Movie, A (1995) .... Additional Voices
Hercules (1998) TV Series .... Additional Voices
Jungle Cubs (1996) TV Series .... Bagheera
Little Rascals, The (1994) .... Froggy
New Woody Woodpecker Show, The (1999) TV Series .... Knothead
Powerpuff Girls, The (1998) TV Series .... Buttercup/Additional Voices
Powerpuff Girls: Twas the Fight before Christmas (2003) Video .... Buttercup
Powerpuff Girls, The (2002) .... Buttercup
Problem Child (1993) TV Series .... Cyndi
Quack Pack (1996) TV Series .... Louie Duck
Rugrats (1991) TV Series .... Thomas "Tommy" Pickles
Rugrats: All Growed Up, The (2001) TV .... Tommy Pickles
Rugrats Go Wild! (2003). .... Tommy Pickles
Rugrats: Still Babies after All These Years (2001) TV .... Herself/Tommy Pickles
Rugrats in Paris: The Movie—Rugrats II (2000) .... Tommy Pickles
Rugrats Meet the Wild Thornberrys (2003) .... Tommy Pickles
Rugrats Movie, The (1998) .... Tommy Pickles
Rugrats Vacation, A (1997) Video .... Tommy Pickles
Teenage Mutant Ninja Turtles (1987/II) TV Series .... Additional Voices
Trumpet of the Swan, The (2001)
Twisted Adventures of Felix the Cat, The (1995) TV Series .... Additional Voices
Wacko (1981) .... Bambi
We Wish You a Merry Christmas (1999) Video .... Ted
What's with Andy? (2001) TV Series .... Additional Voices (2001–2002)

NICOLE (JAFFE) DAVID

There has been no small amount of speculation about what became of Nicole Jaffe, who starred as nerdy intellectual Velma Dinkley on the original *Scooby-Doo, Where Are You?* series. Although the popular cartoon actress never did another animated show since leaving the tremendously successful series in 1974, none of the many criminals she helped to "unmask" over the years got revenge on the smartest of the "meddling kids." In fact, the actress, who now goes by her married name, Nicole David, is still very much a part of show business. But now she works behind the scenes as a highly influential Hollywood agent, representing high-profile clients such as John Travolta and Elijah Wood. However, her journey from cartoon voice artist to being named as one of the entertainment industry's top fifty female executives by the *Hollywood Reporter* is less a Cinderella story than a reflection of David's hard work.

Born in Montreal, Canada, David knew from a young age that she wanted to be in the entertainment business. Aspiring to be an actress, she started her career as an apprentice in summer stock, concentrating on her craft before moving to New York to pursue parts and to continue her studies. She landed a small role in a Broadway production and soon relocated to Los Angeles where she became a member of the Actor's Studio.

Once in Hollywood, David began landing small, but memorable parts in film and television. Her first film role was in Walt Disney's 1968 *The Love Bug*, playing a hippie girl. It was, as she describes it, "a tiny, tiny part," but it led to other jobs, including the television series *Room 222* and the role of goofy and flirtatious Betty Smith in the 1969 Elvis movie, *The Trouble with Girls*. She was fascinated by her work with Elvis, finding him "an incredibly sexy, lonely, sad person with the most magnetic eyes I'd ever seen." But the film was also significant because it featured actor Frank Welker, who would go on to play Freddie, her costar on the *Scooby-Doo* series.

Her most famous role practically found her—with a little help from Hanna-Barbera director Gordon Hunt. At the time, David was starring as Peppermint Patty in the stage version of *You're a Good Man, Charlie Brown*. Hunt came backstage afterwards and asked her if she would be interested in auditioning for the role of Velma. David, who had never done voice-overs and was admittedly less concerned with earning a place in animation history than a paycheck, jumped at the chance. "I thought it was a Godsend because I was a very, very struggling actress. I had done the Elvis Presley movie and a couple of other things, but not that much. I was very grateful to have the opportunity to work. Gordon Hunt was the nicest person in the world, and the cast was great."

Although David was now cast in a regular series, other work in film and television was sporadic. She gradually began feeling unfulfilled by her profession, and the passion for acting that she felt as a young girl began to wane. David's talent agent at the time had a suggestion that she took to heart. She was told, "You know, you're not getting a lot of work, and you're always helping everybody else. Why don't you be an agent?" David had found her calling.

Starting afresh, David embarked on her new career within the entertainment industry. She and an associate, Arnold Rifkin, launched a small talent agency called Rifkin/David and the pair proved to be a good match. Rifkin, a former entrepreneur who dealt in the manufacturing of shoes and sold furs, may have seemed an unlikely choice; but he knew how a business should be run, and David knew the ins and outs of the acting profession. Diligence and hard work paid off, and what started out as a small venture soon made industry giants take notice. The agency merged and expanded, eventually becoming Triad Artists, which was subsequently acquired by the William Morris Agency.

David, who rose through the ranks of WMA to become senior vice president of Motion Picture Talent, has built a roster of clients that reads like the who's who of Hollywood's A-list. Her former partner, Arnold Rifkin, had very high praise for her work in an article published in the *Independent*, opining that female agents develop their clients from the "inside out." He was reported to have said of David, "Nicole is the master practitioner. In this business you are only as good as the people you represent, and Nicole has made her people so much better by giving them somebody to trust."

When asked if she misses acting, David is very quick to reply, "Not an inch. The day I became an agent was the happiest day of my life. At the very beginning I wanted to be an actress, but as I did it, I realized that I was not very good at it. I did not want other people to be responsible for my destiny. . . . I wanted to go to work every day and do something that I knew I was good at. I always knew that I was not good at acting. I looked for something that I could be fulfilled by and that I could make a contribution with, and this is it. . . . I love being an agent."

Even though David self-deprecatingly refers to her acting as "mediocre," it certainly must have had some resonance with the audience, as her character's popularity has only increased over time, with several fan sites now devoted to Velma and the cast of *Scooby-Doo*. David downplays her contribution: "I think it's a fluke. I think it was due to the efforts of Gordon Hunt and the fact that I *was* Velma. I was always independent. I always believed that I was equal and that I could do things that boys could do, and I think that part of the charm of the character is her sense of independence and feeling. I could never have done the part of Daphne. You have to be that character somewhat to play it. It's hard to play that regular a character if you're not."

Very much the Hollywood insider, David was quite surprised at the continued interest in the thirty-year-old program, saying that she learned of its popularity through one of her clients, poet and hip-hop sensation Lauryn Hill. "I certainly had no idea that this show was a tremendous success at all. . . . Lauryn Hill heard that I did *Scooby-Doo*, and she was so excited. She told me what a great show it was, and how hip it is . . . and I was stunned. I thought, 'Gee, I never would have done this if I could have gotten a good movie.' I wanted to be the Daniel Day-Lewis of that era. That was my goal . . . so when I got the part of Velma, I had no idea it was anything other than a wonderful opportunity to make a living."

While David now has immense power—able to influence the way movies are scripted and often making million-dollar deals—she does not seem status conscious at all, stating, "I have a lot of respect for people who do things well, whether it's a busboy, a voice-over person, or a movie star. When people do things well, I'm in awe of them." She has especially kind words for her fellow voice actors, remarking, "The people that I worked with at Hanna-Barbera during those years, even the people that came in and did little parts, they were so far superior to me because they did lots of voices." As modest as she may be about her acting, David obviously enjoys it, as she recently teamed up with the original cast of *Scooby-Doo* to do two direct-to-video movies.

David is very conscious of enhancing women's roles in the industry, and not just for her clients; she also actively mentors her assistants. For the women who do plan to follow in her footsteps in the acting profession, she offers her motto: "Be the master of your destiny!" She reiterates the wisdom she has gained from years of being both an actress and an agent, "Learn your craft. Be an entrepreneur. Don't leave your destiny in other people's hands because there is no person on a white horse coming along to save you. You'd better do it for yourself, and that goes for anything you do."

In retrospect, it seems only fitting that David was able to make her own luck in her rise to a Hollywood mega-agent whose clients, past and present, have included Emma Thompson, Franka Potente, Melanie Griffith, Julie Andrews, Eve, Whitney Houston, and Salma Hayek, just to name a few. "*Jinkies*," Velma always was the smart one.

CREDITS

New Scooby-Doo Movies, The (1972) TV Series . . . . Velma Dinkley
Scooby-Doo, Where Are You! (1969) TV Series . . . . Velma Dinkley
Scooby-Doo and the Legend of the Vampire (2003) Video . . . . Velma Dinkley
Scooby-Doo and the Monster of Mexico (2003) Video . . . . Velma Dinkley
Scooby-Doo's Creepiest Capers (2000) Video . . . . Velma Dinkley
Scooby-Doo's Greatest Mysteries (1999) Video . . . . Velma Dinkley

JUNE FORAY

She is, without a doubt, the First Lady of Animation. It is difficult not to seem overly profuse when describing June Foray and her work; but to simply impress it is not necessary to do any more than rattle off a list of credits, achievements, and awards she has amassed over her decades-long career. A pioneer of the animation industry, Foray has been recognized for not just giving voice to her characters, but for the way she endows them with a personality and depth using a robust voice that projects from her diminutive frame.

Describing her parents as "artistic and cultured," Foray may have been destined to be a performer. She began her career path in entertainment at the age of six when her mother, herself a pianist and singer, insisted that her daughter have piano and dancing lessons. The young Foray, who was more taken by her aunt's career on stage, hated the piano so much that she counted herself fortunate to break her finger playing baseball, thus ending her lessons. When she finally blurted out, "Mother, what I really want is to be an actress," her parents saw to it that she studied with a series of first-rate acting instructors.

Acting "came naturally," and when Foray was twelve years old, her teacher, former stage actress Elizabeth Larson, tempered and refined her talent until she finally said, "June, I can't teach you anymore; you can do more voices than I can do." Foray says, "I think the genesis of many of the characters that I do now came from the time when I studied with Mrs. Larson and my other teachers, where I also memorized the classics. I was an omnivorous reader, and the little old I lady that I do as Granny, and I use her in a lot of other voices as you probably know, evolved really from *The Old Woman Shows her Medals*, by James M. Barrie. And a lot of the grand dames I did, of course, were from 'Mrs. Malaprop,' and, so this is where it all started, actually, and I realized when I was studying and reading and memorizing that I could do all of these voices."

Having worked in radio professionally from the time she was twelve in her home state of Massachusetts, she came out with her family to California when she was in her early teens. "I started in radio here, and when I started to go to college, it was impossible to meet a college scholastic schedule as well as working. Because in those days when we did radio shows, we did an afternoon show for the East Coast and then we took three hours off and did a show for the West Coast, [in addition to] a lot of local programming. So, that's why I never finished college, and I would like to have had a B.A. in something or other, but it wasn't to be. But I'm just as glad that it wasn't because I've had a very fulfilling life, rewarding career, and I'm still enjoying it."

In the early days of her career, Foray acted on national radio programs such as *The Phil Harris and Alice Faye Show, The Danny Thomas Show*, and *Smile Time with Steve Allen*. In the 1950s, she graduated to recording for various record labels. While under contract for Capitol Records, she worked with other animation voice greats such as Stan Freberg, Daws Butler, Mel Blanc, and Pinto Colvig, who did the original Bozo the Clown, and Goofy for

Disney. But her animation career began in a roundabout way. Starting with her voice work for the Capitol, RCA, Liberty, and Decca record labels, she performed on the Stan Freberg records and various children's albums.

She recalls, "Disney hadn't, nor did Warner Bros. have their own record companies . . . so they would farm out their features, plus their shorts, to Capitol Records or Columbia Records or Liberty or whoever; and so, my being under contract to Capitol records, I did all of the character voices on the records that they [produced for] Disney." When Disney found out about Foray's work on their albums, they hired her for her first animated part, that of Lucifer, the cat in the 1950 *Cinderella*. She followed that up with the 1952 Disney short *Trick or Treat*, where she played a witch christened "Witch Hazel," which caught the attention of Warner Bros. director Chuck Jones. Jones called Foray in to reprise Witch Hazel in *Broomstick Bunny* and various other Bugs Bunny shorts for Warner Bros.

Since beginning her illustrious career, Foray has enjoyed many of her characters, counting the little bun-haired lady who owned Tweety and Sylvester among her all-time favorites. "I loved Granny, of course, in the Warner Bros. Cartoons, but Witch Hazel was a funny character which I first did at Disney's—and I don't know how Chuck got the ability or rights to using the same name, but I've made Witch Hazel at Warner Bros. just a little bit different. The *Trick or Treat* Witch Hazel that I first did at Disney had a bit of a British accent, but Witch Hazel [at Warner Bros.] was all American."

Foray enjoyed her work at Warner Bros., especially for Jones, who became a life-long friend. However, it was during this time that Mel Blanc had made the deal with the studio to get exclusive on-screen credit in lieu of a substantial raise. Foray said that it particularly irritated her, Daws Butler, and Stan Freberg, who continued to perform anonymously. However, she notes that at least the credits have been more recently expanded to include them on the Warners cartoons that now air on television.

Interestingly enough, not only did Foray voice the "Indian Squaw" in Disney's 1953 version of *Peter Pan*, she and Margaret Kerry (Tinkerbell in *Peter Pan*) provided a physical model for the artists as well. "I was also rotoscoped as one of the mermaids in *Peter Pan* after I had recorded. They were ready to go into animation. They rotoscoped many of the characters, and I was called back to get into a bathing suit . . . and so one of the mermaids looks a little bit like me."

Calling her work for Jay Ward "the high-water mark of [her] career," she enjoyed *Rocky and Bullwinkle*, chiefly because its sophisticated humor and gentle satire were far above the Saturday morning fare calculated to condescend to children. Citing the ingenious writing from Bill Scott, who wrote most of the *Bullwinkle* segments, as well as providing the moose's voice, and many others including Allan Burns (*The Mary Tyler Moore Show, Lou Grant*), who worked on *Fractured Fairytales,* Lloyd Turner (*The Odd Couple*), Chris Hayward (*Get Smart, Barney Miller*), Chris Jenkyns, and George Atkins, Foray states, "The plots were simple [and] were brilliantly written. They were all brilliant writers, and so they did not condescend to children. This is why, I think, some of the earlier cartoons were satirical; they were bright; they were brilliant, in many cases." Foray admits that the satirical bent of the series may have offended people, but wryly notes, "We offended people in a nice way."

Foray provided almost all of the female characters and the occasional male voice for the series, including Rocket J. Squirrel, the shapely Natasha Fatale (who was noticeably less "fatale" when the animators gave her a breast reduction at the request of the network and pressure groups), prim Nell Fenwick (who was Dudley Do-Right's lady love), and George of the Jungle's mate, Ursula. Foray was featured on almost every Jay Ward program, even if just playing an array of "walk-on" witches and fairies.

There has been some speculation as to the identity of two women mentioned in the title song for *George of the Jungle*: "Fella" (sometimes erroneously credited as "Velma" or "Thelma") and Ursula. Addressing rumors that George was originally involved in a tawdry ménage à trois until network censors nixed the idea, Foray discounts the idea with a laugh, "It was a joke. The song said Fella and Ursula because George would sometimes call Ursula 'Fella.' Ursula was George's only wife, it was just a joke."

Foray also lauds Ward's technique for the way he did not actively direct the ensemble. Instead, he had the cast of radio veterans gathered around the microphone and allowed them to perform the script as a radio play, only stopping them when someone laughed or they were over time. Foray said this allowed for the rapid-fire repartee (in which it was said that Foray was so fast she had been known to step on her own lines) that would not have been possible in the comparatively isolated recording methods that are now commonplace.

Among her entire repertoire, Foray was particularly fond of Rocky and Natasha and was especially tickled in the many instances where the naïve squirrel often would unknowingly chat with Boris Badenov or Natasha, who had just "disguised" themselves with a scarf or dark glasses. "Well, of course, Rocky was always so square, he'd say, 'Hey, haven't I seen you somewheres before?' I always get a kick out of that."

Writing children's stories and poetry since the age of fifteen, Foray produced "about three hundred" children's stories and performed all the characters for her own radio program for children entitled *Lady Make Believe*. "I think that's what started me on the multiple voices in knowing that that's what I wanted to be in radio." Surprisingly, a box of *Make Believe* scripts was unearthed in the aftermath of 1994's Northridge earthquake. Saying that the innocent, charming fantasies were needed to provide an escape for the children of modern, more troubled times, Foray has since recorded "six wonderful stories" that may be released as CDs.

Foray says that her comprehensive background as both an actor and a writer gave her enough perception to be able to get into any character, "whether they're evil or good . . . but I think it's an intuition that you have that you can crawl into someone else's mind and I think that's the way the personality fits in. However, I must say that I have a lot of ebullience, I have a lot of dynamism, and I have a lot of energy and maybe that hems the character that I do."

If Foray gives inspiration to the animator, it is implied in subtle cues from her performance: "Sometimes one had a special laugh, or one has a special way of reading a line, so that the animator thinks, 'Well, maybe one eyebrow went up, or maybe the chin was tucked in.' And I think the animator, who is a very intelligent, perceptive man himself, can glean ideas from the way characters are read, and I think that's the only suggestion. . . . I would never overtly make any suggestion to an animator, but I think, by my characters that I play, they do have suggestions. I never change a script—sometimes I have an idea where, where perhaps the grammar is wrong. I'm a strict grammarian and maybe the pronunciation is a little incorrect from what they have directed me and I say, 'Well, gee, I'd rather read it this way.' "

In the creation of a new voice, Foray has been known to draw upon her old characters for a new wrinkle. But in the case of her audition for *The Smurfs* (she arrived prepared to audition only for the role Smurfette, which, subsequently, went to Lucille Bliss), she read cold for the part of Jokey Smurf at the suggestion of Hanna-Barbera voice director Gordon Hunt and ultimately won the role on the strength of an improvised funny laugh. Foray also walked away from the audition with the parts of Ma Gargamel and Mother Nature, whom she said are "really almost an impersonation of [late film actress] Mary Boland."

Foray's voices have not been limited to those of cartoon characters. She did looping for Stephen Spielberg [on *Jaws*] when two boys from the Massachusetts location had not redone the exterior recording. "Plus [I did] some of the extraneous characters for Burt Reynolds. I did *Cannonball Run*. I did a couple of the prostitutes and operators. I did the little boy who had been murdered and had come back from the grave in *The Changeling*, with George C. Scott." Foray has even lent her voice to toys, doing the original voice for nostalgic baby-boomer favorite Chatty Cathy dolls and, conversely, the murderous Talky Tina doll, whose favorite refrain was, "I'm Talky Tina and I'm going to kill you," for an unforgettable episode of the *Twilight Zone*.

Far from being opposed to playing characters like the ill-tempered Tina, Foray has an elegant argument about the perception of violence in animation. Reminding the viewer that cartoons are basically just a series of drawings, "it really isn't violence . . . Bugs Bunny may have been turned inside-out or tarred and feathered, but you know what? He was up in the next frame and running around saying, 'Eeh, What's up Doc?' So, I don't feel that, that funny violence in cartoons is actually violence, and I'm putting parenthesis on the 'violence.' I'm a little too young to remember burlesque or vaudeville—I guess that started in the early nineteenth century—but from what I hear, all of the burlesque and all of these characters slipped on banana peels, and everybody laughed at little old ladies falling. I think they still do. So, I think that comedy is predicated on somebody else's misfortune. So, unless you see a human being depicted in full animation where they stab and blood gushes out, to me, that is violence, but I don't see any of that in the humor. Humor is kicking somebody in the derriere, or hitting them on the head, or laughing at somebody falling down."

Foray's achievements include seven semesters of teaching at the University of Southern California in the 1980s. She comments, "It's been a very enjoyable experience. I've never really liked teaching, but I feel, having had the rewarding career that I've had and I am still enjoying, that maybe I should pass it on to the much younger people, and so that's the way I feel about it. It's given me great pleasure to find that some of these people are now working in the various studios, and they say, 'Well, we studied under June Foray.' [Among them, the accomplished Corey Burton] It kind of makes me feel a little bit warm and happy."

Foray has dedicated much of her time serving on various animation-related organizations and panels. Founding the "Annie Awards" (the animation industry's equivalent to the Oscars) in 1972 when she was president of ASIFA (the international animated film society), she was more recently recognized by the organization, which named a juried award for "significant and benevolent impact on the animation industry" in her honor. She was also on the board of the American Center of Film for Children and the National

Academy of Recording Arts and Sciences, and serves as chairman of the Student Academy Awards in the Motion Picture Academy. In 2003, Foray was re-elected to serve what is now approaching three decades on the Board of Governors for the Academy of Motion Picture Arts and Sciences. There, she promoted awareness of animation in the academy and actively fought to keep the Short Subject category from being phased out of the Academy Awards. Of course, all of this was capped off in 2000 by the awarding of her star on the Hollywood Walk of Fame after an apropos nomination by her former director and friend, Chuck Jones. He has been quoted as commenting, "June Foray is not the female Mel Blanc. Mel Blanc is the male June Foray."

It is quite amusing to note that in spite of her good work—or maybe because of it—she claims to be included in Richard Nixon's "enemies list" (along with Bill Cosby, Paul Newman, and several other celebrities). In 1973, she dared to spearhead a successful boycott against the high price of meat. Recalling that, at one point, she was called by Senator Hubert Humprey to testify before Congress. About a week later, she received a call from news-caster Charles Osgood, who told her that Nixon was putting a ceiling on the price. Regardless, she replied the boycott was still on, in part, because the price was still too high. All of which, she says, placed her on the dreaded list. Apparently, the incident became more than just a curiosity as Foray said her taxes were then audited by the IRS for ten years following!

Looking back at a long and illustrious career that still continues to flourish, Foray is justifiably proud of her achievements in a profession in which she feels aptly gratified and rewarded. While she may have started out with the intention of simply making a living, she has since become a living legend.

CREDITS

2 Stupid Dogs/Super Secret Squirrel (1993) TV Series . . . . Additional Voices
51st Annual Primetime Emmy Awards, The (1999) TV (uncredited) . . . . Herself
Adventures of Rocky & Bullwinkle, The (2000) . . . . Rocket J. "Rocky" Squirrel/Natasha Fatale/
    Narrator's Mother
Ah, Sweet Mouse-Story of Life (1965)
A-Haunting We Will Go (1966) . . . . Witch Hazel
Alvin Show, The (1961) TV Series . . . . Daisy Bell/Mrs. Frumpington (1961)
Andy's Gang (1955) TV Series . . . . Midnight, the cat/Old Grandie, the witch
Apes of Wrath (1959)
Baby Looney Tunes (2001) TV Series . . . . Granny
Bedtime Bedlam (1955)
Beetle Bailey and His Friends (1963) TV Series
Bewitched Bunny (1954) (uncredited) . . . . Witch Hazel

Bird in a Bonnet, A (1957) .... Granny

Bongo Punch, The (1957)

Boris and Natasha (1992) (uncredited) .... Autograph Woman

Boston Quackie (1957)

Broken Leghorn, A (1959) (uncredited) .... Miss Prissy/Hens

Broom-Stick Bunny (1956) (uncredited) .... Witch Hazel

Bugs Bunny and Tweety Show, The (1986) TV Series .... Various Characters

Bugs Bunny Mother's Day Special, The (1979) TV .... Granny

Bugs Bunny Show, The (1960) TV Series .... Granny/Witch Hazel

Bugs Bunny/Looney Tunes Comedy Hour, The (1985) TV Series .... Various Characters

Bugs Bunny/Road Runner Hour, The (1968) TV Series .... Various Characters

Bugs Bunny's Easter Special (1977) TV .... Granny

Bugs Bunny's Howl-Oween Special (1978) TV .... Witch Hazel

Bugs Bunny's Looney Christmas Tales (1979) TV .... Clyde Rabbit/Mrs. Claus

Bugs Bunny's Third Movie: 1001 Rabbit Tales (1982) .... Granny/Goldimouse/Mrs. Sylvester/
    Mrs. Elvis Gorilla/Jack's Mother

Bugs 'n' Daffy Show, The (1996) TV Series .... Various Characters

Bullwinkle Show, The (1961) TV Series .... Rocket "Rocky" J. Squirrel/Natasha Fatale/Nell Fenwick

Calvin and the Colonel (1961) TV Series .... Myrtle

Car of Tomorrow (1951)

Cat's Me-Ouch, The (1965) .... Vocal Effects

Catty Corned (1953)

Cheese It, the Cat! (1957) .... Alice Crumden/Trixie Morton

Chipmunk Reunion, The

Christmas Is

Cinderella (1950) .... Lucifer

City That Forgot about Christmas, A

Congratulations, It's Pink (1967)

Cricket in Times Square, The (1973) TV .... Mother

Curiosity Shop (1971) TV Series .... Aardvark/Giraffe/Elephant

Dad, Can I Borrow the Car? (1970) TV .... Various Characters

Daffy Duck's Movie: Fantastic Island (1983) .... Granny

Daffy Duck's Quackbusters (1988)

Danger Team (1991) TV .... Voice of Nit

Death of a Salesman (1966/II) TV .... Jenny

Deduce, You Say (1956) .... Shropshire Slasher's Mother

Dennis the Menace (1985) TV Series .... Mrs. Wilson

Dick Tracy Show (1961) TV Series .... Additional Voices

Don't Axe Me (1958)

Droopy, Master Dectective (1995) TV Series .... Additional Voices

DuckTales (1987) TV Series .... Magica de Spell/Ma Beagle/Mrs. Featherby

DuckTales: The Movie—Treasure of the Lost Lamp (1990) .... Mrs. Featherby

Dudley Do-Right Show, The (1969) TV Series .... Nell Fenwick

Duel Personality (1966) .... Tom/Jerry

Egg-Cracker Suite, The (1943)

Explosive Mr. Magoo, The (1958)

Fabulous Funnies, The (1978) TV Series .... Broom Hilda/Oola/Hans/Fritz/Sluggo

Faeries (1981) TV .... Hag

Farm of Tomorrow, The (1954)

Father of the Bird (1997) .... Cornbread

Father's Day Off (1953)

Father's Week-End (1953)

First Bad Man, The (1955)

Flagstones, The (*The Flintstones* pilot) . . . . Betty Rubble

Flintstones, The (1960) TV Series . . . . Additional Voices (1963–1966)

Flintstones: Wacky Inventions, The (1994) (archive footage) . . . . Additional Voices

Flintstones Kids, The (1986) TV Series . . . . Additional Voices

Flush (1977) (uncredited) . . . . Belle Chance

Flying Feet (1969) . . . . Roland's Mum

Flying Sorceress, The (1956) (uncredited) . . . . Tom's Mistress/Witch

Fractured Fairy Tales: The Phox, the Box, and the Lox (1999) . . . . Milkmaid

Fractured Flickers (1963) TV Series . . . . Various Voices

French Freud (1969)

Fright before Christmas (1979) TV . . . . Clyde Rabbit

Friz Freleng's Looney Looney Looney Bugs Bunny Movie (1981) . . . . Granny

Frosty the Snowman (1969) TV . . . . Teacher/Karen/Various Voices

Garfield and Friends (1988) TV Series . . . . Additional Voices

Garfield Gets a Life (1991) TV . . . . Mona/Librarian

George of the Jungle (1967) TV Series . . . . Ursula Van Horn/Marigold/Gertie

Get Lost (1956) . . . . Knothead/Splinter

Giftwrapped (1952) . . . . Granny

Greedy for Tweety (1957) . . . . Granny

Gummi Bears, The (1985) TV Series . . . . Granni Grammi/Moblile Tree/Most Peaceful Dragon in the World/Councilor Woodale

Hare-Less Wolf (1958) (uncredited) . . . . Mrs. Wolf

Hawaiian Aye-Aye (1964) . . . . Granny

Hawks and Doves (1968) . . . . Roland's Mom/Rattfink's Mom

Heathcliff (1980) TV Series . . . . Grandma (1980–1982)/Crazy Shirley/Sonja/Marcy

Heathcliff and Marmaduke Show TV Series . . . . Marcy

Here Comes the Gump (1969) TV Series . . . . Additional Voices

Hiss and Make Up (1943) (uncredited) . . . . Granny

Honey-Mousers, The (1956) . . . . Alice Crumden/Trixie Morton

Honey's Money (1962)

Hoppity Hooper (1964) TV Series . . . . Rocky

Horton Hears a Who! (1970) TV . . . . Jane Kangaroo

How the Grinch Stole Christmas! (1966) TV (uncredited) . . . . Cindy Lou Who

How the Grinch Stole Christmas! Special Edition (1994) TV (archive footage)

How to be a Detective (1952)

I Yabba-Dabba Do! (1993) TV . . . . Additional Voices

Incredible Book Escape, The (1980) TV

Incredible Hulk and Amazing Spiderman, The (1982) TV Series . . . . Rita

Inspector, The

International Woodpecker (1957) . . . . Knothead/Splinter

Jet Cage, The (1962) . . . . Granny

Jetsons, The (1962) (1985) TV Series . . . . Additional Voices

Kiddie's Kitty, A (1955)

Last Hungry Cat, The (1961) (uncredited) . . . . Granny

Le Ball and Chain Gang (1968) . . . . Edna/Mother

Let's Stick Together (1952) (uncredited) . . . . Spike's Wife/Various Kids

Little Drummer Boy, The (1968) TV . . . . Aaron's Mother

Little House, The (1952)

Little Nemo: Adventures in Slumberland (1992) . . . . Librarian/Lone Ranger

Looney, Looney, Looney Bugs Bunny Movie, The (1981) . . . . Granny

Looney Tunes: Back in Action (2003) Video . . . . Granny

Looney Tunes: Reality Check (2003) . . . . Granny
Looney Tunes: Stranger Than Fiction (2003) Video . . . . Granny/Witch Hazel
Love Me, Love My Mouse (1966)
Magical World of Chuck Jones, The (1992) . . . . Herself
Man Called Flintstone, The (1966) . . . . Tanya Malichite
Merrie Melodies: Starring Bugs Bunny and Friends (1990) TV Series . . . . Various Characters
Mickey's House of Villains (2002) . . . . Witch Hazel (segment: "Trick or Treat")
Miss Switch to the Rescue (1982) TV . . . . Bathsheba/Saturna
Mixed Master (1956) (uncredited) . . . . Alice
Mouse for Sale (1955) (uncredited) . . . . Woman
Mouse-Placed Kitten (1959) . . . . Matilda/Junior's Mistress
Mr. Magoo (1960) TV Series . . . . Additional Voices
Mr. Magoo's Christmas Carol (1962) TV . . . . Ghost of Christmas Past
Mulan (1998) . . . . Grandmother Fa
My Smurfy Valentine TV Series . . . . Jokey/Smurfberry Bird
Of Feline Bondage (1965) . . . . Jerry/Fairy Godmouse
Off to See the Wizard (1967) TV Series . . . . Dorothy
One Cab's Familly (1952)
Pet Peeve (1954) (uncredited) . . . . Woman
Peter Pan (1953) (uncredited) . . . . Mermaid/Squaw
Phantom Tollbooth, The (1970) . . . . Faintly Macabre/Additional Voices
Pizza Tweety-Pie, A (1958) . . . . Granny/Spaghetti Bird
Pogo Special Birthday Special, The (1969) TV . . . . Pogo Possum/Mam'selle Hepzibah
Pound Puppies Special (1985) . . . . Mother Superior/Old Lady
Problem Child (1990) TV Series
Problem Child 2 (1991) . . . . Puppet
Punch Trunk (1953)
Pup Named Scooby-Doo, A (1988) TV Series . . . . Addtional Voices (1988–1991)
Quackodile Tears (1962) (uncredited)
Rabbit Romeo (1957) . . . . Millicent
Raggedy Ann and Andy
Really Scent (1959) (uncredited) . . . . Narrator
Red Riding Hoodlum (1957)
Red Riding Hoodwinked (1955) . . . . Granny
Redux Riding Hood (1997) . . . . Grandma
Rikki-Tikki-Tavi (1975) TV . . . . Nagaina the Cobra, Wife of Nag/Teddy's Mother/Darzee's Wife
Road Runner Show, The (1966) TV Series . . . . Various Characters
Rocket-bye Baby (1956) (uncredited) . . . . Hospital P.A./Martha Wilbur/Old Lady
Rockhound Magoo (1957)
Rocky and His Friends (1959) TV Series . . . . Rocket J. Squirrel/Natasha Fatale/Various Others
Scooby-Doo Meets the Boo Brothers (1987) TV (uncredited) . . . . Poor Old Witch
Simpsons, The (1990) . . . . Rubber Baby Buggy Babysitting Service Lady
Smurfic Games, The . . . . Jokey Smurf
Smurfily Ever After . . . . Jokey Smurf
Smurfs, The (1981) TV Series . . . . Jokey Smurf/Mother Nature
Space Jam (1996) . . . . Granny
Speaking of Animals (1941–1949)
Spider-Man and His Amazing Friends (1981) TV Series . . . . Aunt May Parker
Star Is Bored, A (1956) (uncredited) . . . . Lolly
Stop! Look! and Laugh! (1960) (uncredited) . . . . Cinderella
Street Cat Named Sylvester, A (1953) (uncredited) . . . . Granny

Strong Kids, Safe Kids (1984) . . . . Jokey Smurf
Super Ducktales (1989) TV . . . . Ma Beagle
Super President and Spy Shadow (1967) TV Series
Sylvester and Tweety Mysteries, The (1995) TV Series . . . . Granny
Sylvester and Tweety Show, The (1976) TV Series . . . . Various Characters
Teen Wolf (1986) TV Series . . . . Grandma/Mrs. Sesslick
That's Warner Bros.! (1995) TV Series . . . . Various Characters
These Are the Days (1974) TV Series
This Is a Life? (1955) . . . . Granny
Three Little Woodpeckers (1965)
Thumbelina (1994) . . . . Queen Tabitha
Tiny Toon Adventures (1990) TV Series . . . . Additional Voices
Tom and Jerry (1965) TV Series . . . . Various Characters (1965–1972)
Tom-ic Energy (1964)
Tree Cornered Twenty (1956)
Trick or Treat (1952) . . . . Witch Hazel
Trip for Tat (1960) . . . . Granny
Trouble with Miss Switch, The (1980) TV . . . . Bathsheba/Saturna
Tugboat Granny (1956) . . . . Granny
Tweet and Sour (1956) . . . . Granny
Tweet Dreams (1959) . . . . Granny
Tweety and the Beanstalk (1957) . . . . Granny
Tweety's High Flying Adventure (2000) . . . . Granny
Unbearable Salesman, The (1957) . . . . Knothead/Splinter
Unexpected Pest, The (1956)
Unnatural History (1959)
Unsafe and Seine (1966)
Vanishing Duck, The (1958) (uncredited) . . . . Joan
Waggily Tale, A (1958)
White Seal, The (1975) TV . . . . Mackah
Who Framed Roger Rabbit (1988) . . . . Wheezy (weasel)/Lena Hyena/Toon Hag
Witch's Tangled Hare, A (1959) . . . . Witch Hazel
Wolf Hounded (1959)
Woody Woodpecker Show, The (1957) TV Series . . . . Splinter/Knothead
Year of the Mouse, The (1965)
Yogi Bear Show, The (1960) TV Series

PAUL FREES

The flamboyant Paul Frees made it clear that he never did "retakes;" he did "encores." Certainly the most complex character in animation, Frees was lauded as "brilliant" by peers and friends for his talent and faultless ear and, almost in the same breath, was criticized as "impossible," "arrogant," and something of an eccentric. There can be no doubt that with his outlandish dress sense, which included wearing firearms to recording sessions, and a dangerous evening pastime of assisting the Los Angeles Police Department on drug raids, Frees' exotic biography rivals the plot of any cartoon he ever voiced.

The man who would be Boris Badenov was born Solomon Hersh Frees in Chicago, Illinois, on June 22, 1920. Although he displayed creative talents as a child, he had no intention of becoming an actor. In 1932, Frees was working toward his dream of becoming a painter until an "accident" landed him in show business. Twelve-year-old Frees and his best friend, Sid Clayton, worked on the twenty-third floor at 75 East Wacker Drive in downtown Chicago, cleaning the studio of their idol, painter Frederick Meyerson, just to have the privilege of watching him paint. But the two soon discovered that radio amateur-hour auditions were being held on the eighth floor at advertising agency Schwimmer and Scott and would sneak down to watch during their lunch breaks.

"We would sit in the booth and watch guitar players, impersonators, whatever it might be, and the next thing I knew, Sid pushed me into the studio, because a kid had just gotten up there, and he was awful." When Clayton told the producer that his friend was "a hundred times better," Frees got his turn in front of the microphone. Doing impersonations of famous stars of the era such as Wallace Beery and Charles Boyer, Frees passed the impromptu audition and was asked back to compete on the live program the following week. He subsequently won the first prize of seventy-five dollars and a watch—a veritable fortune in the midst of the Great Depression. The following week, Frees entered and won first prize in another talent show, effectively ending his painting ambitions.

That summer, Frees put together and was the emcee for little shows, even "a pony line of young girls from dancing school." Learning how to tap dance, he sang and toured with this group as "Buddy Green, the Prince of Impersonators." He spent the next couple of years touring during the summer, and, he said, "The next thing I knew, I was in full-time show business." Frees, who was gaining experience in Chicago's dramatic radio scene, eventually talked his parents into letting him quit high school to join an adult theater troupe and toured night clubs throughout the United States and Canada.

As did most of his peers, Frees enlisted in the military during World War II and was awarded the Purple Heart after being wounded in battle at Normandy. To pass the hours while recuperating at a San Diego hospital, he turned to painting again as a part of his recovery. As had happened years before, a friend took the initiative to showcase Frees' talent and submitted his first completed painting to a contest. The piece won first prize and was selected for showing in the National Gallery in Washington, D.C. The honor won him an art scholarship, and Frees was once again on his way to becoming a professional painter.

According to Frees' biography from Milton Kahn Associates, he did not have a chance to register for classes before tragedy struck—his young bride,

Annelle, passed away. Knowing he had to find employment to offset mounting bills, he got his start by simply appearing at Hollywood's front door. "I was hanging around the CBS studios and one day one of the producers saw me. I was still walking around with a cane and Ray Buffum asked about my injury and told me that he was a World War I vet." When Buffum asked Frees if he wanted to come in and see some shows, Frees characteristically replied, "Heck, no, I want to be in them!"

The novice actor was then given a chance to show what he could do. Although his first professional radio work consisted of one line of dialogue on *The Lux Radio Theater*, Frees soon graduated to other popular shows of the time, eventually working on up to two dozen different series simultaneously, including a stint as the host of *Suspense*. In 1948, he won the industry's top honor, the Radio Life Award. When the medium started to fade, Frees made the move to cross over to television—there performing in commercials, guest starring on *The Jack Benny Show*, and playing the voice of John Beresford Tipton on *The Millionaire*. For a short time, Frees hosted his own late-night talk show, *Frees on Two*. He obtained small on-camera roles in motion pictures such as *The Thing from Another World* and Elizabeth Taylor's first picture, the Oscar-winning *A Place in the Sun*, but Frees was heard on the silver screen more than he was seen.

Having earned a sterling reputation for voice-overs, Frees was used in films as a narrator, radio announcer, television announcer, and for varieties of off-camera voices. One of his specialties was also dialogue replacement for actors who were unavailable to redo their lines. Frees did impeccable work "looping" dialogue for stars such as Orson Welles, Peter Lorre, Cary Grant, and Boris Karloff. When Humphrey Bogart was ill with cancer, Frees replaced one-third of his dialogue in the 1956 film *The Harder They Fall.*

But movie stars were not the only ones whose dialogue Frees replaced. He also worked to redub entire roles for inexperienced actors or those with accents that were hard for American audiences to understand. In the 1963 film *A Time to Live and a Time to Die*, Frees' personal best was dubbing the voices of seventeen German actors who could not speak a word of English. In some scenes there were three or four characters interacting on the screen at once, and Frees expertly captured the essence of all.

By 1959, Frees had done voice-overs in theatrical cartoons, playing the crow in Columbia Pictures *Fox and the Crow* series for famed animator and Jerry Lewis director Frank Tashlin. He also took over the role of Barney Bear from actor Billy Bletcher in the MGM Barney Bear series and worked with Fred "Tex" Avery and Woody Woodpecker creator Walter Lantz, but Frees considered working with Jay Ward on *Rocky and His Friends* to be the high-light of his career. "I think *The Bullwinkle Show* is one of the best written of all the cartoon series. It was more adult. The other things, even Ludwig Von Drake (for Disney studios), [were] more kids' stuff. Anything that Hanna-Barbera did was more juvenile. I frankly don't care for any of that. At Jay Ward we've always been a very close, tight-knit family for many, many years. You have to remember how many different shows we did together. But it wasn't just that; it was how good the shows were."

When Frees came to the animation recording studio—Ward's included—he was a larger-than-life presence, reportedly involved in practical jokes on the set to "holding court" over all other actors. In *The Enchanted World of Rankin/Bass*, fellow voice-over actor Dick Beals recounts Frees' attitude in the recording studio: "Paul Frees was exactly three minutes late for his recording sessions. He was always docked by AFTRA for his tardiness, too. It was his way of showing the animation directors that he was just as impor-tant." Veteran voice actor Hal Rayle, who worked with Frees on Kellogg's commercials during the 1970s, comments that "Paul Frees was not known as the 'Great Intimidator' for nothing. He had his days where he just had to rule! This is what Paul Frees wore on a usual day: soft pink on the shirt, . . . ivory-bone three-piece suit with a huge gold chain across the middle. One side was a watch; the other side was a derringer. [Paul Frees' son Fred explained, 'In the army, my father worked for the special services, and after his discharge he continued to carry firearms with him at all times.'] Could be any one of a number of different derringers. He always had a different gun on him. Always in bone slip-on shoes, pink socks, pink carnation, and dark glasses, usually with an orangish tint. And he always wore the same colors—different styles but always the same colors. Quirky guy."

However, his reported antics in the recording studio for Jay Ward reflected more of what Hanna-Barbera voice actor Doug Young termed "what we in the business call 'The Mickey Rooney Syndrome.' In other words, the guy was always on, but very funny. Finally, the director would have to say, 'Paul, come on, shape up. We've got work to do.' He had to get really mean, because Paul just didn't want to stop." Director Bill Hurtz was quoted in the *L.A. Times* as saying that while castmate Hans Conreid as villain Snidely Whiplash was reading his lines, Frees set fire to his script. Hurtz concluded, "It became a matter of professional pride to read it through before becoming consumed in flames." According to Keith Scott's 2000 book, *The Moose That Roared*, Frees was responsible for getting *Rocky and Bullwinkle* announcer William Conrad, who had been acting with Frees since 1945, hired at Jay Ward studios. Frees was known to mercilessly tease his friend—who was probably most famous for playing the television detective Cannon—often reducing the imposing figure to "shrieks of laughter." Reportedly, when Conrad made a failed attempt at a character voice, which came out sounding exactly like his own, Frees for years subsequently referred to him as "The man of a thousand voice."

Aside from the ensemble work with Conrad, June Foray, and Bill Scott, Frees was employed on several Jay Ward series, voicing Otto Von Clutch on *Tom Slick*, Fred the valet on *Superchicken*, the ape named Ape and the narrator on *George of the Jungle*, Inspector Fenwick on *Dudley Do-Right* of the Mounties, Captain Peter Peachfuzz of *Rocky*, and many incidental characters on all of the above. Of all the cartoons he worked on in his career, Frees cites Badenov as one of his favorite characters, but claims to have almost never seen the work he did for Jay Ward. "Throughout the years, I've only seen about four or five segments. I never go looking for the things that I've done for any particular purpose. I'm not interested. I was interested in the *Bullwinkle*s to see how they came out, but, you see, I worked sixteen to eighteen hours a day. Sometimes I would work until four or five o'clock in the morning."

Although the work he did for Jay Ward studios was the most creatively satisfying for Frees, any perks that Ward could have offered (although Ward took a perverse pride in not offering any) would have been no match for what he received from the producers of *The Beatles* cartoons in the mid-1960s. According to Frees, he was flown to England about every two or three weeks and did "a whole slug" of shows with all expenses paid. Frees was ensconced at premier hotels like the Dorchester, with access to a Rolls Royce and a chauffeur. Best yet, he claims that the privileges culminated with dinner once accompanied by the Beatles and Princess Margaret.

While there were a few critics who were incensed at the pseudo-Liverpudlian accent Frees affected to play George Harrison and John Lennon—Lennon was supposed to be especially "amused" by its inaccuracy—Frees defends his rendition as not being due to lack of ability. "It was done for the American market, and not for Europe. They wanted an approximation of the flavor, but not the heavy accent, so that the American market could understand it. . . . When they finally did the cartoons for the Australian and the European markets, they dubbed in English actors."

The Beatles were not the only rock-and-roll stars Frees associated with throughout his career. Frees worked with the Osmond Brothers on *The Osmonds* cartoons and also with the Jacksons on *The Jackson 5* animated series, both for Rankin/Bass. But it was outside his professional duties that Frees made his most bizarre rock-and-roll connection. According to Frees' son, editor and musician Fred Frees, "He continued to do undercover work for the United States government while he pursued his career in voice-over work."

In the 1970s, according to Peter Guralnick, author of the well-reviewed Elvis Presley biography, *Careless Love, the Unmaking of Elvis Presley*, Elvis was out for dinner with noted ex–Los Angeles narcotics officer John O'Grady (who had previously helped Presley with a spurious paternity case) at famous Hollywood eatery Chasen's. There, O'Grady introduced Frees to Presley, who was immediately enchanted with the federal badge that Frees had been granted by John Ingersoll, then director of the Bureau of Narcotics and Dangerous Drugs.

Fred Frees confirms that not only was his father the assistant to the head of the Narcotics Bureau in Washington D.C., "which not many people knew about," but at one point he actually worked undercover with Elvis Presley. The iconic singer, in 1971, successfully petitioned President Nixon through Senator George Murphy to also grant him a similar narcotics badge. (According to Guralnick, the senator had even promised Elvis an appointment with FBI director J. Edgar Hoover.) But, ultimately, the most lasting record of Frees' involvement is the still much published bizarre-looking photo of Presley and Nixon shaking hands as Presley received his narcotics badge.

However, it is unclear to the younger Frees what role Presley played in narcotics operations. Although rumors in rock-and-roll circles persist that Frees and Presley provided information to the FBI to assist in deportation proceedings against ex-Beatle John Lennon, his son discards them as nonsense. "I don't believe that my father would actively work to deport a person that he knew and liked." But for the criminals that did get caught, Rayle recalls Frees would "actually use his limo to deliver people to jail. He was a wild man, Paul Frees."

Apart from the roles he played in the Rankin/Bass rock-and-roll cartoons, Frees appeared in every special the studio produced, playing an assortment of voices including one of his all time favorites, the Burgermeister from *The Year without a Santa Claus*. In an interview with author Rick Goldschmidt for his book *The Enchanted World of Rankin/Bass*, Arthur Rankin states, "Paul Frees was my good luck charm! Paul was in everything I ever did." Rankin has a favorite anecdote involving Frees, legendary dancer Fred Astaire, and Astaire's agent, Shep Fields. "I walked into the studio one morning, and waiting to work for me for the first time was Fred Astaire with his manager/agent, Shep Fields. . . . The three of us were sitting side by side in the conference room when Paul Frees walks in. I said, 'Good morning, Paul, I'd like you to meet

Shep Fields and Fred Astaire.' Paul walks down the line of chairs passing the three of us [ignoring Astaire] and says outloud, 'Not *the* Shep Fields?'"

Even though Frees appreciated the work given to him with Rankin/Bass and considered Arthur Rankin and Jules Bass two of his closest friends, he was also grateful to them on a more personal level. "Rankin and Bass introduced my wife and I. My wife was from England and she was a friend of Arthur Rankin's. So he and this girlfriend of his decided that we were both perfect for each other, but neither of us wanted to meet. One day, we both gave in and said, 'Yes,' for one drink at the Polo Lounge in the Beverly Hills Hotel." Two weeks later, the woman and admittedly "much older" Frees were married in his sixth such ceremony. Frees quipped slyly, "Although in show business there is no such thing as much older, is there?"

By the mid 1980s, Frees decided to forgo the often sixteen-hour days in the recording studio and retire in the Northern California Bay area, commenting that he was happy to leave Hanna-Barbera, dismissing his later work with the studio as his least favorite. "There are quite a few that I did just because I had to do them, but they weren't characters that I cared for. I've done so many characters that I didn't even think twice about, and they usually came from Hanna-Barbera." Frees quickly became so enamored to the San Francisco area that he refused any work that brought him to L.A. Even an offer from *The Jackson 5* to appear in a music video and travel with them as the narrator on their 1980s reunion tour could not persuade him to leave. Though he continued to do commercial voices such as the Pillsbury Doughboy and Froot Loops icon Toucan Sam from his home studio, Frees claimed that nothing could get him to leave the bay area short of Jay Ward Studios starting up again or Rankin/Bass producing new holiday specials. Unfortunately, neither studio beckoned, and Frees never returned to Los Angeles.

On November 1, 1986, Paul Frees succumbed to heart failure in Tiburon, California. After Frees died, his son Fred found items such as a disguise kit full of fake beards and mustaches while going through his personal effects. In keeping with his spirit, according to friend Lee Harris, at Frees' memorial service actor Lorne Greene eulogized Frees with the following story: "'Years ago, I was getting these strange phone calls in the middle of the night. It was a sultry, deep-voiced woman who made all sorts of obscene suggestions. I was married, so it was irritating and I couldn't figure out who it was and how she got my phone number. Sometime later, I was on the lot when I heard the voice behind me say 'Hi, there, big boy!' I turned around and it was Paul! I had worked with him for months and I had no idea he was the woman! He was just that good!'"

In his biography from his public relations agency—Milton Kahn Associates—written in the early 1980s, Frees states, "I can duplicate any voice and dialect I hear." When questioned about the boast for this publication, Frees, without missing a beat, repeated the question in the interviewer's voice. As to Frees being occasionally called a "braggart," it can be said that it is not really bragging if one can really pull it off.

CREDITS

101 Dalmatians (1961) . . . . Dirty Dawson
A-Hunting We Won't Go (1943) . . . . Crow
Adventures of Hoppity Hopper from Foggy Bogg (1962) TV Series . . . . Narrator
Alvin Show, The (1961) TV Series (voice) . . . . Additional Voices
Ape Suzette (1966) . . . . Cockney Sailor
Aquaman (1967) TV Series (voice) . . . . Kyro/Guardian of the Universe
Atlantis, the Lost Continent (1961)
Atom Ant/Secret Squirrel Show, The (1967) TV Series . . . . Morocco Mole/Squiddly Diddly
Baby Butch (1954)
Bally Hooey (1960)
Banana Splits Adventure Hour, The (1968) TV Series . . . . Evil Vangor
Barney's Hungry Cousin (1953) (uncredited) . . . . Barney Bear
Bats in the Belfry (1960)
Be Patient, Patient (1944) . . . . Crow
Beany and Cecil (1962) TV Series (voice). . . . Additional Voices
Bear That Wasn't, The (1967) . . . . Narrator
Beatles, The (1965) TV Series . . . . John Lennon/George Harrison
Beatniks, The (1960) . . . . Various Voices
Beetle Bailey and His Friends (1963) TV Series . . . . Barney Google/Snuffy Smith/Ignatz Mouse/
    Officer Bull Pupp/Mr. Kolin Kelly
Bomb Voyage (1967) . . . . Commissioner
Bozo the Clown (1959) TV Series (voice) . . . . Additional Voices
Bugged in a Rug (1965) . . . . Charlie Beary
Bullwinkle Show, The (1961) TV Series . . . . Boris Badenov/Captain Peter
    Peachfuzz/Cloyd/Inspector Fenwick
Bunglin' Builder, The (1971) . . . . Charlie Beary
Busybody Bear (1952) (uncredited) . . . . Barney Bear/Buck Beaver
Calvin and the Colonel (1961) TV Series . . . . Oliver Wendell Clutch
Carpetbaggers, The (1964) (uncredited) . . . . Narrator
Casanova Cat (1951)
Cellbound (1955) (uncredited) . . . . Prisoner/George the Warden/Little Wife
Charlie in Hot Water (1970) . . . . Charlie Beary
Charlie the Rainmaker (1971) . . . . Charlie Beary
Charlie's Campout (1969) . . . . Charlie Beary
Charlie's Golf Classic (1970) . . . . Charlie Beary
Charlie's Mother-in-Law (1963) . . . . Charlie Beary
Chump Champ, The (1950)

Cirrhosis of the Louvre (1966) .... Commissioner

Clash and Carry (1961)

Cobs and Robbers (1953) (uncredited) .... Barney Bear/Joe Scarecrow/Crows

Cock-a-Doodle Deux-Deux (1966) .... Commissioner

Cool It, Charlie (1969) .... Charlie Beary

Corny Concerto (1962) .... Doc

Cosmic Capers (1957) .... Narrator

Cruise Cat (1952) (uncredited) .... Ship's Captain

Davey Cricket (1965) .... Charlie Beary

Dick Tracy Show, The (1961) TV Series .... BB Eyes/The Brow/Cheater Gunsmoke/Flat Top (II)/
   Go Go Gomez (II)/Itchy/The Mole/Mumbles/Oodles/The Retouchables

Disneyland (1954) TV Series .... Ludwig Von Drake (1961–1983)

Disney's DTV Valentine (1986). . . . Ludwig Von Drake/Announcer

Doc's Last Stand (1961) .... Doc

Donald and the Wheel (1961)

Donald in Mathmagic Land (1959) (uncredited) .... The True Spirit of Adventure/Narrator

Down Beat Bear (1956) (uncredited) .... First Radio Announcer

Dream Kids, The (1944) .... Crow

Dudley Do-Right Show, The (1969) TV Series .... Inspector Ray K. Fenwick

Egg-Yegg, The (1945) .... Crow

Et Tu Otto (1962) (uncredited) .... Champlain/Cosmo/Rocky/Various Voices

Eyes into Outer Space (1959)

Famous Adventures of Mr. Magoo, The (1964) TV Series .... Various Voices

Fantastic Four, The (1967) TV Series .... The Thing (Benjamin J. Grimm)/The Watcher/Additional
   Voices

Farm of Tomorrow, The (1954) (uncredited) .... Narrator

First Easter Rabbit, The (1976) TV .... Zero

Fish Story, A (1972)

Flight of Dragons, The (1986) (uncredited) .... Antiquity

Fly with Von Drake (1963) .... Ludwig Von Drake

Foot Brawl (1966) .... Charlie Beary

Fowled-up Birthday (1962) .... Charlie Beary

Fowled-up Falcon (1960)

Foxey Flatfoots (1946) .... Crow

Fractured Flickers (1963) TV Series .... Voice

Framed Cat, The (1950)

Francis in the Haunted House (1956) .... Francis the Talking Mule

Frankenstein Jr. and the Impossibles (1966) TV Series .... Fluid Man

Freeloading Feline (1960) .... Doc

Freewayphobia (1965) .... Narrator

Frosty the Snowman (1969) TV .... Santa Claus/Traffic Cop/Various Voices

Frosty's Winter Wonderland (1976) TV .... Jack Frost

Gay Purr-ee (1962) .... Meowrice/Railway Cat

George of the Jungle (1967) TV Series .... Narrator/Ape Named Ape/Commissioner/Plumtree/
   Weevil/Fred/Baron Otto Matic/Dick Two-Lane/Additional Voices

Goliath II (1959)

Good Friend, The (1969)

Goofy's Freeway Troubles (1965) (uncredited) .... Narrator

Goose in the Rough (1963) .... Charlie Beary

Goose Is Wild (1963) .... Charlie Beary

Gopher Broke (1969) .... Charlie Beary

Great De Gaulle Stone Robbery, The (1965) . . . . Three-Headed Villain
Guest Who? (1965) . . . . Charlie Beary
Half-Pint Palomino (1953) (uncredited) . . . . Barney Bear
Ham and Hattie: Spring (1958)
Hat, The (1962)
Heir Bear (1953) (uncredited) . . . . Barney Bear/Gopher/Tax Collector
Here Comes Peter Cottontail (1971) TV
His Mouse Friday (1959)
Hobbit, The (1978) TV . . . . Bombur/Troll #1
Homesteader Droopy (1954) (uncredited) . . . . Narrator
Hoppity Hooper (1964) TV Series . . . . Narrator
Impossible Possum, The (1954) (uncredited) . . . . Barney Bear
In Shape with Von Drake (1964) . . . . Ludwig Von Drake
In the Bag (1956)
Incredible Mr. Limpet, The (1964) . . . . Crusty
Jack Frost (1979) TV . . . . Kubla Kraus
Jerky Turkey (1968) . . . . Charlie Beary
Jerry's Cousin (1951) (uncredited) . . . . Cousin Muscles
Keeping up with Krazy (1962) . . . . Ignatz Mouse/Officer Pupp
Krazy Kat (1963) TV Series (uncredited) . . . . Ignatz Mouse/Officer Pupp
Last Unicorn, The (1982) . . . . Mabruk
Laurel and Hardy Cartoon, A (1966) TV Series . . . . Various Characters
Le Bowser Bagger (1967) . . . . Commissioner
Le Escape Goat (1967) . . . . Commissioner
Le Great Dane Robbery (1968) . . . . Commissioner
Le Quiet Squad (1967) . . . . Chief
Let Charlie Do It (1972) . . . . Charlie Bear/Junior
Little Drummer Boy, The (1968) TV . . . . Aaron's Father/Magi
Little Runaway (1952)
Little Wise Quacker, The (1952) . . . . Barney Bear
Magic Fluke (1949) . . . . Crow
Magic Peartree, The (1967)
Man Called Flintstone, The (1966) . . . . Rock Slag/Bo-Bo/Triple X/Mario/Shady Character
Man Is His Own Worst Enemy (1962) . . . . Ludwig Von Drake
Mars and Beyond (1957)
Mary Poppins (1964) . . . . Horse
Matty's Funday Funnies (Beanie & Cecil) (1959) TV Series . . . . Additional Voices
Method and the Maw, The (1962) . . . . Barney Goggle/Snuffy Smith
Missing Mouse, The (1953) (uncredited) . . . . Radio Announcer
Moochin' Pooch (1971) . . . . Charlie Beary
Mother's Little Helper (1962) . . . . Charlie Beary
Mouse Blanche (1962) . . . . Ignatz/Officer Pupp
Mouse in the House (1967) . . . . Charlie Beary
Mouse Trapped (1959) . . . . Doc
Mr. Magoo (1960) TV Series (voice) . . . . Tycoon Magoo/Additional Voices
Mr. Magoo's Christmas Carol (1962) TV . . . . Charity Man/Fezziwig/Eyepatch Man/Tall Top-Hat Man
Mr. Moocher (1944) . . . . Crow
Music for Everybody (1966) . . . . Ludwig Von Drake
Mysto-Fox (1946) . . . . Crow
Nestor, the Long-Eared Christmas Donkey (1977) TV . . . . Olaf/Donkey Dealer
New Adventures of Huck Finn, The (1968) TV Series (voice) . . . . Additional Voices

Noah's Ark (1959) . . . . Noah/God

Osmonds, The (1972) TV Series . . . . Fugi the Dog

Paste Makes Waste (1968) . . . . Charlie Beary

Pest of Show (1962) . . . . Doc

Phoney Baloney (1945) . . . . Crow

Pink Panther Show, The (1969) TV Series . . . . Commissioner (1971–1978)

Pink Panzer (1965) . . . . Narrator

Pinkfinger (1965) (voice)

Pique Poquette of Paris, The (1966) . . . . Spider Pierre

Plastered in Paris (1966) . . . . Commissioner

Plenty below Zero (1943) . . . . Crow

Point, The (1971) TV . . . . King Leaf Man

Primitive Pluto (1950) (uncredited) . . . . Primo

Psychological Testing (1962) . . . . Lt. Fuzz/Lt. Forbes/Sgt. Tortoise

Punchy de Leon (1950) . . . . Crow

Punchy Pooch (1962) . . . . Doc

Puppetoon Movie, The (1987) . . . . Arnie the Dinosaur/Pillsbury Doughboy

Rah, Rah, Ruckus (1964) . . . . Charlie Beary

Rain, Rain Go Away (1972)

Reaux, Reaux, Reaux Your Boat (1966) . . . . Crab Louie

Return of the King, The (1980) TV . . . . Goblin/Elrond

Robin and the Seven Hoods (1964) (uncredited) . . . . Radio Announcer

Robin Hoodlum (1948) . . . . Crow

Rocky and His Friends (1959) TV Series . . . . Boris Badenov/Captain Peter Wrongway Peachfuzz/
    Various Voices

Roof-Top Razzle Dazzle (1964) . . . . Charlie Beary

Room and Bored (1943) . . . . Crow

Rudolph and Frosty's Christmas in July (1979) TV . . . . Winterbolt

Rudolph's Shiny New Year (1975) TV . . . . Santa Claus/Eon/General Ticker/Seventeen-Seventy-Three
    "Sev"

Sacré Bleu Cross (1967) . . . . Hassan the Assassin

Santa Claus Is Comin' to Town (1970) TV . . . . Burgermeister Meisterburger/Grimsby/Soldiers/
    Townsmen

Scarlet Coat, The (1955) (uncredited) . . . . Narrator

Secret Squirrel Show, The (1965) TV Series . . . . Morocco Mole

Sink Pink (1965)

Slay It with Flowers (1943) . . . . Crow

Sleepy-Time Squirrel (1954) (uncredited) . . . . Barney Bear/Jimmy Squirrel

Sleepy-Time Tom (1951)

Snuffy Smith (1963) TV Series . . . . Barney Google/Snuffy Smith

Snuffy's Song (1962) . . . . Barney Google/Snuffy Smith

Space Ghost/Frankenstein Jr. Show (1976) TV Series . . . . Fluid Man

Space Mouse (1959) . . . . Doc

Square Peg in a Round Hole (1963) . . . . Ludwig Von Drake

Stingiest Man in Town, The (1978) TV . . . . Ghost of Christmas Past/Ghost of Christmas Present

Stowaway Woody (1963)

Super President and Spy Shadow (1967) TV Series (voice) . . . . President James Norcross/Super
    President/Narrator

Super Six, The (1966) TV Series . . . . Brother Matzoriley #1/Captain Zammo

Symposium on Popular Songs, A (1962) . . . . Ludwig Von Drake

Take Me to Your Gen'rul (1962) . . . . Snuffy Smith/Barney Google

Tale of a Wolf (1960)
That's No Lady—That's Notre Dame (1966)
Three Tall Tales (1963) . . . . Ludwig Von Drake
Tin Can Concert (1961)
Tin-Tin (1963) TV Series . . . . Detective Thompson/Additional Voices
Toll Bridge Troubles (1942) . . . . Crow
Tom and Jerry (1965) TV Series (voice)
Tooth or Consequences (1947) . . . . Crow
Top Cat (1961) TV Series . . . . Various Voices
Treasure Jest (1945) . . . . Crow
Tree for Two (1943) . . . . Crow
Tricky Trout (1961)
TV of Tomorrow (1953)
Twice upon a Time (1983) . . . . Narrator/Chef of State/Judges/Bailiff
Uncle Waldo's Cartoon Show (1966) TV Series . . . . Fillmore the Bear
Unhandy Man, The (1970) . . . . Charlie Beary
Unlucky Potluck (1972) . . . . Charlie Bear/Junior
Unsafe and Seine (1966) . . . . Commissioner/Pub Waiter/Patrons
Unsure Runts (1946) . . . . Crow
Von Drake in Spain (1962) . . . Ludwig Von Drake
Way Down in the Corn (1943) . . . . Crow
Wee-Willie Wildcat (1953) (uncredited) . . . . Barney Bear/William Wildcat
Wind in the Willows, The (1987) TV . . . . Wayfarer
Window Pains (1967) . . . . Charlie Beary
Witty Kitty (1960) . . . . Doc
Woodsman, Spare That Tree (1942) . . . . Crow
Woody Woodpecker and His Friends (1982) Video . . . . Various Voices
Woody Woodpecker Show, The (1957) TV Series . . . . The Beary Family/Doc/Paw/Wally Walrus

STERLING HOLLOWAY

His voice is one of the most instantly recognizable voices in the world—once it is heard, it is indelibly etched on the mind of the listener. While aficionados of older films may recognize Sterling Holloway as the tall, lanky, red-headed soda jerk, messenger, and country bumpkin of the films of the 1930s and '40s; more than a decade after his passing, millions of viewers continue to be charmed by his distinctive velvety rasp that graces both Disney cartoon heroes and villains. In his voice lies the elusive Cheshire Cat in *Alice in Wonderland,* the quiet menace of Kaa, the snake from *The Jungle Book,* as well as the wistful "Oh, bother" of the beloved Winnie the Pooh.

The actor, born January 14, 1905, in Cedartown, Georgia, was the son of a prominent businessman. Like his father, he was the namesake of Confederate general Sterling "Pap" Price, but the younger Holloway convinced his parents to let him bow out of his military education at Georgia (now Woodward) Military Academy when his first brush with acting in an amateur theatrical production led to an interest in dramatics. Holloway claimed that his show business career began at fifteen when he subsequently enrolled in the American Academy of Dramatic Arts in New York. Judging from the stature of some of his classmates, including the likes of Spencer Tracy, Pat O'Brien, and Georgia Neese (the first woman to become the secretary of the U.S. Treasury), Holloway already seemed destined for greatness.

After graduation, the actor then spent much of his early career shuffling between the coasts, first touring the West with a stock company called the Shepherd of the Hills. Upon his return to New York, he signed with the Theater Guild to gain notoriety in the first Broadway production of Rodgers and Hart's *Garrick's Gaieties* for famed director David Garrick. During the different productions of the various revues, he wrote some sketch material, introduced the Rodgers and Hart standard song "I'll Take Manhattan" in 1925 and, in the following year, "Mountain Greenery" before he left for Los Angeles to try his luck in films.

Ironically, for an actor whose legacy is his vocal characterizations, it was the advent of sound that initially hampered his efforts at a film career. In a biographical article published on a Disney-affiliated web site, author Jim Fanning quotes Holloway as commenting, "I came to Hollywood at a bad time. The movies were in a state of turmoil. . . . Sound was coming in and silents were going out. I made a silent two-reel comedy called *The Fighting Kangaroo.* Then I did a silent feature, *Casey at the Bat,* with Wallace Beery for Paramount, and all of a sudden I was a has-been. Nobody thought I was suitable for talkies. . . . So I returned to New York." Despite success in the various revues, vaudeville, night clubs, and radio jobs, Holloway decided that he was more interested in the innovations being made in film and returned to Los Angeles. This time, he said, he was "determined to make it."

Holloway made an attempt to be noticed by agents and motion picture producers by appearing at the Pasadena Playhouse; patronized by film executives, it was considered a showcase for actors wishing to make the move into motion pictures. Holloway said it was exposure there that prompted

Frank Capra to offer him a part in his 1932 film *American Madness*. Fanning quoted Holloway as concluding, "I guess they liked me in it because they then cast me in *Blonde Venus* with Marlene Dietrich. I played this student walking through the woods and I find Marlene in the nude taking a bath. I wrote my mother about it and she wanted to know what they were doing to me out here."

However, Holloway's image could not have been more wholesome when he began a forty-year-long association with Walt Disney in 1942. Evidently, Disney was an admirer of the actor and wanted him for the studio's breakthrough first feature, *Snow White and the Seven Dwarfs*. Disney was known to designate voice talent not just for vocal quality or acting ability, but to aid in the development of the characterizations. According to a memo from 1934, Holloway was his initial choice for the voice of Sleepy, although ultimately the part went to studio musician and gagman Pinto Colvig, who performed Grumpy as well. It was not until eight years later that the actor made his vocal debut—with even his bumbling image used as an animation model—for the bumbling stork who delivers baby Dumbo.

However, it was not only Holloway's expressive inflections but the experienced actor's ability to use subtle shadings and nuances to convey any emotion that were instrumental in the creation of his extraordinary characters. While Holloway's virtuous straight-forward parts in features include a turn as (the adolescent) Flower the skunk in the 1942 *Bambi* and Roquefort the mouse for *The Aristocats* (co-starring with Zsa Zsa Gabor and Phil Harris in the 1970s release), the testament to his talent lies more in his complex, understated villains.

In *The Disney Villain*, two of Disney's famed veteran "nine old men" animators and authors Ollie Johnston and Frank Thomas directly attribute the success of *Alice in Wonderland*'s cool Cheshire Cat character to Holloway as a welcome contrast to the "all-out, wild gyrations" of the other frenetic characters. In animator Ward Kimball's estimation of the actor's dreamlike performance, "His quiet, underplayed subtleties consequently stole the show!" Thomas and Johnston also give Holloway much of the credit for envisioning Kaa in 1967's *The Jungle Book* as the magnetic and affecting villain of the final version. At first, the production team was having difficulty with casting, as eight different voices had been tested and then rejected, until an anxious Disney then personally approached him with a request to audition during a session for Winnie the Pooh.

In the role, Holloway then not only delivered Kaa's lines with an inspired menace and arrogance, but also ad-libbed dialogue that further inspired the animators. As Disney had often done before (and did on the same project with the casting of Phil Harris as Baloo), he then changed the characterization to better suit the voice and judged Holloway's Kaa so appealing that a new scene was added in the form of the snake's confrontation with George Sanders's icy tiger Shere Khan. However, the scene stealer in the film is probably Kaa's "Trust in Me." Ironically, the composers, the Sherman brothers, had originally created the song (presumably with a very different slant) for *Mary Poppins*, but it was reworked to lure Mowgli to the hypnotic snake. Inspired by Holloway's "sandpaper voice" the composers were quoted to explain that they created a "weaving kind of melody with a thousand sibilant sounds" for Holloway to slither his tongue around as Kaa.

But even with such major characterizations in feature films and the occasional live-action television parts on shows like *The Life of Riley* program of the early 1960s, Holloway's all-time favorite part remained Disney's beloved Winnie the Pooh. While he may have not been an obvious choice, it is now difficult to imagine any other voice to convey the childlike innocence of A. A. Milne's "bear of very little brain." There are only four productions starring Holloway: 1966's *Winnie the Pooh and the Honey Tree*, 1968's *Winnie the Pooh and the Blustery Day*, and 1974's *Winnie the Pooh and Tigger Too* (which were combined with new animation to make 1977's feature, *The Many Adventures of Winnie the Pooh*). While subsequent Pooh projects have featured Hal Smith and Jim Cummings as the title character, of course, it was Holloway who set the standard.

By his later years, the actor had won numerous awards and achieved gold records for several children's albums and had become an avid collector of contemporary art. Although he had retired from the business in the 1970s, aside from the occasional children's theatrical production, he counted among his fans Amy Carter, who reportedly once asked that her father, President Jimmy Carter, call to wish the actor a happy birthday. Honored on October 22, 1991, as a Disney legend, the eighty-seven-year-old Holloway passed away a little more than a year later on November 22, 1992, at Good Samaritan Hospital in Los Angeles. With a Cedartown street named for him, a bronze marker in front of his birthplace, and a local museum exhibit devoted to his achievements, Cedartown's favorite son is memorialized, if not in his hometown, then in his many animated classics for generations of future fans to come.

CREDITS

Alice in Wonderland (1951) . . . . Cheshire Cat
Aristocats, The (1970) . . . . Roquefort
Bambi (1942) . . . . Flower (adolescent)

Ben and Me (1953) . . . . Amos Mouse
Christmas at Walt Disney World (1978) TV (voice) . . . . Sleeping Beauty Narrator
Dumbo (1941) . . . . Mr. Stork
Goliath II (1959) . . . . Narrator
Jungle Book, The (1967) . . . . Kaa
Lambert the Sheepish Lion (1952) . . . . Narrator/Mr. Stork
Linus the Lionhearted (1964) TV Series (voice) . . . . Sugar Bear/Lovable Yours Truly
Little House, The (1952) . . . . Narrator
Make Mine Music (1946) . . . . Narrator (Peter and the Wolf)
Many Adventures of Winnie the Pooh, The (1977) . . . . Winnie the Pooh
Mickey and the Beanstalk (1947) . . . . Narrator
Pelican and the Snipe, The (1944)
Peter and the Wolf (1946) . . . . Narrator
Speaking of Animals, No. Y7-1: Dog Crazy (1947) . . . . Dog Owner
Susie the Little Blue Coupe (1952) . . . . Narrator
Three Caballeros, The (1945) . . . . Narrator for "The Cold-Blooded Penguin"/Professor Holloway
Tukiki and His Search for a Merry Christmas (1979) . . . . North Wind
Winnie the Pooh and the Blustery Day (1968) . . . . Winnie the Pooh
Winnie the Pooh and the Honey Tree (1966) . . . . Winnie the Pooh
Winnie the Pooh and Tigger Too! (1974) . . . . Winnie the Pooh

MIKE JUDGE

When Mike Judge finished his first Beavis and Butt-head film, *Frog Baseball*, he deemed it "the stupidest piece of junk [he] ever made." After screening the film for his friends and family, he said the reaction ranged from mild revulsion to amused disgust. At times, Judge has been so unsure of his work that he once considered leaving his name off the credits to spare his mother and older family members the embarrassment. But rarely has success so stunningly defied expectations as it has for the self-taught animator. By 1998, he was ranked number sixteen on the *Forbes* list of richest entertainers, with an estimated income of $53 million. This came as a most welcome surprise for Judge, who at the age of thirty believed his wife might have to support him for the rest of his life. Certainly, the worldwide sales of books, movies, and subsequent television shows like *King of the Hill* will ensure his place on the list for years to come.

Still seeming too quiet and self-effacing to have a celebrity-sized ego, the son of an archaeology professor and a school librarian was born in Guayaquil, Ecuador. The family moved several times for his father's job, eventually settling in Albuquerque, New Mexico. Naming his earliest cartoon influences as old Warner Bros. shorts which aired on a children's show hosted by local celebrity "Captain Billy," Judge's skewed sense of humor may have been influenced by how his first hero met his untimely end. "Captain Billy was caught fooling around with some guy's wife and the guy shot him. It was in the news and I remember my mom trying to sugar-coat it by telling me something like, 'Captain Billy was just hugging her to say she'd done a good job and her husband came in.'"

No doubt it was about this time he was first exposed to Butt-head's spiritual father, Goofus, of "Goofus and Gallant" from the children's magazine *Highlights.* "Of course, all the kids like Goofus. It was such a bizarre little comic strip because then, at least, Goofus seemed to always have this angry look on his face and he seemed to do things wrong just for the sake of doing things wrong. Of course, when my brother and I were real little we used to play Goofus and Gallant, and both of us would always want to be Goofus."

Ironically, the younger Judge was someone Beavis and Butt-head would have written off as a "wuss." An animal lover and excellent student who also played in the school orchestra, he felt like a nerd who did not belong in any of the cliques, not even the "weirdo crowd." Whatever measure of popularity he had was earned by imitating the people who later popped into his cartoon landscapes, particularly his teachers. While his band director was the model for Principal McVicker, Tom Anderson and Hank Hill were based on a conglomeration of retired military men, some of whom were on his paper route. Even in naming his characters he says, "There was actually a guy named Neil Butt in junior high and he had a brother, Mike Butt. At roll call, it never failed. . . . I don't know how many hundreds of days, but even at the end of the last semester the teacher would go Armstrong . . . Bakka . . . *Butt*. And some-body would always laugh every day. It didn't matter if they'd heard it a hun-dred times." "Beavis" was a popular football player, the antithesis of his namesake, but Judge "just liked the name Beavis."

After surviving the public school bullies who regularly robbed and harassed him, then the rigors of a Catholic high school, Judge majored in physics at the University of California at San Diego. Graduating with a B.A., he was hired to work for a Dilbertesque government contractor which made weapons systems for F-18 jets. A conscientious objector, he soon quit to become a full-time musician and toured the country for a year as a blues bassist. In 1989, after Judge married his college sweetheart, Francesa Morroco, he realized that he had to get serious about his career. A vision of playing dives until he was sixty and "being around drunk people all the time" persuaded him to attend graduate school at the University of Texas, Dallas, with the intention of possibly teaching math at a community college.

A big fan of Monty Python and Second City, Judge vaguely wanted to do "something in comedy and filmmaking." By chance, he attended an animation festival in Dallas and left obsessed with the need to make an animated film. He checked out a how-to book from the library and bought an old Bolex 16-mm camera. Having no real expectations beyond making his friends laugh, Judge drew on his work experiences to create *Office Space*, a character study of Milton, a disgruntled engineer. When he picked up the processed film, he was encouraged by the laughter of his first fans, the developers at the film lab, and it made him wonder if there was a wider market for his sense of humor. After he finished a second film, *Huh?* he mailed tape copies to every suitable festival and TV show, not really anticipating any response. Comedy Central eventually licensed *Office Space*; the Sick and Twisted Animation Festival wanted *Huh?* and his third film, *The Honkey Problem*, but his biggest success was yet to come.

The unlikely breakthrough happened at the end of 1991, when Judge filmed the two "bastard children of the sexual revolution," as he christened them in an online interview. As in all his other cartoons, it was a one-man production: writing the script, doing all the voices, drawing the animation, and even com-posing and performing the theme song. Like his previous efforts, Beavis and Butt-head developed from life experience—this time as a synthesis of the cre-ator's adolescence and his relationship with his brother. He discovered an early version of Butt-head in one of his old notebooks. "I was trying to draw a guy I went to high school with. It didn't really look like him, but I thought it was funny, so I kept drawing it like that." His sidekick came about as yet another failed attempt to draw the same classmate.

Next, it was time to record the voices. Judge said he found that Butt-head was comparatively easy, as Judge's natural voice sounds like a soft-spoken, slightly higher-pitched version. For greater authenticity, he simulated talking through Butt-head's braces by curling his lip back when he did the character. Beavis's voice was scratchy enough to hurt his throat, but the distinctive laugh was one remembered from a high-school calculus classmate who always bit his lip, then went "*Heh, Heh.*"

Judge recalled, "Normally I'd record the voice on a cassette in my own house when no one was around. With this one, I actually went to a guy who had a little studio set up. Actually, I wouldn't call it a studio. It was a room in an office building. Sitting on a desk he had a reel-to-reel eight track, and I went in there and was just going '*Huh-Huh-Huh-Huh.*' I wanted a scary, dumb, embarrassing moronic laugh; so I just conjured it up on the spot. I recorded the theme music and the voices all in about two hours, because I remembered I had to come home for the baby-sitter."

Although Judge had promised the piece to Spike and Mike, he realized that the cartoon was perfect for MTV's 1991 animation anthology *Liquid Television*. He then cold-called MTV, only to be rejected by ultra-cool "real snotty interns" who gave him the runaround. Eventually, talent won out, and *Liquid Television*'s production company saw and wanted all of his work. However, the Beavis and Butt-head short, *Frog Baseball*, was an unprecedented hit at the MTV focus group, with one test member refusing to leave until he had a copy of the tape for himself. MTV vice president Abby Terkule wasted no time in setting up a meeting to order thirty-five more *Beavis and Butt-head*s.

Stunned by the decision, its novice creator panicked, assuming it was still going to be a one-man production, and sat at the meeting worrying, "I can't even think of one more thing these guys could do." Well, MTV had some definite ideas. Their creative, if not commercial, vision was that the two idiot-savants be nothing more than animated VJs. Judge ultimately agreed to a compromise: a story would be interwoven with the music video segments. In fact, Judge quickly found out that the video segments turned out to be a blessing in disguise, as they cut down substantially on the necessary scripting and animation work.

When the show went into production, Judge's segment producer was assigned to choose the best and the worst videos MTV had to offer, then forward them to Judge for the final selection. Judge watched the tapes and picked out a few of his own. Then, while they ran, he improvised the commentary in real time, usually without help from writers. To further save time, the character animation for the video segments was continually recycled stock shots. Although Judge was not that enthused with doing the segments at the time, he said after the show ended production in 1997, he could watch them with a new appreciation. "When I haven't seen the show in a while and I watch it on TV, it's usually the video stuff that makes me laugh."

Judge's vocal versatility enabled him to perform all the main male characters (except Stewart and Todd, in later shows), though a few gave him trouble. "Originally, I wanted to get someone else to do Beavis. I didn't like to do it and didn't want to do it, but we had no budget and no resources, so I couldn't go out and find anyone. I just did the voice and ended up really liking it. Now I'd say that Beavis is probably my favorite." As for a least favorite character, his choice is obvious. "I don't like doing [Coach] Buzzcut. The only way to sound like him is to yell. Sometimes the story doesn't call for yelling and I have to yell anyway. It's a hard one to pull off."

Although AC/DC has commented that it was "cool" that Butt-head has been their best advertising ever, Judge does not think the show increased the sales of the featured bands. "People don't buy a record because Beavis and Butt-head say they're good; I think successful bands just got exposure on the show. On the other hand, there are bands like Bon Jovi that I've had Beavis and Butt-head rail on, and it hasn't affected their success. . . . It's funny because there's all these 'rock majesty–type' videos on MTV which are pretentious or artsy, and the fact is that the audience are guys like Beavis and Butt-head just sitting there going '*Huh, Huh, Huh, Huh*. You can see her boobs.' We had a few complain, but MTV was pretty good about letting us say what we wanted. I don't know if it's really ruined any bands, though some people bring up Winger."

Never conceived as commercial programming, Judge sees *Beavis and Butt-head* as a disgusted reaction to dumb, but safe, politically correct television. He dismissed the hand-wringing essays at the time about the show signaling the downfall of Western civilization, saying, "Some people just don't understand satire. Most people who like the show are fairly smart and like it for the right reasons. I get a lot of letters from women in their fifties who have teenagers and they see exaggerated versions of their sons in it. Many of the high and mighty who claim to be above such vulgarity will hear that [revered film director] Bernardo Bertolucci said he is a fan, or Patrick Stewart [who had guest starred as an animated Captain Picard] or David Letterman [who voiced Butt-head's father in the movie *Beavis and Butt-head Do America*]; then they'll start to change their opinion."

Certainly, adult-oriented animators like Ralph Bakshi should have disproved it long ago, but many parents had wrongly assumed all cartoons are meant as children's programming; and many of the show's image problems stemmed from that fact. Judge explains, "*Beavis and Butt-head* definitely was not meant for kids—not by me or anyone at the network." As a father of two daughters, Judge was greatly saddened by the 1993 incident in which the mother of a five-year-old Ohio boy claimed her son was imitating Beavis when he set a fire which killed his younger sister. Although the home was not wired for cable television and the mother had reportedly left her children unsupervised, *Beavis and Butt-head* became the new scapegoat of the political Right. In a particularly surreal moment, in a congressional hearing on violence, even U.S. Senator Ernest Hollings was compelled to publicly denounce the threat that, as he deftly put it, "Buffcoat and Beaver" represented.

Noting that kids have been playing with fire long before television was invented, Judge contends that it is a natural tendency to grasp for someone or something to blame when faced with a situation that traumatic. He pointed out that parents who object to any of MTV's programming can lock-out the channel or opt not to order cable at all. He likens lack of parental supervision to buying a copy of *Hustler* and "leaving it on the coffee table for the kids to read, then complaining to the publisher." However, in *Beavis and Butt-head's* case, MTV eventually caved in to pressure from watchdog groups, adding a disclaimer, moving the time slot to a much later hour, and scrapping all references to fire. Although Judge approved of the decisions, he was shocked to learn MTV had also censored the fire references by erasing them from the *master tapes*. "I couldn't believe it. The only place the shows exist in their original form is on tapes in people's houses."

Despite the controversy, *Beavis and Butt-head* garnered surprisingly favorable reviews from conservative publications like the *National Review*, the *New York Times*, and *Time* magazine. Judge is proudest of the third and subsequent season's beginning with Beavis's sugar-fueled frenzy of "The Great Cornholio." He debunks the elaborate theories many fans have had on the meaning of the Cornholio character. "That is probably one of my favorites just because we did that without a script. We needed an extra show to fill out the season and we were a script short, so Kris Brown, the head writer, and I just kind of wrote it as I was recording it. There is no meaning to what Beavis is actually saying. I figure he's just regurgitating things he has heard. It's kind of the stuff I used to do to annoy my sister and brother when I was a kid."

In 1996, ignoring the naysayers in the movie industry who did not see the potential of adult-oriented animation, Paramount approached Judge for a movie version. At the time, Judge was characteristically sardonic. "The original joke was these two had absolutely no business on television, and they certainly don't belong on a movie screen at eight dollars a throw." But the studio was grimly determined to reach the market before the show's popularity peaked, and production was pushed ahead as quickly as humanly possible. The voice recordings were being done practically the minute those sections of the script were written, and Judge had sold *King of the Hill* to Fox, all while the *Beavis and Butt-head* television series was still in production—Judge had long since reached the burnout point and was *literally* dreaming in cartoons. With the constant commuting between production centers of New York, London, Los Angeles, and back to Austin, it was obvious what had to go. In November of 1997, after 220 episodes, MTV aired the final installment of the series, entitled "Beavis and Butt-head Are Dead."

But, of course, they were not. The movie, *Beavis and Butt-head Do America*, ensured their survival when it opened a month later to good reviews and broke the record for December releases to that point. But, most importantly, it finally made Judge a millionaire. Originally forced to sign over the television rights to MTV in a fairly standard contract, Judge had to settle for the fame while MTV owned the fortune. Although he figured the show would initially hit big, quickly peak, and die, Judge did have the foresight to reserve the right to negotiate a percentage of the movie; and he certainly laughed last the day the film premiered. The film made the entertainment industry take notice by earning a domestic gross more than sixty times the production cost. Since then, there have been rumors about a sequel—recent market research in 2002 has proved that there is still an interest in a *Beavis and Butt-head* revival— but Judge has been hesitant, stating that he has not had the two and a half years to produce the sequel, and he is unwilling to hand his creations over to someone else.

Since 1998, Judge has teamed up with Greg Daniels of *The Simpsons* to create "the alternative Andy Griffith," Hank Hill. Although Judge believes he will never create pop-culture icons on the level of his first success, one of the pleasures that *King of the Hill* affords is allowing him to play Hank, a character, he admits, that is closest to his own personality. When Fox approached him looking for "the next Homer Simpson," Judge looked back through his sketchbooks. Inspired by his childhood neighbors, so-called "Bubba" types, who used to get together on Saturday mornings to compare power tools, he then created a socially conservative, "Ross Perot"–type family who is firmly grounded in Arlen (think Garland), Texas, reality. Staying close to his material, Judge still spends much of his time working in his Austin studio and staying in touch with Los Angeles via videolink.

Unlike his earlier solo productions, *King of the Hill* is definitely an ensemble show. Judge is one of more than eighty people involved in its creation and voices only two of the main characters—Hank and Boomhauer. While Hank sounds reminiscent of Tom Anderson, Boomhauer was inspired by a garbled voice-mail message left by a ranting *Beavis and Butt-head* fan; Judge had to listen to the message forty times before he finally deciphered that the fan was calling simply to complain that the show did not start on its scheduled time. Beyond the regular cast (including Kathy Najimy as Peggy Hill, Pamela S. Adlon as Bobby Hill, Brittany Murphy as Luann Platter, Johnny Hardwick as Dale Gribble, and Stephen Root as Bill Dauterive), there have also been a fair number of celebrity guest stars. Although the show has featured guests who are Judge's favorites (he singles out Snoop Doggy Dog and Carl Reiner), Judge says guest celebrities are not as big a priority for him, personally, as the Fox network; he prefers to cast actors solely on who would be right for the part.

Although Judge has done some occasional work on productions other than his own, most recently cameos on the *Spykids* films, he rarely appears as an on-camera performer. He also rarely voices other animated projects because, he says, "No one thinks of me as a voice person." With a full schedule that includes his current projects (like co-founding 2003's Animation Show Festival), family, and indulging his hobby of surfing, one thing he does miss, since the studios first entered the picture, is personally drawing the characters. He laments, "I was just getting good at it when I stopped." Although the current animation is much cleaner than his initial efforts, he had dictated that there is a minimum standard of stylistic crudeness to be met. Judge is determined that his signature look continue to be "high school doodles," never sophisticated Disney-type productions in which he jokes all of the heroes look like (1970s actor) "John Davidson."

In 1999, coming full circle while making a start into live-action films, his first non-animated movie was *Office Space*. Directing a film for a major studio with high-profile actors like Jennifer Aniston was a sharp contrast to his "no budget" first animated movie also of the same name. When David Letterman asked him, in a *Lateshow* interview for the film's promotion, how live-action compares to animation, Judge sheepishly replied that, although the down side of live-action projects is "you can't erase people," it was a good experience as "the quality and quantity of people kissing my ass went way up." If he ever decides to continue in that area, it is quite possible that someday he may be known as something other than, as *Forbes* once referred to him, "the king of the pile of cartoon money."

CREDITS

51st Annual Primetime Emmy Awards, The (1999) TV . . . . Himself
Airheads (1994) . . . . Beavis/Butt-head
Austin Powers: International Man of Mystery (1997) (uncredited) . . . . Beavis/Butt-head
Beavis and Butt-head (1993) TV Series . . . . Beavis/Butt-head/Tom Anderson/David Van Driessen/
    Bradley Buzzcut/Principal McVicker/Mr. Stevenson(1993–1997)/The Great Cornholio (1994–1997)
Beavis and Butt-head Do America (1996) . . . . Beavis/Butt-head/Tom Anderson/Mr. Van
    Driessen/Principal McVicker
Beavis and Butt-head Do Christmas (1995) TV . . . . Beavis/Butt-head/Tom Anderson/David Van
    Driessen/Mr. Stevenson/Burger World Manager/Principal McVicker/Bradley Buzzcut/Maxi-Mart
    Owner
Frog Baseball (1992) . . . . Beavis/Butt-head
Inbred Jed (1991) . . . . Inbred Jed
King of the Hill (1997) TV Series . . . . Henry "Hank" Rutherford Hill/Jeff Boomhauer/Additional
    Voices
Mene Tekel (1997) . . . . Beavis/Butt-head
MTV Video Music Awards 1992 (1992) TV . . . . Beavis/Butt-head
Office Space (1991) . . . . Milton/Others
South Park: Bigger, Longer, & Uncut (1999) . . . . Kenny McCormick saying Goodbye

TOM KENNY

As the voice of SpongeBob Squarepants, Tom Kenny now lives a life of his childhood fantasies from a time when he and his brother "lived and breathed" cartoons. He was obsessed with Bugs Bunny, Daffy Duck, Rocky and Bullwinkle, and what he jokingly calls Hanna-Barbera's "total con-man characters" in the form of Yogi Bear, the picnic basket thief; Snagglepuss, the out-of-work actor looking for a free meal, and Top Cat, who lives "in an alley with his friends running from the cops," which may have been questionable role models for more impressionable viewers. But Kenny's journey into his world of "dumb sweet yellow characters" began as a "total obsession" with another nautical cartoon icon—Popeye the sailor.

Aware at a very early age that there were actual people making cartoons, Kenny and his brother read the jackets of the cartoon records to see the pictures and biographies of Hanna-Barbera's Don Messick and Daws Butler. Claiming that he would discuss different voice actors the way other kids analyze baseball players, for his fifth-grade writing assignment to profile a famous American, Kenny chose legendary Warner Bros. cartoon director Chuck Jones. This was in part because Jones was responsible for the short *One Froggy Evening*, starring Michigan J. Frog—the singing top-hatted character that has since become the icon for the Warner Bros. television network. For Kenny, the cartoon was and remains "profound"; he explains, "It's life and aging and death and everything right in a nutshell."

Contrary to expectations, the comedian denied being the class clown, claiming he was much too shy and introverted to ever "have the balls to do it [him]self." However, he was not too shy to supply material for others. One of the "clowns" was classmate/future stand-up comedian Bobcat Goldthwait. Their friendship continued beyond high school when the two even spent a summer as seasonal help playing monsters in a haunted house for the local carnival, then dabbling in the local bands scene, Kenny forming a group called the Tearjerkers.

Then inspired by comedians like Woody Allen, Richard Pryor, George Carlin, and Rodney Dangerfield, Kenny tried his hand at sketch comedy with the Generic Comics—recalling that the group basically rehashed material that they saw on SCTV the week before. Still, he found the local scene easy to conquer for both rock and comedy; finding an opportunity to perform was fairly effortless. "The line between spectator and participant was pretty easy to break; basically all you had to do was do it." And, in the mid-1980s, his circle of friends gained a reputation as "the court jesters of the local punk rock scene."

By the time Kenny turned eighteen, he was already tired of bad day jobs and, although the band had opened for popular 1980s acts such as the Go-Gos and Nick Lowe, he saw little future in the Tearjerkers. Telling his father that he was going to take a year off to "find" himself, Kenny headed to Boston to try stand-up comedy at the local clubs. He had not been in Boston very long when Goldthwait offered him the opportunity to join him in San Francisco as his opening act. Kenny welcomed the more unconventional environment and said he quickly became a headliner in his own right. More importantly, after gaining experience and exposure in many clubs all over the country and the West Coast, Kenny's true ambitions were about to be realized. At the time he had already been dubbed the "human cartoon" because watching his act "was like watching a cartoon come to life," and, in 1991, Hanna-Barbera's Kris Zimmerman and Nickelodeon's Mary Harrington made it official. After a performance at a Santa Monica club, they asked if he had ever considered doing cartoons. Kenny was dumbfounded, "I just looked at them and said, 'Only every day of my life have I wanted to do cartoons!'"

But on his first day, he came to the studio "nervous as a cat." Hired to play Heffer on 1993's *Rocko's Modern Life*, it suddenly dawned upon him, "Here I am doing the job that I always wanted to do and I've never really done it. I don't really know how to do it and I'm thrown in the room with people who were just great at it." Even more daunting was the sight of Charlie Adler recording his lines as the leads of Cow, Chicken, and the Red Guy for Cartoon Network's *Cow and Chicken*. "The whole show is him." Adler was conducting a conversation between three different characters and when the director asked if he would like to record the lines separately, Adler replied, "No, no, I can do [it this way.]" Kenny recalls that Adler, without skipping a beat, "just fired out this rapid-fire conversation. . . . It was his first time looking at the stuff and he just knocked it out of the park." Kenny's first reaction was, "Oh shhooooooooooot. I don't want to be here," but he bluffed his way through the first session and took confidence in the thought that he was "just as smart as the next guy."

Although he was at first unsure of his footing, the actor earned his standing during the first *Rocko* session in which he had to fill in for Adler. The producers needed him to do multiple parts and perform a song, allotting him only ten minutes in which to learn it. After accomplishing the feat, Kenny said that he felt he could stand "toe to toe" with the other actors and remained on *Rocko's Modern Life* for the entire fifty-two-episode run.

Reflecting on his work in the series, he especially enjoyed working with his co-stars, only railing against the fact that friend Carlos Alazraqui (who provided the lead voice of Rocko) lost his side job as the voice of the Taco Bell chihuahua ("Yo Quero Taco Bell") in the popular ad campaign. Kenny explains that Latino pressure groups forced the cancellation of the promotional character, citing it as an offensive stereotype. Although that had happened a few years ago, Kenny is still incensed—urging people on such matters of political correctness to "lighten up!" He then cracks, "You don't see Romanian people picketing the cereal aisle [in a Bela Lugosi accent], '*Count Chocula is unfair. It makes everyone think that we are a race of chocolate-loving vampires. Do not buy the cereal, PLEASE!*'"

The follow-up role to *Rocko's Modern Life* came courtesy of Craig McCracken, creator of the *Powerpuff Girls* (formerly entitled the hilarious, but cable unfriendly *Whoopass Girls*). Kenny was hired to replace commercial and sports announcer Ernie Anderson, who was slated to be the mayor of Townsville, but, unfortunately, had passed away right before the show started taping. Like Hank Azaria—who has explained that his many characters on *The Simpsons* began as failed impressions of other established actors, so unrecognizable that they then can become original character voices—Kenny created the voice of the "knucklehead" who calls the girls to fly into action as an eclectic mix of unsuccessful impersonations of the Wizard of Oz, Joe Flynn (of *McHale's Navy* fame), and a touch of character actress Ruth Gordon's performance from Clint Eastwood's *Every Which Way but Loose*. Kenny called his experience with the *Powerpuff Girls* a "blast," citing the voices behind the huge-eyed, Margaret Keanesque girls, (Buttercup) E. G. Daily, (Bubbles) Tara Charendoff-Strong, and (Blossom) Cathy Cavadini, as "amazing" actors.

It was not until *CatDog* that Kenny had some qualms about working for a large organization like Nickelodeon. *CatDog's* creator, Peter Hannan, former cartoonist from the Chicago alternative paper *The Reader,* had sold the show to the network, with Kenny quickly cast as Dog. Nickelodeon executives hired, then fired, a steady stream of actors who recorded the pilot as "Cat." Kenny joked that it was like being in Vietnam. "I didn't want to get too close to whoever was playing Cat because I knew he was going to get picked off." While he was impressed by some, including Kevin McDonald, an alumnus from *The Kids in the Hall,* he said, "All it takes in this business is one dopey suit to go, 'I don't get it,' and you're gone." Ultimately, Kenny recorded the pilot with ten different actors before they settled on Jim Cummings. Then the executives continued to complicate matters when they demanded not one episode a week, but five, which, Kenny recalls, "made for an incredibly insane schedule for which everybody was just knocked out," and the show suffered accordingly.

When executives realized the vast commercial potential of Kenny's next project and Nickelodeon's most popular show to date, they were justifiably motivated to make the same demands. In 1996, *SpongeBob Squarepants* began when *Rocko's Modern Life* animator Steve Hillenberg called Kenny over to his house to discuss the appeal of his cheery little sponge character before he pitched it to Nickelodeon. Hillenberg—a former marine biologist and illustrator who had been inspired by shows like Ralph Bakshi's *Mighty Mouse* and *Pee-Wee's Playhouse* to learn animation at CalArts—drew upon "all these weird little invertebrates" he liked from his former occupation. Wanting the star to have the appeal of the "innocent childlike" character that is "faced with the trials of life," he looked to Laurel and Hardy and Pee-Wee Herman for inspiration. Kenny said he was instantly amazed at the "thoroughly thought out universe" that Hillenberg had sketched on storyboards and model sheets, down to the now familiar landmarks like SpongeBob's pineapple house. When the animator finally asked what he thought of the idea, Kenny said he gushed, "It's completely stupid and insane! I love it!"

Nickelodeon was also pleased and agreed to fund the so-called *"SpongeBoy"*—with a caveat or two. After they already recorded the pilot, the legal department discovered that there was a commonly sold floor mop of the same name and the character was quickly rechristened with only a slight variation to have as little an impact as possible on the production already in progress. But less agreeable to the creative team had been the studio's request for a celebrity voice, to which Hillenberg absolutely refused. Countering that Kenny's voice had been his inspiration since his initial doodles of the character, Hillenberg argued that, by the time of the taping, Kenny already knew how to ad-lib, laugh, cry, and sing as SpongeBob. The network executives then conceded and Kenny was joined by the regular cast, Roger Bumpass (the cranky clarinet-playing Squidward), Bill Fagerbakke (the dim-witted starfish Patrick), Carolyn Lawrence (the perky squirrel Sandy), and Doug Lawrence as the tight-fisted Mr. Krabs.

Hillenberg "went to the mat" for him with Nickelodeon, and Kenny remains very grateful, saying he never gets tired of doing SpongeBob—although the part is often very draining to perform. Describing his character as "the Mayor of Munchkinland meets Elroy Jetson" who is "highly emotional, falling apart at the slightest provocation," Kenny contends that there are some days when the session "is nothing but screaming and crying for four solid hours." Almost as demanding is his braying laugh, for which Kenny explains, "We knew that we wanted an annoying, irritating laugh that would just make everybody that heard it want to strangle him; in the tradition of Pee-Wee Herman." Combining the "in-your-face" cackle of Woody Woodpecker and that of his idol Popeye, Kenny then added one last fitting element—the chatter of a dolphin calling above water.

One of the creative forces on the show (he was a writer on HBO's 1995 series *Mr. Show*), Kenny has had a definite impact beyond simply performing the voice. Having once worked for a Mr. Krabs–type at a department store, certainly Kenny's work experiences seem to be played out on many episodes written around SpongeBob's employment at the Krusty Krab fast-food emporium. Kenny expounds on his first job ever as a McDonald's employee: "I lasted a day and a half and I had seniority. That's how terrible these jobs are."

Even Kenny's physical appearance has had an influence on SpongeBob's character. Kenny said when he first made the mistake of wearing a new pair of glasses to a session, every animator immediately began drawing them on his animated alter-ego. They finally made their debut on the show as SpongeBob's jelly fishing glasses, and, certainly, collectors of the oceans of SpongeBob merchandise can continue to see Kenny's latest eyewear depicted on future items, if not on the show itself.

While many fans are usually clamoring to see their favorite voice-over artist—some of the mall signing tours and lectures have prompted newspapers to make comparisons to the excited crowds waiting for the Beatles—Kenny was surprised that the fans (more than a third are adults) of the show were less than pleased when he debuted on camera as *SpongeBob*'s host, "Patchy the Pirate." Intended to be a send-up of the local cartoon kiddie hosts, Nickelodeon was inundated by angry letters from fans who felt they were being swindled of their *SpongeBob* time. Those who do wish to see Kenny performing can always rent films like *How I Got into College* or Bobcat Goldthwait's 1992 *Shakes the Clown*, in which he portrayed Binky, a "psychotic coke-snorting" clown.

Looking back on his good fortune, Kenny marvels not only that he has been successful in his chosen career but at the caliber of the talent throughout the animation industry. "The biggest difference I found was that, even though animation was really much harder for me to break into, . . . the guys at the top that worked all of the time really were the best guys. The best musicians don't sell the most records; the funniest people don't have the sitcoms. . . . But you walk into a voice-over session and the people, guys like Jim Cummings, these guys are just drop-dead amazing."

Now an accomplished comedian and voice actor, Kenny has had a chance to share the spotlight with his childhood hero, if just by proxy. Upon visiting his local grocery store, he discovered the August 3, 2002, edition of *TV Guide* sporting a feature story entitled "The 50 Greatest Cartoons Characters of All-time." One of the four covers featured in that issue was SpongeBob being fished out of the ocean by none other than Kenny's longtime idol, Popeye. Kenny, who as a child had dressed as Popeye every Halloween and continues to be an avid collector, then felt as if "his whole crazy life had come full circle." Even his wife, Jill Talley—the accomplished comic actress whom he met on the 1990s Fox series *The Edge*—who has since forbidden him from sneaking any more *Popeye* memorabilia into an already extensive collection, certainly would be able to forgive him this one final *pièce de résistance.*

CREDITS

3-South (2002) TV Series . . . . Various Voices
Animated Adventures of Bob and Doug McKenzie, The (2003) TV Series
Cartoon Cartoon Fridays (2000) TV Series . . . . Mayor/Lenny Baxter
CatDog (1998) TV Series . . . . Dog/Cliff
CatDog: The Great Parent Mystery (2001) TV . . . . Dog/Cliff
Cow and Chicken (1997) TV Series . . . . Additional Voices
Crank Yankers (2002) TV Series (voice) . . . . Larson Grier (2003)
Dave the Barbarian (2004) TV Series . . . . Shadow Official
Dexter's Laboratory (1996) TV Series . . . . Valhallan
Dilbert (1999) TV Series . . . . Asok/Ratbert
Dragon Ball Z (1996) TV Series . . . . Additional Voices
Duck Dodgers (2003) TV Series . . . . Additional Voices
Dumb and Dumber (1995) TV Series . . . . Weenie
Fairly OddParents, The (2001) TV Series . . . . Cupid
Fairly OddParents: Abra-catastrophe, The (2003) TV . . . . Cupid/Muffin Man/Others
First 13th Annual Fancy Anvil Awards Show Program Special Live in Stereo, The (2002) TV
   (uncredited) . . . . Himself/Professor Utonium
Flintstones: On the Rocks, The (2001) TV . . . . Bellboy/Mammoth Vendor/Bed Monkey/Bowling
   Announcer
Futurama (1999) TV Series . . . . Yancy Fry Jr./"That Guy"/Joey Mousepad/Adlai/Abner Doubledeal
Game Over (2004) TV Series . . . . Arthur/Various Voices
Godzilla: The Series (1998) TV Series . . . . N.I.G.E.L.
Harvey Birdman, Attorney at Law (2001) TV Series . . . . Boo Boo Bear
I Am Weasel (1999) TV Series . . . . Additional Voices
Johnny Bravo (1997) TV Series . . . . Carl Chryniszzswics (1999–2001)
Lilo & Stitch: The Series (2003) . . . . Various Voices
Looney Tunes: Reality Check (2003) Video . . . . Emeril
Looney Tunes: Stranger Than Fiction (2003) Video . . . . Vampire Tweety Bird/Stone Cold
   Duck/Emeril/ Tech Support Narrator
Mission Hill (1999) TV Series . . . . Wally
Mummy: The Animated Series, The (2001) TV Series . . . . Jonathan
Orange County (2002) (uncredited) . . . . SpongeBob SquarePants/Gary
Powerpuff Girls, The (1998) TV Series . . . . Narrator/Mayor/Mitch Mitchelson/Additional Voices
Powerpuff Girls, The (2002) . . . . Mayor/Narrator/Mitch Mitchelson/Snake/Li'l Arturo
Rocko's Modern Life (1993) TV Series . . . . Heffer Wolfe/Mr. Smitty/Peaches (1993–1996)
Samurai Jack (2001) TV Series . . . . Additional Voices
SpongeBob SquarePants (1999) TV Series . . . . SpongeBob SquarePants/Gary/Mr. SquarePants/
   Narrator/Patchy the Pirate
SpongeBob SquarePants Movie (2004) . . . . SpongeBob SquarePants
Stripperella (2003) TV Series . . . . Various Voices
Xiaolin Showdown (2003) TV Series . . . . Raimundo

JOHN KRICFALUSI

In the late 1980s, the Nickelodeon cable channel was conceived by parent company Viacom to provide quality children's programming. Its stated mission at the time of its inception was that the network would provide material that was suitable for kids, their parents, and even "nervous PTA members." It is ironic, then, that one of its first successful original cartoon series became much more than the simple entertainment for which the network's executives may have originally bargained. Through John Kricfalusi's subversive, scatological, and absurdist classic *Ren & Stimpy*, he and his company Spumco almost single-handedly attempted to bring the art form of animation back from the brink of creative oblivion and to resurrect the artist-run production system similar to that which created the classic American cartoons from the First Golden Age of Animation.

Who better to take up that challenge than Kricfalusi (alias John K.), who has spent much of his life watching, studying, dissecting, and, finally, creating animation? After spending an early childhood in Germany as an army brat, he and his family moved back to Ottawa, Canada, where the seven-year-old "wasted his youth watching and drawing cartoons." In the Kricfalusi household, the viewing of *Quick Draw McGraw* and *Huckleberry Hound* and other Hanna-Barbera productions was not a mindless activity, but a daily event—complete with a special Huckleberry Hound cereal bowl that he made his mom wash so he could properly perform the ritual.

Certainly, by age eleven, when he was already drawing cartoons and (unsuccessfully) mailing off movie ideas to Disney, his career path seemed determined. Despite the fact that he is considered by many in his field as something of a genius, he jokes that he failed art class every year in high school, but was eventually enrolled in animation classes at Ontario's Sheridan College. Although the school is well respected in the animation industry, Kricfalusi, who has some harsh assessments of animation training programs in general, lamented the fact that Sheridan's emphasis was on "really basic technical things. How to draw? No. How to act? No. How to compose? No. No animation skills do you learn in animation school." However, it was at this time that a local resident in the form of local movie buff Reg Hart introduced Kricfalusi to classic MGM and Warner Bros. cartoons. Kricfalusi described his enlightenment as "the wildest experience I ever felt, like taking acid or something." No doubt wanting to have a chance to produce that level of work, he decided to leave school for a brilliant career in Hollywood.

During the marketing blitz of the 1980s, he quickly became disillusioned with studios stuck in what he calls the "Dung Age" of animation. He spent much of the '80s working his way through a series of cartoon mills, noting—not quite tongue-in-cheek—that many of his talented co-workers became depressed to the point of alcoholism at having to squander their talents on programs that were, basically, half-hour commercials. He worked at many of these studios, singling out the now defunct Filmation for his choice as "the worst animation studio in history." (One of the animators justified his time there by calling the house he bought with the profits he made on 1983's

He-Man and the Masters of the Universe "Casa de He-Man.") There Kricfalusi was hired to "ruin" many of his childhood favorite cartoon characters, such as Tom and Jerry and Droopy, which the studios wanted to "revive" for contemporary audiences. On the subject, he noted sardonically in 1995, "I hate to use the word 'revive.' Whenever they 'revive' or 'revile' an old character—bring one back from the grave—they always take what you liked about it and remove it. They take out the ingredients that made it successful in first place. So, it completely stuns me. . . . Why not just invent a new character? Why take an old one and then make him different from what we liked about him in the first place?"

However, during the time he and his animator friends spent in "cartoon purgatory" they were able to ponder at length what was wrong with the industry and brainstorm their own solutions in the form of radically original characters such as Ren and Stimpy, Jimmy the Idiot Boy, and George Liquor, and they made presentation after presentation for studios and networks throughout the 1980s without much success. Only after being further "tortured" on fare like *Richie Rich, Hero High,* and *Laverne and Shirley in the Army,* and some slightly more enjoyable experiences with the 1987 Ralph Bakshi revival of Mighty Mouse, did he and his equally disenfranchised artists—Lynne Naylor, Jim Smith, and Bob Camp—form the Spumco studio, whose primary mission was to give control of the cartoons back to the cartoonists.

Their first break came in 1990 when Kricfalusi showed the model sheets for *Ren & Stimpy* and *Jimmy the Idiot Boy* to Vanessa Coffey, then Nickelodeon's vice president of Animation. Coffey, who also had been underwhelmed with the popular animation of the 1980s, was impressed with originality and audacity of *Ren & Stimpy.* He was then flown to New York to pitch it to Nickelodeon executives, where, as is the custom of many venerable animators including Walt Disney, Kricfalusi not only described his story to the executives but exuberantly acted out all the parts in the would-be show. Even though Coffey recalls the unabashed performance scared them half to death, Nickelodeon's president Gerry Laybourne offered him a deal on both series. Kricfalusi said that Laybourne especially liked Jimmy. However, like *Simpson's* creator Matt Groening, who sold the rights to *The Simpsons* rather than give up his copyright to his "Life in Hell" characters, Kricfalusi choose to hold onto the copyright to Jimmy and let them have Ren & Stimpy instead. So began the relationship on a good note—albeit, however fleeting.

The new entrepreneurs then had to build the Los Angeles Spumco studio from the ground up and hire talent, including the voices for the original characters. Kricfalusi already had a concept of Ren's voice from the time of his creation when he was employed as an in-betweener at (commercial studio) Calico Creations. "I just used to do this weird Chihuahua drawing and I think somebody suggested to me, 'Why, don't you use Peter Lorre's voice for him?'" By the time the series was finally in production, he had yet to find the Kirk Douglas–type "intensity," "insanity," and "fierce drive" for Ren and ended up voicing the character himself—all this despite his assertion that he is "no voice actor, by any stretch of the imagination," to the point that he claims, "I can't stand to listen to my voice, even on the answering machine."

Kricfalusi was already familiar with the man who would be Stimpy, Billy West, from Kricfalusi's work as producer on the 1988 remake of the *Beany and Cecil Show*. At the time, he was involved in finding voice actors for the (Bob) Clampett family, which was resurrecting the legendary animator's successful program of the 1960s. Although Kricfalusi was impressed with the audition of veteran voice actors like John Stephenson (best known as Mr. Slate on *The Flintstones* and Dr. Benton Quest of *Jonny Quest*), he credits the Clampett family for discovering West. "They played me a tape of him on the radio doing all these different voices and I thought, "Well, that's just great. Let's get him out here." West did the audition and Kricfalusi was "sold on him instantly." He remembers telling the Clampetts, "'Even if he's not one of the star characters, we've got to use this guy. He's really, really talented.'" Kricfalusi heard West's Larry Fine impersonation and "just fell off [his] chair laughing." "I always loved *The Three Stooges* and Larry, of all of them! It's the last one you would think to mimic. . . . I always loved Larry, so I kept trying to find a character in *Beany and Cecil* to use that voice."

However, Kricfalusi says that although he had previously recorded West doing a Fine-inspired voice for an unfinished episode of *Beany and Cecil*, West did not come up with the idea to incorporate the Fine impersonation into the voice of Stimpy. Kricfalusi says that for the *Ren & Stimpy* pilot he "thought of Billy instantly" and then asked West to come up with some voices for Stimpy, specifying that it not be clichéd: "One thing I didn't want was just a stock stupid character voice, because every time you have a big dumb character, it's [imitating the Warner Bros. cartoon caricature of Lennie from *The Grapes of Wrath*, voiced by Stan Freberg], *'Which way did he go, George? Which way did he go?'*"

"So, we played around with a few things, and finally, I said, 'Why don't you try that Larry Fine thing,' thinking that Nickelodeon would instantly reject it, which they did. I thought, 'This is not what I thought of when I first thought about Stimpy.' That is such a weird voice to come out of that, but we got used to it. . . . He only had two lines in the pilot and then, when we started the series, Nickelodeon wanted another Ren, even though I did the Ren in the pilot." Kricfalusi contends that, contrary to what had been said in the popular media of the time, initially, "There was never any consideration of Billy doing Ren."

The show successfully premiered in August of 1991 and quickly became the highest rated show in cable history up to that point. According to Kricfalusi, while the network outwardly reveled in its first success, the executives secretly "hated" the show. One of the problems might have been that they had envisioned children as the target market and had reserved approval of every stage of the process from the initial treatment, outline, and storyboard up to the actual production. But even though the network quickly found that the show was a hit with college students and adults, they still assigned two story editors to make notes to tone down the gross humor, nonsequiturs, and surreal elements that attracted in much of the older audience. After less than two years of production, the relations between Nickelodeon and Spumco became so strained that, amid accusations of missed deadlines and production cost overruns, Nickelodeon took over his brainchild and, according to Kricfalusi, "dulled it down by degrees." He says that he unsuccessfully tried to make amends by offering concessions such as reducing costs by using more limited animation, but ultimately concludes he was surprised that the relationship lasted as long as it did.

Still, in detailing his thoughts on the industry, Kricfalusi has been unapologetically candid—writing many articles in various animation magazines in which he has detailed some of the issues he has encountered by years of experience working for the various animation studios. One reoccurring theme of these articles has been his concern that the control of the medium sometimes rests with those who may not necessarily understand or care about animation.

He is not alone in deploring that with the current system of production, there are too many people between the artist and the audience, maintaining that "getting the product from the creator to the audience takes four hundred steps," suffering some mid-level employees working in the animation field not because they have any enthusiasm for the subject, but because they view it as a stepping-stone into live-action. Animation, Kricfalusi has emphatically stated, should be left to the artists.

He has been quoted many times on the pitfalls faced by writers in the animation field, citing the voice tracks for classic animation done at Disney and Warner Bros., which were created not by writers per se, but "by sharing the storyboard—not a script—with the actors." Kricfalusi stated in 2003 to

Animation World Magazine, "There are difficulties that writers who are not artists face." He then explains, "Not every artist is a writer. Not every musician is a writer, but would you want somebody to write a symphony who wasn't a musician? Would you want somebody to write a science book who didn't know science? You write what you know. So why would you come into the animation business not able to draw and all of a sudden you want to tell all the people who do know how the stuff works and what to do?"

Of course, the script is integral with the performances of the voice actors. Even in composing the lines of actual dialogue, Kricfalusi warns that the writer must be aware that the writing done for cartoons may be difficult for an actor who is expected to perform with minimal rehearsal time. "You've got to remember that that kind of writing is not natural. This is . . . *a really* important point. If you don't have natural lyrical flowing dialogue that's easy to read, it doesn't matter how good an actor is, he'll stumble over it. And I learned that the hard way. Write a line that when you read it looks good, then you get some clever words in it or something—nine syllables in one of the words and you're congratulating yourself. But then you find out the actor can't read it. He just keeps stumbling over it. It doesn't have rhythm to it. You've got to stop writing like that. Well, they don't stop writing like that in cartoons. They continue to write like that and that makes the acting even worse; even if you are a good actor."

Although Kricfalusi has had the highest regard for actors such as Billy West, he is pessimistic that the voice-over field will be able to recapture the "golden age of cartoon voices" and produce luminaries such as his personal favorites, Mel Blanc and Daws Butler. "There was a great training ground in the '30s and '40s radio [and] that doesn't exist anymore. Every day, it was hours and hours and hours of dramatic acting on the radio. This was an art form that was completely sound. . . . People's ears are very acute if you are not looking at any picture—if you are not distracted by cameras and camera angles and dramatic lighting, you are just going to listen to the voices and those voices are going to get really good."

In lieu of a strong theatrical, vaudevillian, or radio background, Kricfalusi is concerned that contemporary and upcoming voice actors are only listening to Daws Butler or Mel Blanc to copy particular inflections that they created for specific characters. "Doing a voice isn't the same thing as acting in character. Everybody in Saturday morning cartoons, that I'm aware of, is doing a voice. Even *The Simpsons,* they're all doing voices. Mel Blanc didn't do voices; he acted the voice. The voice came as part of it. He happened to have a great sounding voice that could . . . make it sound like different characters, not only in their inflections, but in the vocal quality."

One of the greatest problems he sees are the studios who want to cash in on the interest in animation, but recently have gone about it by adapting animated programs for live-action film. He calls it "a shame" because the continuing interest proves how much the audience loves cartoons. "But never would anybody in power today think, for a second, 'Well, maybe we should discover some new cartoonist who can create some new cartoons that will make us a fortune.' Instead, they hire live-action people who say, 'Watch some of these old Tex Avery cartoons and steal everything you can and we'll put $60 million into this for ya,' instead of saying, 'For $15 million, we'll go find a new Tex Avery.'" That being said, this did not stop Kricfalusi from renting a bus for the day to take the Spumco staff in 1994 to see the first major cartoon live-action adaptation, *The Flintstones* movie. Thinking it was going to be the worst movie of all time, he concluded dryly, "It wasn't quite; Spielberg has made other movies, too."

It is not that he does not see the necessity of having profit motivate production, contending that the secret of Warner Bros.' success was the fact that Warners executive Leon Schlessinger was never at the studio. "He couldn't be caught dead hanging out with the cartoonists. . . . I have nothing against greed. I would love to find a really greedy honest businessmen who just wants to make billions of dollars because, if there was such a thing, they would hire the artists. They'd say, 'All right. I'm going to the racetrack. You sit down and make the cartoons and I'll collect the money and I'll put my name all over it.' I'd love to find a guy like that!"

At the turn of the century, Kricfalusi continues to be at the forefront of animation, by referencing its past. He has since created 2001's *The Ripping Friends*, a quartet of buff, but insipid superheroes who are meant to parody the *GI Joe* and *He-Man* toy-oriented shows that he was once compelled to create. Also, in 2003, he has made a return to earlier successes with the production of all new episodes of *Ren & Stimpy*, commissioned for the Spike cable network. While he says the "revival" was basically motivated by financial considerations, he has commented that he is having a great time resurrecting Spumco from scratch, which includes training animators to his specifications. With Kricfalusi reprising the voice of Ren, not surprisingly, the project that put him on the map is, Kricfalusi maintains, "the best project I ever worked on, the most fun I ever had, the most creatively rewarding." While the new studio began with six episodes, some from unproduced scripts from the original Nickelodeon series, Kricfalusi hopes that, if this run is successful, it could eventually lead to a feature-length project.

In the meantime, the cartoon aficionado who has also been noted for his send-up of Yogi Bear and music videos for Bjork and Tenacious D is still striving to create a new golden age of cartoons. He has been the Hollywood route and back to his native Ottawa for this latest venture. Perhaps his determination has been partially due to necessity. Even at the height of his contentions with Nickelodeon in 1995, when asked if he had reached a point when he wanted to throw up his hands and say the heck with the business, Kricfalusi laughed and replied, "All the time. The only thing is I'm no good at anything else!"

CREDITS

Boo Boo Runs Wild (1999) TV . . . . Boo Boo
Day in the Life of Ranger Smith, A (1999) TV . . . . Boo Boo
Goddamn George Liquor Show, The (1999) TV Series . . . . Jimmy the Idiot Boy
Ren & Stimpy Show, The (1991) TV Series . . . . Ren Hoek (1991–1993)/Various Characters
Ren & Stimpy Show, The (2004) TV Series . . . . Ren Hoek
Ripping Friends, The (2001) TV Series . . . . Citricet (2001)

MAURICE LaMARCHE

Maurice LaMarche, most famous as the voice of the megalomaniacal lab mouse, the Brain, in Steven Spielberg's *Pinky and the Brain,* was a "painfully shy child who would escape into cartoons to shed his inhibitions." Making his way through the Toronto school system, LaMarche discovered he could do different voices. He would often walk to school mimicking his favorite Warner Bros. cartoon characters. That, of course, brought derisive laughter from his classmates.

"Unfortunately, I didn't know the difference between laughing with me and laughing at me. I thought as long as I was getting laughs, it was okay." Eventually, his strange voices earned him periodic trips to the school psychologist and the same diagnosis came back nearly every year: Maurice just wanted attention. The need to be noticed was so compelling that it prompted him to drop out of high school and develop a stand-up comedy routine. By the age of nineteen he began to work the Toronto comedy club circuit. It was at Yuk Yuks that Arlene Berman, from the Canadian animation company Nelvana, recognized his talent for impressions and signed him for "Easter Fever," a comedic roast of the Easter Bunny. "I played Don Rattles (Don Rickles) and Steed Martin (Steve Martin). That was the first time I ever heard my voice come out of an animated character on television, and that was the coolest high I'd ever felt. It was like I'd stepped into that alternate universe that I'd always kind of imagined when I was a kid, but they personified in *Roger Rabbit.*"

LaMarche admits that before moving to Los Angeles, he had the typical starstruck dreams of life in Hollywood. He describes his career as "a failing upwards." Although he loves his work and makes it clear that he casts no disparagement on the voice-over business, it is not exactly what he wanted to do as an actor. "I love what I do now. I think it's almost providential that I'm in this rather than what I wanted for myself. What I wanted was the big TV series, the big sitcom, the stardom . . . not being able to eat in a restaurant without being bothered for my autograph. I have a lot of friends who went on to that, and I think if I'd have gone that path, I probably would have become a very self-destructive person."

He soon found that the hard reality of Hollywood was the constant "auditioning and not getting it." To support himself, he struggled through the worst working experience of his life. "I'm the only actor in Los Angeles that never worked as a waiter. I wasn't even talented enough to get a job as a waiter. I had to make do with telephone sales. I was one of those annoying people who called you at your office . . . and tell you that you have a back order of pens and toner . . . and 'just go run over and get a purchase order number for me.' That's the worst job I ever had because I knew I was doing something dishonest. I feel very bad about that since it was not a terribly moral thing to do, but I had to eat, and I had to pay the rent. I made eight thousand dollars in my first year in Los Angeles."

Although he had no formal training in acting, it was his work in stand-up comedy that gave him the confidence to audition. The training he received from stand-up was "the craft of the immediacy of working with an audience, doing impressions, and [his] own sensibilities about what's funny, what reading on a line will tickle the funny bone."

All the while, his "sensibilities" caught the attention of voice-over extraordinaire Frank Welker, who gave him unsolicited, but welcomed support. "I was auditioning, and people kept saying to me, 'Oh, you're the guy Frank Welker keeps talking about.' I learned that Frank had been boosting me throughout the small community for about a year. It's such a complement, a nice guy of Frank's stature trying to help me, so I really owe him a huge debt." The combination of persistence and Frank Welker's lobbying led to his first big job as the Chief on 1983's *Inspector Gadget*. During these recording sessions, LaMarche, a long-time *Get Smart* fan, was thrilled to have the opportunity to work with Don Adams, who played the title role.

It soon became apparent that the animation business might not be so bad after all. "I did the Chief and various villains and there's Don Adams sitting there. In between takes he would regale us with stories of the making of *Get Smart*, and nobody tells a story like him. It was really great. So, I thought, this animation stuff is pretty cool. You sit in a chair. You talk in between takes, and at the end of the day you get a nice check. Wow, this is cool!"

The future was finally unfolding as planned. He went from *Inspector Gadget* to another DIC production, *The Real Ghostbusters*. His stand-up career was thriving; he was opening for big name acts like Rodney Dangerfield. He was also delighted and grateful to have signed with William Morris agent Nina Nisenholtz. But in March of 1987, a life-altering tragedy occurred. "My dad was murdered by his best friend and I really spiraled into a deep depression and didn't feel like doing stand-up, couldn't do stand-up. Part of it was because I didn't have the energy to make people laugh one on one. And the other part was, my dad would come see just about every show, and I knew he was there. Knowing that he'd never be there anymore was painful for me. So, I left stand-up for quite a while and just concentrated on the cartoons."

In the two years that followed, he was able to gradually piece his life together and return to the comedy clubs when the family suffered another devastating loss. "My little sister was killed in a car crash; she was eighteen years old. I'll confess to you, I had started drinking heavily after my father's murder. I stopped drinking and within that first year my sister was killed. . . . I did not go back to drinking, but that was the death knell for my stand-up career. I just didn't have the energy. There was too much sadness; but the cartoons were always there, and I always loved doing it. It was a way of returning to my childhood. It was a way of expressing myself artistically."

From that point on, LaMarche immersed himself in voice-over work. He remains "very indebted" to Marsha Goodman, who put him in just about every incidental part on other DIC shows. In show business, if you are talented, work brings more work, and LaMarche's talent was beginning to be rewarded. When *Tiny Toons* was announced, he naturally wanted to work on a Steven Spielberg project, but was less than optimistic about his chances. Convinced there was no way anyone of Spielberg's stature would hire a "shloob" like him, he auditioned anyway, and was subsequently hired to do Dizzy Devil, among various parts on the show. The 1990s *Tiny Toons* led to another Spielberg show, *Animaniacs*, which spun off *Pinky and the Brain*.

When *Pinky and the Brain* was cast, it was an odd bit of serendipity that led LaMarche to the most popular role of his career to date. Years ago, he learned to mimic a hysterically funny Orson Welles outtake that has long made the rounds in Hollywood. Captured during the taping of a commercial, a flustered Welles mercilessly intimidated his woefully inexperienced director. After hearing the tape, LaMarche learned to recite Welles's tirade verbatim. From that day forward, any director who dared to cross him has had to endure a live rendition. Although he shows no remorse in poking fun at Welles, he does not want people to misunderstand. "Welles is one of my heroes, but it's a double-edged sword. I like to parody him at his worst moments." The session that became a nightmare for Welles turned out to be a godsend for LaMarche.

On the day of the audition, the actors were given the first look at the characters. "When they drew the Brain, he was a physical rendering of [animation writer] Tom Minton, sans the ears. [Tom] was working on *Animaniacs* at the time, and he had a partner named Eddie Fitzgerald, who is about six foot two and very driven and . . . not a Cockney, but he is very, very high energy and manic like Pinky, and Minton is just very somber. Apparently they were inseparable. . . . I didn't know Tom Minton at the time. He talks in a monotone, and if I would have known that I probably would've never gotten the job. I just took one look at the drawing of the Brain and said, 'This looks like Orson Welles!' I launched into my Orson Welles, which everybody was damn sick of by that time, because at recording sessions I launch into my Orson Welles impression in between takes. The executives said, 'Boy, that works for that character.' Andrea Romano [animation director] told me after I did that, they stopped looking. 'We didn't let anyone else audition for the Brain. You were the Brain at that point.'"

LaMarche is quick to point out that the voice he uses for the Brain is not a bang-on Welles impression. "I've always had an ear for mimicry. It's been tough to fight that and actually create my own characters, but over the years I've managed to learn to cross-pollinate voices. The Brain is two-thirds Orson Welles, one-third Vincent Price. Consequently, he's his own character." The only direct Welles impersonation is the *Animaniacs* episode "Yes, Always," which is a "rip-off" of the Welles outtake tape. "People who know the tape are floored by that particular thing. It's basically a $200,000 inside joke."

LaMarche is as much a fan of the show as anyone. He has two personal favorite episodes: "Bubba Bo Bob Brain," in which the Brain becomes a country music singer whose hit song has a controlling subliminal message, and the 1995 Christmas special in which the two mice disguise themselves as elves to infiltrate Santa's toy shop and send out hypnotic "Noodle Noggin" dolls that mesmerize the recipients and bend them to the will of the Brain. That is the only episode thus far in which the Brain's plan succeeds. However, instead of enslaving the world, he can only give an emotionally wrought speech ordering everyone to "have a Merry Christmas." "I just felt so good doing that final speech as the Brain. It flowed. The feeling came. He had the world in his hands and he couldn't do it. I don't know if he couldn't do it because it was Christmas. . . . But he gives it all up. The key to *Pinky and the Brain* is not necessarily the world takeover plots, although they're fun . . . and the struggle to get it done even if we don't get anywhere near the plot, even if it's just the get-rich-quick scheme to finance the plot, that's fun too. But the thing that makes this work is these two guys, despite their antagonistic relationship, really love each other."

Ironically, one of the funniest lines in the Christmas special completely eluded LaMarche. Pinky invites the Brain to a party at reindeer Donner's house, to which the Brain replies, "Somehow the prospect of joining the Donner Party doesn't appeal to me." "I will confess to you, being Canadian, I didn't get a lot of American history. I didn't get the joke when I read it. In fact, I was embarrassed to ask, so I didn't ask for another two weeks after we recorded it. The fact that the joke works serves to illustrate that it is possible for an actor to deliver a joke without understanding it if they're true to the character. . . . What strikes me about *Pinky and the Brain* is it reminds me a lot of *Rocky and Bullwinkle* because it works on different levels. Kids can watch it, but there are a lot of jokes they wouldn't understand, like the Donner Party, but they can really love the show."

LaMarche, known affectionately to his friends as "Moe," approached the character of the Brain very seriously. He tried to invest the characterization with considerable depth and even a sense of morality. A plot he strongly dis-approved of was one in which the Brain buys all the real estate on the planet above the thirty-ninth floor. He then devises a plan to cause a flood thirty-nine stories deep by melting the polar ice caps, thus making him the ultimate landlord and giving him global control. "I had an objection to that episode; I said, 'This is the first time that Brain's ever come up with a plan where peo-ple could actually get hurt. I don't like that, and I'm voicing it right now.'" Of course, the plan ultimately fails and the Brain receives his comeuppance from an angry Soviet space dog. "It was very gratifying for me at the end of the episode as a viewer to see the Brain get the absolute living hell kicked out of him for six months by that dog. The little bastard deserved it. It'll teach him for coming up with a plan that could hurt children."

Whatever transgressions the Brain may have made against mankind were evidently forgiven, judging by the enthusiastic crowds at subsequent auto-graph sessions as well as the vast quantities of fan mail, some of it addressed simply to "The Brain." LaMarche did his best to answer all of the letters. "We got very intelligent fan mail. I got one from a marine biologist who wanted to offer his expertise in a plan for taking over the world. We had a lot of univer-sity students and professionals writing to us, so we were very flattered by that."

LaMarche was also able to assist one especially prominent viewer. Director Tim Burton had a problem on the set of the 1994 film *Ed Wood*. Near the end of the film, Wood, in drag, has an epiphany when he meets Orson Welles (Vincent D'Onofrio) at a local bar. "When they finally got the dailies back, they realized that Vincent looked fantastic as Orson Welles, but his voice was thin and reedy. So, Tim saw me, flew me up to San Francisco, and I looped [replaced] the voice. Tim was tremendous to work with. I heard all these hor-ror stories of how eccentric he was. The most eccentric thing he did was sit with his feet up on the chair and his knees up to his chest. . . . Whoa. . . . Oh, boy! . . . How wacky! But other than that he knew exactly what he wanted."

Ed Wood was by no means the only looping job on his long list of credits. Much work is necessary in removing the profanity for films to be shown on commercial television or on air planes. His first looping experience was humble, replacing all of Chuck Barris's expletives for *The Gong Show* movie. But his crowning achievement so far was some added dialogue for *The Pagemaster*. Of that, he says, "I'm very proud of this. I looped Patrick Stewart, and I can't even tell where my lines are, so I must have done a good job, 'cause I don't know when it's me and when it's Patrick."

LaMarche's ear for mimicry has also earned him work doing voices already established by other actors. He voiced the 1980s incarnations of Popeye on

Popeye and Son, and Dishonest John on the 1988 *Beany and Cecil*. In recreating an established voice, it can be very difficult to separate your own slant on the character from your predecessor. "You can't help but add something of yourself, but for the sheer voice print where they say, 'We want people not to know this guy ever died,' I work as hard as I can to match that. I'll record myself and play it back next to the original, back and forth, until I almost can't tell the difference."

One of the most difficult voices for him to copy was Jack Mercer's Popeye. "My throat actually bled. I assume I was pretty close to the original voice, but it was very tough to get that raspy. I did my best to stay true to the Mercer Popeye of 1950s cartoons that I remembered so well. I loved the black and whites more, but the flavor of the show seemed to be going for more of that '50s kind of feel. It's a show about the kids, with Popeye almost as an incidental character. But I was really thrilled to get that job. It's an honor to me to be cast as all these classic characters." As for *Beany and Cecil*, "It's one of my favorite cartoon shows ever because I was kind of a sad little kid, and Cecil was my hero. I would imagine that I could shout out, 'Help, Cecil, Help!' just like Beany did, and this guardian angel would come along. I was in Catholic school at the time, too, so I related Cecil to guardian angels."

His relentless perfectionism earned him the role of Toucan Sam for Kelloggs when Paul Frees died in 1986. "I worked on his second-to-last Froot Loops commercial and he was sick at the time. Just for timing, I read in Paul's lines for Toucan Sam a few times. They remembered that, so when Paul passed away, I got a good shot at it." After six call-backs and not hearing anything, LaMarche was notified by the creative director. Kelloggs had made the commercial with another actor of their choosing. Liking LaMarche better, the director had him go into the studio to loop the commercial, and then presented two separate tapes to the president of Kelloggs. Not telling him who was who, he asked the president to pick the best one. LaMarche recalls, "Without trying to be right or wrong the president says, 'Well, tape B is closer to Paul Frees. If I didn't know better, I'd think it was Paul.' The creative director said, 'That's Maurice LaMarche from Los Angeles.'"

Sometimes, however, a perfect impersonation does not win the part. When Daws Butler died, LaMarche auditioned for the role of Cap'n Crunch. "I did my Daws Butler impression. Then they said, 'Well, we want him to be younger, more youthful, more energetic.' I said, 'Well, why does he still have a white mustache and white hair? Is he just now taking his vitamins?' So, that's when I began to lose it because I still tried to be true to the character. I'm always sad when somebody passes away. When I'm brought in to sound like somebody whom I admire, I don't look at it as a ghoulish thing. I look at it as if I'm carrying on for them. Paul Frees' ex-wife, Joy, has actually thanked me for doing such a good job with Toucan Sam. . . . I feel I'm entrusted with a legacy in a way."

Being established in the voice-over community affords one the luxury to refuse any offer of work, but actors who are just starting out cannot, and LaMarche was no exception. "I don't know that I'd ever do another show like [1986's] *The Popples*, where it's so blatantly a commercial for a toy. At the time I took it my career was like a snowflake that was starting to grow into a snowball and I dared not turn anything down. But, after I got into it, I just said, 'Jeeze, we're not doing anything here. We're not being funny. We're not being entertaining. We're just making these cutesy commercials for this toy that's based on rolled up socks. You know how you roll up your sock? That's what a Popple is.'" Conversely, sometimes a personal favorite is canceled. "I would give almost anything to bring back *The Critic*, along with *Pinky and the Brain;* those are the two most satisfying jobs I've ever had. In a case like *The Critic*, I did twenty-seven characters in one show. What a treat as an actor to be able to play that and to be able to work with a guy like Jon Lovitz, who's become a friend."

Sadly, the show foundered on ABC and was soon picked up by Fox, but even a tie-in to *The Simpsons* could not save it from so-so ratings and network politics. In an effort to boost viewership, creators (and *Simpsons* producers) Mike Reiss and Al Jean had the main character, Jay Sherman, appear on *The Simpsons* as a judge at the Springfield Film Festival. Although LaMarche worked on that episode, he did not record his lines with the cast. "I did two *Simpsons* episodes, but I always did my lines while I was recording *The Critic*. The crossover episode was the only episode that (*Simpson's* creator) Matt Groening took his name off of. I played George C. Scott getting hit in the groin with a football. I just had to say "Oh, my Groin!" The other thing I did was Jay's burp during the burping contest at the table between Homer and Jay. You know, Homer goes forth with a good-sized belch, and then the Critic goes, 'Oh, that's nice Homer, BEEEELLLCH' Which is my patented sound effect that nobody else seems to be able to do, not even WELKER!"

Although LaMarche's patented belch could not save *The Critic*, this one facet of his character lives on in other shows. "I seem to get a lot of burp-over work. Whenever Wakko burps, when Spork burped in [the *Animaniacs* parody] *Star Truck*, . . . I'm the stunt burp guy. Whenever anyone needs a burp they say, 'We could have Moe do this.'"

LaMarche is also fond of some of the incidental characters he has done on such shows as *The Tick*. "I did my all-time favorite villain role on that, 'The

Evil Midnight Bomber What Bombs at Midnight.' It's on a show called 'The Tick versus the Tick' and it's my little tip of the hat to my late friend Sam Kinison. He's a mad bomber, and he's one of those guys that have three radio stations playing in his head at one time. It was my tribute to Sam. He was a good friend."

Apart from comedy, LaMarche continues to take acting classes, doing scene study. "My wife (Robin Eisenman) is an acting teacher, and one of the best. I'm more and more looking at this as an acting job. When I first came into it, it was just schticking. But lately I've done very dramatic speeches where it had to be almost on the level of the Brain's breakdown in the [1995] Christmas episode. When I did the Brain's speech, I looked in the booth and, apart from me having tears in my eyes, Andrea Romano was wiping tears from her eyes. Touching stuff. I did a [1986 version] *Jonny Quest* with Rob [Paulsen] where I had to play his adopted dad, and I had to tell Rob's character, Hadji, a dark family secret. Even though I wasn't on camera, I treated it like a real acting piece. I did it in one take, and there was a lot of positive feedback afterwards from everybody. I always try to bring a little more of the actors craft to it rather than just walk in with 'What goofy voice can I do today?'"

Whether influenced by great speeches or scripts, many successful actors tend to branch out into writing or directing. With the encouragement of his "writer friends," LaMarche is currently writing a project that involves animation, although he has no directing aspirations. "My wife will direct whatever I write because she's a terrific director, but I really do see myself doing voice-overs in one form or another until it's time for me to go, because it's a great form. You can stretch so much that I don't think people can get tired of you and throw you away. A guy who's on a hit series for seven years may never work again. The four million dollars he made doing that sitcom for over seven years can be spent and he can be out of work. It saddens me to see guys I used to watch on variety television in the '60s drive around in beat-up Honda Civics today. I go, 'Wow, these guys were at the top of their form. What happened?' So, I really do see myself doing this, and being able to do it for a long time. I think you can't be making a living in this business and have more fun. I'm sure there are richer guys, but I don't know if they're as happy as animation voice-over people."

Despite the ridicule he suffered as a child, his favorite cartoons, *George of the Jungle, Super Chicken, Beany and Cecil, Rocky and Bullwinkle,* and *The Flintstones,* helped him develop the skills that eventually turned his life around. In 1996, he concluded, "It actually hit me while watching a *Pinky and the Brain* scoring session. I thought, 'Wow, I'm on the same sound stage that

Carl Stalling used for all those classic Warner cartoons. And that piano is the same piano Carl played. I've come thousands and thousands of miles, and many, many years, but I'm finally here. I'm right where it all came from.' " As far as the need to be in the spotlight, Hollywood certainly provides plenty of company. LaMarche observes, "I've since come to the conclusion that when we watch the Academy Awards, everybody in that audience didn't get enough attention as a child." Like the many Oscar hopefuls in the crowd, Maurice LaMarche may not yet have satisfied his craving for attention; with his experience in *Pinky and the Brain* and *Futurama,* he will just have to settle for the world and the world beyond.

CREDITS

101 Dalmatians II: Patch's London Adventure (2003) .... Horace
Adventures of Hyperman, The (1995) TV Series .... Kidd Chaos/Comptroller
All Dogs Go to Heaven 2 (1996)
Amazing Adventures of Inspector Gadget, The (1986) .... Chief Quimby
Animaniacs (1993) TV Series .... The Brain/Squit Pigeon/Additional Voices
Attack of the Killer Tomatoes (1990) TV Series .... Zoltan
Baby Blues Christmas Special, A (2002) TV
Balto II: Wolf Quest (2001) .... Balto
Barman: The Animated Series (1992) TV Series .... Additional Voices
Beany and Cecil (1988) TV Series .... Dishonest John
Beethoven (1994) TV Series .... Additional Voices
Bonkers (1993) TV Series .... Tuttle Turtle/Mr. Blackenblue/Smarts
Bugs Bunny's Funky Monkeys (1997)
Captain Planet and the Planeteers (1990) TV Series .... Duke Nukem (1990–1993)/Verminous
    Skumm (1990–1993)
Captain Simian and the Space Monkeys (1996) TV Series .... Dr. Splitz/Splitzy
Carrotblanca (1995) .... Yosemite Sam
Channel Umptee-3 (1997) TV Series
Chimp Channel, The (1999) TV Series .... Harry Waller/Bernard the Sarcastic Cockatoo
Comic Book: The Movie (2004) .... Various Voices
Cool World (1992) .... Mash/Drunken Bar Patron/Dr. Vincent Whiskers/Super Jack
Critic, The (1994) TV Series .... Jeremy Hawke/Additional Voices
Critic, The (2000) TV Series .... Other Character Voices
D.C. Follies (1987) TV Series .... Additional Voices
Dennis the Menace (1986) TV Series .... George Wilson/Henry Mitchell
Dennis the Menace in Cruise Control (2002) TV .... Henry Mitchell
Dennis the Menace in Mayday for Mother (1981) TV .... Mr. Wilson
Dexter's Laboratory (1996) TV Series .... Dick McMan/Ratman/Simion/Washington/Additional Voices
Dilbert (1999) TV Series .... Garbage Man/Bob the Dinosaur
Droopy, Master Detective (1993) TV Series .... Additional Voices
Duck Dodgers (2003) TV Series .... Additional Voices
Duckman (1994) TV Series .... Additional Voices

Easter Fever (Special) (1980) Don Rattles/Steed Martin

Extreme Ghostbusters (1997) TV Series . . . . Egon Spengler

Freakazoid! (1995) TV Series . . . . Longhorn

Futurama (1999) TV Series . . . . Donbot/Clamps/LRRR/Hedonism Bot/Lt. Kif Kroker/Morbo/
Walt/ Sun/God/Additional Voices

G.I. Joe (1990) TV Series . . . . Copperhead/Lowlight/Serpentor/Spirt/Destro

Gadget and the Gadgettes (2004) TV Series . . . . Lt. Gadget

Gadget Boy and Heather (1995) TV Series

Gadget Boy's Adventures in History (1998) TV Series

Gravedale High (1990) TV Series . . . . Sid

Harvey Birdman, Attorney at Law (2001) TV Series . . . . Additional Voices

Hey Arnold! The Movie (2002) . . . . Big Bob/Head of Security

Hey Arnold! (1996) TV Series . . . . "Big" Bob Pataki/Additional Voices

Histeria! (1998) TV Series . . . . George Washington/Abraham Lincoln/Additional Voices

House of Mouse (2001) TV Series . . . . Mortimer Mouse/Mickey Moose/Scuttle/Basil of Baker
Street/Ratigan/March Hare/Additional Voices

Inspector Gadget (1983) TV Series . . . . Chief Quimby (1985)

Inspector Gadget: Gadget's Greatest Gadgets (1999) . . . . Inspector Gadget/Chief Quimby (and in
segments "The Capeman Cometh" and "Gadget's Gadgets")

Inspector Gadget Saves Christmas (1992) TV . . . . Chief Quimby

Inspector Gadget's Last Case: Claw's Revenge (2002) TV . . . . Inspector Gadget

Johnny Bravo (1997) TV Series . . . . Additional Voices

Kideo TV (1986) TV Series . . . . Puzzle

King of the Hill (1997) TV Series . . . . Various Voices

Life and Adventures of Santa Claus, The (2000) . . . . Mogorb/King of the Awgwas/Lord of Lerd/
Bo/Master Mariner of the World

Little Mermaid, The (1992) TV Series . . . . Scuttle

Looney Tunes: Reality Check (2003) Video . . . . Yosemite Sam/Wile E. Coyote

Looney Tunes: Stranger Than Fiction (2003) Video . . . . Yosemite Sam/William Shakespeare's
Ghost/Dr. Moron/Pepe le Pew

Mickey Mouse Works (1999) TV Series . . . . Mortimer Mouse

Mickey's Magical Christmas: Snowed in at the House of Mouse (2001)

Oblongs, The (2001) TV Series . . . . Additional Voices

Party Wagon (2003) TV Series . . . . Bumpy Snits

Pepper Ann (1997) TV Series . . . . Chuck Pearson

Pink Panther (1993) TV Series . . . . Additional Voices

Pinky and the Brain (1995) TV Series . . . . The Brain

Pinky & the Brain Christmas Special, A (1995) TV . . . . The Brain

Pinky, Elmyra, & the Brain (1998) TV Series . . . . The Brain

Popeye and Son (1987) TV Series . . . . Popeye

Popples (1986) TV Series . . . . Puzzle

Problem Child (1993) TV Series . . . . Additional Voices

Real Ghostbusters, The (1986) TV Series . . . . Egon Spengler

Road Rovers (1996) TV Series . . . . Radio Announcer

Rock & Rule (1983) . . . . Sailor

Sabrina's Secret Life (2003) TV Series . . . . Salem

Scooby-Doo in Arabian Nights (1994) TV

Siegfried and Roy: Masters of the Impossible (1996) . . . . Additonal Voices

Simpsons, The (1989) TV Series . . . . "George C. Scott"

Slimer! And the Real Ghostbusters (1988) TV Series . . . . Egon Spengler

Sonic Underground (1999) TV Series . . . . Sleet
Space Goofs (1997) TV Series . . . . Eckno/Others
Space Jam (1996) . . . . Pepe le Pew
Stripperella (2003) TV Series . . . . Various Voices
Tale Spin (1990) TV Series . . . . Additional Voices
Taz-Mania (1991) TV Series . . . . Hugh
Tick, The (1994) TV Series . . . . Deadly Bulb/Evil Midnight Bomber
Tiny Toon Adventures (1990) TV Series . . . . Dizzy Devil (1991)
Tiny Toon Adventures: How I Spent My Vacation (1992) . . . . Dizzy Devil
Tom and Jerry: The Magic Ring (2002) . . . . Spike/Alley Cat
Transformers (1984) TV Series (uncredited) . . . . Six-Gun
Twisted Adventures of Felix the Cat, The (1995) TV Series . . . . Additional Voices
Wacky Adventures of Ronald McDonald: Scared Silly, The (1998) . . . . Dr. Quizzical
Wakko's Wish (1999) . . . . The Brain/Squit Pigeon
Whatever Happened to Robot Jones? (2002) TV Series . . . . Robot Dad (2002–)
Where on Earth Is Carmen Sandiego? (1994) TV Series . . . . Additional Voices
Where's Waldo? (1991) TV Series . . . . Additional Voices

NORMA MACMILLAN

Norma Macmillan has spent much of her career playing naïve, non-threatening characters, such as the misunderstood Casper, the friendly ghost not able to "scare up" any friends; the hapless Sweet Polly Purebred from the *Underdog* series, who "couldn't go out for coffee and doughnuts without being kidnapped" (as Hal Erickson quips in his book *Television Cartoon Shows*); or Davey Hanson from *Davey and Goliath*, who, despite his Christian upbringing, had a knack for finding trouble around every turn. Television junkies in the 1980s will also most likely remember Norma

Macmillan as Aunt Martha, the sweet half of an elderly duo of aunts who, as the result of a life-changing epiphany, switched from their normal brand of mayonnaise to Kraft. The Canadian-born actress with the light airy voice may have been the veteran of stage, radio, and the small screen, but her greatest legacy is her animated one.

Born in Vancouver, she recalls that she started acting in her teens. She interjects, "My family tells me [it was] when I was a baby!" Although her parents were "fairly prominent socially," they were very supportive of her acting career and that of her sister, who had ambitions of being a singer. "I really thought I was going to be a singer first, but I found that nobody cared that much for me. They seemed to like it when I acted, so I stuck to acting." It was while a stage actress that she met her future husband, Thor Arngrim, when she joined his Totem Theatre group in 1951. While they might have been long on talent, the company was short on funds and it disbanded in 1954, whereupon Arngrim and Macmillan then married and moved to Toronto. Saying she had not been able to find work with the deep-voiced actresses popular in Vancouver, her light voice seemed perfect for "all the gabby ingenues" in Toronto.

Wanting to be part of the "wonderful radio shows" being produced at the time, she was initially hesitant to admit that she had no radio experience. To break in, she confesses she told the producers at the CBC (Canadian Broadcasting Corporation), "I can do children voices," just assuming that she probably could. "Of course, they were very interested as the radio programs were at night and odd hours when the radio stations did not want real children to work." Macmillan immediately got a call and subsequently voiced up to nine shows a day, working the gamut from the school broadcast in the morning to "mental health dramas," where she was cast as "a disturbed, schizophrenic little boy." After playing children for a couple of years in various series, she says, "I had the voice thing down."

"I also began doing—when television started—voices for their prominent puppet shows, and I was the voice of many of the Toronto shows." After the birth of their son, Stefan, "practically at the CBC," the family relocated to New York City to allow her husband to work as a Broadway producer. With Macmillan's background in radio, her husband was able to connect her with the voice-over/animation studio executives in New York. Her first job was on a Cocoa Puffs commercial directed by Gene Deitch, who was also an animation writer and producer for Paul Terry's studio, Terrytoons.

Deitch hired Macmillan to voice two boys and two girls in a television pilot called *Easy Winners*. According to Leonard Maltin, in *Of Mice and Magic*, CBS executives subsequently rejected the project as "too New Yorker-ish," but while it was not picked up, it was notable as it was written by a now-prominent newspaper cartoonist—Jules Pfeiffer. Macmillan remembers her Terrytoons co-worker as "a very shy young man. I used to get on the train with him from New York and we'd go out to New Rochelle, which is forty-five minutes from Broadway. . . . I was so stunned later when he became such a strong personality." Pfeiffer was frustrated by the fact that Terrytoons seemed to have no interest in actually producing his work (although they kept raising his salary when he would threaten to quit). He finally left when his part-time hobby as a newspaper cartoonist became a full-time occupation.

However, Macmillan characterized her time with Terrytoons as a "good experience." After doing a series called *Luno* with Bob McFadden, she said the show led to "hundreds" of commercials in New York, among them, "Transie," the transagram character who was the logo for a commonly used telegram company. "And I did the Tootsie Roll, Tootsie pop characters, and things like that. . . . There were really in the hundreds and it was really very exciting to do that. During that time, I got a call from Paramount [Famous Studios] and Seymour Mitel, the director. They were looking for someone to match up the Casper voice. Now, my understanding was that there was, first of all, a boy that did Casper, and then another lady [Mae Questel], in the very earliest *Caspers*. . . . I sounded so much like them that I did the next twenty-six with Bradley Bolke [for] *The New Casper Cartoon Show* [1963, Famous Pictures], and I also sang the theme song, which [singing] " *. . . the time has come for me to leave and so I really have to go.* "

With Casper as her first major animated character, she scored another success with her participation on *The First Family Album*, a hit comedy record which parodied the Kennedy family. Macmillan portrayed first daughter Caroline on that and a second First Family album. Although she describes the follow-up as "quite fantastic," it met with disappointing sales.

Still, she was able to stay very productive in the New York animation world. She was hired for Total Television Productions' 1964 *Underdog* as TV news reporter and "doggie damsel-in-distress," Sweet Polly Purebred. Her signature song, "*Oh where, oh where has my Underdog gone? Oh where, oh where could he be?*" was a commonly heard refrain to Wally Cox's Underdog on the numerous occasions she was kidnapped by Riff Raff or Simon Bar Sinister (both Alan Swift), among an assortment of nefarious villains. During this time, there was also a personal production of note—daughter Alison Arngrim was born in New York. (While brother Stefan later starred in 1968's *Land of the Giants*, Alison won lasting fame as the blonde-curled spoiled brat

Nellie Olson of *Little House on the Prairie* and has worked as a stand-up comedian since she was a teenager.)

When the family eventually migrated to the West Coast in the mid-1960s, Macmillan found work on Art Clokey's early claymation effort—*Davey and Goliath*. Her recollections of her beginnings are a little sketchy, "I don't believe that I did Sally originally. . . . I did various things like schoolteachers and other parts, other females." In 1965, she also replaced Dick Beals (after a salary dispute) as Davey in *Davey and Goliath*. Her approach to performing on the programs was similar to that with *Casper*. "Bradley [Bolke] and I divided all the voices. Bradley did all the voices from middle C and below and I did all high ones."

With most of her cartoon work a "buyout," that is, she received a flat fee for her work and only received a residual for *Underdog*, Macmillan's finances dictated that she venture beyond animation. Her favorite theatrical feature film work consisted of dubbing the boys voices for the 1967 classic movie musical *Camelot*. She recalls that director "Josh Logan went to Europe and when he came back he wasn't satisfied with the voices of the young Arthur as a little boy, nor Tom of Warrick (the boy that Richard Harris, King Arthur, sings to at the end of *Camelot*). So they auditioned people and I played these two boys in it. I dubbed the voices for them and worked with Josh Logan, which is very exciting."

In the 1980s, Macmillan also ventured out into television for guest-starring parts on programs such as *Webster*, *Mr. Belvedere*, *Night Court*, and *Colombo*, although she admitted, "Most of the time I prefer voice work, because it so exciting." For her on-camera work, although Macmillan said that the quality of her voice had helped win her on-camera auditions as it amused and arrested the attention of producers, the irony was that, with doing so much voice work, it took some time to readjust to being seen. "When I first came from New York, despite the fact that I had been a stage actress, I had done so much voice work that I was expressing everything vocally only. I had to go to classes to learn how to get my face working and become animated again!"

Of all her many parts, she names the friendly ghost as her favorite. "When my kids were young and in school, I would take them to school and some of the other children would hear about Alison. Alison would tell the children about their mother's voices, but mostly they would say, 'Would you do Casper for me?' And I still get young people, particularly college-age, who say, 'You were Casper?' I have a stock line I read, *"Hi, I'm Casper the friendly ghost and I want to be your friend!"* and then I may sing a few bars of the cartoon song . . . so I've been doing that for now about twenty years." When asked if anyone ever inquired what Casper was when he was, presumably, once a living being (suggestions have included Richie Rich, to whom Casper bears a striking resemblance), she replied simply that she thinks of Casper as "a very sweet, loving, little boy."

A dedicated professional, upon her retirement Macmillan joined a radio production group for seniors, when the couple returned to Toronto in the mid-1990s. Although she has since passed away at the age of seventy-nine in 2001, the actress with the ethereal voice and versatile talent has left an indelible mark on animation which will be enjoyed by her contemporaries as well as generations to come.

CREDITS

Alice of Wonderland in Paris (1966)
Animated Adventures of Tom Sawyer, The (1998) Video . . . . Widow Douglas
Boo Bop (1957) . . . . Casper
Boo Kind to Animals (1955) . . . . Casper
Bull Fright (1955). . . . Casper
Challenge of the GoBots (1984) TV Series . . . . Additional Voices
Davey and Goliath (1962) TV Series . . . . Davey Hansen (beginning 1965)/Various Voices
Dutch Treat (1956) . . . . Casper
Ghost of Honor (1957) . . . . Casper
Gumby Show, The (1957) TV Series . . . . Goo/Additional Voices
Heir Restorer (1958) . . . . Casper
Hide and Shriek (1955) . . . . Casper
Hooky Spooky (1957) . . . . Casper
Howdy Doody (1954) TV Series . . . . Heidi Doody
Ice Scream (1957) . . . . Casper
Keep Your Grin Up (1955). . . . Casper
King Rounder (1964)
Line of Screammage (1956) . . . . Casper
Maggie Muggins (1955) TV Series . . . . Fitzgerald Fieldmouse
Matty's Funday Funnies (1959) TV Series . . . . Casper
Missing Genie, The (1963) . . . .Tim
Moby Dick and the Mighty Mightor (1967) TV Series . . . . Li'l Rok
New Casper Cartoon Show, The (1963) TV Series . . . . Casper/Various Voices
Nightmare on the Thirteenth Floor (1990) TV
Old Mother Clobber (1958)
Out of the Inkwell (1962) TV Series . . . . Kokette
Peakaboo (1957) . . . . Casper
Penguin for Your Thoughts (1956) . . . . Casper
Red, White, and Boo (1955) . . . . Casper
Roc-a-by Sinbad (1964) . . . . Tim
Spooking about Africa (1957) . . . . Casper

Spooking with a Brogue (1955) .... Casper
Tiger's Tail, A (1964) .... Tim
Tom and Jerry (1965) TV Series (voice) (uncredited)
Trouble in Bagdad (1963) .... Tim
Underdog (1964) TV Series .... Sweet Polly Purebred
Wizard of Oz, The (1991) .... Narrator

ROBERT (BOB) McFADDEN

As the lyrics of the theme song state, take "six drops of the essence of terror, five drops of sinister sauce," and too much of "a tincture of tenderness," and the result is "Milton the Monster." Take away the essence of terror and sinister sauce, and you get Milton's alter ego, Robert McFadden.

McFadden, the voice of the lovable monster, was born in East Liverpool, Ohio, on January 19, 1923, and spent much of his youth hanging out in movie houses with his father. McFadden recalled, "My father used to sing with the silent movies. They would have a pianist, and they always had music to go with the silent pictures, no matter how small the theater. Once in a while they would hire a singer if they could find someone good enough to sing during the love scenes, and my father used to do that." McFadden's favorite movies were the westerns, and early on he distinguished himself from the other neighborhood kids by acting out scenes, which included talking and fighting with himself. McFadden would often roam the neighborhood with his toy six guns by his side, taking on all comers. "I was the fastest draw on Third Street. I used to have one of these six guns, like all kids had, but I had the record as the fastest draw because I used to put Vaseline in my holster. I had a leather holster, and the Vaseline would enable me to get my gun out faster." McFadden admitted that his western fantasies were the extent of his early performances.

It was while stationed with the navy in Puerto Rico during World War II that McFadden picked up where he left off as a child. To keep up the troops' morale, the base would put on a talent show once a week. McFadden, who would sing and do impersonations for his friends in his barracks, decided to try his luck on stage. "I would get up and impersonate singers, Vaughn Monroe and other people like that who were big stars at the time, and I figured when I got out of the service, I was going to be a big hit in show business." Unfortunately, when McFadden made the rounds after being discharged from the service, he found that postwar America was not ready for his act, so he went back to his prewar job working in a steel mill.

The drudgery of working at the mill only fueled McFadden's desire to succeed as an entertainer. McFadden formulated a plan and began preparing for his future. "Every payday I would pull twenty dollars of my pay for the day when I got into show business, figuring I would have to have money to live on, plus some kind of wardrobe." The preparedness paid off when, in 1950, a steel strike put McFadden out of work. Taking his unemployment as a sign, McFadden pulled up stakes and headed to the West Coast to visit his brother.

McFadden arrived in California with fifteen hundred dollars, a new shirt, new shoes, and a powder-blue dinner jacket that he thought would look good on stage. While making the rounds of talent agents, McFadden had something more valuable than a new wardrobe at his disposal; he had a phony resume. "I gave them a big song and dance that I was a big star in the East, but that I got married and I got out of the business, and I just got a divorce, and I'm getting back into it. I told them I played all of the best clubs, the Copacabana in New York and all of that." The lies were good enough to convince some of the small-time agents, and McFadden was on his way to the small time, playing Moose lodges and VFW halls. "They figured they could take a chance on me at $75 for a weekend, so that's how I got started. They didn't expect much and they didn't get much either in the way of material."

By playing the small venues in the western states, McFadden built up a solid act. Returning east to New York, he auditioned for and earned a spot on *Arthur Godfrey's Talent Scouts*, where he won first place. The win enabled McFadden to get better bookings in nightclubs and gave him the confidence to stay in New York to try and build up a career in commercials. "My wife and I got a cheap hotel room, and I thought I was going to be an overnight sensation in voice-overs. My first big commercial was on camera for a product called 'Awake.' It was a fake orange juice. But I had to go out and play nightclubs to pay the rent because I could get up to $1,000 per week in Texas and Oklahoma and places like that. That would keep me going for at least a month, as long as I didn't eat too much and stayed in a toilet. But unfortunately, I had to be gone for a couple of weeks and lose any kind of momentum I might have had." It took McFadden almost five years before he was able to make a living without having to leave New York.

Once McFadden became a fixture in the New York voice-over community, he began getting work on comedy albums, such as 1962's best-selling *The First Family*, a spoof of life with the Kennedy family, on which he played Fidel Castro, and on *Johnny Carson's Guide to New York and the World's Fair*. Carson, who was just starting out as a talk-show host, would later cast McFadden as one of the Mighty Carson Art Players on the *Tonight Show*.

By 1964, McFadden had made the transition to animation voice-overs. "I started doing voices first for Terrytoons, which at the time was in New Rochelle, New York. I got the job because I could do a lot of voices. They were paying $150 a cartoon, and that was the end of it. They could play the cartoon for a thousand years and you would never get any more money, but you had to do all of the voices for the $150. That's why they wouldn't write women into the scripts because that would be two people they would have to pay. But I did thirty or forty theatricals for Terrytoons. I did all the voices on a show called *Sad Cat* [Ralph Bakshi's first cartoon] and also [with Norma Macmillan] on *Luno*, the soaring stallion, about a boy who used to rub his artificial toy horse and it would come to life."

McFadden's work on the Terrytoons coincided with an animated television series produced by General Foods called *Linus the Lionhearted* (1964), which featured characters that also doubled as spokespersons for various

General Foods cereals. McFadden voiced the character So-Hi and also mailman Lovable Truly (who hawked Alpha-bits cereal in commercials). The series lasted for twenty-six episodes before entering syndication. Although the series was short lived, it proved to be one of McFadden's favorites. "I liked it because there was one segment where they wanted to create a character while we were doing it, which was unusual. They wanted to see if it could work, so they created a character called Frank Pfass, who spoke double talk. He was pretty funny, but we were the only ones who thought so."

Apparently, the Federal Communications Committee did not find the show to be very funny. In his book *Television Cartoon Shows*, author Hal Erickson writes, "The 26 *Linus* episodes might well have been network-run forever had not the FCC horned in and decided that the series represented more advertising than entertainment." The series would not be McFadden's last brush as a cereal spokesman; he would later go on to be the voice of Frankenberry for the cereal of the same name.

Eventually, McFadden's voice-over work brought him to the attention of animator Hal Seeger. Seeger, who was working on a television cartoon called *Fearless Fly*, hired McFadden to voice both the Superhero insect and his alter ego Hyram (which McFadden did in his best Wally Cox impersonation.) What was intended to be an incidental character on *Fearless Fly* literally ended up stealing the show. McFadden explains, "On the third show of that series, Fearless Fly goes into a place and he meets a benign monster called Milton, and the producers, the animators, and everybody flipped over the character. No one in the public had seen it yet, but everybody was so crazy about the character and what was happening with it that they decided to change the name of the show from *Fearless Fly* to *Milton the Monster* with *Fearless Fly* segments."

Milton the Monster, a Hal Seeger Production, ran on ABC television from 1965 to 1967. Though the series was thought to be a knock off of *The Munsters* and *The Addams Family*, which were also popular at the time, Milton was actually in the planning stages long before either of the other shows aired. Production delays forced *Milton* to air later, making it look like an imitator, but the series, co-written by *Popeye* voice-actor Jack Mercer, was as original as it was funny. The premise was simple. Professor Weirdo, with the aid of his assistant Count Kook, tries to create a terrifying monster as a welcome addition to the denizens of Horror Hill, which include fellow monsters Hee-Bee and Jee-Bee (also voiced by McFadden). By accidentally adding too much of a tincture of tenderness, the professor, to his chagrin, ends up creating goody-goody Milton, a Frankenstein-like monster with a southern accent and a smoke stack for the top of his head. As to the accent, McFadden admits that Milton's voice *was* borrowed. "The producers wanted something that sounded 'country.' I did a few country voices that they didn't like because they sounded too much like farmers. So then I did a Gomer Pyle impersonation, and they said, 'That's it.'"

Recording the voices on *Milton* was a different matter. McFadden remembered, "My God, we recorded them on a magnacorder. Hal Seeger had a little studio with the doors open, and I couldn't understand that because anything else that I've ever done was in sound-proofed studios." McFadden also claimed that sometimes when they were recording, you could hear traffic going by outside. But Seeger defended his methods, "It wasn't a recording studio. We usually recorded in our conference room, but the sound was fine. I didn't own the facilities then; I just had a recorder. There's nothing wrong with the tracks. They're still running them." At least when it came time to record his next job, [1968's] *Cool McCool*, McFadden got to use a real studio and impersonate one of his favorite comedians, Jack Benny, in doing McCool's voice.

Cool McCool, created by Batman creator Bob Kane and produced by King Features, was a bungling Maxwell Smart–type agent who always got his man. McFadden claimed, "It was a mortal sin taking money for that, because Bob Kane, who was the writer on that show, would sit in the studio and say, 'Look, if you want to change a word here or there or make a funny sound effect or anything, just go ahead, feel free.' That was his first mistake." McFadden and co-star Chuck McCann would take advantage of Kane's generosity and ad-lib to their hearts content. "Kane would do like three shows and say, 'Thank you very much; it was great.' And Chuck would look at me and we would walk out and say, 'This is just like stealing money.' I had so much fun." Although the show would only last one season, McFadden had a great time voicing McCool's Keystone Cop father, the unintelligible Harry McCool, who needed another cop to interpret what he said.

One thing that never had to be explained to McFadden was how to get commercials. His approach was unique but effective. On one famous 1970s national commercial for the laundry detergent *Whisk*, McFadden had to audition for a parrot that squawked, "Ring around the collar." When going in for the audition, McFadden thought, "Oh, God. I have to do an audition for a parrot. Who can't do a parrot? Anybody that I know that I compete with can do it upside down." Realizing he had to do something different, McFadden came up with a brainstorm. "I think there were about eleven or twelve guys there, and I was about the last guy to go in. The producer had had a bad day, and so I said, 'Can this parrot act?' and I did a death scene. 'Everything is going black. Somebody get me some Whisk. Goodbye.' And the producer says, 'No, no, no, it's just a regular parrot.' And I said, 'Does the parrot sing?' 'No, no, no, he doesn't sing. He just does two lines.' And I said, 'Are you sure he doesn't sing? *Ring around the collar!* I have just about gone my limit with this guy, so I said, 'Okay,' and in a regular parrot voice said 'pretty shirt' and 'ring around the collar.' This is the thing you leave them with, because the producer has a lot of things on his mind besides you. The actor likes to think that he is the total focus, but if the producer figures, 'I won't have any problems with this guy because he can do it several ways,' that's the thing you want to leave them with."

Apart from commercials, the rest of McFadden's animation career would be for one studio, Rankin/Bass. Rick Goldschmidt, author of the book *The Enchanted World of Rankin/Bass,* notes, "Next to Paul Frees and Alan Swift, Bob McFadden voiced most of the other Rankin/Bass incidental characters over the years. He did Snarf in *Thundercats,* Jingle Bells in *The Year without a Santa Claus,* Baron Von Frankenstein in *Mad, Mad, Mad Monsters,* and Jasper the court jester in *The Enchanted World of Danny Kaye.*" According to McFadden, Jules Bass once confided to him during a session, " 'I've used everybody in the business who does voices, and I think there are two people who are the best in the business, and that's you in New York, and Paul Frees on the West Coast.' He said something interesting to me. He said, 'All these people who do voices, and there are hundreds of them and they are very, very good, but they can't act. They can do impeccable impersonations of somebody, but they cannot act the context of doing that voice, whereas *you* take a voice, and you become that person and you're acting and you're believable.' I never really fully understood that, but he's a big guy, so I was very flattered."

In the 1980s, McFadden decided to leave the hectic life in New York for the more sedate atmosphere of Delray Beach, Florida. Though he continued to do selected commercials, McFadden spent most of his time performing in clubs and condominiums until October 1998.

On January 7, 2000, at the age of seventy-six, Bob McFadden died of Lou Gehrig's disease. Goldschmidt summed it up when he wrote, "Bob was an outstanding talent that certainly was underappreciated in recent years. . . . He will be sorely missed."

CREDITS

Abercrombie the Zombie (1965) TV
Abominable Mountaineers, The (1968) . . . . Sad Cat/Impressario
Adventure by the Sea (1964) . . . . Luno the White Stallion

All Teed Off (1967) . . . . Sad Cat/Impressario
And So Tibet (1964)
Astronut Show, The (1965) TV Series . . . . Oscar Mild/Various Voices
Balloon Snatcher (1969) . . . . Oscar
Batfink (1967) TV Series . . . . Additional Voices
Beggin' the Dragon (1966)
Big Game Fishing (1968) . . . . Sad Cat/Impressario
Boy Pest (1963)
Brother Bat (1967)
Brother from Outer Space (1964) . . . . Oscar Mild/Gadmouse
Cagey Business (1965)
Clean Sweep (1967)
Commander Great Guy (1968) . . . . Sad Cat/Impressario
Coneheads, The (1983) TV . . . . Louie Boucher
Cool McCool (1966) TV Series . . . . Cool McCool/Harry McCool
Courageous Cat and Minute Mouse (1960) TV Series . . . . Courageous Cat/Minute Mouse
Defiant Giant, The (1966)
Don't Spill the Beans (1965) . . . . Fenimore
Drawing Power (1980) TV Series
Dress Reversal (1965) . . . . Sad Cat
Dribble Drabble (1968) . . . . Sad Cat/Impressario
Drum up a Tenant (1963)
Easter Bunny Is Comin' to Town, The (1977) TV . . . . Chugs
Electronica (1960)
Enchanted World of Danny Kaye: The Emperor's New Clothes, The (1972) TV . . . . Jaspar
Fiddle-Faddle (1960)
Fiddlin'Around (1962)
Flight of Dragons, The (1986) . . . . Sir Orin Neville Smythe
From Nags to Witches (1966)
Fuzz, The (1967)
Gadmouse, the Apprentice Good Fairy (1965) . . . . Fenimore/Sad Cat/Gadmouse/Letimore
Galaxia (1960)
Going Ape (1970) . . . . Oscar
Gold Dust Bandit, The (1964) . . . . Luno the White Stallion
Good Snooze Tonight (1963)
Grand Prix Winner (1968) . . . . Sad Cat/Impressario
Harry Happy (1963)
Haunted Housecleaning (1966) . . . . Oscar
Homer on the Range (1964)
Horning In (1965)
Hound about That (1961)
Hound for Pound (1963)
I Want My Mummy (1966)
Itch, The (1965)
Judo Kudos (1967) . . . . Sad Cat/Impressario
Karate Kat (1987) TV Series
King Rounder (1963) . . . . Luno the White Stallion
Kisser Plant (1964) . . . . Oscar
Life & Adventures of Santa Claus, The (1985) TV . . . . Tingler
Little Drummer Boy Book II, The (1976) TV
Loops and Swoops (1967) . . . . Sad Cat/Impressario

Miceniks (1960)

Mike the Masquerader (1960)

Milton the Monster Show, The (1965) TV Series . . . . Milton the Monster/Fearless Fly

Missing Genie, The (1963) . . . . Luno the White Stallion

Molecular Mixup (1964) . . . . Oscar Mild

Mouse Trek (1967)

Nearsighted and Far Out (1964)

No Space like Home (1971) . . . . Oscar

Odor-Able Kitty, The (1945)

Ocean Bruise (1965)

One of the Family (1962)

Oscar's Birthday Present (1971) . . . . Oscar

Oscar's Thinking Cap (1971) . . . . Oscar

Outer Galaxy Gazette (1964) . . . . Oscar

Outside Dope, The (1965)

Penny Ante (1965)

Phantom Moustacher (1961)

Pig's Feat, The (1963)

Pinocchio's Christmas (1980) TV

Poor Little Witch Girl (1965)

Potions and Notions (1966)

Robot Ringer (1962)

Robot Rival (1964)

Robots in Toyland (1965) . . . . Oscar

Roc-a-Bye Sinbad (1964) . . . . Luno the White Stallion

Rudolph and Frosty's Christmas in July (1979) TV

Scientific Sideshow (1969) . . . . Oscar

Scuba Duba Do (1966) . . . . Fenimore

Sheepish Wolf (1963)

Shoe Flies (1965)

Silly Scandals (1931)

Silverhawks (1986) TV Series . . . . Cmdr. Stargazer/Steel Will/Hardware

Sky's the Limit, The (1965) . . . . Oscar

Solitary Refinement (1966)

Sour Gripes (1963)

Space Pet (1969) . . . . Oscar

Squaw Path, The (1967)

T.V. Fuddlehead (1959)

Tell Me a Badtime Story (1963)

Third Musketeer, The (1965) . . . . Fenimore

Throne for a Loss (1966)

Thundercats (1985) TV Series . . . . Snarf/S-s-slithe

Tiger's Tail, A (1964)

Trick or Cheat (1966)

Trick or Tree (1961)

Trouble in Baghdad (1963) . . . . Luno the White Stallion

Turtle Scoop (1961)

Twinkle, Twinkle Little Telestar (1965) . . . . Oscar

Year without a Santa Claus, The (1974) TV Special . . . . Jingle Bells

JACK MERCER

Popeye, the ever popular squinty-eyed, muscle-bound, spinach-eating sailor man first appeared playing a secondary character to regulars Olive Oyl and then-boyfriend Ham in a popular newspaper comic strip called "Thimble Theater." The brainchild of Elzie Crisler Segar, he was created for a single appearance in 1929; however, by 1933 he remained so popular that the Fleischer studio acquired the rights for an animated version. When he made his appearance, it was yet again as a supporting character, this time to Betty Boop in the aptly titled short *Popeye the Sailor*. But, it was only when Fleischer animator Jack Mercer was able to bring his wit and talent as both a writer and voice-actor to the character in subsequent cartoons that Popeye was on his way to becoming a cultural icon.

Mercer was born into a show business family and had been comfortable on stage since he was able to walk and then tap dance. His parents, knowing that show business was a tough lifestyle, wanted their son to earn a living using his artistic talent. His wife, Virginia, recalled that he complied until the seventeen-year-old briefly enrolled in a design school. On the first day, he sold a design for curtains and quickly decided that home-decorating design was not the career path he wanted to take. Fortunately, Mercer's mother—who was a successful enough performer to have worked with entertainers as renowned as Lucille Ball—relented and, through her agent, got him started in the Fleischer brothers' studio as an animation artist.

Mercer seized his opportunity to add "voice artist" to his resume after the first man who voiced Popeye—the vaudeville singer William Costello, better known as "Red Pepper Sam"—was fired. According to Leslie Cabarga in *The Fleischer Story*, Costello had won the part when Dave Fleischer heard his rendition of Gus Gorilla on the Betty Boop radio show and judged his raspy voice fitting for the character of Popeye. But, as Olive Oyl co-star Mae Questel was quoted in *Of Mice and Magic*, "He did it for one year, that's all. Success went to his head so fast it was ridiculous." Demanding a vacation in the middle of a production, Costello found himself unemployed. The Fleischers then conducted a search that grew increasingly desperate for a replacement. A drummer from the Paramount-associated Fred Waring orchestra was hired, only to be promptly let go when he immediately asked Waring for more money. The studio reportedly was so desperate that at least one other man was briefly tried after Dave Fleischer hired him off the street while buying a newspaper.

Meanwhile, Mercer had been entertaining his colleagues in the inbetweener department with his impressions and quirky voices he did while hard at work at the drawing board. When Lou Fleischer overhead him doing a masterful rendition of the *Popeye* theme song, he was instantly impressed, but brother Dave at first rejected the idea on the grounds that they were short of animators. When the part went unfilled, the executives asked him to record a test session as Popeye, then offered him the role. Virginia Mercer recalled that her future husband was not sure he was capable of sustaining the performance. "His natural voice was quite high when he was eighteen, nineteen. . . . But as he would be drawing, he'd make crazy sounds and they all figured, well, he can really do almost anything. He told me he went home and he practiced and he practiced until he could get his voice deep enough that he finally found that he could do it."

At the Fleischer studio, the character underwent something of a transformation as several traits were added that were not in the original comic strip. While his new ardor for spinach and shuffling gait were stylistic choices, the muttered ad-libs became something of a necessity. Although much of the dialogue was scripted by Mercer and the other writers ahead of time, the improvised asides were an attempt to contend with a soundtrack that was recorded "post synch." That is, the voices were recorded after the drawings of the characters speaking were finished and the voice actors then had to record their performance to match the "lip-flaps" that the animators had already drawn. Difficulty arose when the artists would often draw lip movements that could not be matched by the written dialogue. So, Mercer, as one of the writers, would be expected to compensate.

Mercer, a full-time employee of the studio, stayed loyal during the animation strike of 1937 against the Fleischer studio. In sympathy for the living conditions of the animators, picketers from the Commercial Artists and Designers Union had organized protests in theaters and persuaded more than five hundred theaters to ban Fleischer films. According to his wife, Mercer was hardly "Popeye, the union man," as went the strikers' chant. Mercer did not want to get involved with the strikers who were sometimes violent and involved the police, nor did he even wish to discuss the subject, although he hinted to his wife that there had been some attempts at intimidation. "He told me a couple of stories. One day he got on the subway to go home, he was living in Manhattan, and there were two great big goons. Jack wasn't very big and it was sort of intimidating without them saying anything. He was not part of that. He continued working."

According to co-star Jackson Beck, who played Popeye's nemesis Bluto, Mercer's reluctance to make waves even extended to his own situation: "He was the timid soul come to life. When we were doing *Popeye* and some other stuff, I said, 'You know, we need more money.' He said, 'Oh, no, no, no, no, no, no, no. I'm very happy with what we're getting.' I said, 'Look, they're taking advantage of us. I'll put in for a raise for all three of us.' So, of course, Mae [Questel] came right along with me, and we bulldozed him, you know. We talked him into it. He was scared to death he'd get sacked. It was awful. We had to build courage into him to say, 'No, I'm not going to do it unless I get some more money.' We finally succeeded in spite of it. He was happy with that. I said to him, 'Jack, if you don't ask, you don't get.' He was a marvelous little guy. I really liked him a lot."

Mercer's wife pointed out that even in the highly collaborative medium of animation, her husband was so multi-talented that he did not necessarily need to depend on others. For a cartoon short he created about an Italian mouse, Mercer first wrote the song and story. But by the time that they were ready to record the background music, he was told by the head of the music department (who was also the head of the union) " 'Jack, you're aware that we are on strike. You'll have to play the accordion and accompany yourself.' " Mercer's wife continues that it was she who was not too thrilled by that prospect. "I had made him give up the accordion because we also had the piano. I said, 'For Godsakes, in a five-room apartment how many [instruments] can you have?' So, he had to rent one, and he practiced, and all weekend I was going out of my mind. But, he did everything in that one."

Mercer's work helped make the *Popeye* series so successful that by the late 1930s, some polls showed that the character was even more popular than Mickey Mouse. Production did not stop, even with the onset of World War II when Mercer was called into active duty and trained for combat. According to his wife, after the government found out who he was, they wanted him to go into the U.S.O., as many of the other performers spent the war there or in Armed Forces Radio. Mercer was well aware that to do so might help to advance his career. However, out of loyalty, he chose to stay with his friends that he had trained with in the Army and was then assigned to fight as part of an anti-aircraft artillery unit in Germany. In New York, the overly optimistic Fleischers backlogged the scripts, hoping that Mercer could do them on a furlough. Eventually, though, they had to scramble to find a replacement, which sometimes meant even Mae Questel had to double for Mercer on "six or seven" of the wartime cartoons.

When Mercer returned from the war, he went back to work for the studio but also did some moonlighting for onetime Fleischer animator Joe Oriolio, who became the producer/director of a version of *Felix the Cat* syndicated for television in the early 1960s. Mercer was the voice of all of the characters in 260 *Felix the Cat* cartoons, but, according to Mercer's wife, did not have time to write for the *Felix* shows because he was still working full-time for the Fleischers. Going over to Oriolo's after work at night, Mercer found the experience working on the cartoon was not as enjoyable as *Popeye*. Oriolo, who was extremely budget conscious, was trying to instruct his staff of middle-aged former Fleischer animators in the new style of "limited" TV animation perfected by Hanna-Barbera. According to John Canemaker, in *Felix, the*

Twisted Tale of the World's Most Famous Cat, "One of his dictums became well known within the industry: scenes that could not fit under his office door, said Oriolo, held too many drawings." To further limit the need for more elaborate animation and accordingly save money from Oriolo's already stretched budget, Mercer was also asked to enunciate very slowly, which would require less labor-intensive artwork. Mercer was also not particularly pleased that he had to continually alter the pitch of his voice, as he was asked to perform the soundtrack straight through, instead of having the luxury of recording each character separately to be edited together later on—the practice of many studios.

When Fleischer's studio eventually folded, along with it went Mercer's steady nine to five job. According to his wife, Hanna-Barbera then asked Mercer (who now also had previous experience writing for *Milton the Monster* and would go on to write for cartoons like the 1960s version of *Casper, the Friendly Ghost* and *Deputy Dawg*) to come out to Los Angeles to write and perform character voices.

Although she reports that Hanna-Barbera was very accommodating and boarded him in an apartment where he could write and come over to the studio as needed, he was somewhat uncomfortable because he could feel a real sense of competition between the East Coast and West Coast writers. The professional jealousy was aggravated by the fact that the talented artist could also draw his own storyboards, which he did. That he was also encroaching on the other storyboard artists' turf did not endear him to them either. According to Virginia, this culminated when "the [CBS] vice president took all the writers to lunch, except Jack, and he says, 'Oh, my God, what now?' And they all came back and said, 'Ha, teacher's pet!'" It seems the vice president had taken all Mercer's work along to use as an example of the quality of work that the network wanted. "Some of them went up into the Hollywood Hills and got drunk. It was so good for his ego."

Also making for an uncomfortable situation, Mercer knew well that this version of *Popeye* was mired in the beginnings of political correctness and found writing for the show "very restrictive." While the Fleischers had produced the theatricals shorts for more adult audiences, the Saturday morning version was aimed primarily at the younger set. Even though the network executives seemed to ignore that fact that children could still view the originals rerun in various forms on television, CBS demanded that the trademark slapstick violence be toned down for the new series.

Mercer's wife explains, "When Jack was writing, he said that he couldn't go ahead and have Popeye hit Bluto, or vice versa. They couldn't have that kind of violence. All he could do was, let's say, smack a tree, and then the tree might come down and hit Bluto. It was very frustrating writing, because they couldn't write the way that they used to."

Hanna-Barbera produced the muted cartoons for five years beginning in 1978. The short-lived series featured a pipeless Popeye running a health club. Also, with perhaps a nod to the odd conservative protest group that wanted to ban the cartoons on the basis of their perception that Olive Oyl was the unwed mother of infant Swee'pea, Hanna-Barbera decided to marry the couple and give them a nine-year-old son, Popeye Jr., who, mysteriously, did not look like either one of them or like spinach.

While Mercer was working in Los Angeles in 1980, Robert Altman brought *Popeye* to the big screen, becoming the first of the recent wave to translate animated series to live-action films. Robin Williams was chosen to play the title role and even tried to contact Mercer to research the part. According to Virginia Mercer, it was Marilyn Schreffler, Hanna-Barbera's Olive Oyl, who relayed the message to Mercer that Williams wanted to meet him, to which Mercer replied that he was not interested. Virginia claimed that it was not that he had an objection to Williams, but that Mercer had long since tired of the many instances where he was asked to critique others' impression of his original character and, after a while, he began to politely refuse the requests. Assuming that Williams wished to be coached solely on "fine-tuning" the voice he had created for Popeye, Mercer declined.

However, as the cartoon Popeye did have a cameo in the beginning of the film (a hatch opens and a Popeye caricature appears and Mercer's voice says, "I guess I'm in the wrong picture"), the couple was invited to the premiere. Although they could not attend due to medical concerns, his wife recalls that they were not exactly disconcerted as the film did not receive the acclaim usually granted to the revered auteur's other films. Mercer's wife recalled citing criticism of the writing, "You wouldn't believe how many [people] said, 'Jack . . . you're the best thing in a ten million dollar picture.'" However, fifteen years later she was still amused to find that every time the film would appear on the television schedule, she would continue to receive the requisite ten-dollar residual.

Sadly, only four years after Jack Mercer was finally recognized as a voice actor on the big screen, he passed away, leaving an unprecedented body of work for writing and voicing numerous animated shorts and series. For Popeye alone, he had voiced the character for more than four decades in addition to performing the early voices of Wimpy, Poopdeck Pappy, and his nephews Peepeye, Poopeye, and Pipeye—as well as at one point recording 220 episodes in less than a year when King Features Syndicate produced it for television. Given his contribution to animation, it is surprising that Mercer is not more widely known. As an explanation, Mercer's wife cited the original policy at the Fleischer's studio, which she said was afraid of, among other things, losing a key employee to another studio. "On Jack's first contract with the Fleischers, it said, 'We'd like to use you for Popeye, and you're not to do any other voices for any other company outside for the yearly contract.' Then they'd renew it each year. In other words, they never wanted to give the voice people any credit. They didn't want them to get too big; whereas, Mel Blanc, he insisted upon it right away, so he always got screen credit. The Fleischers gave credit to Jack if he wrote the stories, but [he] never, never got screen credit [for the voice] . . . he always got credit for writing [but] since that was only a small part of his work in the beginning, he would write the stories, and then they'd say, 'Hey Jack, we got a *Popeye*, so come on over and we'll record.' But with Mae Questel and Jackson Beck, that was their livelihood. They were just voice actors, you know, but Jack was part of the whole system. He did almost everything for them."

It has been noted that Mercer could have promoted himself publicly, if nothing else, as a voice actor. *Popeye* and *Casper* animator Myron Waldman was quoted in 1995 as saying of Mercer, "He could have made a lot of money doing personal appearances, but he was so shy he wouldn't do it." Despite his varied career and substantive role in the history of the medium (further discussed in Fred Grandinetti's self-published *I Yam What I Yam*), Virginia Mercer said the number one question he was always asked was, "Do you really like spinach?" She concluded with a laugh, "His stock answer and the truth was 'Yes, with vinegar.'"

CREDITS

Adventures of Popeye (1935) . . . . Popeye
Aladdin and His Wonderful Lamp (1939) . . . . Popeye/Aladdin
All-New Popeye Hour, The (1978) TV Series (story) . . . . Popeye
All's Fair at the Fair (1938) . . . . Elmer
All's Fair at the Fair (1947) . . . . Popeye
Alona on the Sarong Seas (1942) (story) . . . . Popeye/Parrot/Lobster
Alpine for You (1951) (story) . . . . Popeye
Ancient Fistory (1953) . . . . Popeye/Fairy Godfather
Anvil Chorus Girl, The (1944) . . . . Popeye
As the Crow Lies (1951) (story)
Assault and Flattery (1956) . . . . Popeye
Audrey the Rainmaker (1951)
Awful Tooth (1952) (story)

Baby Wants a Battle (1953) (story) . . . . Popeye
Baby Wants a Bottleship (1942) (story) . . . . Popeye
Baby Wants Spinach (1950) (story) . . . . Popeye
Balmy Swami, A (1949) (story) . . . . Popeye
Barking Dogs Don't Fite (1949) (story) . . . . Popeye
Base Brawl (1948) . . . . Tommy Tortoise
Be Mice to Cats (1960) (story)
Beach Peach (1950) . . . . Popeye
Beaus Will Be Beaus (1955) . . . . Popeye
Betty Boop and Grampy (1935) (voice)
Betty Boop's Penthouse (1933) (voice)
Big Bad Sindbad (1952) . . . . Popeye/Nephews
Big Chief Ugh-Amugh-Ugh (1938) . . . . Popeye
Big Drip, The (1949) (voice)
Big Flame-Up, The (1949) (voice)
Blunder Below (1942) . . . . Popeye
Boo Hoo Baby (1951) (voice)
Boo Kind to Animals (1955) (voice)
Boo Ribbon Winner (1954) (voice)
Boos and Arrows (1954) (voice)
Boos and Saddles (1953) (voice)
Bopin' Hood (1961) (story)
Bored Cuckoo (1948) . . . . Cuckoo
Boss Is Always Right, The (1960) (story) . . . . Jeepers
Bouncing Benny (1960) (story)
Bout with a Trout, A (1947) . . . . Bob Hope/Jerry Colonna
Bride and Gloom (1954) . . . . Popeye
Bridge Ahoy! (1936) . . . . Popeye
Brotherly Love (1936) . . . . Popeye
Bulldozing the Bull (1938) . . . . Popeye
Busy Buddies (1960) (story) . . . . Jeepers
By the Old Mill Scream (1953) (story)
Camptown Races, The (1948) (voice)
Campus Capers (1949) (story)
Candid Candidate, The (1937) . . . . Constituents
Candy Cabaret (1954) (voice)
Cane and Able (1961) (story)
Cape Kidnaveral (1961) (story) . . . . Spec's Father/Two Friends
Car-azy Drivers (1955) . . . . Popeye
Cartoons Ain't Human (1943) (story) . . . . Popeye/Popeye's nephews/Roger Blackleg/Horse
Case of the Cockeyed Canary, The (1952) (voice)
Casper Comes to Clown (1951) (voice)
Casper Takes a Bow-Wow (1951) (voice)
Casper's Birthday (1959) (voice)
Casper's Spree under the Sea (1950) (voice)
Cat Carson Rides Again (1952) (voice)
Cat in the Act (1957) (story)
Cat Tamale (1951) (voice)
Cat-Choo (1951) (story)
Cheese Burglar (1946) (voice)
Chew-Chew Baby (1958) (voice)

Child Psykolojiky (1941) .... Popeye/Pappy
Child Sockology (1953) (story) .... Popeye
Circus Comes to Clown (1947) (voice)
City Kitty (1952) (voice)
Clown on the Farm (1952) (story)
Cobweb Hotel (1936) (voice)
Comin' round the Mountain (1949) (voice)
Cookin' with Gags (1955) .... Popeye
Cops Is Always Right (1938) .... Popeye
Cops Is Tops (1955) .... Popeye
Counter Attack (1960) (story)
Crazy Town (1954) (voice)
Crystal Brawl, The (1957) .... Popeye
Customers Wanted (1939) .... Popeye
Dandy Lion, The (1940) (voice)
Dante Dreamer (1958) (story)
Date to Skate, A (1938) .... Popeye/Roller Skating Attendant
Deep Boo Sea (1952) (voice)
Deputy Dawg (1959) TV Series (writer)
Disguise the Limit (1960) (story)
Dizzy Dishes (1955) (voice)
Do or Diet (1953) (voice)
Dog Show-Off, The (1948) (story)
Doing Impossikible Stunts (1940) .... Popeye/Movie Director
Doing What's Fright (1959) (voice)
Double-Cross-Country Race (1951)
Down to Mirth (1959) (story) .... Professor Brainstorm
Drinks on the Mouse (1953) (voice)
Drippy Mississippi (1951) (voice)
Dutch Treat (1956) (voice)
Eggs Don't Bounce (1943) (story)
Enchanted Square (1947) (voice)
Farm Foolery (1949) (voice)
Farmer and the Belle, The (1950) .... Popeye
Feast and Furious (1949) (voice)
Felix the Cat (1960) TV Series. . . . Felix/Professor/Rock Bottom/Poindexter/Master Cylinder/
  Vavoom
Females Is Fickle (1940) .... Popeye
Fiddle-Faddle (1960) (story)
Fightin' Pals (1940) .... Popeye/Bluto
Fine Feathered Fiend (1960) (voice)
Firemen's Brawl (1953) (story) .... Popeye
Fit to be Toyed (1959) (story) .... Psychiatrist/Santa Claus/J. P. Grisley's Father
Fleets of Stren'th (1942) (story) .... Popeye
Flies Ain't Human (1941) .... Popeye
Floor Flusher (1954) (story) .... Popeye
Fly's Last Flight, The (1949) .... Popeye
Football Toucher Downer, The (1937) .... Popeye
For Better or Nurse (1945) .... Popeye
Forest Fantasy (1952) (voice)
Fowl Play (1937) .... Popeye

Fresh Vegetable Mystery, The (1939) (voice*)*
Friend or Phony (1952) . . . . Popeye
Fright from Wrong (1956) (story)
Fright to the Finish (1954) (story) . . . . Popeye
Frightday the 13th (1953) (story)
Frighty Cat (1958) (voice)
Frog Legs (1962) (voice)
From Dime to Dime (1960) (story)
From Mad to Worse (1957) (voice)
Fun at the Fair (1952) (voice)
Fun on Furlough (1959) (voice)
Funderful Suburbia (1962) (story)
Gabby's Swing Cleaning (1941) (voice)
Gabriel Church Kitten (1944) (voice)
Gag and Baggage (1952) (voice)
Ghosks Is the Bunk (1939) . . . . Popeye
Ghost of Honor (1957) (voice)
Ghostwriters (1958) (story)
Giddy Gadgets (1962) (story)
Gift of Gag (1955) . . . . Popeye
Git Along Lil' Duckie (1955) (voice)
Gobs of Fun (1950) (voice)
Good Scream Fun (1950) (story)
Goofy Goofy Gander (1950)
Goonland (1938) . . . . Popeye/Pappy
Gopher Spinach (1954) . . . . Popeye
Gramps to the Rescue (1963) (story)
Granite Hotel (1940) (voice)
Greek Mirthology (1954) . . . . Popeye/Nephews
Gulliver's Travels (1939) . . . . King Little/Prince David (speaking)/King Bombo/Sneak/Snoop/Snitch
Gym Jam (1950) (story) . . . . Popeye
Happy Birthdaze (1943) . . . . Popeye/Shorty/Neighbor
Haul in One, A (1956) . . . . Popeye
Hector's Hectic Life (1948) (voice)
Hello, How Am I? (1939) . . . . Popeye/Wimpy
Henpecked Rooster, The (1944) (story)
Hep Cat Symphony (1949) (story/voice)
Her Honor the Mare (1943) (story) . . . . Popeye/Popeye's Nephews
Hiccup Hound (1963) (story/voice)
Hide and Peek (1956) (voice)
Hi-Fi Jinx (1962) (story)
Hill-billing and Cooing (1956) (story) . . . . Popeye
Hold That Lion, Please (1951) (voice)
Hold the Wire (1936) . . . . Popeye
Hooky Spooky (1957) (voice)
Hospitaliky (1937) . . . . Popeye
Hot-Air Aces (1949) . . . . Popeye
Hound for Pound (1963) (story)
Houndabout (1959) (story) . . . . Julius
House Builder-Upper, The (1938) . . . . Popeye
House Tricks? (1946) . . . . Popeye

How Green Is My Spinach (1950) . . . . Popeye
Huey's Father's Day (1959) (story)
Hull of a Mess, A (1942) (story) . . . . Popeye
Hungry Goat, The (1943) . . . . Popeye/The Admiral/Kid
Hunky and Spunky (1938) (voice)
Hysterical History (1953) (voice)
I Don't Scare (1956) (story) . . . . Popeye
I Likes Babies and Infinks (1937) . . . . Popeye
I Never Changes My Altitude (1937) . . . . Popeye
I Wanna Be a Life Guard (1936) . . . . Popeye
I Yam Love Sick (1938) . . . . Popeye
Ice Scream (1957) (story)
I'll Be Skiing Ya (1947) . . . . Popeye
I'll Never Crow Again (1941) . . . . Popeye/Crows
I'm in the Army Now (1936) . . . . Popeye
Impractical Joker, The (1937) . . . . Irving
In the Nicotine (1961) (story)
Insect to Injury (1956) . . . . Popeye
Invention Convention (1953) (voice)
I-Ski Love-Ski You-Ski (1936) . . . . Popeye
It's a Hap-Hap Happy Day (1941) (voice)
It's the Natural Thing to Do (1939) . . . . Popeye/Bluto
Jeep, The (1938) . . . . Popeye
Jitterbug Jive (1950) (story) . . . . Popeye
Job for a Gob, A (1955) . . . . Popeye
Jolly Good Ferlough, A (1943) . . . . Popeye/Popeye's Nephews/Twinkletoes
Jumping with Toy (1957) (story)
Katnip's Big Day (1959) (voice)
Keep Your Grin Up (1955) (voice)
Kick in Time, A (1940) (voice)
Kickin' the Conga' Round (1942) . . . . Popeye
Kid from Mars (1960) (story)
King for a Day (1940) . . . . The Little King
King of the Mardi Gras (1935) . . . . Popeye
Kozmo Goes to School (1961) (story) . . . . Truant Officer/School Bully
Land of Lost Watches (1951)
Land of the Lost, The (1948) (voice)
Learn Polikeness (1938) . . . . Popeye
Leave Well Enough Alone (1939) . . . . Popeye
Let's Celebrake (1938) . . . . Popeye
Let's Get Movin' (1936) . . . . Popeye
Let's Stalk Spinach (1951) . . . . Popeye
Line of Screammage (1956) (story)
Lion in the Roar (1956) (voice)
Lion's Busy, The (1961) (story/voice)
Little Boo Peep (1953) (voice)
Little Brown Jug (1948) (voice)
Little Red School Mouse (1949) (story)
Little Stranger, The (1936) (voice)
Little Swee' Pea (1936) . . . . Popeye
Loose in a Caboose (1947) (voice)

Lost and Foundry (1937) . . . . Popeye
Lumberjack and Jill (1949) (story) . . . . Popeye
Lunch with a Punch (1952) (story) . . . . Popeye/Nephews
Many Tanks (1942) . . . . Popeye
Marry-Go-Round, The (1943) . . . . Popeye/Shorty
Matty's Funday Funnies (Beany & Cecil) (1959) TV Series (writer) . . . . Additional Voices
Me Feelins Is Hurt (1940) . . . . Popeye/Bluto
Me Musical Nephews (1942) (story) . . . . Popeye/Nephews
Mess Production (1945) . . . . Popeye
Mice Capades (1952) (voice)
Mice Meeting You (1950) (voice)
Mice Paradise (1951) (story)
Miceniks (1960) (story/voice)
Mighty Hercules, The (1963) TV Series. . . . Various Characters
Mighty Navy, The (1941) . . . . Popeye
Mighty Termite, The (1961) (voice)
Mike the Masquerader (1960) (story)
Milton the Monster (1965) TV Series (writer)
Mister and Mistletoe (1955) (story) . . . . Popeye/Nephews
Mite Makes Right, The (1948) (voice)
Monkee Doodles (1960) (voice)
Morning, Noon, and Nightclub (1937) . . . . Popeye
Mouse Blanche (1962) (story)
Mousetro Herman (1956) (story/voice)
Mouseum (1956) (story)
Mousieur Herman (1955) (voice)
Moving Aweigh (1944) . . . . Popeye/Shorty/Cop/Mailman
Mr. Bug Goes to Town (1941) . . . . Mr. Bumble/Swat
Mr. Money Gags (1957) . . . . Tommy Tortoise
Musical Lulu (1946) (voice)
Musical Mountaineers (1939) (voice)
Mutiny Ain't Nice (1938) . . . . Popeye
Mutt in a Rut (1949) (story)
My Artistical Temperature (1937) . . . . Popeye
My Pop, My Pop (1940) . . . . Popeye/Pappy
Nearlyweds (1957) . . . . Popeye
Never Kick a Woman (1936) . . . . Popeye
Never Sock a Baby (1939) . . . . Popeye
New Casper Cartoon Show, The (1963) TV Series. . . . Various Voices
Newshound (1955) (story)
Nix on Hypnotricks (1941) . . . . Popeye/Professor I. Stare/Taxi Driver
North Pal (1953) (voice)
Northern Mites (1960) (story/voice)
Northwest Mousie (1953) (story)
Not Ghoulty (1959) (story)
Nurse to Meet Ya (1955) (story) . . . . Popeye
Nurse-Mates (1940) . . . . Popeye
Of Mice and Magic (1953) (voice)
Off We Glow (1952) (voice)
Oily Bird, The (1954) (voice)
Okey-Dokey Donkey (1958) (story)

Olive Oyl and Water Don't Mix (1942) (story) .... Popeye
Olive Oyl for President (1948) .... Popeye
Olive's $weep$take Ticket (1941) .... Popeye
Olive's Boithday Presink (1941) .... Popeye/Geezle
One Funny Knight (1957) (story)
One of the Family (1962) (story)
One Quack Mind (1951) (story)
One Weak Vacation (1963) (story)
Onion Pacific (1940) .... Popeye/Bluto
Organ Grinder's Swing (1937) .... Popeye
Our Funny Finny Friends (1949)
Out of This Whirl (1959) (story)
Out to Punch (1956) .... Popeye/Ringside Announcer
Paneless Window Washer, The (1937) .... Popeye
Parlez Vous Woo (1956) .... Popeye
Party Smarty (1951) (story)
Patriotic Popeye (1957) .... Popeye
Peck Your Own Home (1960) (voice)
Peekaboo (1957) (voice)
Peep in the Deep (1946) .... Popeye
Penguin for Your Thoughts (1956) (voice)
Penny Antics (1955) .... Popeye
Perry Popgun (1962) (story)
Pest Pilot (1941) .... Popeye/Poopdeck Pappy/P.A. Announcer
Pest Pupil (1957)
Pig's Feat, The (1963) (story)
Pilgrim Popeye (1951) (story) .... Popeye/Nephews/The Turkey
Pip-eye, Pup-eye, Poop-eye, an' Peep-eye (1942) .... Popeye/Nephews
Pitchin' Woo at the Zoo (1944) .... Popeye
Planet Mouseola (1960) (story)
Pleased to Eat You (1950) .... Hunter/Zoo Dietitian
Plumbing Is a "Pipe" (1938) .... Popeye/Wimpy
Poop Goes the Weasel (1955) (story/voice)
Popalong Popeye (1952) (story) .... Popeye/Nephews
Popcorn and Politics (1962) (story) .... Vice President
Popeye (1956) TV Series. ... Popeye/Wimpy
Popeye, the Ace of Space (1953) (story) .... Popeye
Popeye and the Pirates (1947) .... Popeye
Popeye for President (1956) (story) .... Popeye
Popeye Makes a Movie (1950) .... Popeye/Nephews
Popeye Meets Hercules (1948) .... Popeye
Popeye Meets Rip Van Winkle (1941) .... Popeye/Rip Van Winkle
Popeye Meets William Tell (1940) .... Popeye/William Tell
Popeye Presents Eugene, the Jeep (1940) .... Popeye
Popeye the Sailor Meets Ali Baba's Forty Thieves (1937) .... Popeye
Popeye the Sailor Meets Sindbad the Sailor (1936) .... Popeye/Wimpy
Popeye's 20th Anniversary (1954) .... Popeye/Bob Hope/Dean Martin/Jerry Lewis/Jimmy Durante
Popeye's Mirthday (1953) (story) .... Popeye/Nephews
Popeye's Pappy (1952) .... Popeye/Pappy
Popeye's Premiere (1949) .... Popeye
Pop-Pie a la Mode (1945) .... Popeye

Possum Pearl (1957) (story)
Pre-hysterical Man (1948) (story) . . . . Popeye
Private Eye Popeye (1954) . . . . Popeye
Problem Pappy (1941) . . . . Popeye/Poopdeck Pappy
Protek the Weakerist (1937) . . . . Popeye
Punch and Judo (1951) . . . . Popeye/The Ringside Referee/Champ/Orphan
Puppet Love (1944) . . . . Popeye
Puttin' on the Act (1940) . . . . Popeye
Quack-a-Doodle-Doo (1950) (story) . . . . Fox
Quick on the Vigor (1950) (story) . . . . Popeye
Quiet! Pleeze (1941) . . . . Popeye/Pappy/Construction Worker
Rabbit Punch (1955) . . . . Tommy Tortoise
Raggedy Ann and Raggedy Andy (1941) . . . . Paint Brush/Doctors
Rail Rodents (1954) (story)
Ration fer the Duration (1943) (story) . . . . Popeye/Nephews/Gianty
Red, White, and Boo (1955)
Rhythm on the Reservation (1939)
Right off the Bat (1958) (story) . . . . Pee Wee/Team Scout/Rube Clodhopper
Riot in Rhythm (1950) . . . . Popeye/Nephews
Robin Hood-Winked (1948) . . . . Popeye/Little John
Robin Rodenthood (1955)
Royal Four-Flusher, The (1947) . . . . Popeye
Safari so Good (1947) . . . . Popeye
Sally Swing (1938) . . . . College Dean
Santa's Surprise (1947)
Scout Fellow (1951) (story)
Scouting for Trouble (1960) (story) . . . . Jeepers
Scrap the Japs (1942) . . . . Popeye
Scrappily Married (1945)
Seapreme Court, The (1954)
Seein' Red, White, 'n' Blue (1943) . . . . Popeye
Self-Made Mongrel, A (1945)
Service with a Guile (1946) . . . . Popeye
Shakespearian Spinach (1940) . . . . Popeye/Bluto
Shaving Muggs (1953) . . . . Popeye
She-Sick Sailors (1944) . . . . Popeye
Ship A-Hooey (1954)
Shoe Must Go On, The (1960) (story) . . . . Luigi the Blacksmith/Concert Promoter/Conductor
Shootin' Stars (1960) (story)
Shuteye Popeye (1952) . . . . Popeye
Sight for Squaw Eyes, A (1963)
Silly Hillbilly (1949) . . . . Popeye
Silly Science (1960) (story)
Sir Irving and Jeames (1956)
Sky Scrappers (1957)
Sleuth but Sure (1956) . . . . Tommy Tortoise
Slip Us Some Redskin (1951) . . . . Older Indian
Small Fry (1939)
Snooze Reel (1951)
Snow Foolin' (1949)
Snow Place like Home (1948) (story) . . . . Popeye

Snubbed by a Snob (1940)
Sock-a-Bye Kitty (1950) (story)
Space Varmit (1962) (story)
Spinach fer Britain (1943) .... Popeye
Spinach Packin' Popeye (1944) .... Popeye
Spinach Roadster, The (1936) .... Popeye
Spinach vs. Hamburgers (1948) .... Popeye/Nephews
Spook and Spin (1938)
Spook No Evil (1953)
Spooking about Africa (1957) (story)
Spooking of Ghosts (1959) .... Ghost
Spooking with a Brogue (1955)
Spooky Swabs (1957) .... Popeye/Ghosts
Sporticles (1958)
Spree Lunch (1957) (story) .... Popeye
Spring Song (1948)
Spunky Skunky (1952) .... Tommy Tortoise
Starting from Hatch (1953) (story)
Stealin' Ain't Honest (1940) .... Popeye
Stork Market, The (1949)
Stork Raving Mad (1958)
Sudden Fried Chicken (1946)
Suddenly, It's Spring! (1944)
Superman (1941) .... The Mad Scientist
Superman in Destruction, Inc. (1942) .... Jimmy Olsen
Superman in Jungle Drums (1943) .... Jimmy Olsen
Superman in Showdown (1942) .... Jimmy Olsen
Superman in the Eleventh Hour (1942) .... Jimmy Olsen
Superman in the Japoteurs (1942) .... Military Officer/Japoteur Leader
Surf and Sound (1954)
Swab the Duck (1956)
Swimmer Take All (1952) (story) .... Popeye
Symphony in Spinach (1948) .... Popeye
T.V. Fuddlehead (1959) (story)
Talking Horse Sense (1959) (story)
Tar with a Star (1949) (story) .... Popeye
Taxi-Turvy (1954) .... Popeye
Tell Me a Bad-Time Story (1963) (story)
Terry the Terror (1960) (story)
Thrill of Fair (1951) (story) .... Popeye
To Boo or Not to Boo (1951)
Too Weak to Work (1943) .... Popeye
Tops in the Big Top (1945) .... Popeye
Toreadorable (1953) (story) .... Popeye
Tots of Fun (1952) .... Popeye
Toys Will Be Toys (1949)
Travelaffs (1958)
Trigger Treat (1960) .... Sheriff
Trouble Date (1960) (story)
True Boo (1952)
Turning Fables, The (1960) (story)

Turtle Scoop (1961) (story)

Twinkletoes—Where He Goes Nobody Knows (1941) (voice)

Twisker Pitcher, The (1937) . . . . Popeye

Ups and Downs Derby (1950) (story)

Vacation with Play (1951) (story) . . . . Popeye

Vim, Vigor, and Vitaliky (1936) . . . . Popeye

Vitamin Hay (1941)

Way Back When a Nightclub was a Stick (1940)

Wedding Belts (1940)

We're in the Honey (1948) (story/voice)

We're on Our Way to Rio (1944) (story) . . . . Popeye

What—No Spinach? (1936) . . . . Popeye

Which Is Witch (1958)

Whiz Quiz Kid (1963) (story)

Wigwam Whoopee (1948) (story) . . . . Popeye

Will Do Mousework (1956)

Wimmin Hadn't Oughta Drive (1940) . . . . Popeye

Wimmin Is a Myskery (1940) . . . . Popeye/Nephews

Win Place and Showboat (1950)

Winner by a Hare (1953) . . . . Tommy Tortoise

With Poopdeck Pappy (1940) (story) . . . . Popeye/Poopdeck Pappy

Wolf in Sheik's Clothing, A (1948) . . . . Popeye

Wood-Peckin' (1943) . . . . Popeye

Wotta Knight (1947) . . . . Popeye/Little King

Wotta Nitemare (1939) . . . . Popeye/Bluto

Yankee Doodle Donkey (1944) (story)

Yoke's on You, The (1962) (story)

You Said a Mouseful (1958) (story)

You're a Sap, Mr. Jap (1942) . . . . Popeye

You're Not Built That Way (1936) . . . . Butcher

Zero the Hero (1954) (story)

DON MESSICK

Ventriloquist, soldier, "Scooby-Doo"—Don Messick's long climb up the career ladder culminated in the voice of the world's most famous animated dog. Although it's been over thirty-five years since it was originally produced, *Scooby-Doo* is more popular than ever, airing twenty-three times a week in the United States and broadcast in forty-five other countries, and with two live-action feature adaptations. Messick, who became a cartoon icon doing characters like *The Jetsons* dog Astro, Boo Boo and Ranger

Smith on *Yogi Bear*, Pixie of *Pixie & Dixie*, Dr. Quest on *Jonny Quest*, and Papa Smurf on *The Smurfs*, is considered almost as much a cornerstone of Hanna-Barbera as its famous founders.

In the 1930s, the twelve-year-old "country hick kid back in Maryland" discovered that his first love was radio, which he listened to during the summertime for seventeen or eighteen hours per day. Charlie McCarthy and Edgar Bergen were his favorites, so, naturally, he couldn't resist the ad in *Popular Science* whose copy screamed, "Boys, throw your voice!" "When my voice changed, I discovered its flexibility, so it seemed to me that the most logical thing was to learn ventriloquism. I still remember the ad, which showed a picture of a man with a trunk on his back and a voice coming out of the trunk and a kid off on the side snickering because he's throwing his voice into the trunk. I knew I had to try it." After spending a quarter on the ventriloquism kit, Messick found that he couldn't make the mouthpiece work, but the instruction book was instrumental in developing his ventriloquist act. "I was a rather shy, introverted kind of kid, smaller than most for my age, and was picked on and teased a lot by my peers, so it was a surprise when all of a sudden I turned to doing my own radio show when I was fifteen."

"I had appeared on a [radio] talent show in Salisbury and I won first prize on that broadcast. And that led to my being called upon by the station, which acted as a talent agency. When an organization like the Lions or the Elks would be seeking entertainment, they would call the radio station, which had a roster of singers and various kinds of comedic talents. So, I started appearing and making five dollars here and seven dollars there all around the area, and that led to my first weekly radio program—a fifteen-minute thing on Monday nights on WBOC in Salisbury. I played the harmonica. I did about two harmonica duets with an organ and interspersed that with dialogue that I wrote for my characters."

Over the two-year period that Messick did the program, he gradually dropped the harmonica and went to strictly writing and performing a one-man situation comedy show. For those wondering what style his comedy was in those days, the answer is an emphatic "CORNY! I bought a lot of joke books and thumbed through them, and depending on the little situation that I was writing, I would incorporate some of those. I also studied books on radio and production, so I was self-taught in that respect." Messick also gained valuable experience by learning from his mistakes.

Coming into WBOC early one evening with his ventriloquist dummy Kentworth DeForrest, Messick wanted to practice his routine that was to air at 7:30 that night. "I was sitting at the piano, and I was just playing *MMM bump bump . . . MMM bump bump*, and Kentworth was singing 'Shortnin'

Bread.' There was a network newscast, by Fulton Lewis Jr., that was being fed out of Washington, D.C., on the Mutual Radio Network. This was before the pre-taped commercial days, so they had to break away from Washington for a local commercial. There was a woman announcer, which in those days was rare, but, because all the male announcers had been drafted, they were down to using women. So, she was waiting at the broadcast desk for the red light to come on and the engineer to give her the cue to read a commercial for the Wyconico Garage. I was sitting there banging on the piano, when all of a sudden I had this strange feeling come over me. I looked across at the control booth and the engineer was staring back at me with a strange look on his face, and the lady announcer had her head down on the desk in front of the microphone, doubled over in hysterics. I realized what the listeners at home must have heard was Fulton Lewis Jr. saying, 'And now, here's your announcer.' Then the next thing they heard was a high-pitched voice singing, *'Three little children lying in bed, one of them sick and the other most dead.'* The lady announcer tried to gain control of herself and she choked her way through the commercial. I was terribly embarrassed. I thought I would certainly be thrown out of the place bodily, but that didn't happen. I don't think we ever did get back to Fulton Lewis Jr. for his goodnight from Washington."

After high school, Messick put the mortification of the experience behind him and moved to Baltimore to study acting. "I think I had pretty good timing right from the time I started performing, because of listening to the radio [performances of] Jack Benny and Jim Jorden, *Fibber McGee and Molly*, people like that. You can't listen to hours and hours of that sort of thing without some of it rubbing off. But I entered a small dramatic school, no longer in existence, run by one man. He had been a Broadway actor and a graduate of the American Academy of Dramatic Art in New York. His name was William Ramsey Streett. We were known as the 'Streett Players.' Going to that school further developed my timing and delivery and helped me get rid of my down-home Eastern Shore accent."

"One of the productions I starred in was *Night Must Fall*, which is a murder mystery. I played the lead—Danny, a psychopathic, homicidal maniac. That was one of my favorites. I also appeared in *Arsenic and Old Lace*, in which I played Dr. Einstein with a Peter Lorre–type voice. At the time I didn't know a movie was going to be made, and Peter Lorre was going to be doing the part of Dr. Einstein in the movie! We did *George Washington Slept Here* and *The Man Who Came to Dinner*. I preferred playing character roles."

Unfortunately, World War II disrupted many plans, among them, Messick's burgeoning acting career. "I was drafted in January of 1945. I was put into basic training in a special division of the infantry, the message center.

When I had written that I did radio work, they, in their infinite wisdom, assumed that it was technical radio. So they figured I could learn Morse code and operate the 'Tick-Tick' thing. Well, needless to say, I wasn't very good at that, but it was better than being a basic rifleman trainee."

If the army did nothing else for Messick, it brought him to the West Coast. "They put me on a troop train again and shipped me to California—Fort Ord. That's the first time I saw California. I was then eighteen years old, and I fell in love with it. By then I was with Special Services, which was the entertainment branch of the infantry, and I took my ventriloquist dummy that I had renamed 'Woody' DeForrest with me. My mother had made him a uniform and we started entertaining almost right from day one. Woody got me out of a lot of dirty detail while in the service."

It was during one of these shows that Messick was faced with a performer's worst nightmare. Inexplicably, his entire audience suddenly stood up and walked out leaving a bewildered Messick staring at an empty hall. "In the middle of the act, I started hearing a shuffling of chairs and the guys started getting up. I finished my act as hastily as I could and dashed offstage into the wings. I asked the MC what was happening and he says, 'Well, can't you smell it?' I had a serious sinus problem at that time so I said, 'No,' and he said, 'Skunk.' The ventilation ducts were open to the outside and a skunk had crawled into the shaft and let loose. The stench was filling the entire auditorium in the middle of my act."

After about a year and a half in the military, Messick received his discharge in 1946 and decided to take his chances in Hollywood. "I got into a thing that was sponsored by the radio actors' union, which was then known as AFRA, the American Federation of Radio Artists, not AFTRA [changed in 1952 to include television actors]. It was a workshop kind of thing which met a couple of times a week, and we recorded half-hour radio dramas. The man who headed up the workshop was named Robert Light, who was the head of the Southern California Broadcasters Association. Robert Light was friendly with Paula Stone, a well-known actress at the time. She and her husband were connected with the workshop and developed a fifteen-minute radio show for RCA Victor called *The Raggedy Ann Show*, based on the dolls. I was Raggedy Andy. That was my first continuing radio series, and it ran for thirty-nine weeks."

When the show was ended by a musician's strike, there seemed to be no work in Los Angeles to be found. "I went on the road for a while in the Midwest, playing theaters and doing my ventriloquist act. I then dumped myself in New York, where I had a few starving months, and made the rounds of producers' offices. I performed over the weekends either up in the Catskills or over in New Jersey in second-rate supper clubs."

At a time when desperation forced him to resort to selling his blood, Messick's fortune turned for the better. While he was in New York, actress Joan Gardiner recommended him to her employer, legendary animator Bob Clampett. "She told him that she knew this guy who could do voices, was a ventriloquist, and who could do puppets. Well, I had never done hand puppets before, but they [the producers] paid my way back to Hollywood, and so for six years I was under contract to Bob Clampett. He had developed *Beany and Cecil* and was developing other shows, including *Buffalo Billy*. It was a half-hour Sunday afternoon live children's puppet show, adventures in the Wild West–type of thing starring Buffalo Billy and his aunt, Ima Hag. So, for six months I practiced in his garage while he tried one contact and then another to get this show on the air. It finally did go on the air in 1949 or 1950 in New York. . . . Again, I was back in New York!"

Thirteen weeks later that show had ended, as well as, apparently, his association with its producer. "Bob Clampett dropped me, but I think he sort of kicked himself for having dropped my contract." Messick went back to the other coast for yet another puppet show; after which, Clampett promptly rehired him to work for the next five years. Besides acting, this stint with Clampett also included the duties of writer and production coordinator on the new live children's adventure puppet productions. Included were the revamped *Adventures of Buffalo Billy*, *The Willy the Wolf Show*, and *Thunderbolt the Wondercolt*, in which he also had a chance to do some on-camera acting.

Messick's cartoon career finally began when friend Daws Butler put in a good word for him. "It's due to Daws that I got my first cartoon job. It was back in the '50s, and Tex Avery was looking for a voice. Daws recommended me to Tex while he was at MGM doing the *Droopy the Dog* theatrical cartoons. The actor who regularly did the voice of Droopy was not available for some reason or other and they needed to get this cartoon completed, so I wound up doing the voice of Droopy on two of the cartoons. Daws was certainly generous with sharing his professional contacts with me as well as just being a great, good friend. I certainly owe Daws, if not for my start in show business, then for the opportunity to grab onto the next rung of the ladder."

His success solidified in 1957 when William Hanna and Joe Barbera decided that Messick and Butler should have the honor of breaking new ground with them. "Daws and I were the first voice men with the first series that Bill and Joe did on their own when they left MGM; that was, of course, *Ruff and Reddy*. I was the voice of Ruff, Professor Gizmo, and the narrator."

The series became a hit. From then on Messick was offered part after part at the studio and eventually came to see Hanna-Barbera as a second home. "My association with Hanna-Barbera has been over twenty-seven years long. I've worked with them on something every year since they formed their own company." In that time, he enjoyed the Hanna-Barbera approach of recording as an ensemble cast, a practice he was familiar with from the old radio programs. He stated that his ambition was always not to just do funny voices for a paycheck, but to approach it as a serious actor. During the course of his series, he took pride in letting his characters evolve and, subsequently, refining them along with his craft.

"Well, I think there is always something of me, of Don Messick, involved inside the character that I do because, basically, I am not an impersonator. That's the way a lot of people who do voices develop them, and that's usually what the producers want. They say, 'We want such and such a type.' So, it's pretty much an acting job for me. The development of a character comes from inside my imagination and expresses itself outwardly, hoping that it conforms pretty much to what the producers had in mind and adding a little bit more to it. Daws was always complimentary about my work in saying that a lot of the other people who do similar things to what I do lack the warmth in the character that I seem to project."

Messick was especially fond of some of his most popular characters. "Boo Boo Bear was kind of special and one of my favorites because he was such a simple naïve little guy, and in a sense Yogi Bear's conscience, because he would always strive to steer him away from his incorrigible acts of stealing 'pic-i-nic' baskets. There's something warm and friendly and nice about Boo Boo. Then there's Muttley. He was always complaining about Dick Dastardly. One of my favorite shows was *Dastardly and Muttley and Their Flying Machines*."

If pressed for an all-time favorite, Messick picked the most famous of Hanna-Barbera creations—*Scooby-Doo*. Messick helped create the character and performed the voice for the first twenty-two years that *Scooby-Doo* shows were in production. When asked about the cartoon canine's enduring popularity, Messick was thoughtful: "I think kids identify with the human characters on *Scooby-Doo*, and bringing with that humanism into Scooby himself makes them further identify with the dog. I mean, everybody loves dogs. And, I think we all project our own personalities onto our pets. Scooby with his vulnerability is a lot like us. We are not all the bravest people in the world. We all have our own hang-ups, and Scooby's hang right out there up front! He's cowardly; yet he always seems to come out on top in spite of himself."

Finding the voice for Scrappy-Doo, Scooby's nephew, became a little more complicated than expected. "When Scrappy was first introduced, they auditioned several people, and they offered it to another actor, but they finally ended up using me. I think we were doing sixteen episodes that season. 'Long about the fourteenth, Joe Barbera and the ABC producer decided they didn't like my Scrappy, so they had Lenny Weinrib (of H. R. Puffenstuff fame) do it. And he had to re-do everything that I'd already recorded, which meant that he had to 'loop' them, which is longer and more complicated. Well, it went on the air that way with Lennie Weinrib's kind of Jerry Lewis mean little kid voice. Then the network decided they didn't like that. 'We prefer Don Messick.' So I didn't redo them, but I started with the next season's shows." Of course, being network executives, first they had to reaudition Messick to make sure that he was really what they wanted.

He also found work on *Jonny Quest*, the second actor to portray Dr. Benton Quest, opposite Tim Matheson as Jonny and Mike Road as Race Bannon. "They started out with John Stephenson, who did six of twenty-six [shows]. They decided to change the voice, have a different actor do it because they found a conflict between John's voice and the voice of Mike Road. So they got me to do it. I also did Atom Ant for the last six or eight episodes [after Howard Morris]."

One of the highlights of Messick's career was his time spent as Bamm-Bamm, Arnold, the paper boy, and various other characters on *The Flintstones*, a show he concisely describes as "one big pun well done." Among the talent he had the honor of working with was one of his childhood idols, Alan Reed, who voiced Fred Flintstone. "I remember Alan Reed when I was a child, listening to the Fred Allen show. He did various characters on many, many radio shows. . . . He seemed to genuinely enjoy the character things I did. He and Mel [Blanc] would be sitting back and I'd glance up, out of the corner of my eye, when I was doing something. They'd be looking at each other and kind of nodding affirmatively, which made me feel good because they were ahead of me and I looked up to them."

Certainly, judging by the continual interest in characters like Scooby-Doo, Astro, and Boo Boo Bear, Messick's peers are not the only admirers of his work. Hanna-Barbera was especially grateful that for all that Messick struggled through at the beginning of his career, he never felt like giving up on showbiz. "I have felt that maybe I should get a steady job as a staff announcer at a radio station. But usually when such an opportunity would present itself, something else would come up to pull me away from going that route."

Sadly, after a long battle with Alzheimer's disease, Don Messick passed away on October 24, 1997, at the age of seventy-one, of a stroke. While

Messick had respected Joe Barbera as a "perfectionist" and a "tough" director to work for at times, Barbera may have given Messick the most flattering tribute when summing up his work and that of his former partner, Daws Butler. "Daws and Don Messick—it was like a goldmine with those two guys. Between them, they could do almost every voice you could think of."

Messick was grateful for his professional success, but he also recognized greater and lasting value to society in his life's work in animation. "We need escapism. I think the world takes itself too seriously. There are so many serious things to think about and deal with. It's nice to have a release, a departure, something that gets us away from the worries of the day, to help us not take ourselves too seriously and deflate our egos, if at all possible. I think that cartoons poke fun at our pomposity and our stuffiness, and so it helps us place a different perspective on some of our real-life situations. If it does nothing else but make us laugh, that in itself is therapeutic, healthy, and good."

CREDITS

13 Ghosts of Scooby-Doo, The (1985) TV Series . . . . Scooby-Doo/Scrappy-Doo (1985–1986)
Abbott and Costello Show, The (1966) TV Series
Addams Family, The (1973) TV Series
Adventures of Gulliver, The (1968) TV Series . . . . Glum/Egger
All-New Scooby and Scrappy-Doo Show, The (1983) TV Series . . . . Scooby-Doo/Scrappy-Doo
Amazing Chan and the Chan Clan, The (1972) TV Series . . . . Chu-Chu the Dog
Animal Follies (1988) . . . . Ruff
Archie's Bang Shang Lalapalooza Show (1977) TV Series . . . . Harvey
Atom Ant Show, The (1965) TV Series . . . . Atom Ant/Shag Rugg/Precious Pupp
Atom Ant/Secret Squirrel Show, The (1967) TV Series . . . . Atom Ant
Auggie Doggie and Doggie Daddy (1959) TV Series . . . . Additional Voices
Bailey's Comets (1973) TV Series . . . . Gabby
Banana Splits Adventure Hour, The (1968) TV Series . . . . Snorky/Professor Carter/Aramis/Shagg Rugg
Barkley's, The (1972) TV Series . . . . Additional Voices
Beany and Cecil (1962) TV Series . . . . Additional Voices
Beef for and After (1962)
Birdman and the Galaxy Trio (1967) TV Series . . . . Falcon 7/Vapor Man
Bungle Uncle (1962)
Bunnies Abundant (1962)
C.B. Bears (1977) TV Series . . . . Clyde
Cantinflas (1980) TV Series . . . . Cantinflas
Cartoon All-Stars to the Rescue (1990) TV . . . . Papa Smurf
Catch Meow (1961)
Cattanooga Cats, The (1969) TV Series . . . . Happy
Charlotte's Web (1973) . . . . Jeffrey
Cheese It, the Cat! (1957)
Chicken Fracas-See (1963)

Child Sock-Cology (1961)

Common Scents (1962)

Creepy Time Pal (1960)

Crook Who Cried Wolf (1963)

Curiosity Shop (1971) TV Series

Dastardly and Muttley in Their Flying Machines (1969) TV Series . . . . Muttley/Klunk/Zilly/Yankee Doodle/Pigeon

Diamonds Are Forever (1971) (uncredited) . . . . . Announcer at Circus Circus

Dinky Dog (1978) TV Series . . . . Additional Voices

Doctor Dolittle (1970) TV Series . . . . Various Animals

Do-Good Wolf, The (1960)

Don Coyote and Sancho Panda (1990) TV Series . . . . . Sancho Panda

Drak Pack, The (1980) TV Series . . . . . Toad/Fly

Droopy: Master Detective (1993) TV Series

Drum-Sticked (1963)

Duck Factory, The (1984) TV Series . . . . . Wally Wooster

Dynomutt, Dog Wonder (1978) TV Series . . . . Scooby-Doo/Mumbly/The Gimmick/Lowbrow

Elephantastic (1964)

Fallible Fable, A (1963)

Fangface and Fangpuss (1979) TV Series . . . . Additional Voices

Fantastic Max (1988) TV Series . . . . Additional Voices

Fee Fie Foes (1961)

First Thirteenth Annual Fancy Anvil Awards Show Program Special Live in Stereo, The (2002) TV (uncredited) (archive footage) . . . . . Scooby-Doo

Flight of Dragons, The (1986) . . . . . Giles of the Treetops/Lo Tae Shao the Golden Wizard

Flintstones, The (1960) TV Series . . . . Bamm-Bamm Rubble/Arnold the Newsboy/Hoppy the Hopperoo (1963–1966)/Additional Voices

Flintstones: Fred's Final Fling, The (1981) TV . . . . Doctor/Fish #1/Fish #2/Parrot/Pigasaurus

Flintstones: Wacky Inventions, The (1994) . . . . Bamm-Bamm Rubble

Flintstones Christmas Carol, A (1994) TV . . . . Bamm-Bamm Rubble/Joe Rockhead

Flintstones Comedy Hour, The (1972) TV Series . . . . Schleprock

Flintstones Meet Rockula and Frankenstone, The (1979) TV

Flintstones' New Neighbors, The (1980) TV . . . . . Bamm-Bamm Rubble/Vulture

Fonz and the Happy Days Gang (1980) TV Series . . . . Additional Voices

Foofur (1986) TV Series . . . . Pepe

Frankenstein Jr. and the Impossibles (1966) TV Series . . . . Multi Man

Fred and Barney Meet the Shmoo (1979) TV Series . . . . Bamm-Bamm Rubble

Fred and Barney Meet the Thing (1979) TV Series . . . . Bamm-Bamm Rubble

Fred Flintstone and Friends (1977) TV Series . . . . Bamm-Bamm Rubble

Further Adventures of Dr. Doolittle, The (1970) TV Series . . . . Additional Voices

Galtar and the Golden Lance (1985) TV Series . . . . Pandat

Get-along Gang, The (1984) TV Series . . . . Officer Growler

Gidget Makes the Wrong Connection (1972) TV . . . . Killer/Gorgeous Cat/Captain Parker/Radio

Godzilla Power Hour, The (1978) TV Series . . . . . Godzooky

Good, the Bad, and Huckleberry Hound, The (1988) . . . . Boo Boo

Great Grape Ape (1977) TV Series . . . . Additional Voices

Groovie Goolies (1971) TV Series

Harlem Globetrotters, The (1970) TV Series (uncredited)

Heathcliff and Dingbat (1980) TV Series . . . . Nobody/Sparerib/Mr. Post (1981–1982)

Help! It's the Hair Bear Bunch (1971) TV Series

Herculoids, The (1967) TV Series . . . . Gloop/Gleep

Here, Kiddie, Kiddie (1960)

Hey There, It's Yogi Bear (1964) . . . . Boo Boo/Ranger Smith/Yogi's Inner Self

Hobbit, The (1978) TV . . . . Balin/Troll #3/Goblin/Lord of the Eagles

Hollyrock-a-Bye Baby (1993) TV

Hong Kong Phooey (1974) TV Series . . . . . Spot/Narrator

Huckleberry Hound Show, The (1958) TV Series . . . . . Pixie/Boo Boo/Ranger Smith

I Yabba-Dabba Do! (1993) TV . . . . Additional Voices

Inch High, Private Eye (1973) TV Series . . . . Braveheart

It's a Wonderful Tiny Toons Christmas Special (1992) TV . . . . Hampton Pig

Jabberjaw (1976) TV Series

Jack Frost (1979) TV . . . . Snip

Jeannie (1973) TV Series

Jetsons, The (1962) (1985) TV Series . . . . Astro/R.U.D.I

Jetsons: The Movie (1990) . . . . Astro

Jetsons Christmas Carol, The (1985) TV . . . . . Astro

Jetsons Meet the Flintstones, The (1987) TV . . . . Astro/R.U.D.I/Mac/Announcer/Store Manager/Robot

Jokebook (1982) TV Series . . . . Additional Voices

Jonny Quest (1964) TV Series . . . . Dr. Benton C. Quest (1964–1965)/Bandit (1964)

Jonny Quest (1986) TV Series . . . . Dr. Benton Quest/Bandit

Jonny Quest vs. the Cyber Insects (1995) TV . . . . Dr. Quest

Jonny's Golden Quest (1993) TV . . . . Dr. Quest

Josie and the Pussycats (1970) TV Series . . . . Sebastian the Cat

Josie and the Pussycats in Outer Space (1972) TV Series . . . . Bleep/Sebastian

Kwicky Koala Show, The (1981) TV Series

La Feet's Defeat (1968) . . . . Sergeant Deux-Deux

Last Holloween, The (1991) TV . . . . Romtu

Last Unicorn, The (1982) . . . . The Cat

Laurel and Hardy Cartoon, A (1966) TV Series . . . . Various Characters

Magilla Gorilla (1964) TV Series . . . . Ricochet Rabbit

Man Called Flintstone, The (1966) . . . . Additional Voices

Matty's Funday Funnies (Beanie & Cecil) (1959) TV Series . . . . Additional Voices

Mighty Orbots, The (1984) TV Series . . . . Crunch/Rondu

Moby Dick and the Mighty Mightor (1967) TV Series . . . . Scooby the Seal

Mumbly Cartoon Show, The (1976) TV Series . . . . Lt. Mumbly

Nestor, the Long-Eared Christmas Donkey (1977) TV

New Adventures of Huck Finn (1968) TV Series . . . . Additional Voices

New Fantastic Four (1978) TV Series . . . . Additional Voices

New Fred and Barney Show, The (1979) TV Series . . . . . Bamm-Bamm Rubble

New Hanna-Barbera Cartoon Series, The (1962) TV Series . . . . . Mr. Twiddle

New Scooby-Doo Movies, The (1972) TV Series . . . . Scooby-Doo

New Scooby-Doo Mysteries, The (1984) TV Series . . . . Scooby-Doo/Scrappy-Doo

New Tom and Jerry Show, The (1975) TV Series . . . . Mumbly

Oddball Couple (1975) TV Series . . . . Additional Voices

Off to See the Wizard (1967) TV Series

Paw Paws, The (1985) TV Series . . . . Pupooch

Pebbles and Bamm-Bamm Show, The (1971) TV Series . . . . Schleprock

Perils of Penelope Pitstop (1969) TV Series . . . . Zippy/Pockets/Dum Dum/Snoozy

Peter Potamus and His Magic Flying Balloon (1964) TV Series . . . . So-So

Peter Potamus Show, The (1964) TV Series . . . . Richochet Rabbitt/So-So

Pixie & Dixie (1958) TV Series . . . . Pixie

Popeye and Son (1987) TV Series . . . . . Eugene the Jeep

Pufnstuf (1970) TV . . . . Additional Voices

Pup Named Scooby-Doo, A (1988) TV Series . . . . Scooby-Doo

Quick Draw McGraw (1963) TV Series . . . . . Additional Voices

Real Adventures of Jonny Quest, The (1996) TV Series (uncredited) . . . . Dr. Benton C. Quest (alternating) (1996–1997)

Return of the King, The (1980) TV

Richie Rich/Scooby-Doo Hour, The (1980) TV Series . . . . . Scooby-Doo/Scrappy-Doo (Scooby's Nephew)

Rockin' with Judy Jetson (1988) TV . . . . Astro

Rudolph and Frosty's Christmas in July (1979) TV

Rudolph's Shiny New Year (1975) TV

Ruff and Reddy Show, The (1957) TV Series . . . . Ruff/Narrator/Various Voices

Sabrina, the Teenage Witch (1971) TV Series . . . . . Cousin Ambrose

Sabrina and the Groovy Ghoulies (1970) TV Series . . . . . Cousin Ambrose/Mr. Kraft

Samson and Goliath (1967) TV Series . . . . Additional Voices

Scooby and Scrappy-Doo (1979) TV Series . . . . . Scooby-Doo (1979–)/Scrappy-Doo (1980–1983)

Scooby and Scrappy-Doo Puppy Hour, The (1982) TV Series . . . . Scooby-Doo

Scooby-Doo, Where Are You! (1969) TV Series . . . . Scoobert Scooby-Doo

Scooby-Doo and the Ghoul School (1988) TV . . . . Scooby-Doo/Scrappy-Doo

Scooby-Doo and the Reluctant Werewolf (1989) TV . . . . Scooby-Doo/Scrappy-Doo

Scooby-Doo Goes Hollywood (1979) TV . . . . Scooby-Doo

Scooby-Doo in Arabian Nights (1994) TV . . . . Scooby-Doo/Boo Boo Bear

Scooby-Doo Meets the Boo Brothers (1987) TV . . . . Scooby-Doo/Scrappy-Doo/Hound

Scooby-Doo/Dynomutt Hour, The (1976) TV Series . . . . Scooby-Doo

Scooby-Doo's Creepiest Capers (2000) . . . . Scooby-Doo

Scooby-Doo's Greatest Mysteries (1999) . . . . Scooby-Doo

Scooby's All-Star Laff-a Lympics (1977) TV Series . . . . Boo Boo Bear/Mr. Creeply/Mumbly/Pixie/Scooby-Doo

Scooby's Mystery Funhouse (1985) TV Series . . . . Scooby-Doo

Shazzan! (1967) TV Series . . . . . Kaboobie

Skatebirds, The (1977) TV Series . . . . Scooter Penguin

Smurfs, The (1981) TV Series . . . . Papa Smurf/Azrael/Dreamy Smurf/Sleepy Smurf

Space Ghost and Dino Boy (1966) TV Series . . . . Blip/Bronto/Zorak

Space Kidettes, The (1966) TV Series . . . . Countdown/Pup Star

Space-Stars (1981) TV Series . . . . . Astro/Gloop/Gleep

Spider-Man (1981) TV Series

Spunky and Tadpole (1958) TV Series . . . . Additional Voices

Story of the First Christmas Snow, The (1975) TV

Strong Kids, Safe Kids (1984) . . . . Papa Smurf/Scooby-Doo/Scrappy-Doo

Super President and Spy Shadow (1967) TV Series

Superfriends (1980) TV Series . . . . Scarecrow

Tabitha and Adam and the Clown Family (1972) TV . . . . Second Cyclone/Trumpet/Voice

Tales of Washington Irving (1970) TV

These Are the Days (1974) TV Series

Tiny Toon Adventures (1990) TV Series . . . . Hamton J. Pig

Tiny Toon Adventures: How I Spent My Vacation (1992) . . . . Hamton J. Pig

Tiny Toon Adventures: Night Ghoulery (1995) TV . . . . . Hamton J.Pig

Tiny Toons Spring Break (1994) TV . . . . Hamton J. Pig

'Tis the Season to Be Smurfy (1984) TV . . . . Papa Smurf

Tom and Jerry (1965) TV Series

Tom and Jerry: The Movie (1992) . . . . Droopy

Top Cat (1961) TV Series . . . . Additional Voices

Transformers (1984) TV Series . . . . Gears/Ratchet/Scavenger/Additional Voices

Transformers: The Movie, The (1986) . . . . Scavenger/Ratchet

Trollkins (1981) TV Series . . . . Additional Voices

Wacky Races (1968) TV Series . . . . Muttley/Professor Pat Pending/Sawtooth/Ring-a-Ding/Little Gruesome/Gravel Slag

Wake, Rattle, and Roll (1990) TV Series . . . . Muttley

Wally Gator (1962) TV Series . . . . . Mr. Twiddle

What's a Nice Kid like You Doing in a Place like This? (1966) TV . . . . . Dormouse/Fluff

Wheelie and the Chopper Bunch (1974) TV Series . . . . Scrambles/Deputy Fishtail

Where's Huddles (1970) TV Series . . . . Fumbles

Yogi and the Invasion of the Space Bears (1988) . . . . Boo Boo Bear/Ranger Smith

Yogi Bear and the Magical Flight of the Spruce Goose (1987) . . . . Boo Boo Bear/Mumbley

Yogi Bear Show, The (1960) TV Series . . . . . Boo Boo Bear/Ranger John Francis Smith

Yogi the Easter Bear (1994) TV . . . . Boo Boo Bear

Yogi's Ark Lark (1972) TV . . . . Boo Boo Bear/Atom Ant/So-So/Moby Dick/Touché Turtle

Yogi's First Christmas (1980) . . . . Boo Boo Bear/Ranger Smith

Yogi's Gang (1973) TV Series . . . . Boo Boo Bear/Ranger John Smith/Touché Turtle/Squiddley Diddly/Atom Ant

Yogi's Great Escape (1987) . . . . Boo Boo Bear/Ranger Smith

Yogi's Treasure Hunt (1978) TV Series . . . . Boo Boo Bear

GEORGE O'HANLON

"Meet Fred Flintstone. . . . " Well, almost. In 1959, George O'Hanlon auditioned for Joe Barbera to provide the voice of Hanna-Barbera's latest cartoon star, Fred Flintstone. However, one of the show's sponsors decided he did not like his voice, and O'Hanlon did not get the job. Scores of other actors competed for the role, which was eventually given to veteran radio star Alan Reed. That might have been the end of O'Hanlon's chances for animation greatness, but in this case, opportunity knocked twice. The success of *The Flintstones* inspired Hanna-Barbera to create a series in 1962 revolving around a futuristic family called *The Jetsons*. The general consensus was that if a series about a prehistoric family could be a hit, then why not try recreating the magic with a family from the opposite end of the spectrum? When the time came to cast *The Jetsons*, Joe Barbera remembered O'Hanlon and gave him the opportunity to play family head George Jetson. Although the role was seemingly inconsequential at the time (only twenty-four episodes were produced for the first run) and O'Hanlon went on to other things, the character would end up playing a major role in his life.

George O'Hanlon was born in Coney Island, New York, on November 23, 1912. If the O'Hanlon family name sounds vaguely familiar, it may be because in 1897 his cousin Virginia's letter became the subject of a much reprinted editorial, "Yes, Virginia, There Is a Santa Claus." However, his family's notoriety can be traced back to the days of Wyatt Earp and Doc Holliday and the original Birdcage Theatre in Tombstone, Arizona, where his grandmother was a dance hall girl. O'Hanlon's parents both worked the burlesque theater circuit, his mother, Lulu Beeson, being an award-winning dancer. His father, George, under the stage name of Sam Rice, managed a theater in Providence, Rhode Island. He also wrote, produced, and starred in the productions he directed. As a child, O'Hanlon was exposed to the greatest comedy acts of the era. It was only natural that he gravitated toward comedy as he began to mature, and the vaudeville stage was the perfect arena to hone his talents. O'Hanlon started as a bit player and a dancer in the days of vaudeville. He studied comic timing by observing the professionals and was befriended by a young comic named Lou Costello, later of Abbott and Costello fame, who became a mentor to him. He found life in the theater exciting and educational, but also fleeting.

By 1930, the Great Depression had arrived, causing the family to lose the theater and leaving them to start over. Undeterred, the O'Hanlons packed up their belongings and headed across the country to try their luck in Hollywood. Upon arrival on the West Coast, the family, including brother James, signed up for and landed parts as movie extras, which helped them make it through the lean times. O'Hanlon eventually signed on as a chorus boy for producer Busby Berkeley, garnering bit parts in several musicals. With the help of a casting director at Warner Bros. Studio, he won a scholarship to a well-known Beverly Hills drama school—Bliss Haydens. He worked as a salesman during the day and studied his craft at night, and it looked as though his hard work was about to pay off.

In 1942, O'Hanlon was hired by the then fledgling director Richard L. Bare, who would go on to direct the television series *Green Acres*, for a short film sponsored by the University of Southern California, entitled *So You*

Want to Give up Smoking. His character, Joe McDoakes, was a typical all-American average guy facing everyday problems. It was during this period that Warner Bros. decided to test him as a contract player. They liked what they saw and decided to sign the young actor. Then, like so many of his contemporaries, O'Hanlon was drafted.

O'Hanlon served three years in the United States Army during World War II. Upon returning to civilian life, he found that Warner Bros. still wanted him. The studio had picked up an option to produce more Joe McDoakes projects, which became known as the *Behind the 8-Ball* series. He was, once again, teamed up with Richard L. Bare—hired not only to act, but also to write the one-reel comedic shorts. The popular series, which ran from 1946 through 1955, produced a total of fifty-six films and received three Academy Award nominations.

At the end of the *8-Ball* series, O'Hanlon and Bare tried their luck with television. O'Hanlon had already made it onto the small screen playing Gillis, the next-door neighbor on the sit-com *The Life of Riley*. With Bare, he tried his hand at a television pilot, attempting to recreate the big screen success of Joe McDoakes. Unfortunately, not only did the pilot not sell, but O'Hanlon was also fired from the *Life of Riley* series for moonlighting. At that point, Bare and O'Hanlon parted company. O'Hanlon eventually teamed up with his brother, James, and they became a successful writing team, producing scripts for episodes of *Gallant Men, Roaring Twenties,* and *77 Sunset Strip.*

Writing assignments were in abundance, and in 1959 O'Hanlon wrote a screenplay for the film *The Rookie,* featuring Julie Newmar, which he also produced and directed. He continued playing bit parts in movies and television and was always on the lookout to regain the leading-man status that eluded him since his *Behind the 8-Ball* days. The search came to an end when he was called upon to take on the role as George Jetson on the new Hanna-Barbera series *The Jetsons.* Joe Barbera was ecstatic to get O'Hanlon's services opposite *Blondie* star Penny Singleton as Jane.

O'Hanlon also enjoyed his work at Hanna-Barbera, commenting, when he watched the finished product, "I laughed myself silly." Practical jokes also abounded as the fun-loving cast pulled affectionate pranks: Daws Butler, in the voice of Elroy Jetson, used to call the O'Hanlon household and leave messages for "Dad." The only person not in on the fun was O'Hanlon's daughter, Laurie. The then four-year-old would watch the show on Saturday morning and become traumatized to the point of tears as she watched her father get sucked under the conveyor belt at the end of every show; she then would have to rush into his room and "wake him up to make sure he was safe!"

Unfortunately, after only twenty-four episodes, Hanna-Barbera pulled the plug on the series. *The Flintstones* was still going strong, and O'Hanlon could only speculate as to why *The Jetsons* was pulled off the air: "I think that it had to do with the business sense of the thing. Maybe they ran out of money. I don't know." One thing O'Hanlon did know was that he was once more unemployed as an actor.

While O'Hanlon continued to write for television for the next several years, including episodes of *Gilligan's Island*, *Love, American Style*, and, ironically, *The Flintstones*, the twenty-four episodes of *The Jetsons* continued to run year after year on Saturday mornings, capturing countless numbers of new fans. O'Hanlon picked up work playing small roles in a string of minor Disney films including *Million Dollar Duck*, *Charley and the Angel*, and *The World's Greatest Athlete*, and he would occasionally insert a part for himself when given a writing assignment, even though he would still have to audition to get the role.

Laurie O'Hanlon recalls the latter part of her father's career, "There was a period when I was in high school that he was playing a lot of drunks and policemen. . . . He did a lot of writing, and he was out of work a lot. There was a strike . . . and then in 1976, he had a stroke." The stroke, which occurred while O'Hanlon was having by-pass surgery, was so debilitating that it looked as though he would never work again. He went nearly blind and his short-term memory was severely affected. He spent most of the next decade convalescing, while his wife, Nancy, supported the family as an executive with a cosmetics company.

Although the taping of the original *Jetsons* series seemed to be a one-off job at the time, O'Hanlon suddenly found himself obsessed with George Jetson. His wife, Nancy, explains, "He had a premonition of doing them again. . . . For a couple of years he would talk about it every once in a while; he'd say, 'They're going to do more *Jetsons.*' It really was very unlikely at that time because nobody was making anything for syndication. They were just using old stuff. . . . I explained to him that they couldn't make new ones because the old ones were already in syndication. I knew they weren't planning to make any new ones at that time. I had asked [Hanna-Barbera] because he was restless. He couldn't do anything. He just sat around and tried to watch television, but he couldn't see it very well and it was very difficult for him. He'd go over to the Motion Picture Hospital and sit around there for a while, and then he'd get restless and come home. Anyway, he just knew they were going to do it, and he wasn't at all surprised when 'they' called."

"They" turned out to be voice director Kris Zimmerman from Hanna-Barbera. She informed Nancy that over forty new episodes were in pre-production and asked if she would bring her husband in to read for the part. Nancy was hesitant. "I was surprised, and I really didn't think he could do it. He couldn't read, he couldn't memorize, he couldn't concentrate very well, and I just couldn't see how it could be done. . . . I said, 'I just think it would make him feel bad to come over there and not be able to do it. I think it would be better if you just got somebody else.'"

Not wanting to lie, Nancy told her husband about the call. O'Hanlon wanted to try recording using a technique that had worked when he had previously done a few radio commercials for a friend. The director would give a reading line by line, and O'Hanlon would repeat it exactly and it was recorded that way. Despite his wife's reservations that he might not be able to give a performance—Jetson's voice required some effort as it was higher pitched and faster than O'Hanlon's speaking voice—she called Hanna-Barbera to see if they could accommodate him.

Hanna-Barbera sent over a storyboard and a few pages of dialogue for Nancy to try out with her husband. "I would do a line, and he would repeat it. He couldn't even do a whole line of dialogue, because he couldn't retain it that long. We had to cut it into pieces. Anyway, he sounded just the same and I was really excited. But he never doubted for a minute."

Once O'Hanlon completed his test with Hanna-Barbera, they had no doubts either. They knew it would take extra effort to get his voice down on tape, but Joe Barbera was adamant about keeping him in the cast. Barbera recalled, "When we started to work . . . it was agony because he couldn't see. So you had to read him the line, and he would then do it, and that was one line at a time. . . . There wasn't much energy, but he would hang on until he finished it." Because of his obvious handicap and the extra time it took to record him, O'Hanlon did not record with the rest of the cast, who also had to read for their parts again to make sure they still sounded the same twenty years later. O'Hanlon's lines were edited in later.

Although his wife said the process "exhausted" him, she also said, "It was really very pleasant for him to go to work. They fussed over him, and he felt like he was accomplishing something." His daughter, Laurie, also noticed the change: "It really kind of breathed new life into my parents' existence. Dad had nothing to do for a real long time except going to therapy and watching television. Having a chance to work really made a difference . . . to have an income and be the provider again."

The forty-one new episodes of *The Jetsons* aired in 1985 and the renewed popularity prompted Hanna-Barbera to plan a full-length feature with Universal Studios. Although Daws Butler, who provided the voice of the Jetson's son, Elroy, and maintenance worker Henry Orbit, had died in the interim, and, due to the demands of a sponsor, Janet Waldo (original voice of *The Jetson's* daughter, Judy) was unceremoniously dropped by the studio and replaced by the unremarkable pop singer Tiffany, the rest of the cast remained intact, and O'Hanlon was once again called in to reprise George Jetson. But this time, while recording his part, tragedy struck.

Barbera recalled O'Hanlon's professionalism and pride in his work, even to the final recording session. "He had a cane, he had to sit down, and he had to be helped in and out. . . . He really was in a fragile position." But, while he was finishing his lines, O'Hanlon was obviously in distress. "I'm a member on the advisory board at the hospital here, St. Joseph's, so they whisked him over there." The doctor at St. Joseph's was honest about the gravity of O'Hanlon's condition, stating that he may only have hours to live. Barbera concluded, "That's the way it happened, but that's the way he wanted to do it."

George O'Hanlon passed away on February 11, 1989, three days before his thirty-sixth wedding anniversary. Six years later, it was Nancy who had a pre-monition just as her husband did eleven years before. Daughter Laurie recalled, "My mom had a dream that Dad came and sat on the corner of the bed and said, 'I'm going back to work.' The next day when [Nancy O'Hanlon] awoke, Hanna-Barbera called and said they were doing a special, and they were going to use him as George Jetson in it, and that there would be a check."

Although George O'Hanlon's career was primarily spent as a writer and an on-screen actor, ironically, later generations will think of him as a voice actor—undoubtedly forever linked with his futuristic counterpart. But that he was the embodiment of George Jetson was undeniable. As Joe Barbera recalled, "George was a rare find for *The Jetsons* voice. Not many people were absolutely born to do a voice. And of all the people I tried, his voice was it."

ROB PAULSEN

Rob Paulsen is shocked, but in a good way. Paulsen, who has become one of the most versatile and popular contemporary animation voice actors, could never have predicted that thousands would wait patiently for hours just for his autograph as hundreds of others were turned away. But, such was the case for the 1994 publicity tour for *Animaniacs*. Paulsen, who played Warner Brother Yakko on the popular series, went on the road with co-stars Jess Harnell (Wakko) and Tress MacNeille (Dot) expecting "twenty or thirty hard-core toon fans," only to be mobbed at Warner Bros. stores in shopping malls around the country.

The voice of Yakko, Pinky from *Pinky and the Brain*, Arthur on *The Tick*, and Raphael on *Teenage Mutant Ninja Turtles*, among so many others, began his study of animation voices as a fan. Born in Detroit, he was raised in the suburbs until he was a young teen, when his family moved to an area south of Flint. He developed a "keen interest in cartoons"; among his earliest recollections are animated commercials and jingles for Good and Plenty and Tootsie Pops as well as *Captain Kangaroo,* the prime-time original run of *The Flintstones,* and *Jonny Quest.* He was "nuts about the Jay Ward and Bill Scott stuff" like *George of the Jungle, Tom Slick,* and *Fractured Fairy Tales*, taking note of Paul Winchell, June Foray, and Paul Frees in particular. "But, what I remember and really laughing at the most was probably at the Roadrunner and realizing, at some point, that Mel Blanc was the guy that did all [the Warners] stuff." Surprisingly, Paulsen insists that he was never the kid on the playground who could do a dead-on rendition of Bugs and company, but he discovered he did have a knack for dialects and "exploited his talent" as a singer for years to come.

His parents were supportive of his musical interests, allowing him to listen to Led Zeppelin and The Who with the condition that he balance that with Prokofiev and Shostakovich. Having a well-rounded musical background, which also included a disparate variety of singers, along with his early radio work, he believes was the start of a segue into his future vocation. His first radio job was a series of commercials for the owner of a Flint sporting goods store and local radio talk-show host, Bill Lamb. Lamb broadcast from a radio studio in his basement and, in the off time, Paulsen and Lamb's son Bob staged radio plays, with original characters and sound effects, that they would subsequently play for their high school. While Paulsen did the shows for fun, his commercial work became his first paying gig—albeit compensation came in the form of tennis shoes and hockey sticks or other merchandise from the elder Lamb's store.

This was most agreeable to the die-hard Red Wings fan as Paulsen's dream was to be a professional hockey player; but, eventually realizing that he "valued his teeth and his nose too much," he readjusted his career path to that of performer. However, it took a year at the University of Michigan before he realized that his heart was in show business and Paulsen left his academic studies for a year with a Los Angeles–based theater company and toured the United States and Canada.

Upon his return to Michigan, Paulsen found the limelight again as the lead singer for Flint-based "Sass"—a regional rock-and-roll band which was successful enough to open for headliners like Bob Seger. But even though he describes his band mates as "very talented," he knew that, even with good material, the chances of being spotted in the Flint area by talent scouts in the recording industry were remote. So, after two years Paulsen, who still had the acting bug from his prior theater tour, headed for the West Coast.

With high school friend and radio producer Bob Lamb, Paulsen piled into a little blue 1980 Honda and landed in Redondo Beach. Paulsen's plan was to "get into commercials as quickly as [he] could on-camera wise and start making a little money" which he hoped would pay for acting classes. The reality was, of course, that he needed a quick way to pay the bills while getting his acting career started and found a job cleaning apartments. "The nice thing about that was I could make my own hours. But, I found some wacky things. . . . People that would abandon apartments, they'd leave, like, half a trout in their apartment with the refrigerator turned off and that was pretty much of a drag."

Fortunately, with his laid-back manner and all-American, nice-guy-next-door looks, he did get commercial work and progressed to guest star on popular television shows like *Hill Street Blues*, *MacGyver*, and *St. Elsewhere* as well as a few movies. Although he disparages his feature work as "pretty crappy," it did include Brian DePalma's 1984 film, the well-received *Body Double*—a film he was not comfortable with as he later disparaged the misogynist violence as mean-spirited and disconcerting.

Although he says he would have liked to have explored work in the animation field at that time, he was not being sent to audition. But by the early 1980s, he had married Parrish Todd, a former production coordinator; and, after about four years of on-camera work, he says it was his wife who recognized his talent and encouraged him to go into the voice-over field. Paulsen made his first regular appearance in an animated series as the characters of Snowjob and Tripwire in 1983's *G.I. Joe*, but credits the "real" beginning of his successful animation career to Hanna-Barbera casting director Gordon Hunt. "I had auditioned at Hanna-Barbera a number of times doing general readings. But Gordon was never there. It was always one of the assistants that would just sort of hold these general auditions that they do periodically to hear new talent and I didn't get anything. Finally, one day Gordon happened to be there and I got a job. And, after that, the next big thing I landed was Hadji [formerly played by Danny Bravo in the 1960s series] and we did another thirteen *Jonny Quests* and that was a real thrill for me, being a big fan of the show."

The work then began to multiply, but more important to Paulsen was that early in his career he was given the opportunity to work with and learn from "incredible" veterans like June Foray, Don Messick, and "childhood hero" Jonathan Winters as well as meet his peers, such as Frank Welker and Nancy Cartwright. However, he was shocked when he had the first taste of how voice actors, who were an integral part in creating their characters, were sometimes treated as expendable. Hired to play the singing voice of rock-star character Apollo Blue on the 1990 *The Jetsons* movie, he had recorded his part only to learn afterward that the original Judy Jetson, Janet Waldo, was to be entirely replaced by the then-popular singer Tiffany. As many others did, he sympathized with Waldo, adding that he thought it was fitting that the movie received a cool reception.

Although he had had a major career break in the form of 1987's *The Teenage Mutant Ninja Turtles*, it was also, ultimately, touched with a bitter-sweetness reminiscent of Waldo's situation. His involvement began at a casual lunch meeting while he was working on NBC's *Fraggle Rock*, playing Marjorie, the talking trash heap. ("I brought 'trash talking' to a whole new level.") Director Stu Rosen met with Paulsen and Townsend Coleman, among others, and pitched them the Ninja Turtles, asking them to read for parts. "We all sort of read for all the characters and I think, as I recall, they narrowed it down and had me and Barry [Gordon] and Townsend and Cam [Clarke] and we all just kind of mixed and matched, and I don't know why I ended up with Raphael. They thought maybe that I was kind of a smart guy."

The "heroes on the half-shell" quickly became the number one Saturday morning cartoon of its time and garnered the largest rating in CBS's history for kid-oriented programming. Further, on the home video market, Paulsen estimates they sold over 30 million cassettes. Yet, when Newline decided to produce a feature film, no one contacted the TV *Turtle* cast. "At the time we were told that the problem was that Newline wanted to make the movies truer to the comic book. And by that they meant that they wanted it to be a little harder and darker, as opposed to the kind of light kid's show the cartoon was." Even after Cam Clarke had an agent call up and suggest they consider the established voice cast for consistency's sake, there was still no interest at the studio. Evidently, the issue was, according to Paulsen, that "the feature people had no connection to the TV people and certainly were not beholden to them at all."

But, Paulsen adds that the situation taught him a "lesson in humility." He explains, "I think secretly I was hoping that somebody would say, you know, like with Janet Waldo, 'Hey, this isn't Raphael.' Well you know what? . . . It didn't make any difference to any of those kids that Raphael wasn't the same in the movies as he was in the TV show. There were two separate entities. The kids still watch the TV show and they love the movies."

At the height of the *Turtles'* popularity, the program was criticized following isolated reports that children were trying to climb into sewers to search for their heroes. Even Paulsen's own young son, Ashton, thought at the time that his dad worked in the sewer. "He would call 'Hello, Donatello! Where's Michelangelo?'" But, Paulsen comments, there are only so many precautions the media can take to prevent people from imitating the things they watch on television: "You can't dress everybody in a giant condom. Those things are going to happen. I think it's important then for the people who do these things to be as accessible as possible and do things like all of us do, which is call kids on the phone [for charity]. And I've been in situations where parents will ask me to defuse situations at home because kids are getting out of hand, and so Raphael will call and tell them, 'Hey this isn't cool.'"

While Paulsen says he is grateful for the opportunity to do the show for a variety of reasons, including a lot of "cool charity things" like playing on a celebrity hockey team against old-timers of different National Hockey League teams, which also allowed him to live his childhood dream of being a professional hockey player. He has also been very active in the Famous Fone Friends charity, which asks voice actors to cheer very sick kids by calling them and talking with them in character. Paulsen says, "I've gotten to call kids all over the country and North America, really, on the phone as a result of Ninja Turtles."

Although he may claim not to be an impressionist, per se, two of his subsequent characterizations seem to make his self-assessment look modest. Originally considered for the part of Arthur, the Tick's side-kick on the Fox animated version of the program, he lost the part to a celebrity (ex-Monkee, Mickey Dolenz), then regained it by the second season when Dolenz went on tour. Although Dolenz had originated the part, Paulsen recreated it seamlessly; his attitude at the time was, "If it ain't broke, don't fix it. My voice timber is very similar and I'm doing pretty much as close to Mickey as I can. You can't help but bring your own sensibilities to the show. I have a tendency to improvise quite a bit because I just like to do that. Sometimes it works and sometimes it doesn't. But I am trying to do as close to Mickey and they keep me on track."

Just as impressive was his rendition of Hollywood's top film comedian, for which his improvisational skills became a real asset. In 1998, Paulsen got to be Jim Carrey "for a lot less money" in CBS's animated version of *The Mask*.

Paulsen, who is a fan of Carrey's, constructed his approach carefully. In a 1998 article for the Los Angeles Time syndicate, Paulsen was quoted to say, "I would never pretend to try to do Jim Carrey. I mean, he's quite uniquely talented and I don't know that anybody could do what he can do. But, I'm a voice actor and I don't have to worry about contorting my face. . . . I basically used my natural voice for Stanley and then what I do when the Mask happens is dictated by what's written on the page. . . . He morphs into different things and I change my voice accordingly." Paulsen added that Film Roman hired him to "bring something to the show" in the form of his improvisational talent. He must have been gratified at how close he came to his mark. Reviews in the press took notice of his performance more than the animation. As the ultimate compliment, when it came time on Carrey's film *Liar, Liar* and Carrey was unavailable to do the looping—which in this case was to replace some of the swearing for the edited television and airline showings— Universal called Paulsen. It seems that Carrey and his manager had watched the cartoon and Carrey told his manager, "Why don't you get that guy?"

"That guy" is not only the voice of the popular *Animaniacs* characters— Yakko and Pinky of *Pinky and the Brian*—he also had a hand in the brainstorming session which led to the series creation. "It was just after *Tiny Toons* were starting to wind down, Tom Ruegger and Andrea [Romano] and a couple of people called Jim [Cummings] and me and Tress [MacNeille] and Frank [Welker] and we just kind of sat around and at a table at Sound Castle Recording and threw out ideas. They were there with Peter Hastings and Paul Rugg and John McCann and some writers and they said, 'Look, here's what we're thinking about doing—there's this pile of characters and we don't really know what's going to be.' Out of the collaboration came *Animaniacs*, a pastiche of Warneresque classic and modern cartoon characters.

For Paulsen, the two lead characters he created for *Animaniacs* ranked "with the best stuff [he'd] ever done." For his character of Yakko, the idea was to create a character with a "Groucho Marx sensibility," without doing the actual voice, while Pinky, the goofy lab rat, was inspired by English comedians like those of Monty Python and *The Goon Show*. Paulsen thought a Cockney accent would be a perfect contrast for Maurice LaMarche's Orson Welles— inspired voice he performed as the Brain. Paulsen said at the time the show was in production that he enjoyed doing Yakko, who is "really a lot of fun because he gets to sing, . . . but, in the grand scheme of things, it is not that unique a voice. It's just a little kind of helium kind of thing that a lot of people can do." While he was fond of the "smart, quick-talking guy," he preferred Pinky as "a more thoroughly thought-out multidimensional character."

One of his prized possessions from that time is a special cel from producer Stephen Spielberg featuring a caricature of the director holding Yakko and standing beside Dr. Scratchensniff with Pinky perched on his hat. The inscription reads, "To Rob, this is only the beginning of your gallery of characters. Mel would have loved you. Steven Spielberg."

To Paulsen's surprise, the director was, by far, not the only adult fan to feel that strongly about the show. Of his warm reception on the 1994 signing tour throughout the country, Paulsen says, "I didn't expect it to be as big with as many adults as I see. I mean, I knew *Animaniacs* was hip and I knew people would get the joke, but I didn't think they would come out and see us!" Paulsen claims one of the most prevalent comments was, "You must be getting tired of this," to which he quotes hockey player Gordie Howe's reply at a memorabilia show: "I've worked too hard for this privilege." Now, that has become Paulsen's stock answer, and he says, "It really is a privilege when people take the time out of their Saturday or Sunday to spend three hours waiting to talk to you for what amounts to thirty seconds or a minute and they get thrilled out of you signing something." He says the adults whose interest in animation was renewed by the show were especially grateful and almost apologized in admitting that their kids introduced them to the show and they have since become the bigger fans.

When asked why animation has become so popular among adults, Paulsen is reflective. "I think it's because there's something very magical about cartoons and the whole medium. I know that's a real broad statement—but I think by that I mean it sort of touches that kid on Saturday morning in all of us. . . . I can remember sitting in pajamas with the feet in them on a cold winter morning in Michigan watching cartoons on Saturday morning. It's almost a sort of a secure feeling that there are . . . certain things that are around us all the time that remind us how important it is to remember what it was like to just get lost in that. It's one of those mediums that everybody seems to like whether they take the time to watch a show and get involved with characters on a show or whether it's wearing a T-shirt with Bugs Bunny on it. . . . There's something about cartoons that sort of allows people not to take life quite so seriously."

CREDITS

101 Dalmatians: The Series (1996) TV Series . . . . Cecil B. DeVil
2 Stupid Dogs (1993) TV Series . . . . Concession Stand Runner/Additional Voices
Addams Family, The (1992) TV Series . . . . Mr. Normanmeyer

Adventures of Jimmy Neutron: Boy Genius, The (2002) TV Series . . . . Carl Wheezer
Aladdin (1993/I) TV Series . . . . Additional Voices
Aladdin and the King of Thieves (1996) . . . . Additional Voices
Alan Brady Show, The (2003) TV Series . . . . Various Voices
Alvin and the Chipmunks Meet the Wolfman (2000) . . . . Mr. Rochelle
Animaniacs (1993) TV Series . . . . Yakko Warner/Pinky/Dr. Otto Scratchensniff/Additional Voices
Attack of the Killer Tomatoes (1990) TV Series . . . . Additional Voices
Balto II: Wolf Quest (2001) . . . . Terrier/Sumac/Wolverine 2
Belle's Magical World (1997)
Biker Mice from Mars (1993) TV Series . . . . Throttle/Fred/Eon
Bonkers (1993) TV Series . . . . Stand-up Comedian/Wally/Ma's Henchman/Toon Camera Zoom/Pig
Bubsy (1993) TV . . . . Bubsy Bobcat
Bump in the Night (1994) TV Series . . . . Squishington
Butt-Ugly Martians (2001) TV Series . . . . 2-T Fru-T/Mike/Ronald
Capitol Critters (1992) TV Series . . . . Additional Voices
Captain Planet and the Planeteers (1990) TV Series . . . . Additional Voices
Casper (1996) TV Series . . . . Spooky
Challenge of the GoBots (1984) TV Series . . . . Additional Voices
Channel Umptee-3 (1997) TV Series . . . . Ogden Ostrich
Charlotte's Web 2: Wilbur's Great Adventure (2003) Video . . . . Farley
Chip 'n' Dale's Rescue Rangers to the Rescue (1989) TV
Cinderella II: Dreams Come True (2002) . . . . Jacques/Baker/Sir Hugh Clayfighter 6
Comic Book: The Movie (2004) . . . . Various Voices
Danny Phantom (2003) TV Series . . . . Jack Fenton
Darkwing Duck (1991) TV Series . . . . Steelbeak/Additional Voices
Denver, the Last Dinosaur (1992) TV Series . . . . Chet/Motley
Detroit Docona (2004) TV Series . . . . Algernon Montgomery
Dexter's Laboratory (1996) TV Series . . . . Major Glory
Dino-Riders (1988) TV Series . . . . Faze/Kameelian
Droopy, Master Detective (1993) TV Series . . . . Additional Voices
Elvira's Haunted Hills (2001) (uncredited) . . . . Adrian
Extremely Goofy Movie, An (2000) . . . . P.J. Pete
Eyes of Fire (1983) . . . . Jewell Buchanan
Fantastic Max (1988) TV Series . . . . Additional Voices
Fish Police (1992) TV Series . . . . Additional Voices
Flintstone Kids, The (1986) TV Series . . . . Additional Voices
Foofur (1986) TV Series . . . . Additional Voices
Fraggle Rock (1987) TV Series . . . . Boober/Sprocket/Marjorie
G.I. Joe (1983) TV Series . . . . Snow-Job/E6 Harlan W. Moore/Tripwire/E4 Tormod S. Skoog
G.I. Joe: A Real American Hero (1983) TV . . . . Tripwire/E-4 Tormod S. Skoog/Snow-Job/E-6 Harlan
    W. Moore
G.I. Joe: The Movie (1987) . . . . Snow-Job/E-6 Harlan W. Moore
Gnome Named Gnorm, A (1992) . . . . Gnorm the Gnome (as Vocal Magic)
Goof Troop (1992) TV Series . . . . Peter "P.J." Pete Jr.
Goof Troop Christmas, A (1992) TV . . . . Peter "P.J." Pete Jr.
Goofy Movie, A (1995) . . . . "P.J." Pete
Gramps (1992) TV . . . . Alien Co-pilot/Gramps/Mule
Greatest Stories of the Bible, The (1994) TV Series . . . . Mookie
Gummi Bears, The (1985) TV Series . . . . Gusto
Hillbilly Blue (1995) . . . . Cook/Cop/Health Inspector/Woman/Additional Voices
Histeria! (1998) TV Series . . . . Mr. Smarty Pants/Sammy Melman/Histeria Kid Chorus

House of Mouse (2001) TV Series . . . . Jose Carioca
I'm Mad (1994) . . . . Yakko Warner/Dr. Scratchensniff
Izzy's Quest for Olympic Gold (1995) TV . . . . George, Izzy's Dad/Teal Bike Rider/Bike Ride
   Announcer/Medal Awarder
Jetsons: The Movie (1990) . . . . Additional Voices
Jimmy Neutron: Boy Genius (2001) . . . . Carl Wheezer/Carl's Mom and Dad/Kid in Classroom/Kid
Jimmy Neutron's Nicktoon Blast (2003) . . . . Carl Wheezer
Jonny Quest (1986) TV Series . . . . Hadji
Jonny Quest vs. the Cyber Insects (1995) TV . . . . Hadji/Number 425/Computer/Additional Voices
Jonny's Golden Quest (1993) TV . . . . Hadji
Jungle Cubs (1996) TV Series . . . . Akela the Wolf/Hathi
Karate Kid, The (1989) TV Series . . . . Additional Voices
Kog-Head and Meatus (2000) . . . . Kog-Head/Meatus
Lady and the Tramp II: Scamp's Adventure (2001) . . . . Otis
Land before Time II: The Great Valley Adventure, The (1994) . . . . Spike/Strut/Chomper
Land before Time III: The Time of the Great Giving, The (1995) . . . . Spike
Land before Time IV: Journey through the Mists, The (1996) . . . . Spike
Land before Time IX: Journey to the Big Water, The (2002) . . . . Spike/Mo
Land before Time V: The Mysterious Island, The (1997) . . . . Spike
Land before Time VII: The Stone of Cold Fire, The (2000) . . . . Spike/Rinkus
Land before Time VIII: The Big Freeze, The (2001) . . . . Spike
Land before Time X: The Great Longneck Migration, The (2003) Video . . . . Spike
Lilo & Stitch: The Series (2003) TV Series . . . . Experiment #625
Little Mermaid II: Return to the Sea, The (2000) . . . . Eric
Little Troll Prince, The (1995) . . . . Borch/Spectator #1
Magician, The (1998) TV Series . . . . Additional Voices
Major Flake (2001) TV Series
Making of "Jimmy Neutron," The (2001) TV . . . . Himself
Mask, The (1995) TV Series . . . . Stanley Ipkis/The Mask
Mickey Mouse Works (1999) TV Series . . . . Jose Carioca
Mickey's House of Villains (2002) . . . . Hades (singing)
Mickey's Magical Christmas: Snowed in at the House of Mouse (2001) . . . . Jaq
Midnight Patrol, The (1990) TV Series . . . . Additional Voices
Mighty Max (1991) TV Series . . . . Max
Monster in My Pocket: The Big Scream (1992) . . . . Jerk at Drive-In
Mutant on the Bounty (1989) . . . . Newsman
New Kids on the Block (1990) TV Series . . . . Additional Voices
One Saturday Morning (1997) TV Series . . . . Centerville Characters (1999–2000)
Online Adventures of Ozzie the Elf, The (1997) TV
Paw Paws, The (1985) TV Series . . . . Additional Voices
Phantom 2040 (1994) TV Series . . . . Heisenberg/Sean One
Pinky and the Brain (1995) TV Series . . . . Pinky
Pinky and the Brain Christmas Special, A (1995) TV . . . . Pinky
Pinky, Elmyra, and the Brain (1998) TV Series . . . . Pinky
Pocahontas II: Journey to a New World (1998) . . . . Additional Voices
Potsworth and Co. (1990) TV Series . . . . Nightmare Prince
Powerpuff Girls, The (1998) TV Series . . . . Additional Voices
Powerpuff Girls, The (2002) . . . . Hota Wata/Killa Drilla
ProStars (1991) TV Series
Pup Named Scooby-Doo (1988) TV Series . . . . Additional Voices
Raw Toonage (1992) TV Series . . . . Additional Voices

Real Adventures of Jonny Quest, The (1996) TV Series . . . . Hadji Quest-Singh (1997)
Return to Never Land (2002) . . . . Additional Voice
Road Rovers (1996) TV Series . . . . Gas Station Attendant
Rockin' with Judy Jetson (1988) TV . . . . Sky Rocker/Zany
Rude Dog and the Dweebs (1989) TV Series . . . . Rude Dog
Saber Rider and the Star Sheriffs (1987) TV Series
Samurai Jack (2001) TV Series . . . . Additional Voices
Scooby-Doo and the Reluctant Werewolf (1989) TV . . . . Brunch
Scooby-Doo in Arabian Nights (1994) TV
Scooby-Doo Meets the Boo Brothers (1987) TV . . . . Shreako/Dispatcher
Smurfs, The (1981) TV Series . . . . Additional Voices
Snorks, The (1984) TV Series . . . . Corky the Snork Patrol/Additional Voices
Sonic the Hedgehog (1993) TV Series . . . . Antoine
Space Cats (1991) TV Series . . . . Additional Voices
Stitch! The Movie (2003) Video . . . . Experiment #625/Technician
Swat Kats: The Radical Squadron (1993) TV Series . . . . Hard Drive
Tale Spin (1990) TV Series . . . . Ratchet/Additional Voices
Taz-Mania (1991) TV Series . . . . Didgeri Dingo (II)/Axle/Dog the Turtle/Francis X.
  Bushlad/Timothy Platypus/Emu/Additional Voices
Teacher's Pet (2000/II) TV Series . . . . Ian Wazselewski
Teacher's Pet: The Movie (2003) . . . . Ian Wazselewski
Teenage Mutant Ninja Turtles (1987/I) TV Miniseries . . . . Raphael/Others
Teenage Mutant Ninja Turtles (1987/II) TV Series . . . . Raphael/Zach the Fifth Turtle/Mr. Ogg/
  High-Tech
Teenage Mutant Ninja Turtles: Planet of the Turtleoids (1991) TV . . . . Raphael
Teenage Mutant Ninja Turtles: The Cufflink Caper (1990) TV . . . . Raphael
Thumb Wars: The Phantom Cuticle (1999) TV . . . . Oobedoob Scobydoob Benubi
Thumbtanic (1998) . . . . Mr. Prickle/Lice Checker #2/Bartender
Thundercats (1985) TV Series . . . . Additional Voices
Tick, The (1994) TV Series . . . . Arthur (II) (1995–)/Caped Crusading Chameleon/Mucilage Man/
  Charles/Brainchild/The Terror/Forehead/Additional Voices
Time Squad (2001) TV Series . . . . Buck Tuddrussel
Timon and Pumbaa (1995) TV Series . . . . Banzai the Hyena/Additional Voices
Tiny Toon Adventures (1990) TV Series . . . . Fowlmouth/Miscellaneous Voices
Tiny Toon Adventures: How I Spent My Vacation (1992) . . . . Fowlmouth/Banjo the Woodpile
  Possum/Mr. Hitcher
Tom and Jerry Kids Show (1990) TV Series . . . . Additional Voices
Top Cat and the Beverly Hills Cats (1987)
Transformers (1984) TV Series . . . . Air Raid/Chase/Fastlane/Slingshot/Haywire
Ugly Duck-Thing, The (2002) TV . . . . Mother Goose/Home Owner
Uncle Gus in: For the Love of Monkeys (1999) TV . . . . Ali-Ali/Horse Race Announcer/Monkey #2/
  Welfare Officer
Wake, Rattle, and Roll (1990) TV Series . . . . D.E.C.K.S.
Wakko's Wish (1999) . . . . Yakko Warner/Dr. Otto Scratchensniff/Pinky Mouse
Where's Waldo? (1991) TV Series . . . . Additional Voices
Wild West COWBOYs of Moo Mesa (1992) TV Series . . . . Additional Voices
Wildfire (1986) TV Series . . . . Additional Voices
Wizard of Oz, The (1990) TV Series
Yogi's Treasure Hunt (1985) TV Series . . . . Additional Voices

Photo courtesy of King Features Syndicate and Fleischer Studios, Inc.

MAE QUESTEL

It is ironic that the voice actor for animation's first screen siren, Betty Boop, narrowly avoided the retiring life of a prim and proper teacher. The great pioneer voice actor who helped shape the profession of modern animation voice-acting was born in 1909, during the last vestiges of the Victorian era, when respectable young ladies would have never been allowed into a career as "vulgar" as show business. Although Questel displayed a talent for performing early, her parents and grandparents reportedly discouraged her aspirations to become a professional.

Consequently, Questel decided to go into teaching, until she unwittingly began a new career courtesy of popular vaudeville star Helen Kane. Questel's friends in her sorority entered her in a talent contest for the best impersonation of Kane at the RKO (Radio-Keith-Orpheum) Fordham Theater. Questel, who was reportedly the only contestant shrewd enough to observe Kane onstage beforehand, delivered a dead-on impersonation that won the seventeen-year-old a contract with the William Morris Agency for the RKO vaudeville circuit. While her act consisted of impersonations of celebrities like Fannie Brice, Marlene Dietrich, Rudy Vallee, and Maurice Chevalier, of course, it was Questel's Helen Kane impersonation that made her an obvious choice for Max Fleischer's Helen Kane send-up, Betty Boop.

Betty Boop made her first appearance as the secondary character of a nightclub singer in a 1930s Bimbo cartoon entitled "Dizzy Dishes." Her much commented upon strange look came from the fact that she was designed to be part human and part French Poodle—presumably drawn to be attractive to the main character, Bimbo, who was, himself, an anthropomorphized dog. (Although *The Fleischer Story* author Leslie Cabarga quoted animator Grim Natwick as saying he had "a song sheet of Helen Kane and the spit curls came from her," Natwick did not explicitly say if the song sheet was for Kane's "I Want to Be Loved by You.")

Although Questel was not the first voice for Betty, hers remains the best-known characterization. Betty Boop was initially voiced by Margie Heinz, Kate Wright, Bonnie Poe, and Annabell (Little Ann) Little—Little even went on the road to do theatrical shows as the character—but it was Questel who, on the strength of her Helen Kane impersonation, won and held the part the longest amount of time—from 1931's "Betty Co-ed" until the series ended in 1939. She was quoted by Cabarga as saying that she actually "lived" the part of Betty, noting at the series end, "It took me a long time to lower my voice and get away from the character."

As the series became popular, Kane, who did not consent to having her likeness or singing style appropriated for Betty, sued the Fleischers and Paramount in 1934, alleging that her earning power had been diminished by the cartoon. It seems the trial ultimately turned on who had coined Betty's catchphrase of "Boop-boop-ba-doop." Helen Kane had made the phrase famous in her song "I Want to Be Loved by You"; however, according to Charles Solomon, in his book *The History of Animation*, the Fleischers won the case by proving that a black entertainer named "Baby Esther" had previously used the phrase before either Kane or Questel.

Being part of the first wave of cartoon voice actors, Questel was instrumental in setting many precedents for the craft. Most notably, she first displayed the type of versatility in the ability to perform a number of roles now almost expected of contemporary animation actors. This not only included the female roles of Little Audrey and Olive Oyl (whom she modeled after actress Zasu Pitts), but also male roles on "five or six" cartoons as it became necessary to fill in as Popeye when Jack Mercer was stationed overseas during World War II!

Even though Questel refused to leave New York (not even when Fleischer's studios moved to Florida in the late 1930s, thereby prompting the Fleischers to end the Betty Boop series), she was able to build a career which ultimately included many different mediums. Her work in the city included radio versions of *The Green Hornet* and *Perry Mason* and the first interactive television program, 1953's *Winky Dink and You*. She had more offers of work in Los Angeles, but always turned them down, preferring to stay in Manhattan to care for her family. Even so, she was still able to count among her film credits Barbara Streisand's *Funny Girl*, a reprising of Betty Boop for 1988's *Who Framed Roger Rabbit*, and a particularly memorable turn as Woody Allen's Jewish mother in 1989's *New York Stories*.

Although she enjoyed meeting and speaking with her fans whenever it was possible, sadly, Questel was a long-time sufferer of Alzheimer's before passing away on January 4, 1998, at her home in Manhattan. As both Betty Boop and Olive Oyl, Questel has had the distinction of creating what is considered to be one of the sexiest and most repulsive women to ever grace a cartoon. However, despite the lack of new material, the characters she helped create have proved ageless, with Betty Boop still considered au courant with over a billion dollars made in merchandising alone. As Bob Hoskin's character in *Roger Rabbit* confirmed over five decades after she originated the character, thanks to Questel, Betty Boop has "still got it."

CREDITS

51st Annual Primetime Emmy Awards, The (1999) TV (uncredited) . . . . Herself
A Hunting We Will Go (1932) . . . . Betty Boop
Abusement Park (1947) . . . . Olive Oyl
Admission Free (1932) . . . . Betty Boop
Adventures of Popeye (1935) . . . . Olive Oyl
Aladdin and His Wonderful Lamp (1939) . . . . Olive Oyl
All's Fair at the Fair (1947) . . . . Olive Oyl
Alpine for You (1951) . . . . Olive Oyl
Ancient Fistory (1953) . . . . Olive Oyl
Anvil Chorus Girl, The (1944) . . . . Olive Oyl
Any Rags (1932) . . . . Betty Boop
Assault and Flattery (1956) . . . . Olive Oyl
Audrey the Rainmaker (1951) . . . . Little Audrey

Axe Me Another (1934) .... Olive Oyl
Baby Be Good (1935) .... Betty Boop
Baby Wants a Battle (1953) .... Olive Oyl
Baby Wants a Bottleship (1942) .... Olive Oyl
Baby Wants Spinach (1950) .... Olive Oyl
Balmy Swami, A (1949) .... Olive Oyl
Barking Dogs Don't Fite (1949) .... Olive Oyl
Barnacle Bill (1930) .... Betty Boop
Be Human (1936) .... Betty Boop
Be Kind to "Aminals" (1935) .... Olive Oyl
Be up to Date (1938) .... Betty Boop
Beach Peach (1950) .... Olive Oyl
Beaus Will Be Beaus (1955) .... Olive Oyl
Betty Boop, M.D. (1932) .... Betty Boop
Betty Boop and Grampy (1935) .... Betty Boop
Betty Boop and Little Jimmy (1936) .... Betty Boop
Betty Boop and the Little King (1936) .... Betty Boop
Betty Boop for President (1932) .... Betty Boop
Betty Boop Limited, The (1932) .... Betty Boop
Betty Boop with Henry (1935) (uncredited) .... Betty Boop
Betty Boop's Bamboo Isle (1932) .... Betty Boop
Betty Boop's Big Boss (1933) .... Betty Boop
Betty Boop's Birthday Party (1933) .... Betty Boop
Betty Boop's Bizzy Bee (1932) .... Betty Boop
Betty Boop's Crazy Inventions (1933) .... Betty Boop
Betty Boop's Halloween Party (1933) .... Betty Boop
Betty Boop's Ker-Choo (1933) .... Betty Boop
Betty Boop's Life Guard (1934) .... Betty Boop
Betty Boop's Little Pal (1934) .... Betty Boop
Betty Boop's May Party (1933) .... Betty Boop
Betty Boop's Museum (1932) .... Betty Boop
Betty Boop's Penthouse (1933) .... Betty Boop
Betty Boop's Prize Show (1934) .... Betty Boop
Betty Boop's Rise to Fame (1934) .... Betty Boop
Betty Boop's Trial (1934) .... Betty Boop
Betty Boop's Ups and Downs (1932) .... Betty Boop
Betty Co-ed (1931) .... Betty Boop
Betty in Blunderland (1934) .... Betty Boop
Beware of Barnacle Bill (1935) .... Olive Oyl
Big Bad Sindbad (1952) .... Olive Oyl
Big Chief Ugh-Amugh-Ugh (1938) .... Olive Oyl
Bimbo's Express (1931) .... Betty Boop
Bimbo's Initiation (1931) .... Betty Boop
Blow Me Down! (1933) .... Olive Oyl
Boop-Oop-A-Doop (1932) .... Betty Boop
Bride and Gloom (1954) .... Olive Oyl
Bridge Ahoy! (1936) .... Olive Oyl
Brotherly Love (1936) .... Olive Oyl
Bulldozing the Bull (1938) .... Olive Oyl
Butterscotch and Soda (1948) .... Little Audrey
Buzzy Boop (1938) .... Betty Boop

Buzzy Boop at the Concert (1938) . . . . Betty Boop
Can You Take It (1934) . . . . Olive Oyl
Candid Candidate, The (1937) . . . . Betty Boop
Car-azy Drivers (1954) . . . . Olive Oyl
Case of the Cockeyed Canary, The (1952) . . . . Little Audrey
Chess-Nuts (1932) . . . . Betty Boop
Child Sockology (1953) . . . . Olive Oyl
Choose Your "Weppins" (1935) . . . . Olive Oyl
Clean Shaven Man, A (1936) . . . . Olive Oyl
Cookin' with Gags (1955) . . . . Olive Oyl
Cops Is Tops (1955) . . . . Olive Oyl
Crazy Town (1932) . . . . Betty Boop
Crystal Brawl, The (1957) . . . . Olive Oyl
Customers Wanted (1939) . . . . Olive Oyl (in episode "Let's Get Movin'")
Dance Contest, The (1934) . . . . Olive Oyl
Dancing Fool, The (1932) . . . . Betty Boop
Date to Skate, A (1938) . . . . Olive Oyl
Dawn Gawn (1958) . . . . Little Audrey
Ding Dong Doggie (1937) . . . . Betty Boop
Dizzy Dishes (1930) . . . . Betty Boop
Dizzy Dishes (1955) . . . . Little Audrey
Dizzy Divers (1935) . . . . Olive Oyl
Dizzy Red Riding Hood (1931) . . . . Betty Boop
Doing Impossikible Stunts (1940) . . . . Olive Oyl
Double-Cross-Country Race (1951) . . . . Olive Oyl
Dream Walking, A (1934) . . . . Olive Oyl
Farmer and the Belle, The (1950) . . . . Olive Oyl
Firemen's Brawl (1953) . . . . Olive Oyl
Fistic Mystic, The (1947) . . . . Olive Oyl
Flies Ain't Human (1941) . . . . Olive Oyl
Floor Flusher (1954) . . . . Olive Oyl
Football Toucher Downer, The (1937) . . . . Olive Oyl
For Better or Nurse (1945) . . . . Olive Oyl
For Better or Worser (1935) . . . . Olive Oyl
Fowl Play (1937) . . . . Olive Oyl
Foxy Hunter, The (1937) . . . . Betty Boop
Fright to the Finish (1954) . . . . Olive Oyl
Gift of Gag (1955) . . . . Olive Oyl
Grampy's Indoor Outing (1936) . . . . Betty Boop
Greek Mirthology (1954) . . . . Olive Oyl
Gym Jam (1950) . . . . Olive Oyl
Ha! Ha! Ha! (1934) . . . . Betty Boop
Happy You and Merry Me (1936) . . . . Betty Boop
Haul in One, A (1956) . . . . Olive Oyl
Hill-billing and Cooing (1956) . . . . Olive Oyl
Hold the Lion, Please (1951) . . . . Little Audrey
Hold the Wire (1936) . . . . Olive Oyl
Honest Love and True (1938) . . . . Betty Boop
Hoppity Goes to Town (1941) (uncredited) . . . . Bee Scout
Hospitaliky (1937) . . . . Olive Oyl
Hot Air Aces (1949) . . . . Olive Oyl

Hot Air Salesman, The (1937) . . . . Betty Boop
House Builder-Upper, The (1938) . . . . Olive Oyl
House Cleaning Blues (1937) . . . . Betty Boop
House Tricks? (1946) . . . . Olive Oyl
How Green Is My Spinach (1950) . . . . Olive Oyl
Hull of a Mess, A (1942) . . . . Olive Oyl
"Hyp-Nut-Tist," The (1935) . . . . Olive Oyl
I Don't Scare (1956) . . . . Olive Oyl
I Eats My Spinach (1933) . . . . Olive Oyl
I Heard (1933) . . . . Betty Boop
I Likes Babies and Infinks (1937) . . . . Olive Oyl
I Never Changes My Altitude (1937) . . . . Olive Oyl
I Wanna Be a Life Guard (1936) . . . . Olive Oyl
I Yam Lovesick (1938) . . . . Olive Oyl
I Yam What I Yam (1933) . . . . Olive Oyl
I'll Be Glad When You're Dead, You Rascal You (1932) . . . . Betty Boop
I'll Be Skiing Ya (1947) . . . . Olive Oyl
I'm in the Army Now (1936) . . . . Olive Oyl
Impractical Joker, The (1937) . . . . Betty Boop
Is My Palm Read (1933) . . . . Betty Boop
I-Ski Love-Ski You-Ski (1936) . . . . Olive Oyl
Island Fling, The (1947) . . . . Olive Oyl
Jack and the Beanstalk (1931) . . . . Betty Boop
Jeep, The (1938) . . . . Olive Oyl
Jitterbug Jive (1950) . . . . Olive Oyl
Job for a Gob, A (1954) . . . . Olive Oyl
Judge for a Day (1935) . . . . Betty Boop
Just a Gigolo (1932) . . . . Betty Boop
Just One More Chance (1932) . . . . Betty Boop
Keep in Style (1934) . . . . Betty Boop
Kids in the Shoe, The (1935) (uncredited) . . . . Woman in the Shoe/Kids
King of the Mardi Gras (1935) . . . . Olive Oyl
Kitty from Kansas City (1931) . . . . Betty Boop
Klondike Casanova (1946) . . . . Olive Oyl
Land of the Lost Jewels (1950) (uncredited) . . . . Isabel
Language All My Own, A (1935) . . . . Betty Boop
Law and Audrey (1952) . . . . Little Audrey
Learn Polikeness (1938) . . . . Olive Oyl
Let Me Call You Sweetheart (1932) . . . . Betty Boop
Let's Celebrake (1938) . . . . Olive Oyl
Let's Get Movin' (1936) . . . . Olive Oyl
Let's Stalk Spinach (1951) . . . . Olive Oyl
Let's You and Him Fight (1934) . . . . Olive Oyl
Little Audrey Riding Hood (1953) . . . . Little Audrey
Little Nobody (1936) . . . . Betty Boop
Little Soap and Water, A (1935) . . . . Betty Boop
Little Swee' Pea (1936) . . . . Olive Oyl
Lost and Foundry (1937) . . . . Olive Oyl
Lost Dream, The (1949) . . . . Little Audrey
Lumberjack and Jill (1949) . . . . Olive Oyl
Lunch with a Punch (1952) . . . . Olive Oyl

Making Friends (1936) . . . . Betty Boop

Making Stars (1935) . . . . Betty Boop

Man on the Flying Trapeze, The (1934) . . . . Olive Oyl

Many Tanks (1942) . . . . Olive Oyl

Marry-Go-Round, The (1943) . . . . Olive Oyl

Mask-A-Raid (1931) . . . . Betty Boop

Matty's Funday Funnies (1959) TV Series (writer) (uncredited) . . . . Casper/Little Audrey/Additional Voices

Mess Production (1945) . . . . Olive Oyl

Minding the Baby (1931) . . . . Betty Boop

Minnie the Moocher (1932) (uncredited) . . . . Betty Boop

Mister and Mistletoe (1955) . . . . Olive Oyl

More Pep (1936) . . . . Betty Boop

Morning, Noon, and Night (1933) . . . . Betty Boop

Morning, Noon, and Night Club (1937) . . . . Olive Oyl

Mother Goose Land (1933) . . . . Betty Boop

Moving Aweigh (1944) . . . . Olive Oyl

Musical Justice (1931) . . . . Betty Boop

Musical Mountaineers (1939) . . . . Betty Boop

Mutiny Ain't Nice (1938) . . . . Olive Oyl

My Artistical Temperature (1937) . . . . Olive Oyl

My Friend the Monkey (1939) . . . . Betty Boop

My Pop, My Pop (1940) . . . . Olive Oyl

Mysterious Mose (1930) . . . . Betty Boop

Nearlyweds (1957) . . . . Olive Oyl

Never Kick a Woman (1936) . . . . Olive Oyl

New Deal Show, The (1937) . . . . Betty Boop

No! No! A Thousand Times No!! (1935) . . . . Betty Boop

Not Now (1936) . . . . Betty Boop

Nurse to Meet Ya (1955) . . . . Olive Oyl

Oh! How I Hate to Get up in the Morning (1932) . . . . Betty Boop

Old Man of the Mountain, The (1933) . . . . Betty Boop

Olive Oyl for President (1948) . . . . Olive Oyl

On with the New (1938) . . . . Betty Boop

Organ Grinder's Swing (1937) . . . . Olive Oyl

Out of the Inkwell (1938) . . . . Betty Boop

Out to Punch (1956) . . . . Olive Oyl

Paneless Window Washer, The (1937) . . . . Olive Oyl

Parade of the Wooden Soldiers (1933) . . . . Betty Boop

Parlez Vous Woo (1956) . . . . Olive Oyl

Peep in the Deep (1946) . . . . Olive Oyl

Penny Antics (1954) . . . . Olive Oyl

Pilgrim Popeye (1951) . . . . Olive Oyl

Pitchin' Woo at the Zoo (1944) . . . . Olive Oyl

Pleased to Meet Cha! (1935) . . . . Olive Oyl

Plumbing Is a "Pipe" (1938) . . . . Olive Oyl

Poor Cinderella (1934) . . . . Betty Boop

Popeye (1956) TV Series . . . . Olive Oyl/Sea Hag/Swee'pea

Popeye and the Pirates (1947) . . . . Olive Oyl

Popeye for President (1956) . . . . Olive Oyl

Popeye Makes a Movie (1950) . . . . Olive Oyl

Popeye Meets Hercules (1948) . . . . Olive Oyl
Popeye the Sailor Meets Ali Baba's Forty Thieves (1937) . . . . Olive Oyl
Popeye the Sailor Meets Sindbad the Sailor (1936) (uncredited) . . . . Olive Oyl
Popeye the Sailor with Betty Boop (1933) . . . . Betty Boop/Olive Oyl
Popeye's Twentieth Anniversary (1954) . . . . Olive Oyl
Popeye's Mirthday (1953) . . . . Olive Oyl
Popeye's Pappy (1952) . . . . Olive Oyl
Popeye's Premiere (1949) . . . . Olive Oyl
Pop-Pie a la Mode (1945) . . . . Olive Oyl
Popular Melodies (1933) . . . . Betty Boop
Pre-Hysterical Man (1948) . . . . Olive Oyl
Private Eye Popeye (1954) . . . . Olive Oyl
Protek the Weakerist (1937) . . . . Olive Oyl
Pudgy and the Lost Kitten (1938) . . . . Betty Boop
Pudgy Picks a Fight (1937) . . . . Betty Boop
Pudgy Takes a Bow-Wow (1937) . . . . Betty Boop
Pudgy the Watchman (1938) . . . . Betty Boop
Puppet Love (1944) . . . . Olive Oyl
Puttin' on the Act (1940) . . . . Olive Oyl
Quick on the Vigor (1950) . . . . Olive Oyl
Red Hot Mama (1934) . . . . Betty Boop
Rhythm on the Reservation (1939) . . . . Betty Boop
Riding the Rails (1938) . . . . Betty Boop
Robin Hood-Winked (1948) . . . . Olive Oyl
Rocket to Mars (1946) . . . . Olive Oyl
Rodeo Romeo (1946) . . . . Olive Oyl
Roger Rabbit and the Secrets of Toon Town (1988) TV . . . . Herself
Romantic Melodies (1932) . . . . Betty Boop
Royal Four-Flusher, The (1947) . . . . Olive Oyl
Rudy Vallee Melodies (1932) . . . . Betty Boop
S.O.S. (1932) . . . . Betty Boop
Safari so Good (1947) . . . . Olive Oyl
Sally Swing (1938) . . . . Betty Boop
Scared Crows, The (1939) . . . . Betty Boop
Seapreme Court, The (1954) . . . . Little Audrey
Seasin's Greetinks! (1933) . . . . Olive Oyl
Service with a Guile (1946) . . . . Olive Oyl
Service with a Smile (1937) . . . . Betty Boop
Shape Ahoy (1945) . . . . Olive Oyl/Popeye
Shaving Muggs (1953) . . . . Olive Oyl
She Wronged Him Right (1934) . . . . Betty Boop
She-Sick Sailors (1944) . . . . Olive Oyl
Shiver Me Timbers! (1934) . . . . Olive Oyl
Shoein' Hosses (1934) . . . . Olive Oyl
Shuteye Popeye (1952) . . . . Olive Oyl
Silly Hillbilly (1949) . . . . Olive Oyl
Silly Scandals (1931) . . . . Betty Boop
Snow Place like Home (1948) . . . . Olive Oyl
Snow White (1933) (Short) . . . . Betty Boop
So Does an Automobile (1939) . . . . Betty Boop
Sock-a-Bye, Baby (1934) . . . . Olive Oyl

Song a Day, A (1936) . . . . Betty Boop
Song of the Birds (1949) . . . . Little Audrey
Spinach Overture, The (1935) . . . . Olive Oyl
Spinach Packin' Popeye (1944) . . . . Olive Oyl
Spinach Roadster, The (1936) . . . . Olive Oyl
Spinach vs. Hamburgers (1948) . . . . Olive Oyl
Spooky Swabs (1957) . . . . Olive Oyl
Spree Lunch (1957) . . . . Olive Oyl
Stop That Noise (1935) . . . . Betty Boop
Stopping the Show (1932) . . . . Betty Boop
Strong to the Finich (1934) . . . . Olive Oyl
Surf Bored (1953) . . . . Little Audrey
Swat the Fly (1935) . . . . Betty Boop
Swim or Sink (1932) . . . . Betty Boop
Swimmer Take All (1952) . . . . Olive Oyl
Swing School, The (1938) . . . . Betty Boop
Symphony in Spinach (1948) . . . . Olive Oyl
Taking the Blame (1935) . . . . Betty Boop
Tar with a Star (1949) . . . . Olive Oyl
Tarts and Flowers (1950) . . . . Little Audrey
Taxi-Turvy (1954) . . . . Olive Oyl
There's Something about a Soldier (1934) . . . . Betty Boop
Thrill of Fair (1951) . . . . Olive Oyl
Thrills and Chills (1938) . . . . Betty Boop
Time on My Hands (1932) . . . . Mermaid (Betty Boop)
Tops in the Big Top (1945) . . . . Olive Oyl
Toreadorable (1953) . . . . Olive Oyl
Tots of Fun (1952) . . . . Olive Oyl
Training Pigeons (1936) . . . . Betty Boop
Twisker Pitcher, The (1937) . . . . Olive Oyl
Two-Alarm Fire, The (1934) . . . . Olive Oyl
Vacation with Play (1951) . . . . Olive Oyl
Vim, Vigor, and Vitaliky (1936) . . . . Olive Oyl
Wait till the Sun Shines, Nellie (1932) . . . . Betty Boop
We Aim to Please (1934) . . . . Olive Oyl
We Did It (1936) . . . . Betty Boop
We're on Our Way to Rio (1944) . . . . Olive Oyl
When My Ship Comes In (1934) . . . . Betty Boop
Who Framed Roger Rabbit (1988) . . . . Betty Boop
Whoops! I'm a Cowboy (1937) . . . . Betty Boop
Wigwam Whoopee (1948) . . . . Olive Oyl
Wild Elephinks (1933) . . . . Olive Oyl
Winky-Dink and You (1953) TV Series . . . . Winky Dink
Wolf in Sheik's Clothing, A (1948) . . . . Olive Oyl
Wotta Knight (1947) . . . . Olive Oyl
You Gotta Be a Football Hero (1935) . . . . Olive Oyl
You Try Somebody Else (1932) . . . . Betty Boop
You're Not Built That Way (1936) . . . . Betty Boop
Zula Hula (1937) . . . . Betty Boop

ALAN REED

What do a craps game and a warehouse full of rotting pralines have to do with Fred Flintstone? Plenty. If not for an unbearably hot New York summer, which spoiled a large inventory of pralines, Alan Reed might never have taken the role of Fred Flintstone; "Yabba Dabba Doo" would not exist as part of the cartoon lexicon. The evolution of Fred Flintstone was brought about by a career that spanned many mediums and several interesting twists of fate.

Alan Reed was born Teddy Bergman in New York City on August 20, 1907. Growing up, he had an insatiable thirst for knowledge, which led him to graduate early from Manhattan's Washington High School. Planning to attend Columbia University, he found that he was too young to meet their admission requirements. To pass the time until he was old enough to enter, he enrolled at the American Academy of Dramatic Arts in New York City, where he discovered an interest in acting. When he finally enrolled at Columbia University, he continued to act while majoring in journalism and participating in their sports program, winning the Eastern Intercollegiate heavyweight wrestling title. But it was while performing in Columbia's annual variety show that he was spotted by Oklahoma candy tycoon Ralph Rose, who talked Reed into moving to Oklahoma City to star in a stock theater company that Rose bankrolled.

However, Reed's stint in Oklahoma was short lived. Rose went bankrupt, and the stock theater company had to close its doors. Reed then returned to New York City with Rose in tow and the two men pooled what little money they had to enter a craps game. Leaving with $2,400, an enormous sum in those days, they formed a partnership and opened a wholesale candy factory at Ninety-Ninth and Broadway, specializing in pecan pralines. Business was good until the advent of summer—when the bottom fell out. The summer heat turned their entire inventory into what Reed described as "an interesting gray color, like secondhand oatmeal." With their stock depleted and no income, their creditors descended, and they soon found themselves out of the candy business.

Reed once again focused his energy on acting. In 1926, he was a staffer at an upstate New York resort called the Copake Country Club. There, up-and-coming playwright Moss Hart and burgeoning author Herman Wouk were employed writing original plays and revues in which Reed performed. It was while working at Copake that he got a line on his first radio job. A guest of the club, who worked for the Judson Radio Program Corporation, mentioned that his company did all of the radio programs for the networks and told Reed to come up to his office in New York. The guest, however, turned out to be just an office boy who was trying to learn the business himself. But, as fate would have it, there was a role available there as the head mobster for a true detective show. The clerk introduced Reed to the producer's secretary in hopes of getting him an audition, but she took one look at Reed and flatly rejected the nineteen-year-old as "too young." Determined to get the part, Reed slyly waited until the secretary left for lunch, then called the producer's office. When the producer answered, Reed mustered a deep, menacing voice befitting a head mobster and growled, "I'm just going to tell you something. I'm coming into your office in a couple of minutes and you're going to give me a job or you're going for a ride!" The producer was sufficiently impressed, or suitably scared enough, to give him the part and Alan Reed was on his way.

Early in his career Reed had a reputation as a solid actor, but he was still a bit naïve when it came to the business end of the profession. In those days of radio, there were many shows written around the sponsor's product. One show Reed starred in early in his career was sponsored by Henry George Cigars, for which the characters were aptly named "Henry" and "George." For the series, the Judson Radio Program Corporation agreed to pay Reed $50 per show during the first year, $100 per show the second year, and in 1930, during the third season, he received $150 per show. Reed thought that was a respectable salary until he bumped into the show's sponsor at a party. The sponsor informed Reed that his company was being billed $750 per show for Reed's services. When Reed informed the sponsor that his salary was quite a bit less, the sponsor called the Judson Corporation and threatened to pull his backing if they did not give Reed the entire sum. Shortly afterward, a check arrived for a princely sum in the 1930s—$12,500.

For the next two decades, Reed did a variety of characters on various radio programs, establishing himself as a master of dialects. He played the straight man for such legendary comedians as Al Jolson, Jimmy Durante, Bob Hope, Milton Berle, and Burns and Allen. He was so much in demand that, at one point, he was a player on thirty-five different shows in one week. In addition to recurring characters such as Rubinoff, a musical director and violinist who was afraid to speak, for the *Eddie Cantor Show*, Reed was "Daddy" on Fanny Brice's *Baby Snooks* and Finnigan and Clancy the Cop on *Duffy's Tavern;* however, his two favorite roles were Pasquale on *Life with Luigi* and Falstaff Openshaw, which he played for ten years on *The Fred Allen Show*. Falstaff, who became a household name during World War II, was recalled by *Flintstones* co-star Don Messick as one of his favorite characters.

Messick said, "I remember Alan Reed when I was a child on the eastern shore of Maryland, listening to *The Fred Allen Show*. Fred Allen would be wandering down his 'Allen's Alley,' and he would encounter these various characters, one of them who was Falstaff Openshaw. He would knock on the door, and Falstaff would open up and let him in, and immediately want to thrust one of his latest writings upon him. He would say to Fred, 'Have you heard?' and then he would give the title of his latest poem. One poem I recall was, 'From miles around was heard the boom when mother fell out of the

Rainbow Room.' The Rainbow Room was a famous nightclub on top of the RCA building. So many of them involved mother. Another one went, 'Don't roll those dice, mother, they're loaded and so are you.' Alan was a tremendous comedic actor."

By the mid 1930s Reed had become an established radio star, and it was not long before he was given his own program, *The Blubber Bergman Show*. Although he was adept at dramatic roles, with *Blubber*, Reed had built such a reputation as a comedy actor or "stooge" that, by 1939, he was having difficulty landing the dramatic roles for which he longed. Routinely dismissed by the executives with, "All you funny fellows, you want to act," Reed decided that the only way to get serious parts was to reinvent himself. In a 1975 interview with Chuck Shaden for the radio program *Those Were the Days*, Reed explained how the transformation was made. "Reed was a family name of my wife's. . . . Her father's name was Myron Reed Walker. His mother's maiden name was Reed, and we had called our firstborn son Alan Reed Bergman. I started looking around and I said, 'There it is right in front of us! It's an awfully good name.' I just chopped off the 'Bergman.' I had it legally changed in 1939 and that was it." The name change was just part of a makeover that extended to dress and manner, and the new approach won him the dramatic roles.

Having successfully reinvented himself, Reed moved his family to Hollywood in 1943 after signing a movie contract with Fox. He garnered small roles in a string of movies including classics like *The Postman Always Rings Twice*, *Viva Zapata*, with Marlon Brando, and *The Desperate Hours*, with Humphrey Bogart. Although he continued to work in radio, by the 1950s the medium, which had been his bread and butter for many years, was winding down. With the advent of television, he was able to reprise his *Duffy's Tavern* and *Life with Luigi* roles in brief onscreen reincarnations of the popular radio shows, but real small-screen success still eluded him.

Although Reed termed the radio version of *Luigi* as "an enjoyable experience" that made the cast so popular with Italians that Reed said he was an honored guest of the Italian American Society, he explained that the *Luigi* television series became another victim of rabid communist hunters of the McCarthy era. "And this, to give you an idea of the times, the girl who played Rosa was called up before the un-American Activities Committee . . . and the sponsor took advantage of a moral turpitude clause and canceled the program. It cost me a quarter of $1 million in both radio and television shows that we had going. We were just breaking into television. The aftermath of that, six months after it went off—the way times were and rumors got around—I went into a butcher shop that I frequented rather well and as the butcher was wrapping up my stuff, he said, 'Is it true that both you and [producer?] Nash were canceled on the *Luigi* show because you were Communists?' I said, 'What?' "

By 1955, Reed was working in television but had not built up a big enough name for himself to command a large salary, and he needed to find a way to supplement his income to support his growing family. In his first non-show-business venture since the ill-fated candy company in the 1920s, Reed developed Alan Reed Enterprises, a specialty advertising company. Although his new business proved to be a moderate success, he was still on the lookout for a long-term acting job. His search led him to an audition at Hanna-Barbera for a new prime-time animated series reminiscent of *The Honeymooners*, the story of a stone-age family, christened *The Flintstones*.

However, the lead role as the lovable loudmouth Fred Flintstone was initially given to actor Bill Thompson, a veteran cartoon voice-over actor who was best known for his portrayal of Droopy, the sad-faced hound dog made famous in the Tex Avery MGM shorts. Thompson was paired up with Hal Smith, best known as Otis Campbell, the town drunk from *The Andy Griffith Show*, who was cast as Barney Rubble. Although Reed initially failed to land the Flintstone role, fate stepped in to bring him back to the gates of Hanna-Barbera when Joe Barbera decided to recast the part.

Hal Smith explained the reason for the casting change: "Bill Thompson was a good actor, but he had something wrong with his throat. He couldn't sustain that gravel that they wanted in Fred, so Mel [Blanc] and Alan Reed started rehearsing. We had already recorded the first five episodes, and finally, we were recording one night, and Bill would cough and he would stop and he'd say, 'I just can't keep that gravel.' Joe Barbera was directing, and he called us in and said, 'You know, this isn't working.' And I said, 'Well, it really isn't. It's difficult for Bill Thompson to hang onto his voice like that because he just doesn't have it.' So he said, 'Well, Mel and Alan have been rehearsing and practicing this, so I think we're going to let them do it.' " Reed and Mel Blanc re-recorded the five episodes Thompson and Smith had already completed. With seasoned radio actors Jean Vander Pyl and Bea Benaderet in the roles of Wilma and Betty, respectively, the core cast was complete.

The hiring of veteran Alan Reed to portray Fred Flintstone was more fortunate for Hanna-Barbera then they initially realized. An off-the-cuff remark made by Reed not only became a successful tag line for his character, but also added a new phrase to the common lexicon. According to co-star

Jean Vander Pyl (and confirmed by Joe Barbera), at an early reading for *The Flintstones*, the script called for an excited Fred to cry out, "Yahoo," but Reed, uncomfortable with the line, voiced his objection with Barbera. Barbera asked him what he thought Fred should say instead, and Reed replied, "I don't know; how about Yabba Dabba Doo?" The ad-lib has since become one of the most recognizable catch phrases in animation history.

Animation turned out to be the perfect venue for Reed's talents. As it was closely related to radio, the medium afforded Reed the opportunity to use his myriad of character voices and dialects throughout the run of the series. In addition to Fred, Reed was known to do as many as three different characters per show, depending on the script.

Throughout the 1960s, while starring in *The Flintstones*, Reed continued to guest star on television shows such as *The Beverly Hillbillies*, where he played a wrestling promoter, and in movies such as *Breakfast at Tiffany's*, where he played mobster "Sally Tomato," a tough-guy part reminiscent of his very first role in radio.

In 1968, after eight seasons in prime time, the original run of *The Flintstones* came to an end. Throughout the 1970s, Reed kept the character and his income alive with a series of commercials for Flintstone's vitamins, Post's Fruity and Cocoa Pebbles cereals, as well as many other incarnations of the lovable caveman. Reed waxed philosophically to Shaden in 1975 about how much he appreciated his animated alter ego: "In the Screen Actors Guild, 80% of our membership earns less than $2,000 a year, and these are people who made good money at some time or another. Actors who would never take under a minimum of a week's contract are very happy to get a days work. Thank the Lord, *The Flintstones* has taken me out of that mess. I've been a very fortunate man."

Alan Reed died of cancer on June 14, 1977, at the St. Vincent's Medical Center in West Los Angeles, California, at the age of sixty-nine. After he passed away, actor Henry Corden was called in to take over as the voice of Fred Flintstone. Corden, a character actor in television and film, was already very familiar with the role as Corden was Reed's singing voice during the original run of the series. Jean Vander Pyl explained the reason for that: "Alan could sing . . . but he couldn't sing on pitch. That caused complications when they were trying to do harmony and anything long, so they got Henry Corden to do it." Although Corden may have been the better singer, Reed's widow, Finette, summed up the differences between her husband's Fred and Corden's Fred, "Henry has the voice, but Alan had the heart."

CREDITS

51st Annual Primetime Emmy Awards, The (1999) TV (archive) .... Himself
Flintstones, The (1960) TV Series .... Fred Flintstone
Flintstones: Wacky Inventions, The (1994) Video (archive footage) .... Fred Flintstone
Flintstones Comedy Hour, The (1972) TV Series .... Fred Flintstone
Fred Flintstone and Friends (1977) TV Series
Lady and the Tramp (1955) .... Boris
Man Called Flintstone, The (1966) .... Fred Flintstone
New Hanna-Barbera Cartoon Series, The (1962) TV Series .... Dum Dum
Shinbone Alley (1971) .... Big Bill
Space Ghost and Dino Boy (1966) TV Series .... Glasstor
"Weird Al" Yankovic: The Videos (1996) Video (archive recordings) .... Fred Flintstone
What's a Nice Kid like You Doing in a Place like This? (1966) TV .... Talking Caterpillar (Fred Flintstone)
Where's Huddles (1970) TV Series .... Mad Dog Maloney

CHRIS SARANDON

Although Chris Sarandon is a classically trained stage player who is best known for his on-camera work in such top-grossing films as *Dog Day Afternoon, The Princess Bride, Child's Play* and as the lead, vampire Jerry Dandrige in *Fright Night,* in 1993 the star of stage and screen made an auspicious debut into animation with one of the most charming performances ever to grace the art as the voice of Jack Skellington — the romantic lead of Tim Burton's 1993 classic *The Nightmare before Christmas.*

Like Jack's venture in Christmastown, Sarandon's first experience with animation was an amazing journey into another world he had no idea existed when he first toured the production area composed of the many stages and facilities which engulfed an entire San Francisco building. Marveling at the structure which housed everything from the sets to animators and production areas, what he found most insightful into the nature of animation was in the lobby of the building, where, in addition to various pieces of recreational equipment like ping-pong tables and pinball games, there was a punching bag for the use of frustrated animators. With the stop-motion figures being delicately moved at small increments every frame and the effects done in-camera, a blunder in the form of a kicked over light stand or false track of the computer-controlled camera meant that the grueling sequence would have to be shot all over again.

Sarandon, who claims an eclectic taste in animation which includes Tim Burton's earlier effort, *Frankenweenie*, came into the project being able to very strongly identify with the themes of alienation common to Burton's body of work because of his upbringing in the small West Virginia town of Berkley, with a population of about twenty thousand. Sarandon's family was "one of three" Greek families in the area. In the relatively small ethnic community, the son of immigrant parents said, "[I felt] very much like I was from Mars, because I was not a born and bred boy from West Virginia, but, at the same time, I wanted desperately to belong." His solution was to work hard to be popular, but it left him feeling "no more popular inside for the effort." His early turn in the limelight included performing in a high school rock band and acting in the senior class play, but his desire to be noticed ultimately won him a scholarship to West Virginia University as the result of a forensics contest.

Sarandon's theatrical interest began late—during his sophomore year in college. He started in drama primarily because he thought it would be amusing and not as demanding as an academic course and, consequently, would allow him to indulge his other interests which, he laughs, "were basically political at the time." When the drama teacher actually asked him to be in a play, Sarandon initially declined, citing his busy schedule. But, after being assured that it would take only two hours of his time a week, he reluctantly agreed to perform a very small part and, to his surprise, found that he enjoyed the experience immensely.

Of course, the next offer made to the talented beginner was for a larger part: this time, the lead in Moliere's *Tartuffe*. When Sarandon declined again, the response was adamant: "You have a gift and you'll never forgive yourself if you don't, at least, explore the possibility that there's a future in it." Finally finding his calling, Sarandon cleared his schedule, took the lead in the play and "just completely fell in love with the theater." Knowing nothing about the stage, he dropped all of his academic classes and completely immersed himself even to the extent of enrolling in graduate school for the performing arts "because [he] felt that [he] didn't really know enough." After learning stage managing and set design, Sarandon began his professional career traveling for a year with a touring company, which led to many more plays than films—along the way marrying one of his college classmates to become the first husband of future Oscar-winning actress Susan Sarandon.

Some two decades later, after a career on the stage and screen, Sarandon was set to make his mark in animation after winning the part of the dapper skeleton on an ill-fated mission to make Christmas, to the concern of his rag-doll girlfriend Sally (voiced by Catherine O'Hara, who also preformed "Shock") and his Halloween kingdom. Sarandon not only had to meet the challenges of creating a voice for a multi-dimensional character, but had to simply get used to creating a world on mike without the usual accouterments to which stage and screen actors are accustomed, such as costumes and other actors with whom to interact.

But, unlike many voice artists who only have a drawing of the character to use for reference, Sarandon was treated to a wealth of materials as Burton had been developing the concept since his unhappy time spent as a Disney animator in the early 1980s. The project, which began as a three-page poem inspired by Burton's favorite 1970s Rankin-Bass stop-motion classics—*How Grinch Stole Christmas* and *Rudolph the Red-Nosed Reindeer*—was given the green light by Disney (copyright owner of Burton's sketches) in 1990. Then collaborating with former Oingo Boingo front man and film composer Danny Elfman, the script took shape as Burton related the story to Elfman, who composed and performed the songs. By the time Sarandon was hired, the project was well underway and he was provided references in the form of storyboards, animators he could consult, Jack figures in progress, and even an entire animated sequence that had been completed to one of Elfman's songs. Sarandon recalls, "So I had a tremendous advantage in that respect, in that the visuals were basically already set up. . . . I had a preview of who I was in stop-action animation and I was blown away by it."

Sarandon claims not to know why he was cast as Jack's speaking voice since Elfman, who was already Jack's singing voice, reportedly had asked to do his speaking part as well. But, aside from Sarandon's considerable acting qualifications, his natural voice was a seamless match for Elfman's, and he approached the part judging that one of his primary challenges was going to be that he was developing a character which, as a totally imaginary entity, could have no real-life back story. Therefore, his approach was in concert with that of the director—to, in a "collaborative kind of way, come up with an idea of the way that the character behaves . . . and essentially, the character that we came up with was one of great sort of enthusiasm and bravado, but at the same time, with a real sort of naiveté overlaying all that."

Sarandon believes that the "tremendous sort of feeling of ennui and a certain kind of unrest of the soul" that is the starting point for Jack's story is universal. And deciding to not only leave his own [home,] where he is king, which requires a tremendous amount of nerve, but going to another world and saying, 'I can change; I can be someone else,' is tremendously naïve in a lot of ways because we all are ultimately a product of who we were. And, at the same time, there is a tremendous potential in each of us for change; which is why I think the character is so appealing."

To complicate matters, the production process for Sarandon was necessarily sporadic and consisted of being flown to San Francisco each month or two to record a scene at a time with director Henry Selick. "I would do the whole scene—any number of variations on the scene, any number of variations on each line—then I would go home and they would animate that sequence." From the spring of 1992 through and into the summer of 1993, the film was steadily being realized by the hundreds of dedicated artists.

After the satisfactory completion of most of the photography, Sarandon was then called back to meet with Burton to redo a couple of sequences: "Because, as you can imagine, doing everything not only out of sequence, but out of context, that once everything is laid in and animated, that the arc of the character changes to a certain extent. [Then] it became clearer to Tim and to Henry that some changes needed to be made. And I went back into the studio with Tim and we made some decisions based on what we both could see." Sarandon felt free to suggest some of his ideas based on what he saw of the completed sequences, adding that he was thrilled that "both Tim and Henry felt [his suggestions] improved the performance tremendously."

In 1993, not too long before the film was released to financial and critical success, Sarandon was given a preview of the nearly completed version on cassette and although it "wasn't in its final glory"—with a couple of storyboards standing in for small sequences, and the color yet to be corrected—he stated, "My mind was blown." Despite Sarandon's warnings when he screened it for his family that it "might not make total sense," he must have known he had a hit when he noticed that his children watched "with their mouths completely dropped down to their knees and followed every minute of it."

According to Sarandon—who says he now would welcome more animated parts in the future—he found the challenge of voice-overs to be agreeably unlike live action. "Whereas one inhabits, both physically and psychologically, the character when you're actually playing it on the screen or on the stage, when you're doing a voice, you get into a totally different mindset because it's just you and a microphone. And I found it quite a lot of fun and quite challenging in a different way. It requires you, in many ways, to create your own world. . . . And basically, you are out there without a net. I've found it very difficult, but extraordinarily challenging; I thought it was a tremendous way to work."

Hopefully, Sarandon will find subsequent projects in animation that will be worthy successors to his impressive debut.

BILL SCOTT

He may be forever associated first and foremost as the man who provided the nasal baritone for the obtuse moose "Bullwinkle," but Scott was not just a top-of-the-line voice talent who supplied the vocal life to a diverse group of characters, including Mr. Peabody, Dudley Do-Right, George of the Jungle, Super Chicken, and Tom Slick. The former animator and story man has justifiably been described as the "soul" of Jay Ward productions, not only voicing Ward's characters but eventually assuming the mantle as head writer and co-producer for his partner and close friend.

Born William John Scott on August 2, 1920, in Philadelphia and raised in Trenton, New Jersey, Scott found his career calling at the early age of four. In the 2000 book *The Moose That Roared*, characterizing himself as an "animation nut from the word go," Scott says he was dazzled by the silent *Felix the Cat* cartoons which ran on early television. The obsession followed him even through his young adulthood. Stricken with tuberculosis at fifteen, Scott relocated with his family to Denver, Colorado, for the change of climate, where the recovered teenager then spent years immersed in as much of the entertainment industry as Denver had to offer.

By the time he graduated with a B.A. in theater and minor in English, Scott had built a formidable resume as a freelance radio performer, working for local stations KOA, KLZ, and KVOD. At eighteen, he joined the Denver Children's Theatre, where he met his future wife, Dorothy Williams. Yet he continued to toy with the idea of animation and was "one of the thousands who responded to the Walt Disney nationwide talent search by drawing Goofy and Pluto." He also found a kindred soul in the form of friend Bill Turnbull, and the duo polished their fledgling animation skills by animating—although they created some title work for local Denver cinemas, it was mostly for the entertainment value.

While Scott longed to be a commercial artist, he doubted he had the ability, and it took a profound and most unlikely chain of circumstances to bring him to his intended vocation. However, after a false start to his professional career in the form of one "traumatic" semester in 1941 teaching English and drama at a local high school, by the next year Scott was drafted for World War II and—with his prior photographic experience—was assigned to be a photographic lab technician at the Peterson Field Air Force Base in Colorado Springs. Then transferred to California, he arrived at the commandeered Hal Roach studios to find that his new crew—the First Motion Picture Unit, which was responsible for making instructional films for the enlisted men—had already shipped out.

Far from being a setback, this freed Scott to delve into the other activities going on at the studio. The wide-eyed young man from Denver first reported for duty—shocked to find that the personnel officer he was addressing was film star Ronald Reagan. And exploring the building, he was even more shocked to find that it contained an animation unit which encompassed employees of Disney, Fleischer, and MGM. There, Scott met Warner Bros. and MGM cartoon veteran Rudy Ising, who was the acting commanding officer of the unit. Ising was able to transfer Scott to the unit, and his new protégé, "who thought he had died and gone to heaven," began his career in animation as, of all unlikely job descriptions, a cel washer for the air force. Scott then spent World War II performing a range of creative jobs; promoted to the position of painter, then inker and "in-betweener" while doing storyboards and layouts, he desperately struggled to improve his drawing skills until ending his military tenure as an assistant animator.

At the end of the war, in 1945, although he had studied under venerable animators such as one of Disney's famous "nine old men" Frank Thomas, Scott had some trouble getting established in Hollywood. Staying in the army reserve for the next ten years, Scott had approached his former CO Rudy Ising but had no leads until an army buddy from his unit recommended him as new talent for Warner Bros.

The 1940s were a hectic time for Scott. He spent 1946 to 1947 at Warners, where he felt privileged to work as a story man with many of his early heroes like Mike Maltese, Tedd Pierce, and Warren Foster. He left the better for the experience, judging that he had become a sharper writer with a more developed sense of animation timing. In 1947, he moved to Paramount to write for the talking animal shorts, the Oscar-winning *Speaking of Animals*, and it was there that he first met future *Rocky and Bullwinkle* collaborator June Foray, who supplied some of the voices.

After spending 1948 acting on Broadway, Scott was offered a position writing for Bob Clampett's national television series, *Time for Beany*. Although the writer enjoyed the creative leeway the crew was given, when it became a success, there was some animosity among the production staff because actors Stan Freberg and Daws Butler were reportedly making twice the writing staff salaries. Scott—who drew the metaphorical short straw to ask for a raise from Clampett—did so and was unceremoniously fired, to the shock of the rest of the crew.

UPA (United Productions of America) was the next stop for Scott in 1950, after being recommended by old army co-horts Phil Monroe and Bill Hurtz. Teamed with another writer, they worked on (Jim Backus's vocal tour de force) *Mr. Magoo* theatrical features and various shorts. Scott was reportedly doing well until the studio suffered some political unrest due to various factors, including the House Un-American Activities Committee; and the political shake-up that ensued left Scott in the unemployment line, which subsequently led to an unsatisfying four years laboring on corporate industrial films.

But Scott fared better when he left the well-paying, but "ulcerating" experience for an assistant producer spot on CBS's *Gerald McBoing-Boing* series, starring Marvin Miller in the title role, which was UPA's first venture in television. Finding the experience disagreeable because of creative differences with executives who, in his view, remained unconcerned with injecting enough humor in the show, Scott left to freelance for various studios during the 1950s. Finally, Scott was contacted to help pen Hanna-Barbera's first television series effort—*Ruff and Reddy*—and it was there in 1957 that he was introduced to future partner Jay Ward.

Rocky and Bullwinkle were already looming on the horizon when Ward had a falling out with Hanna-Barbera's animator Shamus Culhane over production methods; this left Ward swearing that he would only work for himself. But, enthused over the prospect of working on an animated series, Ward retrieved an old concept, *The Frostbite Falls Review,* which he had been unable to sell. Although Ward brought Scott on board as a writer for the nascent program, Ward was delighted to discover, in creating the storyboards, that Scott had an amazing vocal ability as well, and Ward asked him to be the voice of Bullwinkle (whose off-beat name Ward purloined from a Berkley car dealership) and later the creator and voice of bespectacled canine Mr. Peabody to Walter Tetley's "boy" Sherman.

After the pilot was sold, the voice-acting team was fleshed out with the addition of June Foray as Rocky and Natasha, Paul Frees as Boris Badenov and (the Frees recommended) William Conrad as the breathless narrator. While Scott and Ward channeled the talents of the award-winning staff that had collectively amassed nine Oscars and honors at the Cannes, Venice, and Edinburgh film festivals, Scott also proved himself to be a quick study of professional cartoon voices and took pride in stealing bit parts from professional veteran Frees. Although it has been noted that Scott may have lacked the "rich vocal timbre" of trained actor Conrad and the gifted Frees, he was well-respected by the ensemble, who were impressed by his writing ability, if not his vocal skills.

The world was introduced to Scott's love of puns, wordplay, subversive satire, and the phrase, "Hey Rocky, watch me pull a rabbit out of my hat!" when *Rocky and Friends* premiered in 1959 on NBC. Television's first animated anti-heroes had fast-paced high-brow verbal humor and leftiest political satire which helped earn the show a sizable adult following and did well enough in the Saturday morning time slot to earn a spot on the Sunday night prime-time schedule. While the animation was most kindly described by the *New York Village Voice* as "triumphantly crude," Ward attributed their success to the importance of good storytelling: "Cartoons have a basic appeal, but an audience will tire if presented only action without thought."

The program, which ended production in 1964, has proved to be a classic. In syndication almost every year since then and just released in DVD in 2003, it still has an unparalleled biting sense of satire that remains timely. Scott passed away on November 29, 1985—having worked only for Disney doing voices for *The Wuzzles* and *The Gummi Bears* after Jay Ward studios closed down in mid-1984. Perhaps Daws Butler had the last word on his impressive talent and versatility. In *Daws Butler, Voice Magician*, a PBS documentary taped in 1987, the actor (who worked on *Rocky* uncredited, as his mainstay Hanna-Barbera's main sponsor rivaled Ward's sponsor) lauded Scott as one of the most talented voice artists in town: "His dialects, his characters, the top of his voice, the bottom of his voice, and such inventive ideas. He had a sense of humor all his own."

CREDITS

Fifty-First Annual Primetime Emmy Awards, The (1999) TV (uncredited) (voice)
Adventures of Hoppity Hopper from Foggy Bogg (1962) TV Series (voice) . . . . Fillmore the Bear/
　Bullwinkle Moose
Beany and Cecil (1959) TV Series (writer)
Bone Sweet Bone (1948) (story)
Bowery Bugs (1949) (story)
Bullwinkle Show, The (1961) TV Series (voice) . . . . Bullwinkle J. Moose/Dudley Do-Right/
　Mr. Hector Peabody/Fearless Leader
Crazy World of Laurel and Hardy, The (1967)
Dog Snatcher, The (1952)
Doggone Cats (1947)
Duck Factory, The (1984) . . . . playing Annie Awards Host in "The Annies" (episode # 1.3), March
　22, 1984
Dudley Do-Right Show, The (1969) TV Series (voice and co-creator) . . . . Dudley Do-Right
Flat Hatting (1944) (story)
Fractured Fairy Tales: The Phox, the Box, and the Lox (1999)
Fractured Flickers (1963) TV Series (voice and writer)
George of the Jungle (1967) TV Series (voice and producer) . . . . George/Super Chicken/Tom
　Slick/Gertie Growler
George of the Jungle II (2003) TV Series
Gerald McBoing-Boing (1950) (story adaptation)
Giddyap (1950) (story)
Gummi Bears, The (1985) TV Series (voice) . . . . Toadwort/SirTuxford/Gruffi

Hick a Slick and a Chick, A (1948) (story)

Hoppity Hooper aka *The Adventures of Hoppity Hooper* (1964) TV Series (voice and writer) . . . .
Fillmore/Bullwinkle

Mister Magoo (1964) TV Series (voice)

Porky Chops (1949) (story)

Riff Raffy Daffy (1948) (story)

Rocky and His Friends (1959) TV Series . . . . Bullwinkle J. Moose/Gidney Moonman/Fairy/Various
Voices

Rooty Toot Toot (1951) (story)

Sloppy Jalopy (1952) (story)

Stupor Salesman, The (1948) (story)

Tell-Tale Heart, The (1953)

Time for Beany (1949) TV Series (story)

Two Gophers from Texas (1948)

Uncle Waldo's Cartoon Show (1966) TV Series (producer/writer)

What Makes Daffy Duck (1948) (story)

Wuzzles, The (1985) TV Series (voice) . . . . Moosel/Brat/Tycoon

KATH SOUCIE

For Kath Soucie there was never any childhood angst over "What am I going to do? What am I going to be?" She loved Lucy! "When you're little, in school, we all had to make career notebooks every year about what we wanted to do, and I wanted to be Lucy when I grew up." Commenting that

the comedienne was a "bit of a cartoon" herself, Soucie may have incorporated some of that sensibility in her cartoon characters, but her image is that
of a polished professional—well-spoken and collected, except for a boister-
ous laugh that occasionally breaks her composure. It should also not be surprising that, with her long blond hair, slender frame, and porcelain skin, her
background was as a stage and on-camera actress—where appearance is
inherently important.

Perhaps the industry's superficialities were a part of the reason the
Cleveland native was discouraged by others from going into the profession,
but she says there was only one major set-back to her self-confidence. "I auditioned for my first high school play. And it was *Brigadoon* with a cast of thousands and I didn't make it. And all my life I'd been told, 'You know, it's very
competitive. You can't really this—you can't really that.' And I hadn't bought
it, and I hadn't bought it, and I hadn't bought it! And, at that moment, when I
knew I didn't get it, it all came rushing at me! And I went, 'You're right! If I
can't even get a part in the high school play, I won't be able to be a professional
actress!'" So, while taking a full academic load in high school, Soucie also
studied the culinary arts, intending to become a chef. But, after graduating
from both schools, she found the courage to "risk one more humiliation" and
get her career back on track.

By the mid-1970s, she had made it to New York City and was enrolled at the
American Academy of Dramatic Arts with lofty ambitions of doing "magnifi-
cent beautiful plays that would change people's lives." Quipping that she made
"about a dollar fifty" doing that, she had to make ends meet with odd jobs—
the worst of which was unwittingly selling "hot" jewelry for a couple of days.
Embarrassed by her Midwestern naiveté at the time, she confesses, "I didn't
realize it until someone told me that it was stolen goods that I was selling."

Apparently, Broadway was not for her for technical reasons as well.
Realizing early in her career that she did not have the vocal projection needed
for stage acting—in the 1970s, theaters did not have the extensive microphone
systems that they do presently—she pursued commercial and television work
while shuttling back and forth between both coasts; that is, until a friend
and mentor of hers invited her to come along to a recording session for an
animated TV commercial he was directing.

Watching the voice-over artist perform, she had a moment of clarity in
which she realized, "I can do that!" It remained "in the back of her mind"
until the day she left on-camera for what she says is forever. "It was just right
before Christmas, I was up for three parts, and one was a soap opera, one was
a feature, and one was . . . an episodic. . . . And I left home for Christmas, and

I was just waiting to hear which one it was. . . . I lost all three of them. I lost the soap because I looked too much like the girl who was supposed to be my roommate and not enough like the boy who was supposed to be my brother. I lost the episodic because they decided to go with a brunette instead of a blond. And the other one had to do with age—I think I was either too old or too young. All three of the reasons had to do with *this* [slaps her wrist] . . . with body. *This* business has to do with ability and skill alone. And I can eat potato chips and have my eyes get all swollen and puffy the next day and it doesn't matter!"

According to Soucie, that ability and skill took some time to acquire. She winces at the memory of her first cartoon voice-over session. After cold-calling several directors, she had struck up a rapport with director Michael Hack, who, "out of the goodness his heart," hired her to do three different one-liners on the 1986 animated version of *Rambo*. "And I was so scared and each one was a different accent and they weren't accents that I could do. I was just awful. I was so terrible and if my career had sprung from that one episode. . . . Lord only knows how it happened."

Happen, it did. Since then, she has worked nearly non-stop for virtually all of the major cartoon production studios. Getting her first series was "a real confidence-builder" and "coup" as she beat out several actors for the last four episodes of *My Little Pony*. That is, she cracks, "Before the big barn fire and all ponies died!" then laughs uproariously. Although, she has occasionally had parts which made her briefly question her career choice—like a "Mutant Poodle" from *2 Stupid Dogs*, where she did nothing but "hysterically yip" throughout the episode—she said she is always "so thrilled and proud" when she is hired for a new series.

Of the regular productions she has been on, she has high praise for programs such as *Hey Arnold!* citing the outstanding quality of its scripts. But her favorite seems to be the long-running *Rugrats;* she calls the show "a true work from the heart of everyone," from the cast to crew and writers. "Probably one of my favorite shows that I ever did was one episode of *Rugrats* with David Doyle, and I played his old girlfriend who shows up after—was it forty or fifty years they hadn't seen each other? And they're in their sixties, and it was [a] sweet, touching, moving, very real episode. He is a brilliant actor, and I just left that day feeling like I really had made something. . . . It was just so soul-satisfying to me. That's the kind of stuff I live for."

While she has joked about the necessity of having a college education when a day's work could be nothing more than incidental characters, her dramatic training has proved very helpful. Characterizing animation as "the last bastion of character acting," in which one can play anything the voice box will allow, Soucie says there has also been an unprecedented rise in dramatic series, like *Gargoyles* (1994), which demand a more realistic tone in the voice acting. "They want someone whose voice works for the character, and they want real internal work, and they want it very potent, very directed and real, and I love that."

Although Soucie usually does not do special preparations in advance for a role, the exceptions are shows like *The Critic*, for which she was regularly called to do impressions of celebrity voices. As she is not an impressionist, that type of assignment is a formidable task. "I rent videos . . . and I listen to them over and over again, and I tape my own voice, and I listen to it. It's really very challenging for me because it doesn't come naturally to me." However, most of her characters are not modeled on specific people, but rather are drawn from her experience. "So much of you is an amalgamation of all the people you have ever met, and a lot of your ideas come from places you don't even know where they came from. . . . But once in a while I'll put a little wrinkle in or something of someone that I know, or even maybe someone from an old movie or a character that I saw on one episode of *Cheers* or something like that, and I remember one particular mannerism. I'll weave it in."

Although she enjoys the parts she has played, she admits the ultimate role for her would be a "big splashy Disney heroine in the big wonderful musicals and stuff, but," she laughs, "I sing like a toad!" But even for the parts where a character may actually be as "cartoony" as a singing toad, she says, "What you do is take everything and make it bigger, but it still comes from a core of reality."

Soucie notes that as animation has gone from being considered a children's or niche interest to mainstream adult entertainment, it has now matured into a "highly effective art form." One positive direction that she has noticed as the medium has developed is that the gender gap has narrowed somewhat from when she started in the business. Perhaps it is not surprising that Soucie claims that in the past she was often the only woman on a show. The practice of excluding female characters stems from the Screen Actors Guild rules prior to 1967, which specified that in a voice-recording session for a cartoon under ten minutes, one actor could be asked to do as many voices as the producer specified for a flat rate. As such, it was cost effective to hire a single actor to do all the voices. Accordingly, it was cheaper to then designate all characters as male to reduce production costs, aside from any other possible cultural prejudices.

But revisions in union contracts and cultural changes meant that the inclusion of women happened gradually. Soucie comments, "When I first started doing this, most of the lady characters that were written . . . what they had to say was condensed into one word and that was, basically, 'Help!' Especially during recent years, the routine practice of characterizing women as the damsels in distress has diminished and there are now many more dynamic roles written for girls and women. "They are writing strong, intelligent, aggressive female roles, and they're the ones that are now being the source of help rather than begging and pleading and whining."

She was also surprised and gratified at the new level of respect she gained by just being part of the process. "I know that when I used to go to parties before, when I was being an actress, and people would ask what I did for living, I would tell them I was an actress. They'd get really sort of patronizing, you know: 'Oh, a budding actress.' And, you know, you'd feel all squirmy and just dreadful. And now when I tell them that I do—because this is all I do—I only do voice-overs, they are *so* interested. They just want to know everything about it. They find it utterly fascinating."

As does Soucie, who, even after more than a decade of voice-over work, still enjoys the variety and unpredictability of her busy schedule. With her phone ringing off the hook—despite the intense competitiveness of her field—her then agent, Cory Weisman, explains that she stands out as "one person who takes every script seriously and really makes it her own." Aside from the material rewards—which include a beautiful house on the Pacific Ocean, from which she often kayaks and can be found whale watching—as Soucie concludes in her own article for *Animation World Magazine*, she also succeeded in her childhood ambition, "to do something absolutely unique, be around fascinating and dashing people all day long, and never be bored." In her words, "Mission accomplished."

CREDITS

101 Dalmatians: The Series (1996) TV Series . . . . Rolly/Cadpig/Anita Darling
101 Dalmatians II: Patch's London Adventure (2003) Video . . . . Perdita
2 Stupid Dogs (1993) TV Series . . . . Mutant Poodle/Additional Voices
51st Annual Primetime Emmy Awards, The (1999) TV (uncredited) . . . . Herself
Adventures from the Book of Virtues (1996) TV Series . . . . Annie
Adventures of Raggedy Ann and Andy, The (1988) TV Series . . . . Raggedy Cat
Aladdin (1993/I) TV Series . . . . Additional Voices
All Growed Up (2003) TV Series . . . . Phil/Lil
Animaniacs (1993) TV Series . . . . Additional Voices

Animatrix, The (2003) Video . . . . Pudgy/Masa/Sara
Annabelle's Wish (1997) . . . . Young Annabelle
As Told by Ginger (2000) TV Series . . . . Blake Gripling
Attack of the Killer Tomatoes (1990) TV Series . . . . Tara
Baby Blues (2000) TV Series . . . . Rodney Bitterman/Megan Bitterman/Various Characters
Beauty and the Beast (1991) . . . . Bimbette
Beauty and the Beast: The Enchanted Christmas (1997) . . . . Enchantress
Beethoven (1994) TV Series . . . . Emily Newton
Beyond (2003) TV Series . . . . Pudgy
Big Sister, The (1995) . . . . Mom
Biker Mice from Mars (1993) TV Series . . . . Harley
Book of Pooh, The (2001) TV Series . . . . Kanga
Brave Little Toaster Goes to Mars, The (1998) . . . . Tieselica
Bruno the Kid (1996) TV Series . . . . Grace (Bruno's Mom)
Bruno the Kid: The Animated Movie (1996) . . . . Grace
Butt-Ugly Martians (2001) TV Series . . . . Angela
Buzz Lightyear of Star Command (2000) TV Series . . . . Additional Voices
Camp Candy (1989) TV Series . . . . Additional Voices
Captain Planet and the Planeteers (1990) TV Series . . . . Linka
Casper (1996) TV Series . . . . Kat
Christmas Carol, A (1997) . . . . Mrs. Cratchit
Clerks (2000) TV Series
Clifford the Big Red Dog (2000) TV Series . . . . Jetta
Clifford's Puppy Days (2003) TV Series . . . . Caroline Howard
Cramp Twins, The (2001) TV Series . . . . Lucien Cramp
Critic, The (1994) TV Series . . . . Various Voices
Danny Phantom (2003) TV Series . . . . Maddie Fenton
Darkling, The (2000) TV . . . . Additional Voices
Darkwing Duck (1991) TV Series . . . . Morgana MacCawber/Aunt Nasty/Additional Voices
Denver, the Last Dinosaur (1992) TV Series . . . . Casey/Heather
Detroit Docona (2004) TV Series . . . . Suzy Anders
Dexter's Laboratory (1996) TV Series . . . . Dexter's Mom/Agent Honeydew/LeeLee/Dexter's
  Computer
Disney Sing-along-Songs: The Lion King Circle of Life (1994) (archive footage) . . . . Bimbette
Don Coyote and Sancho Panda (1990) TV Series . . . . Additional Voices
Droopy, Master Detective (1993) TV Series . . . . Additional Voices
Duckdaze
Ducktales (1987) TV Series . . . . Additional Voices
Dumb and Dumber (1995) TV Series . . . . Waitress
Earthworm Jim (1995) TV Series . . . . Princess What's-Her-Name
Extremely Goofy Movie, An (2000) (uncredited) . . . . Co-Ed
Fly Girls (1999) . . . . Cornelia Fort
Gargoyles (1994) TV Series . . . . Princess Katherine/Weird Sisters/Maggie "the Cat" Reed/Orphelia/
  Cornelia Stallman/Additional Voices
Gargoyles: The Goliath Chronicles (1996) TV Series . . . . Additional Voices
Gargoyles: The Heroes Awaken (1994) . . . . Princess Katherine
Gen 13 (1998) . . . . Additional Voices
God, the Devil, and Bob (2000) TV Series . . . . Andy Allman
Goof Troop (1992) TV Series . . . . Additional Voices
Gramps (1992) TV . . . . Alien Kid #1
Gummi Bears (1985) TV Series . . . . Additional Voices

Hercules (1998) TV Series .... Additional Voices
Hey Arnold! (1996) TV Series .... Miriam Pataki/Marilyn Berman/Additional Voices
Hey Arnold! The Movie (2002) .... Miriam/Mona/Reporter
Hollyrock-a-Bye Baby (1993) TV .... Pebbles Flintstone-Rubble
House of Mouse (2001) TV Series .... Perdita/Kanga/Bimbettes/Additional Voices
Indescribable Nth, The (1999) .... Otis
Invasion America (1998) TV Series .... Rita Carter/Sonia
It's A Wonderful Tiny Toons Christmas Special (1992) TV .... Little Sneezer
James Bond, Jr. (1991) TV Series .... Additional Voices
Jem! (1985) TV Series .... Minx/Ingrid Krueger
Johnny Bravo (1997) TV Series .... Aunt Katie/Additional Voices
Jungle Cubs (1996) TV Series .... Winifred
Karate Kid, The (1989) TV Series .... Additional Voices
Kim Possible: A Stitch in Time (2003) TV. ... Various Voices
Lady and the Tramp II: Scamp's Adventure (2001) .... Collette/Danielle
Life & Adventures of Santa Claus, The (2000) .... Natalie Bessie Blithesome, Princess of Lerd/
   Little Mayrie
Lilo & Stitch (2002) .... Additional Voices
Little Dracula (1991) TV Series .... Mrs. Dracula/Millicent
Magician, The (1998) TV Series .... Additional Voices
Majo no takkyubin (1989) .... Kiki's Mother
Marvel Action Universe (1988) TV Series .... Additional Voices
Mickey Mouse Works (1999) TV Series .... Additional Voices
Mickey's Magical Christmas: Snowed in at the House of Mouse (2001) .... Kanga
Mighty Max (1991) TV Series .... Bea
Mike, Lu, and Og (1999) TV Series .... Margery
My Freaky Family (2001) TV .... Nadine
My Little Pony (1986) TV Series .... Additional Voices
Nick and Noel (1993) TV .... Noel
Olive, the Other Reindeer (1999) TV
Online Adventures of Ozzie the Elf, The (1997) TV .... Clover
Pepper Ann (1997) TV Series .... Cissy Rooney/Nicky's Mom
Phantom 2040 (1994) TV Series .... Additional Voices
Piglet's Big Movie (2003) .... Kanga
Pink Panther, The (1993) TV Series .... Additional Voices
Pocahontas II: Journey to a New World (1998) .... Additional Voices
Powerpuff Girls, The (1998) TV Series .... Additional Voices
Pryde of the X-Men (1989) TV .... Kitty Pryde
Pup Named Scooby-Doo, A (1988) TV Series .... Additional Voices (1988–1991)
Quack Pack (1996) TV Series .... Daisy Duck
Raw Toonage (1992) TV Series .... Additional Voices
Real Ghostbusters, The (1986) TV Series .... Janine Melnitz (II) (1987–1991)
Recess (1997) TV Series .... Butch
Recess: School's Out (2001) .... Counselor
Return to Never Land (2002) .... Wendy
Rugrats (1991) TV Series .... Phillip "Phil" Deville/Lillian "Lil" DeVille/Elizabeth "Betty" DeVille
Rugrats: All Growed Up, The (2001) TV .... Phil DeVille/Lil DeVille/Betty DeVille
Rugrats: Still Babies after All These Years (2001) TV .... Herself/Phil Deville/Lil Deville
Rugrats in Paris: The Movie—Rugrats II (2000) .... Phil DeVille/Lil DeVille/Betty DeVille
Rugrats Go Wild! (2003) .... Phil DeVille/Lil DeVille/Betty DeVille
Rugrats Meet the Wild Thornberrys (2003) .... Phil DeVille/Lil DeVille/Betty DeVille

Rugrats Movie, The (1998) . . . . Phil DeVille/Lil DeVille/Betty DeVille
Rugrats Vacation, A (1997) . . . . Phil DeVille/Lil DeVille/Betty DeVille
Santa Clause 2, The (2002) . . . . Chet
Savage Dragon, The (1996) TV Series . . . . Alex Wild
Scooby-Doo in Arabian Nights (1994) TV
Secret Files of the Spy Dogs, The (1998) TV Series . . . . Collar Communicator Voice
Siegfried and Roy: Masters of the Impossible (1996) . . . . Additional Voices
Slimer! And the Real Ghostbusters (1988) TV Series . . . . Janine Melnitz
Smurfs, The (1981) TV Series . . . . Additional Voices
Sonic the Hedgehog (1993) TV Series . . . . Princess Sally Acorn/Nicole (Sally's Computer)
Space Jam (1996) . . . . Lola Bunny
Spawn (1997/II) TV Series . . . . Cyan/Additional Voices
Speed Buggy (1973) TV Series . . . . Additional Voices
SpongeBob SquarePants Movie (2004) . . . . Kid Fish #1/Kid Fish #2/Fish Cop Woman
Super Dave (1987) TV Series . . . . Additional Voices
Superhuman Samurai Syber-Squad (1994) TV Series . . . . Elizabeth Collins (Sam's Sister)
Swat Kats: The Radical Squadron (1993) TV Series . . . . Turmoil
Tale Spin (1990) TV Series . . . . Additional Voices
Tales of Tillie's Dragon, The (1998)
Tigger Movie, The (2000) . . . . Kanga
Tiny Toon Adventures (1990) TV Series . . . . Fifi La Fume/Little Sneezer
Tiny Toon Adventures: How I Spent My Vacation (1992) . . . . Fifi La Fume/Little Boo/Sneezer
Tiny Toon Adventures: Night Ghoulery (1995) TV . . . . Fifi La Fume
Toonsylvania (1998) TV Series
Toxic Crusaders, The (1991) TV Series . . . . Additional Voices
Trumpet of the Swan, The (2001) . . . . Paramedic/Newscaster/Serena
Ugly Duck-Thing (2002) TV . . . . Dot/Woman/Librarian/Baby Duck
Wacky Adventures of Ronald McDonald: Scared Silly, The (1998) . . . . Fry Kid #1
Weekenders, The (2000) TV Series . . . . Tish Katsufrakus
Whatever Happened to Robot Jones? (2002) TV Series . . . . Mom Unit
What's with Andy? (2001) TV Series . . . . Additional Voices (2001–2002)
Where on Earth Is Carmen Sandiego? (1994) TV Series . . . . Additional Voices
Widget, the World Watcher (1990) TV Series . . . . Brian/Christine
Wild West COWBOYs of Moo Mesa (1992) TV Series . . . . Additional Voices
Yo, Yogi! (1991) TV Series . . . . Additional Voices

JEAN VANDER PYL

Jean Vander Pyl's work on *The Flintstones* was an extreme case of life imitating art. Already playing the part of Wilma, when it came to casting for the first cartoon baby ever born in an animated series, Vander Pyl immediately volunteered. As she was quoted on the Cartoon Network website in 1995, "I'm not usually that bold, but I wanted to do Pebbles. I wanted just the right voice for that cute face."

Vander Pyl, who claimed she always shared a "kinship" with her sensible yet sardonic cartoon persona, was also pregnant during the recording, although she shared the good news only with good friend and cast mate Bea Benaderet (Betty Rubble). The crew learned when, she said, "One day I wore a dress that made me show more in the tummy, and Joe Barbera looked at me and said, 'Jean, that dress on you, it makes you look pregnant.' I looked at Bea and she looked at me and I said, 'Well, I am. . . .' Their faces all dropped, after which there were congratulations, hugs, and some razzing. Joe said, 'Well, you didn't have to go that far, Jean. I know you want realism, but this is ridiculous!'" At the actual taping, Vander Pyl remembers it as a special show for her and Alan Reed (Fred): "I had a lump in my throat and I looked at Alan and we both welled up with tears." As if it were scripted, of course, her son Roger would have to be born on the same day that millions watched Pebbles's birth. Of course, Pebbles's real-life mother "didn't see that until later reruns!"

Vander Pyl made her own debut on October 11, 1919, in Philadelphia, but her father's sales job meant the family never really had a fixed address. One of her earliest childhood memories is of the Midwest winters she spent in the northern Chicago suburb of Evanston, on Sheridan Road near the Lake Michigan shoreline. "I remember it well because I got the worst paddling I ever had—and I didn't get many—when my mother looked out the window and saw me with my friends sliding on a wave that had frozen over on the lake."

Realizing that she was meant to be an actress from her first performance in a kindergarten play, she was fortunate that her family finally settled in Long Beach, California. There in 1934 the teenager studied drama privately and, while at Beverly Hills High school, landed her first professional radio show in the form of a series called *Calling All Cars*—which netted her a grand total of $7.50 per day. While continuing her radio work, she went on to college at UCLA until deciding to pursue a career in radio full time.

After marrying advertising executive Carroll O'Meara, she steadily built a career in such radio shows. Her numerous comedies included *Fanny Brice, Eddie Cantor, Our Miss Brooks, Blondie, Corliss Archer,* and *Amos and Andy,* for which she spent three years portraying all of Andy's girlfriends. In drama, her best-known role was as the mother, Margaret Anderson, in *Father Knows Best,* but she also appeared on *Lux Radio Time, Playhouse 90,* and *The Cisco Kid,* among many others.

When the new studio Hanna-Barbera put a call out for a female voice, Vander Pyl had more than enough experience developing and communicating characters only using her voice to become an animation voice actor. In 1959, she was offered the role that was her greatest claim to fame—Wilma Flintstone—although in those days Hanna-Barbera had an extremely informal auditioning process. "Joe would call us up. . . . He'd say, 'Jean, I got a couple of characters coming up in this show. What have you got for a voice for such and such?'"

Obviously, Vander Pyl's quick thinking made her the choice for the cartoon pastiche of *The Honeymooners* (of which both Hanna and Barbera were big fans), and the show was off to an auspicious beginning. Concerning the program which premiered as *The Flagstones* (recristened after it was judged too close to the Flagstons, the family in the *Hi and Lois* comic strip), Vander Pyl told David Martindale in an interview for *Ultimate TV* of her interpretation of the part of Wilma, "What I was doing was trying to do an Audrey Meadows. Not an impersonation, but something inspired by that type of character. They were New Yorkish. They had that New York sound. And so I put it up in the nasal thing. 'Ra-alph,' she'd say. So I'd go, 'Fre-ed.'"

Almost instantly, the cast of veteran actors became close friends; Vander Pyl reminisced that it was "a sweet and wonderful time." In a radio interview done at the time of the show's production, she explained that the recording was "just as though it were the old radio days" and the ensemble cast had as much fun making the series as the audience did watching it. "It was such a small group of radio people. They all knew everybody. . . . We certainly all knew each other because when they'd have auditions, which they did for every show, you'd end up with the same people in the hall waiting to audition every time. And then we worked together."

Vander Pyl also credits the writing staff for the show's early success. "We did such human comedy. One of my favorite lines was in the very first show: the paperboy throws the [stone] paper at Fred and it spins him around and knocks him down and he gets back up and says, 'Oh, I hate the Sunday paper.' I broke up in recording. They had to start over again because I just fractured. I don't know why it struck me as so funny, except, every time that I go out to pick up the Sunday paper, I think of it because the damn thing is so heavy. And as long as they have newspapers, that line is going to get a laugh."

When pressed for a favorite episode, she had an unexpected choice. She was particularly fond of a Halloween special in which the Flintstones won a trip to Transylvania: "We all had such wild parts!" In the story, Dracula rises from a five-hundred-year sleep, thinks Wilma is a dead ringer for his wife, and the rest of the plot consists of Dracula trying to get rid of Fred. They manage to run away with Dracula on their heels all the way to Bedrock.

Vander Pyl recalls that, on the very last page of the script, Wilma finally agrees to marry him providing he can adjust to suburban life. Wilma outlines his new domestic responsibilities in a rant that lasts for five minutes at top speed. "I said, 'You'll have to pick up the kids' and yadda yadda yadda . . . and Dracula grabs his head [in consternation] and flies back to Transylvania. I've never read anything so fast in my life. I loved the triumph! When I finished, the cast applauded."

As with their closest successors of prime-time prosperity, the cast of *The Simpsons*, the cast of *The Flintstones* was also thrilled to watch the parade of celebrities who recorded their own voices for their animated guest-starring roles—including the appropriately recristened Ann-"Margrock" and "Stoney" Curtis. Vander Pyl stated, "We didn't record with Tony Curtis, and that was the biggest disappointment. All the girls were disappointed because Tony Curtis was in his heyday and I said, 'Oh, shoot. Here I am making love to Tony Curtis, and he didn't show up to the studio.' Ann-Margaret did come and Hoagy Carmichael did come and do it with us, and that was fun."

A veteran of Hanna-Barbera productions by the time *The Jetsons* was produced in the early 1960s, Vander Pyl remarked that she found she "adored" playing Mrs. Spacely to Mel Blanc's blustering president of Spacely Sprockets—Jetson's pint-sized boss. However, her distinctive vocal tones are probably better recognized as Rosie, the Robot Maid, whom Barbera instructed her simply to pattern as a robot version of Shirley Booth from the 1960s sitcom *Hazel*.

If there was any aspect of her career that she regretted, it was that she eventually recognized the need to join Smoker's Anonymous. While it may seem unthinkable now, in the 1950s, family-oriented programming like *The Flintstones* could be sponsored by companies like Reynolds tobacco; and, along with her *Flintstones* cast mates, Vander Pyl is immortalized in some black-and-white commercials touting the benefits of Winston cigarettes. The cast was not hesitant to patronize their sponsors. "All of us smoked like fiends. In those days, nobody ever told us there was anything wrong with it; and you sit around rehearsals with nothing to do and everybody else is smoking, and you take it up. That's what I did. It was a nervous tension reliever. Alan Reed, Mel [Blanc], Bea Benederet, and myself, we all smoked." According to her son Michael, smoker's hack was directly responsible for Betty's and Wilma's distinctive giggles: "That cute little laugh that Betty and Wilma did with their mouths closed? They came up with that when they normally laughed, because they were smokers, they coughed." In 1995, Vander Pyl expressed her hope that the younger generations "were smart enough not to start" and worked on some anti-smoking promotional advertisements before she became the last original Flintstones cast member to die—at the age of seventy-nine, on April 11, 1999—of lung cancer.

Perhaps the most fitting legacy for Vander Pyl as well as for all *The Flintstones* cast is that, because of syndication, *The Flintstones* is on somewhere in the world every minute of every day. As long as there are families, it is likely to remain so.

CREDITS

All-New Scooby and Scrappy-Doo Show, The (1983) TV Series
Atom Ant Show, The (1965) TV Series . . . . Maw Rugg/Floral Rugg
Atom Ant/Secret Squirrel Show, The (1967) TV Series . . . . Maw Rugg
Bear Up (1963)
Bearly Able (1962)
Big Mouse Take (1965)
Creepy Time Pal (1960)
Deep in My Heart (1954) (uncredited) . . . . Miss Zimmermann
Dinky Dog (1969) TV Series . . . . Additional Voices
Do Good Wolf, The (1960)
Fallible Fable, A (1963)
Fee Fie Foes (1961)
Flintstone Christmas, A (1977) TV . . . . Wilma Flintstone/Pebbles Flintstone
Flintstone Kids, The (1986) TV Series . . . . Doris Slaghoople
Flintstones, The (1960) TV Series . . . . Wilma Flintstone/Pebbles Flintstone
Flintstones: Fred's Final Fling, The (1981) TV . . . . Wilma Flintstone/Pebbles Flintstone/Elephant
Flintstones: Jogging Fever (1981) TV . . . . Wilma Flintstone/Pebbles Flintstone
Flintstones: Wacky Inventions, The (1994) Video . . . . Wilma Flintstone/Pebbles Flintstone
Flintstones Christmas Carol, A (1994) TV . . . . Wilma Flintstone
Flintstones Comedy Hour, The (1972) TV Series . . . . Wilma Flintstone
Flintstones Little Big League, The (1979) TV . . . . Wilma Flintstone
Flintstones Meet Rockula and Frankenstone, The (1979) TV . . . . Wilma Flintstone
Flintstones Movie, The (1994) . . . . Mrs. Feldspar (conga line dancer)
Flintstones' New Neighbors, The (1980) TV . . . . Wilma Flintstone/Pebbles Flintstone
Fred and Barney Meet the Shmoo (1979) TV Series . . . . Wilma Flintstone/Pebbles Flintstone
Fred and Barney Meet the Thing (1979) TV Series . . . . Wilma Flintstone/Pebbles Flintstone
Fred Flintstone and Friends (1977) TV Series . . . . Wilma Flintstone
Fred's Final Fling (1980) TV . . . . Wilma Flintstone/Pebbles Flintstone
Here Kiddue, Kiddie (1960)
Hey There! It's Yogi Bear (1964)
Hollyrock-a-Bye Baby (1993) TV . . . . Wilma Flintstone
Hong Kong Phooey (1974) TV Series . . . . Rosemary
I Yabba-Dabba Do! (1993) TV . . . . Wilma Flintstone/Mrs. Slate
Inch High, Private Eye (1973) TV Series . . . . Mrs. Finkerton
Jetsons, The (1962) TV Series . . . . Rosie the Robot/Mrs. Starla Spacely
Jetsons: The Movie (1990) . . . . Rosie the Robot

Jetsons Christmas Carol, The (1985) TV .... Rosie the Robot
Jetsons Meet the Flintstones, The (1987) TV .... Wilma Flintstone/Rosie/Mrs. Spacely/
Just a Wolf at Heart (1963)
Kooky Loopy (1961)
Little Bo Bopped (1959)
Magilla Gorilla (1964) TV Series .... Ogee
Man Called Flintstone, The (1966) .... Wilma Flintstone/Pebbles Flintstone/Nurse/Baby/Old Lady
New Fred and Barney Show, The (1979) TV Series .... Wilma Flintstone/Pebbles Flintstone
New Tom and Jerry Show, The (1975) TV Series .... Additional Voices
No Biz like Shoe Biz (1960)
Not in Nottingham (1963)
Raggedy Rug (1964)
Rockin' with Judy Jetson (1988) TV .... Rosie
Santa and the Three Bears (1970) ....
Scooby-Doo, Where Are You! (1969) TV Series .... Additional Voices
Slippery Slippers (1962)
Snoopy Loopy (1960)
Swash Buckled (1962)
Top Cat (1961) TV Series (uncredited) .... Goldie
Where's Huddles (1970) TV Series .... Marge Huddles
Wind-up Wilma (1981) TV .... Wilma Flintstone/Pebbles Flintstone
Yogi Bear Show, The (1960) TV Series
Yogi's Ark Lark (1972) TV .... Maw Rugg/Floral Rugg/Woman

JANET WALDO

Janet Waldo, the voice of the perpetually perky young women of animation — Judy Jetson, Josie of *Josie and the Pussycats*, and Penelope Pitstop — was born with the desire to act. However, the actress from Yakama Valley, Washington, had her heart set on a Broadway theatrical career until it was diverted to Hollywood instead, by way of Bing Crosby.

Given Waldo's heritage, it is surprising that she did not become a musician. Although her parents were not career performers, she says her mother had a beautiful singing voice, and as a little girl she would wake in the midnight hours to music when her father returned from the late shift on the Northern Pacific Railroad to play the violin and cello. Waldo's sister, Elizabeth, found her calling as a violinist and as a composer with several albums to her credit. But although Janet liked the piano, the toddler loved her bit part as a doll in a school play. "I bent over and said 'mama' and got a laugh. I was three and I said, 'That's what I want to do!' "

An acting prodigy, Waldo worked steadily in local radio until Bing Crosby changed her life. Waldo was hired for her first professional job at ten, when the local Seattle radio station chose her to do a commercial for a brand of flour. By the time she was a young teenager, Crosby (who was originally from Spokane) came back to Washington State on a publicity junket. He saw Waldo in a comedic play and, impressed with her potential as a comedienne, asked her back to Hollywood (with her mother and a small group of hopefuls).

Waldo says Crosby and his brothers—who referred to her as the "little girl with the little boyish figure"—acted as her agents and were very concerned because she was so young and not ready to do film. Waldo then found her niche with Crosby on the radio, eventually becoming a household name in the title role of the radio comedy *Meet Corliss Archer*. But she is also grateful for more personal reasons. While on *Archer,* she met her husband, playwright Robert E. Lee (who, before he passed away in 1994, wrote *First Monday in October, Auntie Mame,* and *Inherit the Wind* with partner Jerry Lawrence). If not for Crosby bringing her to California, she noted that she would never have met her husband.

Although Waldo loved the dramatic acting roles—she worked in both drama and comedy with such legends as Bob Hope and Kirk Douglas—she soon discovered her talent for voices. Auditioning to play opposite Crosby in a radio show based on an Alice Faye film, she won the part over ninety other people with her impersonation of Faye. "They didn't expect me to win it, but I was determined that I was going to play opposite Bing Crosby. I wore my black hat with a veil and the black dress and aged myself up a bit, because we always worked in front of an audience. Bing, of course, just about died when he saw me playing opposite him, but I had the opportunity in radio to do real acting and that's what I've always loved."

She segued into her animation career at Hanna-Barbera courtesy of her then agent Jack Wormser. Working on an on-camera series at the time and with a background in radio, Waldo was mainly called for radio spots. One day,

Wormser casually asked her if she would like to audition for a new cartoon series called *The Jetsons*. The naturally youthful-voiced Waldo had fun auditioning for the part of daughter Judy. "I just did my own voice pretty much in those days and I just exaggerated a little bit. But I did it and I won it and I couldn't believe it! Of course, in doing *The Jetsons* I had no idea they were going to become the national phenomenon because we only did twenty-four."

Waldo was especially delighted at the high quality of the original series and believes the charm of *The Jetsons* stems from the fact that it was intended to be prime-time television. "I think that the people love seeing a normal, darling, real family in outer space in the future and, of course, the gadgets. . . . There was so much imagination. So many things were contrived that were going to be in the future and people are totally fascinated by that. The clothes were so offbeat and wild and wonderful. And I think the scripts were just delightful." Although the program was written to appeal to an all-ages audience, it ultimately could not compete against the top-rated *The Wonderful World of Disney* and *Dennis the Menace*—sending the twenty-four episodes into perpetual reruns after cancellation.

Of course, that those same twenty-four episodes of *The Jetsons'* only season were so popular for the next fourteen years on three different networks convinced Hanna-Barbera to commission a new series in 1985. Although Waldo enjoyed working on the series (and it was a good opportunity for people like future *Ren & Stimpy* auteur John Kricfalusi to gain experience), she questioned some of the changes, including the addition of an alien character named "Orbity." "I think that's true because everyone doesn't want anything changed about *The Jetsons*. They want it just the way it was."

She attributes the quality of original programs that were "so very, very special" to Joe Barbera's perfectionism; Barbera was directing each one and insisting upon every sound he wanted. Waldo says, "He would not let us go until he heard it, and I don't care if it was Paul Lynde or Daws Butler or Bea Benaderet or me or anybody else, even Alan Reed, who did Fred Flintstone; he would make them do it over and over again until they got it just the way he thought it should be." Although she says the cast felt the pressure of limited rehearsal and production schedules, Barbera's sessions "sometimes would take as long as six hours."

Of course, no grueling production schedule prepared Waldo for the shock she would receive on the taping of 1990's *The Jetsons* movie. After voicing Judy Jetson for almost two decades, due to a decision by the sponsor MCA, she was suddenly replaced by the fleeting teenage pop star of the time—Tiffany. Waldo recalls, "The reason that I was totally unprepared for it was that Joe came to the first session [for the film]. In fact, he stuck his head in a lot of the recording and said, 'Ah, thank God for Janet.'" When the news broke, Waldo was incensed to be the only one missing from the original surviving cast. "I didn't say this to Joe, but to my family and everybody I talked to—if they're going to do *The Jetsons* with a new cast, I wouldn't have felt bad at all ... but the fact that it was the original cast except I wasn't in it!" In addition, Waldo, who regularly did press for *Jetsons* projects, was particularly upset since the day before they called with the news she had just finished five hours of nationwide promotion for *Jetsons* home videos.

Still, Waldo could have conceivably kept Judy's speaking part—it is common for singers to double for actors on singing parts—but Tiffany proved not to be a good singing match for Waldo and, therefore, needed to record the speaking part as well. Although Waldo said she later read in *People* magazine that voice director Gordon Hunt had played her tape for Tiffany and she tried to impersonate Waldo to the best of her ability, Waldo remained unconsoled. "She was not right casting for Judy, anyway, because she is a totally different sound from me, from the way I played Judy Jetson. Her voice is a whole different register."

Waldo recalled the reaction as swift and widespread—letters immediately poured into Hanna-Barbera. "The director, everybody felt bad. The secretaries felt bad. Some of the people in the press cried and one girl threatened to quit." On a personal level, Waldo said of the decision, "[It] really rocked me and I actually grieved for a couple of weeks." But Hanna-Barbera tried to smooth the relationship by offering a part on *The Smurfs*. Ever the professional, Waldo took the job and accepted an apology from Joe Barbera for the circumstances beyond their control. "He was very, very sweet and, of course, I didn't say to him some of things I felt like." Nevertheless, because she "loves everybody at Hanna-Barbera and we get along so beautifully," just months after the movie fiasco, Waldo found herself in Las Vegas, returning to the *Jetson* press junket tour.

While Waldo has preformed ADR work for performers as diverse as Sally Field, Aretha Franklin, and Natalie Wood, she loves her work in animation, calling it "glorified radio," where roles are "quite a bit bigger than life." With Judy Jetson as her favorite character, surprisingly, she also has fond memories of Penelope Pitstop. Of the Hanna-Barbera series based on the 1941 serial *The Perils of Pauline,* Waldo says, "I always have thought that they would do a new series of *Penelope Pitstop*, but, of course, Paul Lynde [archvillain Sylvester Sneekly/the Hooded Claw] isn't here now. . . . Penelope was just so happy and she never worried about anything and she'd just say,

'Well, lucky for me; I've just got this or this or this.' She was just such a bland sort of naïve, wonderful character. I loved playing her."

If Waldo has any advice to impart for the next generation of voice actors, aside from learning the craft of acting and immersing oneself in the character, it is "be original. Because when you look at the truly outstanding voices, the voices that live on—it's always the original ones that last. Other people . . . are just trying to do imitations of the original, but if you come up with something that is yours, then you're off and running . . . . To your own self be true!"

Waldo seems to have followed her own advice. As proof of her inspired beginning, along with the cels of her characters, including Morticia Addams from the 1973 animated version of the *Addams Family* and Josie of *Josie and the Pussy Cats*, she still has a memento in the form of a picture of Crosby that he had autographed. Waldo said she was grateful for the opportunity to work with him shortly before he died, and to have the chance to thank him for changing her life and her life's work—taking her from stage actress to voice-over artist extraordinaire.

CREDITS

Abbott and Costello Show, The (1966) TV Series
Addams Family, The (1973) TV Series . . . . Morticia Addams/Granny
Adventures of the Little Prince, The (1982) TV Series . . . . Additional Voices
All-New Scooby and Scrappy-Doo Show, The (1983) TV Series
Amazing Chan and the Chan Clan, The (1972) TV Series . . . . Various Characters
Atom Ant Show, The (1965) TV Series . . . . Granny Sweet
Atom Ant/Secret Squirrel Show, The (1967) TV Series . . . . Granny Sweet
Battle of the Planets (1978) TV Series . . . . Princess/Susan
Bear Hug (1964)
Bear Knuckles (1964)
Cattanooga Cats, The (1969) TV Series . . . . Jenny Trent
Habit Rabbit (1964)
Heidi's Song (1982) . . . . Tinette
Help! It's the Hair Bear Bunch (1971) TV Series
Honeymoon in Bali (1939) (uncredited) . . . . Fortune Girl's Companion
I Yabba-Dabba-Do! (1993) TV . . . . Additional Voices
Jabberjaw (1976) TV Series
Jack and the Beanstalk (1967/I) TV . . . . Princess Serena
Jetsons, The (1962) TV Series . . . . Judy Jetson
Jetsons Christmas Carol, The (1985) TV . . . . Judy Jetson
Jetsons Meet the Flintstones, The (1987) TV . . . . Judy Jetson/Female Computer
Josie and the Pussycats (1970) TV Series . . . . Josie McCoy
Josie and the Pussycats in Outer Space (1972) TV Series . . . . Josie McCoy
Laurel and Hardy Cartoon, A (1966) TV Series . . . . Various Characters
Man Called Flintstone, The (1966) . . . . Miss Soapstone/Nurse/Stewardess/Girl #2

Miss Switch to the Rescue (1982) TV . . . . Miss Switch/Guinivere
New Adventures of Superman, The (1966) TV Series . . . . Lana Lang
New Tom and Jerry Show, The (1975) TV Series . . . . Additional Voices
Once upon a Forest (1993) . . . . Edgar's Mother
Perils of Penelope Pitstop (1969) TV Series . . . . Penelope Pitstop
Planète sauvage, La (1973) (uncredited) (English-language version)
Puppy Saves the Circus, The (1981) TV . . . . Gloria Goodbee
Puppy's Amazing Rescue, The (1980) TV . . . . Mother
Puppy's Further Adventures, The (1983) TV Series . . . . Mother
Rockin' with Judy Jetson (1988) TV . . . . Judy Jetson
Roman Holidays (1972) TV Series . . . . Henrietta
Scooby and Scrappy-Doo (1979) TV Series . . . . Additional Voices
Secret World of Og, The (1983) TV . . . . Mother/Old Lady
Shazzan! (1967) TV Series . . . . Nancy
Smurfs, The (1981) TV Series . . . . Hogatha (1982–1989)
Space Kidettes, The (1966) TV Series . . . . Jenny
Superman/Aquaman Hour of Adventure, The (1967) TV Series . . . . Lana Lang
These Are the Days (1974) TV Series (voice)
Tom and Jerry (1965) TV Series (voice)
Trouble with Miss Switch, The (1980) TV . . . . Miss Switch
Wacky Races (1968) TV Series . . . . Penelope Pitstop
Yogi's First Christmas (1980) . . . . Cindy

FRANK WELKER

"Do you hear the frog?" Well, if you heard this from an educational toy as a child just learning your ABCs, then the first voice actor you probably remember is Frank Welker. In addition to countless credits in cartoons and live-action, his vocal talents can also be found on many of the educational toys generations of children have grown up with, such as Mattel's "See and Say Clock" and "The Farmer Says." Not many people realize that cartoon

legend Welker is the person responsible for teaching them that *"The cow says, 'Mooooooo.'"*

Actor, musician, stand-up comedian, and voice-over legend, Welker has spent the last three decades covering the spectrum of entertainment. Although famous in animation circles for his many straightforward characters—such as Freddie Jones, the hip, scarf-wearing blond leader of the mystery-solving gang in *Scooby-Doo, Where Are You?* Hefty and Poet Smurf on *The Smurfs*, Kermit and Skeeter on *Muppet Babies*, rock-and-roll drumming shark Jabberjaw on *Jabberjaw*, and seven different characters on *Transformers*, including Megatron, leader of the evil Decepticons, in the series about warring, morphing robots—Welker's bread and butter relies heavily on his uncanny ability to imitate members of the animal kingdom and to amaze with his alien creature voices.

Over the past thirty years, Welker's vocal acrobatics in live-action productions have surreptitiously graced characters such as the evil gremlin Spike in *Gremlins*, the poisoned monkey in *Raiders of the Lost Ark*, Spock's screams in *Star Trek III: The Search For Spock*, barnyard animals in *Big Top Pee Wee*, the gopher in *Caddyshack II*, as well as characters in countless television shows, including *The X-files*, *MacGyver*, cult favorite *Get a Life* (where he voiced Chris Elliot's alien friend Spewey), and *Return to Green Acres*, where he played the pig, Arnold Ziffel.

While most voice-over artists are commonly associated with the characters they portray, Welker is a specialist, respected in the industry for the quality and quantity of his vocal effects, especially the four-legged kind. An apt title for a Welker biography would be "My Life as a Dog," since he seems to have cornered the canine market in the entertainment industry. A sampling of Welker's cartoon dogs include Bart's dog, Santa's Little Helper, on *The Simpsons*; Richie Rich's dog, Dollar, on *Richie Rich*, Fonzie's dog, Mr. Cool, on *Fonz and the Happy Days Gang*, Foofur, a bloodhound that inherits a mansion and turns it into a haven for his homeless buddies, on *Foofur*; and Dynomutt, Dog Wonder, on *The Scooby-Doo/Dynomutt Hour*. Live-action dog dubbing includes the Grinch's dog, Max, in the live-action Jim Carrey project, *How the Grinch Stole Christmas*; Elvira's dog, Gonk, in *Elvira—Mistress of the Dark*, the terrorizing Saint Bernard Cujo in the adaptation of Stephen King's *Cujo*; a rottweiler in the Chris Farley vehicle *Tommy Boy*; and various dogs in such films as *K-9 II* and *101 Dalmatians*. But long before Welker was lauded for barking and growling his way to stardom on the big screen, he was known as somewhat of a street performer.

Franklin W. Welker was born in Denver, Colorado, on February 16, 1945. The youngest of three boys proved to be a showman at an early age. By the time he was seven, he could be found outside his home standing atop an ash pit entertaining his neighbors and friends. What his parents assumed to be a stage the young lad was going through proved to be an ongoing obsession, as Welker then progressed to doing impersonations of his family, friends, and pets. At times, he was a prankster, confusing callers to his home by answering the phone in funny voices.

In grade school, it was only natural for a boy with Welker's talent to be the class clown. It did not take him long to realize that he could use his unique vocal qualities to attract the opposite sex, and, consequently, in an effort to impress a group of girls, twelve-year-old Welker was kicked out of his seventh-grade class for making dog sounds. In many classrooms, he would have been given detention for his indiscretion and the incident would have been forgotten, but a perceptive teacher decided to enter Welker into a school competition where he could display his talent without fear of retribution. The success of his performance and the sound of applause was addictive, and he craved more. The next year, performing in Colorado's Summer Showagon, he was chosen as one of the top 20 finalists out of 250. The *Rocky Mountain News* named the thirteen-year-old one of the best acts of the year and prophetically dubbed him a star of tomorrow.

Upon entering high school, Welker switched gears, becoming active in sports and music. Co-captain of his football team, he was honored to be chosen as a member of the all-city team as well. Earning letters in wrestling and track, he still found time to perform in one of Denver's most popular folk groups, the Coachmen. With a broad range of interests, the multi-faceted Welker's future was wide open. Not long after his high school graduation, he obtained a job as a prop boy for CBS television affiliate KLZ in Denver, but because of his crazy vocal antics, he was soon assigned to do sound effects and gags for the local *Fred 'n' Fae Show*.

In 1965, Welker left KLZ and headed west to California to attend Santa Monica College, where he studied acting and performed in a series of plays. Two years later, while continuing his education at UCLA, he also began his professional career, obtaining his first acting job in a commercial for Bold laundry detergent. Other commercials followed, and although the young actor was beginning to gain momentum as an on-camera actor, he decided to expand his repertoire.

With plays and commercials under his belt, Welker was determined to try his hand at stand-up comedy. Developing a routine and making the rounds to audition for local clubs, he landed a stint at a West Hollywood club called Ledbetters, then frequented by comedian Steve Martin. The burgeoning comedian proved to be a crowd pleaser and was subsequently hired as an MC for a Hollywood strip club called the Losers, which gave him experience in performing burlesque-style comedy. While in the club's employ, Welker was spotted by a talent agent who booked him in night clubs in San Francisco and Atlantic City, which led to him touring with the Righteous Brothers as their opening act.

After a year of touring with different musical groups, Welker returned to acting, snagging a role in the Elvis Presley film *The Trouble with Girls*. There he appeared with his future animation co-star Nicole Jaffe, the future Velma on the *Scooby-Doo* series. Between takes, Welker entertained the cast and crew by making animal sounds; this so amused Presley that, whenever he saw Welker on the set, they would greet each other by making choking dog noises. The film, which would prove to be the last for the king of rock and roll, was the first for Welker, who would go on to appear in several more, including *The Computer Wore Tennis Shoes* and *Now You See Him, Now You Don't* for Disney Studios and the Don Knotts comedy *How to Frame a Figg*.

But it was Welker's stand-up routine that started him on the road to voice-overs. After recreating a dog-and-cat fight on stage at Ledbetters, Welker was approached by a producer who observed his act and offered him a job as the voice of a dog's tail in an upcoming Friskies commercial. Welker, who had never done a voice-over before, was not even quite sure what one was, but agreed to do the job.

When Welker showed up for the spot, the producer's girlfriend, who happened to be casting ABC's *Scooby-Doo, Where Are You?* witnessed his stellar talking-tail performance and decided that he would be perfect for the role of the dog on the new Hanna-Barbera series. Welker then walked into Hanna-Barbera convinced that he "would get the dog, hands-down." But when the auditions were over and the smoke cleared, veteran voice actor Don Messick had the lead role, leaving Welker earmarked for the role of Freddie. Welker recalled his chagrin in an interview with writer Bob Miller in *Animation World Magazine*, "I said, 'Freddie? He's the straight guy. Maybe I could do Shaggy because it is such a character voice.'" (Coincidentally, the actor who would be Shaggy, Casey Kasem, thought *he* was best for Freddie). Little did he know that the character he resisted would go on to become a career staple for the next thirty years.

Once Welker had his foot in the door at Hanna-Barbera, he soon became a fixture in their studios, working alongside established voice-over veterans such as Henry Corden, June Foray, and Paul Winchell, among others. As the new kid on the block, Welker initially found it hard to convince director Barbera to let him voice more than incidental characters. Welker told *Animation World Magazine*, "Here I was, brand new, and I was sitting around the table with Don Messick and John Stephenson and Henry Corden and all these really great voice actors, and Joe Barbera would say, 'Okay, you've got the part of the villain and it's a guy named Coal Miner and he's a real bad dude! John, you want to take a try at it?' and John would read four or five lines. And Joe would say, 'Okay, that sounds good. Messick, you want to try?' Don would read it and Joe would go, 'Okay, anybody else?' and he wouldn't look at me because I'm twelve years old." After feigning disappointment in not being asked, Welker would eventually get to give the character a try, usually to end up losing the part to a more established actor.

Welker's saving grace was, once again, his ability to do animals and strange creatures. Because there was an animal of some type in every show, Welker was almost always guaranteed a spot. But he admitted to *Animation World Magazine* in 2000, "In the early days, Joe Barbera hired me a lot—not because he felt I was such a great voice guy, but because he thought I was funny. He was really perceptive in the people he hired, because my readings weren't quite as good as some of the polished guys. But I think he liked that I would bring him the weird stuff, and he liked that I would ad-lib."

As his voice-over career was taking off in the 1970s, Welker continued to work on-camera, appearing in such shows as *Love American Style* and *The Don Knotts Show*. But his experience as a stand-up comedian once again earned him a coveted role when, while he was performing his act at the Comedy Store, Paul Keyes, the producer of Rowan and Martin's *Laugh-In*, spotted him and asked him to appear on the opening show of the season with featured billing. After the initial episode, Welker was asked back for four more shows and offered a spot as a *Laugh-In* regular for the following season. Unfortunately, there was no following season: NBC canceled the groundbreaking show. Welker countered the cancellation by diving headfirst into other projects. Continuing with television, he made several appearances on *The Merv Griffin Show* and was a regular on *The Burns and Schreiber Comedy Hour*. But by the mid 1970s, he decided to phase out on-camera work, not only for the anonymity factor, but also to afford him the freedom to continue working in other areas of the business, namely, on his night club act.

Though the 1970s found Welker performing a number of animated voices, including Marvin (Junior Super Friend) and his pet, Wonder Dog, on *Super Friends*, Curly on *The Three Robonic Stooges*, Fangface on *Fangface*, and the

Shmoo on *Fred and Barney Meet the Shmoo*, he also performed on two comedy albums, *The Watergate Comedy Hour*, in which he played Richard Nixon, and comedian Bill Dana's record *Jose Supersport*. In addition, Welker took his comedy act on the road, opening for such notables as Glen Campbell, Ricky Nelson, and Ann-Margaret. Ironically, Welker was opening for Ann-Margaret at the Las Vegas Hilton (Elvis Presley's Vegas home base) the night his old friend and iconic former co-star passed away.

In the mid 1980s, the animation business boomed with the advent of cartoon syndication. Studios and actors were kept busy year round, whereas before the work was seasonal, usually from March to September. Welker found himself immersed in voice-over work, sometimes averaging three shows per day, with commercials and radio shows thrown into the mix.

In 1984, when Hanna-Barbera announced that they were going to produce new episodes of their 1960s futuristic space-age family, *The Jetsons*, the studio assembled the original cast. Although each member had to re-audition for their parts to make sure the now venerable actors could still maintain their former energy levels and the voice quality of their characters, each person passed the test, including a now disabled George O'Hanlon, who did the part of patriarch George Jetson. In Hanna-Barbera tradition, a new character was added to the cast, a space alien named Orbity, which Welker was hired to voice.

Joe Barbera explained, "We used to do that with *The Flintstones*. We used to try and add something each year. One year was the birth of the baby, one time we brought in Gazoo, a character from outer space. In this particular case, we were asked by our salespeople, 'Could we add any new elements?' So we tried Orbity." Adding Orbity to the cast gave Welker a chance to work with a dream ensemble cast of voice-over legends, including Mel Blanc, Daws Butler, and Don Messick (Welker once referred to Blanc as the Beatles and Butler and Messick as the Rolling Stones of voice-over artists). Although Welker was thrilled to be a part of the cast, he admitted to being a "Jetsons purist" and thought that the studio should not have tampered with the characters, even though he "had fun with Orbity."

As time passed, many of the great voice-over actors from the early days of cartoons, including Daws Butler, Don Messick, and Mel Blanc, passed away, leaving Welker the new elder statesman of animation. Although only in his fifties, Welker was working with young actors such as Mary Kay Bergman, Rob Paulsen, Jeff Glen Bennett, and Maurice LaMarche, who had grown up with his work.

Ironically, Welker faced the same fate as the *Jetsons'* cast when called upon to do the voice of Freddie for a new *Scooby-Doo* video release. Welker explained to Bob Miller of *Animation World Magazine*, "When we were doing the direct-to-video movie *Scooby-Doo on Zombie Island*, I was basically the only one left from the original group. I thought they might replace me because they thought my voice had gone down an octave. I personally feel I can do Freddie right up front . . . [as] that happens to be close to my original voice. When we were recording it, the director kept saying, 'Higher and higher,' and I kept saying, 'No, no, I don't think so. I did that for a lot of years,' and I went back and looked at some tapes, just to make sure, because I don't want to be doing something that's wrong for the studio, either. And so they were looking at some old tape, 'cause they were worried about some of the old voices and matching them. [The director] listened to the Freddie voice and said, 'I'll be darned. He's absolutely right. He sounds exactly like Freddie.' It's a double-edged sword."

The fault of the voice change possibly lies with television stations. In order to have more time for commercials and promos, the networks often time-compress episodes of many shows, including *Scooby-Doo*, which then also speeds up the audio. Thus, it makes the character voices sound higher pitched than they actually were in the initial recording.

By the beginning of the new millennium, Welker had pretty much mastered all aspects of show business, including releasing his own comedy album, *Frank Welker—Almost Sold-Out*, in 1987. Though he sometimes gets jobs based solely upon his formidable reputation, there are times that he has found himself so typecast in the minds of some studio clients that it has taken the intervention of the recording staff to ensure that he is being fairly considered for new and original projects. But as long as Welker gets a chance to audition for roles, he is happy. As to what the future holds for him, he claims that getting older will have no effect upon his career. Although he finds it harder to maintain the vocal stress of monster characters or otherwise screaming for long periods of time, he sees no real restrictions to his abilities. As he concludes, "In terms of performing, I see no limitations. I'll just do older dogs."

CREDITS

101 Dalmatians: The Series (1996) TV Series . . . . Scorch
13 Ghosts of Scooby-Doo, The (1985) TV Series
2 Stupid Dogs (1993) TV Series
Adventures from the Book of Virtues (1996) TV Series . . . . Socrates
Adventures of Don Coyote, The (1988) TV Series . . . . Don Coyote
Adventures of Hyperman, The (1995) TV Series . . . . Entrobe
Adventures of Jimmy Neutron: Boy Genius, The (2002) TV Series . . . . Goddard

Aladdin (1992) .... Abu the Monkey
Aladdin (1993/I) TV Series .... Abu/Xerxes/Additional Voices
Aladdin and the King of Thieves (1996) .... Abu the Monkey
Aladdin's Arabian Adventures: Creatures of Invention (1998) .... Abu
Aladdin's Arabian Adventures: Fearless Friends (1998) .... Abu
Aladdin's Arabian Adventures: Magic Makers (1998) .... Abu
Aladdin's Arabian Adventures: Team Genie (1998) .... Abu
All-New Popeye Hour, The (1978) TV Series .... Dinky
Alvin and the Chipmunks (1983) TV Series .... Additional Voices
Amazing Adventures of Inspector Gadget, The (1986) .... Brain/Dr. Claw/M.A.D Cat/Lesser Wambini
   (segments: "Magic Gadget" and "The Great Wambini's séance")/News Reporter/Animals
   (segment: "The Great Wambini's séance")/M.A.D Agent (segment: "The Capeman Cometh")
Amazing Bunjee Venture, The (1984) TV
Animaniacs (1993) TV Series .... Ralph the Guard/Thaddeus Plotz/Buttons/Runt/Flavio
   Hippo/Chicken Boo/Additional Voices
Annabelle's Wish (1997) .... Additional Voices
Atlantis: Milo's Return (2003) Video .... Mantell/Obby
Bailey's Comets (1973) TV Series .... Pudge
Batman Beyond: Return of the Joker (2000/I) .... Woof the Hyena-Man/Ace the Bathound
Beauty and the Beast (1991) .... Footstool (dog)
Beauty and the Beast: The Enchanted Christmas (1997) .... Phillippe/Sultan
Belle's Magical World (1997) .... Sultan
Berenstain Bears, The (1985) TV Series .... Raffish Ralph/Weasel McGreed/Farmer
   Ben/Henchweasels/Others
Best of Roger Rabbit, The (1996) .... Various Voices
Bionic Six (1987) TV Series .... Glove/Mechanic/Chopper
Blackstar (1981) TV Series .... Gossamear/Burble/Rif
Blondie and Dagwood (1986) TV .... Dagwood Bumstead
Bobby's World (1990) TV Series .... Roger the Dog
Bonkers (1993) TV Series .... Toon Handbag/Quark/Elmo/Groucho-like Toon/Gentle Ben
   Butterman/Toon Ghost
Bruno the Kid (1996) TV Series .... Additional Voices
Buddy (1997) .... Buddy
Burns and Schreiber Comedy Hour, The (1973) TV Series .... Regular
Butch Cassidy and the Sundance Kids (1973) TV Series .... Elvis
Buzz Lightyear of Star Command (2000) TV Series .... Grubs
Buzz Lightyear of Star Command: The Adventure Begins (2000) .... Grubs/Self Destruct/Ranger
   #1/Rhizomian Man/Cadet Flarn
Caddyshack II (1988) .... Gopher
Capitol Critters (1992) TV Series .... Presidential Felines
Captain N: The Game Master (1989) TV Series .... Gameboy (1990)
Captain N & the Adventures of Super Mario Bros. 3 (1990) TV Series .... Additional Voices
Captain Planet and the Planeteers (1990) TV Series .... Suchi (1990–1993)/Lead
   Suit(1990–1993)/Tank Flusher (1990–1993)/Additional Voices
Captain Simian & the Space Monkeys (1996) TV Series (uncredited) .... Apax/Additional Voices
Cartoon All-Stars to the Rescue (1990) TV .... Slimer/Baby Kermit
Casper and the Angels (1979) TV Series
CatDog: The Great Parent Mystery (2001) TV .... Bessie the Sea Monster
Cats Don't Dance (1997) .... Farley Wink
Centurions, The (1985) TV Series
Challenge of the GoBots (1984) TV Series .... Scooter/Zeemon/Rest-Q/Blaster

Channel Umptee-3 (1997) TV Series

Charlotte's Web 2: Wilbur's Great Adventure (2003) Video . . . . Animal Voice Effects

Chipmunk Adventure, The (1987) . . . . Sophie/Arab Prince/Additional Voices

Christmas Carol, A (1997) . . . . Debit

Cinderella II: Dreams Come True (2002) . . . . Pom Pom/Lucifer

Clifford the Big Red Dog (2000) TV Series . . . . Manny

Completely Mental Misadventures of Ed Grimley, The (1988) TV Series . . . . Sheldo

Crane Brained (1976) . . . . Crane Jr./Dragonfly

Cro (1993) TV Series . . . . Gogg/Bobb/Earle

Darkwing Duck (1991) TV Series . . . . Additional Voices

Dave the Barbarian (2004) TV Series . . . . Faffy

Deep Blue Sea (1999) . . . . Parrot Noises

Denver, the Last Dinosaur (1992) TV Series . . . . Additional Voices

Dexter's Laboratory (1996) TV Series . . . . Monkey/Krunk/Additional Voices

Dink, the Little Dinosaur (1989) TV Series . . . . Scar/Crusty

Dino-Riders (1988) TV Series . . . . Krulos/Rasp/Glyde

Dirty Little Billy (1972) . . . . Young Punk

Dogfather (1974)

Don Coyote and Sancho Panda (1990) TV Series . . . . Don Coyote/Dapple

Don Knotts Show, The (1970) TV Series . . . . Regular

Donkey Kong Jr. (1983) TV Series . . . . Donkey Kong Jr.

Doug's First Movie (1999) . . . . Herman Melville

Droopy: Master Detective (1993) TV Series

DuckTales (1987) TV Series . . . . Bubba Duck/Bigtime Beagle/Baggy Beagle

DuckTales: The Movie—Treasure of the Lost Lamp (1990) . . . . Additional Voices

Ducktales: Treasure of the Golden Suns (1987) TV . . . . Bigtime Beagle

Dukes, The (1983) TV Series . . . . Flash/Smokey/General Lee

Dungeons and Dragons (1983/I) TV Series . . . . Uni/Additional Voices

Dynomutt, Dog Wonder (1978) TV Series . . . . Dynomutt the Dog Wonder/Freddy Jones

Evil Con Carne (2000) TV . . . . Boskov the Bear

Faeries (1981) TV . . . . Puck/Fir Darrig/Trow/Hunter

Fangface (1978) TV Series . . . . Sherman Fangsworth/Fangface/Baby Fangs/Fangpuss

Fangface and Fangpuss (1981) TV Series . . . . Fangface/Fangpuss

Fantastic Max (1988) TV Series . . . . Additional Voices

First 13th Annual Fancy Anvil Awards Show Program Special Live in Stereo, The (2002) TV
    (uncredited) (archive footage) . . . . Fred Jones

Fish Police (1992) TV Series . . . . Mussels Marinara/Doc Croaker

Flintstones: On the Rocks, The (2001) TV . . . . Dino/Monkey/Elevator Guy

Flintstones: Wacky Inventions, The (1994) . . . . Barney Rubble

Flintstones Christmas Carol, A (1994) TV . . . . Barney Rubble/Dino

Flintstones Little Big League, The (1979) TV . . . . Bamm-Bamm

Flintstones' New Neighbors, The (1980) TV . . . . Creeply/Mother Pterodactyl

Fonz and the Happy Days Gang (1980) TV Series . . . . Mr. Cool

Freakazoid! (1995) TV Series . . . . Mr. Chubbikins

Fred and Barney Meet the Shmoo (1979) TV Series . . . . Shmoo

Fred Flintstone and Friends (1977) TV Series

Friz Freleng's Looney Looney Looney Bugs Bunny Movie (1981)

Futurama (1999) TV Series . . . . Nibbler

G. I. Joe (1983) TV Series . . . . Short Fuse (E-4 Eric W. Friestadt)/Wild Bill (W-4 William S. Hardy)/
    Torch (Tom Winken)/Copperhead

G. I. Joe: A Real American Hero (1983) TV . . . . Short Fuse (E-4 Eric W. Friestadt)/Wild Bill
    (W-4 William S. Hardy)

G. I. Joe: The Movie (1987) .... Torch/Tom Winken of Dreadnok/Order
Galtar and the Golden Lance (1985) TV Series .... Tuk/Thork/Koda
Garfield: His Nine Lives (1988) TV .... Mendelsen
Garfield and Friends (1988) TV Series .... Bo/Booker/Sheldon/Fred Duck
Garfield Gets a Life (1991) TV .... Lorenzo/Gunner
Gargoyles (1994) TV Series .... Bronx/Boudicca/Cagney
Gargoyles: Brothers Betrayed (1998) .... Bronx
Gargoyles: The Force of Goliath (1998) .... Bronx
Gargoyles: The Goliath Chronicles (1996) TV Series .... Bronx
Gargoyles: The Heroes Awaken (1994) .... Bronx
Get-Along Gang, The (1984) TV Series .... Braker Turtle
GoBots: War of the Rock Lords (1986) .... Scooter/Zeemon/Rest-Q/Pulver-Eyes/Sticks/Narliphant
Goof Troop (1992) TV Series .... Waffles/Chainsaw
Goof Troop Christmas, A (1992) TV .... Grizz/Waffles/Chainsaw
Goofy Movie, A (1995) .... Bigfoot
Gravedale High (1990) TV Series .... Frankentyke/J. P. Ghastly
Grim & Evil (2001) TV Series .... Boskov the Bear
Grinch Grinches the Cat in the Hat, The (1982) TV
Hägar the Horrible (1989) TV
Happily Ever After (1993) .... Batso
Heathcliff (1980) TV Series .... Dingbat (1980–1982)
Heckle and Jeckle Show, The (1956) TV Series .... Heckle/Jeckle (1979–1982)
Heidi's Song (1982) .... Schnoddle/Hootie
Hercules (1998) TV Series .... Pegasus/Cateblas/Additional Voices
Histeria! (1998) TV Series .... Father Time/Fetch/Pule Howser
Hollyrock-a-Bye Baby (1993) TV .... Barney Rubble/Dino/J. Rocko
House of Mouse (2001) TV Series .... Gus Goose/Mountain Lion/Figaro/Aracuan Bird/
   Salty the Seal/Dodger/Beagle Boys/Abu/Cri-Kee/Pegasus/Butch the Bulldog/Additional Voices
How the Grinch Stole Christmas (2000) .... Voice of Max the Dog
How to Frame a Figg (1971) .... Prentiss Gates
Hudson Hawk (1991) .... Bunny the Dog
Hunchback of Notre Dame, The (1996) .... Baby Bird
Hunchback of Notre Dame II, The (2002) .... Achilles/Djali
I Yabba-Dabba Do! (1993) TV .... Barney Rubble/Dino
In Search of Dr. Seuss (1994) TV .... Additional Voice-Over
Incredible Detectives, The (1979) TV .... Hennesy
Inspector Gadget (1983) TV Series .... Brain/Dr. Claw/M.A.D. Cat
Inspector Gadget: Gadget's Greatest Gadgets (1999) .... Dr. Claw/Brain/M.A.D Cat/Dr. Noodleman
   (segment: "Gadget's Gadgets")/M.A.D Agent (segment: "The Capeman Cometh")
Inspector Gadget Saves Christmas (1992) TV .... Brain/Dr. Claw/M.A.D. Cat/Santa Claus
It's a Wonderful Tiny Toons Christmas Special (1992) TV .... Gogo
It's Punky Brewster (1985) TV Series .... Glomer
It's the Pied Piper, Charlie Brown (2000) .... Mayor
Itsy Bitsy Spider, The (1992) .... Itsy Bitsy Spider
Itsy Bitsy Spider, The (1994) TV Series .... Itsy
Jabberjaw (1976) TV Series .... Jabberjaw
Jetsons, The (1962) TV Series (uncredited) .... Orbity
Jetsons: The Movie (1990) .... Additional Voices
Jetsons Christmas Carol, The (1985) TV .... Ghost of Christmas Present/Orbity/Young Mr. Spacely/
   Teenage Mr. Spacely
Jetsons Meet the Flintstones, The (1987) TV .... Dan Rathmoon/Johnny/Mr. Goldbrick
Jimmy Neutron: Boy Genius (2001) .... Goddard/Orthgot/Worm/Demon

Jimmy Neutron's Nicktown Blast (2003) . . . . Goddard
Jonny Quest (1986) TV Series . . . . Additional Voices
Jonny Quest vs. the Cyber Insects (1995) TV . . . . Bandit
Jonny's Golden Quest (1993) TV . . . . Bandit
Kangaroo (1984) TV Series . . . . Monkey Biz Gang
Kissyfur (1985) TV Series . . . . Claudette/Uncle Shelby
Kitchen Casanova, The (1996) . . . . Pudge
Kwicky Koala Show, The (1981) TV Series
Lady and the Tramp II: Scamp's Adventure (2001) . . . . Reggie (vicious street dog)
Land before Time III: The Time of the Great Giving, The (1995) . . . . Velociraptor
Land before Time IV: Journey through the Mists, The (1996) . . . . Tickles
Last Holloween, The (1991) TV . . . . Scoota
Last of the Mohicans, The (1975) TV . . . . Magua/Soldier
Legend of Calamity Jane, The (1997) TV Series . . . . Joe Presto
Legend of Tarzan, The (2001) TV Series . . . . Manu
Life with Feather (1978) . . . . Crane Jr./Dragonfly
Lilo & Stitch: The Series (2003) TV Series . . . . Additional Voices
Lion King, The (1994) . . . . Additional Voices
Little Giants (1994) . . . . Animation Vocal Sound Effects
Little Mermaid, The (1989) . . . . Additional Voices
Little Mermaid II: Return to the Sea, The (2000) . . . . Max
Little Troll Prince, The (1995) . . . . Prag 2
Looney, Looney, Looney Bugs Bunny Movie, The (1981) . . . . Lawyer/Interviewing Dog
Looney Tunes: Back in Action (2003) . . . . Scooby-Doo
Marvin: Baby of the Year (1989) TV . . . . Announcer/Marvin (baby sound effects)
Mayflower Voyagers, The (1988) TV
Meatballs and Spaghetti (1982) TV . . . . Woofer
Mickey Mouse Works (1999) TV Series . . . . Butch the Bulldog/Mountain Lion/Salty the Seal/
    Aracuan Bird/Additional Voices
Mighty Ducks (1996) TV Series . . . . Chameleon
Mighty Ducks the Movie: The First Face-Off (1997) . . . . Chameleon
Mighty Max (1991) TV Series . . . . Warmonger
Mighty Mouse Playhouse, The (1955) TV Series . . . . Heckle/Jeckle/Quackula
Monchichis (1983) TV Series . . . . Patchitt
Monster in My Pocket: The Big Scream (1992) . . . . Big Ed/Swamp Beast/Projectionist
Mulan (1998) . . . . Khan the Horse/Little Brother the Dog/Cri-Kee the Cricket
Munchies (1987) . . . . Munchies
Muppet Babies (1984) TV Series . . . . Kermit/Beaker/Skeeter (1986–1992)
My Little Pony: The Movie (1986) . . . . Bushwoolie #3/Grundle
New Adventures of Mighty Mouse and Heckle and Jeckle, The (1979) TV Series . . . . Heckle/Jeckle/
    Quacula
New Adventures of Tom and Jerry, The (1980) TV Series . . . . Droopy/Slick/Spike/Barney Bear
New Fantastic Four, The (1978) TV Series . . . . H.E.R.B.I.E.
New Scooby-Doo Movies, The (1972) TV Series . . . . Fred "Freddy" Jones
New Shmoo, The (1979) TV Series . . . . Shmoo
New Tom and Jerry Show, The (1975) TV Series . . . . Additional Voices
Night of the Living Doo (2001) TV . . . . Freddy Jones/Jabberjaw
Our Friend, Martin (1999) . . . . Bull Connor/Chihuahua
Pac-Man (1982) TV Series . . . . Chomp Chomp
Pagemaster, The (1994) . . . . Horror/Dragon
Partridge Family, 2200 A.D., The (1974) TV Series . . . . Orbit

Pinky and the Brain Christmas Special, A (1995) TV

Pinocchio and the Emperor of the Night (1987) . . . . Igor

Pirates of Darkwater (1991) TV Series . . . . Niddler the Monkey-Bird

Plastic Man Comedy/Adventure Show, The (1979) TV Series . . . . Yukk

Pocahontas (1995) . . . . Flit

Pocahontas II: Journey to a New World (1998) . . . . Flit

Pound Puppies (1986) TV Series . . . . Catgut/Nabbit

Powerpuff Girls, The (1998) TV Series . . . . Additional Voices

Powerpuff Girls, The (2002) . . . . Whole Lotta Monkeys

Prince and the Pauper, The (1990) . . . . Archbishop/Dying King

Pryde of the X-Men (1989) TV . . . . Toad/Lockheed

Pup Named Scooby-Doo, A (1988) TV Series . . . . Additional Voices (1988–1991)

Puppy Saves the Circus, The (1981) TV . . . . Tiger/Lead Pony/Clown

Puppy's Amazing Rescue, The (1980) TV

Puppy's Great Adventure, The (1979) TV

Q*bert (1983) TV Series . . . . Q*mungus/Q*ball/Q*Dad/Coilee Snake/Ugh/Wrong Way/Sam Slick

Real Adventures of Jonny Quest, The (1996) TV Series . . . . Bandit (1996–1997)/Dr. Jeremiah Surd (1996–1997)/Dr. Zin/Ezekiel Rage

Real Ghostbusters, The (1986) TV Series . . . . Ray Stantz (1986–1991)/Slimer (1986–1991)/Additional Voices

Rescuers Down Under, The (1990) . . . . Joanna, McLeach's sidekick Lizard/Special Vocal Effects

Return of Jafar, The (1994) . . . . Abu the Monkey

Return to Never Land (2002) . . . . Additional Voices

Richie Rich/Scooby-Doo Hour, The (1980) TV Series . . . . Dollar (the Rich's Family Dog)/Frederick "Freddy" Jones

Road Rovers (1996) TV Series . . . . Shag/Muzzle

Road to El Dorado, The (2000) . . . . Altivo/Various Others

Robotix (1985)

Roller Coaster Rabbit (1990) . . . . Bull

Rude Dog and the Dweebs (1989) TV Series . . . . Caboose/Seymour/Rot

Rusty: A Dog's Tale (1997) . . . . Boss Duck

Sabrina, the Teenage Witch (1971) TV Series . . . . Big John Sullivan

Saintly Switch, A (1999) TV . . . . Voltaire

Schnookums and Meat Funny Cartoon Show (1993) TV Series . . . . Meat

Scooby and Scrappy-Doo (1979) TV Series . . . . Frederick "Freddy" Jones (1979–1980)

Scooby and Scrappy-Doo Puppy Hour, The (1982) TV Series . . . . Freddy Jones

Scooby-Doo (2002) . . . . Creature Voices

Scooby-Doo, Where Are You! (1969) TV Series . . . . Freddy Jones

Scooby-Doo and the Alien Invaders (2000) . . . . Freddy Jones

Scooby-Doo and the Cyber Chase (2001/I) . . . . FreddyJones/Cyber Freddy

Scooby-Doo and the Ghoul School (1988) TV . . . . Matches/Papa Werewolf/Well Dweller

Scooby-Doo and the Legend of the Vampire (2003) Video . . . . Scooby-Doo/Freddy Jones

Scooby-Doo and the Monster of Mexico (2003) Video . . . . Freddy Jones

Scooby-Doo and the Reluctant Werewolf (1989) TV . . . . Crunch

Scooby-Doo and the Witch's Ghost (1999) . . . . Freddy Jones

Scooby-Doo Goes Hollywood (1979) TV . . . . Freddy Jones

Scooby-Doo in Arabian Nights (1994) TV . . . . Freddy Jones

Scooby-Doo on Zombie Island (1998) . . . . Freddy Jones

Scooby-Doo Project, The (1999) TV . . . . Freddy Jones

Scooby-Doo/Dynomutt Hour, The (1976) TV Series . . . . Freddy Jones/Dynomutt

Scooby-Doo's Creepiest Capers (2000) . . . . Freddy Jones

Scooby-Doo's Greatest Mysteries (1999) . . . . Freddy Jones

Scooby's All-Star Laff-a-Lympics (1977) TV Series . . . . Dynomutt the Dog Wonder/Magic Rabbit/Mildew Wolf/Sooey Pig/Tinker/Yakky Doodle

Scooby's Mystery Funhouse (1985) TV Series . . . . Freddy Jones (1985–1986)

Secret Garden, The (1994) TV . . . . Robin

Sectaurs (1986) TV Miniseries . . . . Skulk/Trancula/Raplor

Shadow, The (1994) . . . . Phurba

Skatebirds, The (1977) TV Series . . . . P.O.P.S. (segment: "Mystery Island")/Jerome/Curly Howard

Simpsons, The (1989) TV Series . . . . Santa's Little Helper/Animal Effects

Slimer! And the Real Ghostbusters (1988) TV Series . . . . Ray Stantz/Slimer

Smurfs, The (1981) TV Series . . . . Clockwork Smurf/Hefty Smurf/Peewit/Poet Smurf/Puppy

Snorks, The (1984) TV Series . . . . Tooter/Occy

Sonic the Hedgehog (1993) TV Series . . . . Additional Voices

Space Jam (1996) . . . . Charles the Dog

Space-Stars (1981) TV Series . . . . Cosmo/Blip

Spider-Man and His Amazing Friends (1981) TV Series . . . . Iceman (Bobby Drake)/Flash Thompson

Spiral Zone (1987) TV Series . . . . Dr. Lawrence/Razorback/Rawmeat

Sport Billy (1982) TV Series . . . . Willy/Sporticus XI/Sipe

Stitch! The Movie (2003) Video . . . . Various Voices

Super Dave (1987) TV Series . . . . Additional Voices

Super Ducktales (1989) TV . . . . Bigtime Beagle/Megabyte Beagle/M.E.L.

Super Globetrotters, The (1979) TV Series . . . . Crime Globe

Super Mario Bros. (1993) . . . . Creatures

Super Powers Team: Galactic Guardians, The (1985) TV Series . . . . Mr. Mxyzptlk

SuperFriends (1973) TV Series . . . . Marvin

SuperFriends: The Legendary Super Powers Show (1984) TV Series . . . . Darkseid/Kalibak

Swat Kats: The Radical Squadron (1993) TV Series . . . . Dr. Elrod Purvis/Dr. Viper/Volcanus/A-1/Captain Snow/Additional Voices

Sylvester and Tweety Mysteries, The (1995) TV Series . . . . Hector

Tabitha and Adam and the Clown Family (1972) TV . . . . Mike

Tale Spin (1990) TV Series . . . . Wildey Pole/Additional Voices

Tales of Tillie's Dragon, The (1998)

Teenage Mutant Ninja Turtles II: The Secret of the Ooze (1991) . . . . Rahzar/Tokka

Three Robonic Stooges, The (1977) TV Series . . . . Curly

Tigger Movie, The (2000) . . . . Additional Voices

Tiny Toon Adventures (1990) TV Series . . . . Gogo Dodo/Furball Cat/Various Voices

Tiny Toon Adventures: How I Spent My Vacation (1992) . . . . Uncle Stinky/Byron Basset/Furball Cat/Little Beeper

Tiny Toons Spring Break (1994) TV

Tom and Jerry: The Magic Ring (2002) . . . . Jerry Bear/Elephant/Elmer/Surveillance Guard/Mouse/Scarecrow/Squirrel/Vulture/Venus Flytrap

Tom and Jerry Kids Show (1990) TV Series

Top Cat and the Beverly Hills Cats (1987)

Trail Mix-Up (1993) . . . . Bear/Beaver

Transformers (1984) TV Series . . . . Blades/Buzzsaw/Chromedome/Frenzy/Galvatron/Groove/Laserbeak/Megatron/Mirage/Mixmaster/Ratbat/Ravage/Rumble/Skywarp/Sludge/Soundwave/Superion #1/Trailbreaker/Wheelie/Pinpointer/Pop-Lock/Teletran 2/Additional Voices

Transformers: Scramble City Hatsudôhen (1986) . . . . Jaguar

Transformers: The Headmasters (1987) TV Series . . . . Soundwave/Soundblaster (U.S. edition)

Transformers: The Movie (1986) . . . . Megatron/Soundwave/Rumble/Frenzy/Laserbeak/Wheelie/
   Junkion
Treehouse Hostage (1999) . . . . Kato
Turbo Teen (1984) TV Series . . . . Flip/Rusty/Dark Rider
Uncle Gus in: For the Love of Monkeys (1999) TV . . . . Dwayne/Monkey #1/TV Interviewer
Wakko's Wish (1999) . . . . Baron Thaddeus von Plotz III/Ralph the Security Guard/Runt
Watch the Birdy (1975) . . . . Puggs/Louie
Waynehead (1996) TV Series . . . . Tripod
What's New Scooby-Doo? (2002) TV Series . . . . Freddy Jones/Scooby-Doo
Wheelie and the Chopper Bunch (1974) TV Series . . . . Wheelie/Chopper
Where's Waldo? (1991) TV Series . . . . Additional Voices
Wish for Wings That Work, A (1991) TV . . . . Santa Claus
Wizard of Oz, The (1990) TV Series . . . . Toto
Wolf Rock TV (1982) TV Series . . . . Bopper
Xyber 9: New Dawn (1999) TV Series
Yogi Bear and the Magical Flight of the Spruce Goose (1987) . . . . Merkin

BILLY WEST

If there is anyone worthy to succeed the mantle of Mel Blanc, one of the top contenders would have to be Billy West, the actor who is now voicing some of Blanc's most popular characters. In addition to his dead-on impressions, West has been all over the dial with an astonishing diversity of characterizations, including Ren & Stimpy, many of *Futurama's* leads—Philip Fry, Professor Farnsworth, Dr. Zoidberg, and Zapp Brannigan—and advertising staples like the current Cherrio's Honeybee and the red M & M, whom he has tried to play as "a candy-covered Leonardo DiCaprio."

Although West is blessed with a flexible voice that can go to the "basement" or up into the "stratosphere," in retrospect, his future profession may have seemed an unlikely choice for the admittedly shy child. At his childhood home in Detroit, radio was a frequent source of entertainment and West was inspired to imitate the singers and announcers. One of his earliest childhood memories is of doing an Elvis impersonation at the age of two, which, he says, "basically consisted of me jumping up and down on the bed naked, except for a pair of my father's shoes, singing 'Blue Suede Shoes.'" While West insists that he "was never a class clown," he was known to do imitations of his teachers, which, when caught, would result in a command performance in front of the entire class.

The young cartoon fan first had a glimpse of his future career when he was just old enough to read. Watching the credits fly by at the end of the cartoons, West was puzzled that even though he had heard twenty or more voices, there were only one or two actors mentioned in the credits. "I was hit in the head with lightning when it occurred to me that it was one or two people doing multiple voices and it blew my mind! I knew that some wackball adult was responsible, somehow." The adults that he saw most often mentioned, Hanna-Barbera's Daws Butler and Don Messick, as well as *Popeye's* Jackson Beck, quickly became his heroes and inspirations.

As he grew to adulthood, a passion for music and for performing voices grew and eventually became more intertwined. For years West sang and played guitar for various bands and would take advantage of appearing on stage by throwing in some "goofy" improvisational comedy between songs and sets; but he was disappointed when he tried his hand at serious stand-up comedy in 1978. "The problem was that nobody told me that you're supposed to have an act. I used to go out and do whatever I felt like doing. Sometimes it would be great and other times people would throw rocks. . . . I think that's why I took to radio."

For that, West was granted a unique opportunity courtesy of a friend. In 1980, his friend was hired to install burglar alarms at the home of a Boston disc jockey and convinced the DJ to listen to West's demo tape. West was then called to WBCN in Boston, where he was given carte blanche to perform character voices and impressions and write comedy bits. But West soon realized that creating a daily radio show was far more difficult than playing around on stage between musical sets. "Radio is such a disposable form of medium that you'd be drained at the end of every morning—because I was doing like fifteen or sixteen voices per morning sometimes." His routines also included women as "no one would get paid in those days; they didn't stick around for very long. And that was my first stuff—was doing radio comedy."

By 1989, West made the move to WXRK in New York City, only to find himself relegated to inane contest promotion, where he was required to repeat incessantly, "New York, home of classic rock 'n' roll!" Knowing that he was going to lose his mind if he stayed in the dead-end job, he found his lifeline was a short walk down the hallway. There he joined forces (albeit part-time) with Howard Stern's infamous crew—performing offbeat characters and celebrity impressions.

By the mid-1990s, following an unsuccessful attempt to join Stern full-time, West's wife, Violet, urged him to try Los Angeles. With commercial and series work to his credit, his demo tape found its way into the hands of the Bob Clampett family, who were working on a 1988 revival of the 1960s hit *Beany and Cecil*. Although the assistant producer on the program, future *Ren & Stimpy* creator John Krisfaluci, gives credit to the Clampett family for discovering West, it was Krisfaluci who was knocked out by West's Larry Fine impersonation, among his other assorted characterizations. Krisfaluci said he persuaded the Clampetts that West would be an excellent choice for the program. With that, West began his cartoon career in earnest.

Of course, it was Krisfaluci's eventual collaboration with West on *Ren & Stimpy* that put both the animator and voice actor squarely on the map. Kricfalusi says that while he interviewed a few voice people for the *Ren & Stimpy* pilot, he "thought of Billy instantly." Although Krisfaluci initially performed Ren to West's Stimpy at the beginning of the series, West recalls that in the planning stages, he was asked to do both leads at Krisfaluci's request. But whatever occurred, by the second season Krisfaluci became too busy with his responsibilities as an animator to double as voice actor and the character fell to West. West recalls that the character bible describes the psychotic Chihuahua as "impatient and easy to anger. . . . He was a manipulative, real dysfunctional dad, kind of—quintessential asshole ala Jackie Gleason." West infused the character with different emotional shades through the root of different actors—what he terms as "the two phases of Peter Lorre, the real manic screaming one and the real quiet menacing one." West graced Ren with a touch of Kirk Douglas, using "emotional quotes" and actual lines from different old movies as well as a touch of Burl Ives ("not the nice Burl Ives, the folk singer, [but] the real bastard that was in *Cat on a Hot Tin Roof* and *Ensign Pulver*"). Finally, since Ren was a Chihuahua, he was subject to the occasional Mexican accent. "It was the weirdest amalgam, because it was always mutating."

Kricfalusi was also looking for a fresh and original voice for the large, mindlessly cheerful feline, specifying that it not be some "stock stupid character voice." West, who agrees that the audience always wants to hear something that is rooted in some kind of reality, certainly different than the stereotypical "cloying" cartoony voice, tried a few options before they hit on a variation of the Larry Fine voice. What came out was, as West concludes, "a very strange amalgam of many different voices" that did not sound exactly like Fine. Although Kricfalusi agreed it was "not what [he] thought of when [he] first thought about Stimpy," West comments that Stimpy "had to be able to live and exist in a cartoon universe by role-playing or being able to do lots of things." Therefore, he saw an impression of Fine's "beautiful non-voice" as "a good jumping-off point because you couldn't have a retarded cartoon cat just sound like a depressed old Jewish guy."

When the program premiered, West was delighted that it was an immediate smash and was amazed that the program was part of an important trend in animation. Citing the fact that there was an effort to capitalize on adult-oriented animation and that this had reached a new level of awareness in the 1990s, West noted that the upstart networks wanted to define their corporate identities with animated characters. Fledgling Warner Bros. network used Michigan J. Frog as a logo, following Fox, whose flagship animated program was *The Simpsons,* and MTV, which wanted to be identified with their biggest ratings accomplishment—*Beavis and Butthead.* Especially considering that there was so much publicized animosity between Nickelodeon and Kricfalusi's Spumco production studio, West found it amusing that Nickelodeon wanted their public identity inexorably linked with *Ren & Stimpy.* West recalls, "I saw on billboards in New York City—at every bus stop there for a while—a big picture of Stimpy next to a bunch of pissed-off rival network executives. [The copy read] our ratings are up over theirs and this and that. But they hung their whole identity on this stupid retarded cat."

West's lower-key follow-up to the infamous cartoon duo was Doug Funnie of the self-titled show. *Doug,* which was pitched by Nickelodeon executive Vanessa Coffey practically in the same breath as *Ren & Stimpy* and *Rugrats,* was designed to "present a role model with a positive point of view." West conceived of him as "an anti–Bart Simpson. He was not in-your-face and he was not a wise guy. . . . Funnie was just kind of thoughtful—real sensitive," while the character of "Boomer" was inspired by "Flo" of the rock veteran duo Flo and Eddie. West was especially impressed by the visuals and the storylines in which the morality was "story driven" and not as "preachy" as straightforward morality plays.

In 1999, West was hired by some of the finest talent in Hollywood—in the form of *Simpson*'s creator Matt Groening's new production company—to provide the voice for several of the leads on Fox's science fiction send-up, *Futurama*. West came closest to his own voice with Philip Fry, a cryogenically frozen twentieth-century pizza delivery man who wakes up in the next century. While West enjoyed his time on the show, the program began on a bitter note when Phil Hartman (best known for his work on *Saturday Night Live* and in *The Simpsons*) suffered a particularly tragic death just before he was to assume the role of *Futurama*'s pompous captain, Zapp Brannigan. Fry was then christened "Philip" in Hartman's honor and West followed up with a Hartmanesqe impression for Brannigan. Calling the show his greatest professional accomplishment to date, West performed an astonishingly diverse assortment of characters, which demanded a formidable range and imagination—from the crab-like Dr. Zoidberg to the 147-year-old Professor Farnsworth.

While West performed in various original projects, he also gradually inherited some of Mel Blanc's choicest roles. For Fox Kids' *The Woody Woodpecker Show* in 1999, West had to copy Blanc's trademark laugh as well as Grace Stafford Lantz's vocals. This was in addition to Elmer Fudd, whom West characterizes as "tough" because of his "delicate, brain-dead delivery" interspersed with "full-fledged yelling and hollering." However, his most amazing Blanc characterization has to be that of a dead-on Bugs Bunny, which he has performed in 1999's *Space Jam* and the 2004 short *Hare and Loathing in Las Vegas*.

West recalls the intense competition for the Bugs Bunny role in 1995. At the time, he was living in New York and traveled to Hollywood at the suggestion of his agent, thinking, "'Oh, my God, wouldn't that be a kick in the ass to say that you were the guy that replaced Mel Blanc?' And I know that every voice guy was secretly dreaming about that. . . . I figured on the plane going out there—I said, 'How many guys do you suppose are in the United States of America? Suppose everybody that's any good in the United States goes to California to try out for this? How many, do you suppose, that are really any good at all? Five? Six?'"

When West reached California, he arrived at the audition to find "eight million Daffy Ducks" and "twenty Bugs Bunnys." He recalls, "The sign-in sheet went from the desk it was sitting on to around the block of people auditioning for Mel Blanc's roles. And it dawned on me. They got one nut that can do a perfect Bugs Bunny from 1939 to 1944. And then there's some screwball who could do the perfect Bugs Bunny from the war years to the "Tang" Bugs Bunny in the '60s."

Although he has remarked that he has been concerned that much of the now famous Warner Bros. cartoons of animation's Golden Age were of their time and the "best work was done before we were born," he has deftly continued in Blanc's tradition as Bugs Bunny in 1996's *Space Jam* and Elmer Fudd for 2003's *Looney Tunes: Back in Action*. West paid tribute to the virtuoso in a 1999 *Chicago Sun-Times* article: "All roads lead to Mel Blanc. He did it all. . . . He was a great actor, more than someone who could do goofball voices. He could provide solid dimension to characters. That's always on my mind, to flush it out and give some dimension."

At the same time, West is cognizant that he cannot be considered the next Mel Blanc by simply impersonating Blanc's voices, rather than attaching his name to characters he is able to personally fashion. Although he has passion for his art, he views himself as ultimately having a "kind of a journeyman mentality." Saying that he believes he is currently working at a fraction of his potential and that he may one day try his hand at writing, he focuses on one objective for all of his cartoon and advertising voice-over work. "If somebody wants to hire me, I hope I'm the best person for the job . . . whether it's a Lego's commercial or *Ren & Stimpy* or an AT&T voice-over or the Honeynut Cheerios Bee or Doug. It's kind of all of equal importance because it's part of the craft. And you can't always get the coolest job in the world." Invoking the later work of Orson Welles, West comments that Welles must have known that his last job on 1984's *Mighty Orbots* was not "high art." He then reasons, "He just probably wanted to work. . . . He was Orson Welles. He wanted to bring something to the party; I kind of feel like that." But in the animation voice-over business, West concludes, he cannot take himself too seriously; after all, he says "One day you are a talking armpit and the next day you're a bottle of beach."

CREDITS

Aero-Troopers: The Nemeclous Crusade (2003) Video
CatDog (1998) TV Series . . . . Rancid Rabitt/Mr. Sunshine/Randolph
Cats & Dogs (2001) . . . . Ninja Cat
Comic Book: The Movie (2004) . . . . Leo Matuzik
Crank Yankers (2002) TV Series . . . . Moo-Shu
Detention (1999) TV Series . . . . Emmitt Roswell
Dinosaur (2000) . . . . Additional Voices
Doug (1991) TV Series . . . . Douglas "Doug" Funnie/Roger M. Klotz
Escape from Atlantis (1997) TV . . . . Voice Characterizations
Extreme Ghostbusters (1997) TV Series . . . . Slimer/Mayor McShane

Futurama (1999) TV Series .... Philip J. Fry/Professor Hubert Farnsworth/Dr. Zoidberg/Captain
   Zapp Brannigan/Leo Wong/Additional Voices
Histeria! (1998) TV Series .... Confucious/Benjamin Franklin/Additional Voices
Invader Zim (2001) TV Series .... Invader Zim
Jimmy Neutron: Boy Genius (2001) .... Poultra/Girl Eating Plant/Oyster/Yokian Officer/Jailbreak
   Cop/Guard/Robobarber/Anchor Boy/Old Man Johnson/Flurp Announcer/Bobby's Twin
   Brother/Butch
Joe's Apartment (1996) .... Ralph Roach
Looney Tunes: Back in Action (2003) .... Elmer Fudd/Peter Lorre
Looney Tunes: Stranger Than Fiction (2003) Video .... Elmer Fudd
Magician, The (1998) TV Series .... Cosmo Cooper
Mind Meld: Secrets behind the Voyage of a Lifetime (2001) Video .... Narrator
Museum Scream (2003) .... Tweety
My Generation G . . . G . . . Gap (2003) .... Porky Pig
Oblongs, The (2001) TV Series .... George Klimer/Anita Bidet/James/Others
Olive, the Other Reindeer (1999) TV .... Mr. Eskimo
Phobophilia: The Love of Fear (1995) TV (voice)
Project G.e.e.K.e.R. (1996) TV Series .... Geeker
Ren & Stimpy Show, The (1991) TV Series .... Stimpson J. Cat (1991–1996)/Ren Hoek (1993–1996)
Rugrats in Paris: The Movie—Rugrats II (2000) .... Sumo Singer
Scooby-Doo on Zombie Island (1998) Video .... Norville "Shaggy" Rogers
Space Jam (1996) .... Bugs Bunny/Elmer Fudd
Stooges: The Men behind the Mayhem (1994) TV .... Himself
Super Santa in Vegetation (2002) TV .... Dr. Miranda/Kid/Potato
Tom and Jerry: The Magic Ring (2002) Video .... Freddie
Toonsylvania (1998) TV Series (voice)
Voltron: The Third Dimension (1998) TV Series .... Pidge
Weird Al Show, The (1997) TV Series .... Announcer/Various Characters

PAUL WINCHELL

The most impressive aspect of Paul Winchell's career is not that he has
become one of the country's most respected ventriloquists or one of the
earliest television stars or the fact that he provided the voice for *Winnie
the Pooh's* Tigger, Dick Dastardly, or Gargamel on *The Smurfs*. These
accomplishments pale in comparison to his efforts in the field of medicine
as the co-creator of an early version of the artificial heart. But in reaching his impressive achievements in his three major interests — theater,
medicine, and art — he had to quell some personal demons, in the process,
coming to terms with his ultra-religious upbringing and forging a new relationship with himself.

Born on December 21, 1922, in Manhattan and raised in Coney
Island, Winchell recounts his restrictive childhood in his 1982 book, *God
2000*. "I was brought up with orthodox old Testament standards. . . .

The celebration of Passover was mingled with angry threats [from his mother] that God would punish me for my transgressions—"sins" no greater than those committed by any little boy as he grows up. . . . She was a very disturbed woman, but I didn't know that then. If I did anything that upset her, it was greeted by my mother's curses: 'God should only strike you dead! . . . God will punish you for being bad—you should only burn in Hell!' And as soon as anything happened that hurt me, there came the reinforcer: 'See, God punished you.'" Winchell writes that she was obsessed with death and the afterlife and constantly made promises and threats about what would happen after her death. "'Oh, my son, my son, who will take care of you after I'm gone? Without me you will die too.'"

Winchell said he was then saddled with an unrelenting, obsessive guilt, but managed to channel his energy in a positive direction. He had hoped to one day become a doctor, but knowing his Depression-era family had no money for medical school tuition, the thirteen-year-old turned his attention to something far less expensive—ventriloquism. While recovering from a bout with polio, Winchell found an ad in a magazine, invested ten cents and sent away for a kit. Of course, the whistle designed to help throw voices did not work, but Winchell studied the accompanying booklet intently. "I was going to an art school where we were doing sculpturing and painting and lettering. I asked my teacher if I could possibly create a ventriloquist's dummy, and if that would be applicable toward credit." With the permission of his art teacher, Jerry Magon, Winchell fashioned a dummy and named it Jerry Mahoney, using his teacher's first name as a way of thanking him. It was not too long before he started entertaining the class with ad-libbed routines.

As Winchell focused his energies into his burgeoning career, he gradually "put away" the tortuous memories of his childhood, believing "it was over and forgotten." He took his comedy routine, five minutes of jokes culled from a magazine, and competed on a coast-to-coast radio show called *The Major Bowes Amateur Hour*. "I went on the radio show and won first prize. I received an offer to go touring, playing vaudeville theaters with the *Major Bowes* review. I was then discovered by an orchestra leader named Ted Weems. He came to see me with his two vocalists, Perry Como and Marilyn Maxwell, who were unknown at the time, and they made me an offer to go touring with them. That's when I turned professional." At the age of fourteen, Winchell dropped out of high school and began playing various theaters and nightclubs, which eventually led to a five-year stint on his own radio show. Then came the advent of television, though not in the form anyone can imagine today.

Television pioneer Allen Dumont had been working on electronic receivers throughout the 1930s, and in the early '40s began his own network: WABD, channel 5 in New York City. Though many people saw television as a passing fad, Winchell saw a great opportunity. "They were doing television experimentation, and my very first television series (*Winchell and Mahoney Show*) was in 1947 when there were only three hundred sets in the entire country. If I wanted someone to see my show, I used to have to invite them down to the department store. We did our show in the department store because there weren't any studios. . . . Then performers began to get into it. Many more sets began to be purchased, and I began to appear as a guest. I appeared on Ed Sullivan's show and Milton Berle's *Texaco Star Theatre* several times."

Having seen Winchell as a guest on other shows, Bigelow rugs offered to sponsor him in a series of his own. "It was a very unusual kind of show because there was no connection between me and the other star, whose name was Dunninger. We went on the air in 1949, and Dunninger did the first half of the program and I did the second half, totally disjointed. In those days when you went to the network, if they liked the performer, they bought the show. They didn't care what you were going to do. When you asked them what kind of format they were going to have, they'd just shrug their shoulders and say, 'I don't know; do what you think is right.' TV has changed considerably since then."

After the demise of the *Dunninger/Winchell Show*, Winchell was hired for a show called *What's Up*, a variety show that, in addition to his ventriloquism, featured Hollywood guests, singers, dancers, and dramatic acting. The show proved to be very popular, but around 1954, after several years of doing television variety, Winchell became interested in entertaining children. This ultimately led to *Jerry Mahoney's Clubhouse*—a children's show that not only was entertaining but also had educational elements. However, Winchell soon realized that when pitching a new show, producers found "education" to be a dirty word. "If you're going to sell a show and you mention educational, you've lost it, so I decided to call it an entertaining show with enlightening overtones."

Winchell used his children's format to explain ordinary, everyday occurrences that might otherwise frighten kids. "When a kid wakes up in the middle of the night because he hears a strange noise, he begins to get anxiety. If he comes from a family that is religiously oriented, then what's coming along could be ghosts or souls. If he comes from a family that is not religiously oriented, then it could be a burglar or an intruder. They don't have an option. I had a song called 'Night Noises' that explained that the house itself makes noise because it goes through so many climactic changes. I designed the show to give them something valuable." *Jerry Mahoney's Clubhouse* was followed in rapid succession by *Toyland Express* (ABC, 1955), *Circus Time* (ABC, 1956), *Five Star Comedy* (ABC, 1957), and *The Paul Winchell Show* (ABC, 1957). It looked as though Winchell had secured a permanent position in the relatively new medium.

Enjoying his newfound fame, Winchell had no idea that his amazingly good fortune would, just as quickly, turn into a long, unstoppable slide—which ended with him on the inside of an asylum. "In the '50s, with the advent of television, I seemed to function as a totally different person in my bid for stardom as a ventriloquist. I was achieving a good measure of success when a call summoned me to my dying mother's bedside. She lingered for a week, during which she rekindled all the terror of God, death, and ghosts, in a mind I had assumed had matured."

With the death of Winchell's mother, he wrote that he became acutely aware of his own mortality. Though successful, he regretted that his academic education had been sorely neglected. At thirty-five, he realized he now had the money to pursue his interest in medicine, so he enrolled in pre-med at Columbia University. There he went on rounds with interns and had the opportunity to watch all kinds of operations. Ever conscious of his mother's death due to heart failure, he watched open-heart surgery and was suddenly struck with the idea of the artificial heart. The authorities refused to take his concept seriously. "People think you are what you do. I'm a ventriloquist, but I'm just a person who *learned* how to do ventriloquism. I was told to go home and play with my dummies."

Undaunted by derisive comments from the "experts," Winchell continued his medical research until, as he detailed in *God 2000*, his world was once again shattered by his mother; this time from beyond the grave. "About a year after her death, at the unveiling of her tombstone, the hammers of Hell began to pound in my head . . . and suddenly—she was back! My mother had returned from the grave just as she said she would. From that day on she was with me every moment. I developed pathological terror and began to lose control. I finally fragmented and was committed to a psych ward. . . . Haunted by my mother's ghost, I could no longer function as an entertainer, so I walked out on my career and myself."

Winchell recalls the horror of that period of his life. "I was so riddled with anxiety that I turned to drugs, alcohol, and sexual debauchery. I looked to psychiatrists for help. What they gave me were labels: 'manic depressive' and 'obsessive compulsive.' I attempted to end my life and wound up in mental institutions on three occasions. I have been tied hand and foot to psychiatric slabs for twenty-four-hour periods, locked in padded rooms where no one responds to imploring pleas for help. If you need to go to the toilet, too bad. If the restraints are too tight, too bad. Perhaps you have seen the film *One Flew over the Cuckoo Nest* or read the book. They are only too accurate."

While those kinds of difficulties may be looked upon with a sympathetic eye in the current day, it was a far different world almost forty years ago. When Winchell finally came out of the nightmare with the help of years of more modern therapy, he relocated to California in 1962 to pick up the pieces and start all over again. He proved extremely resilient, doing guest spots on shows, including *The Beverly Hillbillies*, and resuming his ventriloquism with dummies Jerry Mahoney and Knucklehead Smiff, while success in commercial voice-overs established him as a reliable pitchman. Soon he found himself working for the legendary animation team of Hanna and Barbera, all the while continuing his medical research.

Finally, on July 16, 1963, he was granted U.S. patent 3,097,366 for an early version of the artificial heart. But when he asked the American Medical Association and the American Heart Association for funds to build a prototype of the breakthrough invention, his request was politely denied. The project was shelved until Dr. William Kolff, the inventor of the first heart-lung machine and artificial kidney machine, began designing his own version of the artificial heart. Kolff soon found, to his surprise, that they had independently derived the same basic design and he was infringing on the ventriloquist's patent. Winchell subsequently signed over his rights to Dr. Kolff and the University of Utah so they could continue with development. However, Winchell says, part of the contractual agreement included giving Winchell access to the hospital, clinics, and labs to continue his own research.

By 1968, Winchell's career in the field of animated voice-overs was only beginning. In that year, his long association with Hanna-Barbera began when he was heard as the voice of Dick Dastardly for the *Wacky Racers*. Dastardly, with his snickering canine sidekick, Muttley, garnered enough attention to warrant a spin-off series the following year, *Dastardly and Muttley in Their Flying Machines*, in which their attempts to "Stop that pigeon!" were foiled weekly. But it was another assignment in 1968 which became his mainstay for thirty years, one of the most endearing characters of all time, and his personal favorite.

Disney introduced "Tigger" in the Academy Award—winning *Winnie the Pooh and the Blustery Day*. Although the character is not too far from his natural speaking voice, Winchell was very surprised to be chosen to play the lovable, bouncy tiger. At the auditions, it seemed as if everybody in the Hollywood voice-over community was vying for the role. "Paul Frees was there, and Shepard Menken, Daws Butler, and Don Messick. The place was just filled with all of Hollywood's talent." The fact that Winchell went in knowing nothing of the character or the script made him somewhat anxious. "The studio has you come in ice cold. You walk in, they show you storyboards of what the character is, and . . . GO! At the drop of a hat you have to improvise and make it all up. It's only on the way home that you begin to digest all of this stuff and think creatively; then you say, 'Oh my. Why didn't I do this kind of a voice?' An old gag about voice people is that they do their best reading on the way home in the car." Fortunately, Disney liked his studio reading, and he was on his way to becoming an animation icon.

The 1970s found Winchell's animation star on the rise with no sign of fading. An abundance of television work for Hanna-Barbera, including Fleegle on *The Banana Splits Adventure Hour*, Bubi Bear on *Help, It's the Hair Bear Bunch*, and Goober of *Goober and the Ghost Chasers*, balanced nicely with his work on Disney theatricals. After playing the Chinese Cat in *The Aristocrats* and Boomer in *The Fox and the Hound*, he reprised his role as Tigger in *Winnie the Pooh and Tigger Too*, for which he won a Best Recording for Children Grammy in 1974 for the film's soundtrack. He kept his live-action skills honed as host of the children's game show *Runaround* (1972) and with guest-starring roles such as a hippie director of detergent commercials on *The Brady Bunch*.

But the 1970s also found Winchell keeping up with his medical studies. In 1974, he graduated from Acupuncture Research Institute College (and later co-authored the 1984 book *Acupuncture without Needles* with Keith E. Kenyon). The following year, he received a D.S.C. degree from National Christian University. "I work on a lot of things. I'm a hypnotherapist and I work with paraplegics and quadriplegics, trying to get them motivated to begin some new techniques because when they come to us, they are absolutely hopeless. They've been told by their doctors that they'll never ever walk or move, and I have to work to try and dispel all of that. I get them fired up, because there are new things that can help."

Winchell has tried to use his position as voice-over artist to innovate cartoons as well. He even saw the ultimate in politically correct cartoons, *The Smurfs*, as a possible forum for social concerns. "I think they should have dealt with racial issues because the Smurfs are all blue. What if a red Smurf showed up and no one wants to deal with him because he's red? Without getting specific, you are already dealing with a racial issue. I had another idea I thought was funny. I said, 'Let's make a lawyer Smurf. We'd call him Smurfy Smurf. Whenever you ask him something, he pulls out a paper and says, 'According to Smurfy's law . . . ' Hanna-Barbera didn't like that. They didn't like the red Smurf idea either. They usually ignored any ideas I came up with."

Regardless, Winchell still saw *The Smurfs* as an educational show with "the same kind of appeal as *Snow White and the Seven Dwarfs*." He enjoyed giving voice to Gargamel, as he saw it as more of an acting challenge than just coming up with another voice. In developing the character Gargamel, Hanna-Barbera wanted an evil, lascivious kind of guy, but not really frightening. "Make him evil, but make him funny. That's why I added the laugh . . . so it doesn't sound that diabolical. I didn't want to scare the kids." He enjoyed doing so throughout *The Smurfs* nine-year run.

By the 1990s, his demons were behind him and his plans for the future seemed unstoppable, until fate took another turn. Despite preventive measures, including abstinence from smoking and weight-training with a low cholesterol diet, Winchell was forced to undergo double by-pass surgery. It had been more than thirty years since his mother succumbed to heart disease, and now it had been revisited upon him. Ironically, the artificial heart that he had labored on over the years was not an option since, due to eventual multiple organ failures in long-term usage, its only function was to buy time for transplant candidates.

Moreover, during the course of the surgery, Winchell suffered a stroke which left him with diminished vision. While he was recovering, Jim Cummings, who was already doing the voice of Winnie the Pooh, took over the job of Tigger on the 1998 film *Tigger's Family Tree*. According to a report in *USA Today*, Winchell's voice was deemed "too raspy" by Disney executives and he was let go after one day's work on the film. Disney executives publicly defended themselves by claiming that they considered his day's work an "audition." Although his then agent Don Pitts complained, saying that previous client Mel Blanc was allowed to perform his characters until he passed away, executives refused to listen to appeals or public comment. Undaunted by Disney's decision, and once again proving his boundless resiliency and optimism, Winchell successfully underwent physical rehabilitation and concentrated on planning future projects.

Recovered and regaining his professional momentum, Winchell has channeled his energy into a myriad of projects, including the Kids World Network (kwn.com), which utilizes video streaming to showcase children's television shows from the past and present. in 2004, he published a brutally honest autobiography entitled *Winch*, which details his bouts with mental illness and his struggles with personal demons. Winchell cautions those looking for a wholesome trip down memory lane. "It's not at all like anybody would expect ... that it's about show biz and it's got all the celebrities, like all the rest of them; believe me, it is not. It's totally frank, open, honest, laid out there in front with all the mental problems and everything. There's nothing private about me that I want to hide. I don't care what skeletons are out there." If, after finishing Winchell's autobiography the reader is still wanting for more, the Internet site paulwinchell.com keeps his fans up to date on current events in his life.

If Winchell ever considers the entertainment field too mundane, he's still excited about the progress of science and medicine and constantly conjures up new ideas, including a new device to create energy from ocean waves. Although he already holds thirty patents, he has been soured on the patenting process. "Too many of my patents have been knocked off, too many have been stolen, and if I want to bring an injunction to stop them, I have to put up almost a half million dollars before I begin as a bond." To document his claim to his innovations, he says, "I keep a log of every phase of development. I have these signed by people as witnesses to the date, the pictures, and drawings. Ultimately, that gives me pretty good protection."

If his inventions, his part at television's inception (with his puppet sidekicks on permanent display at the Smithsonian Institution), or his establishing the voice of Tigger (a character that has now earned, literally, more than a billion dollars for Disney) are not a fitting legacy, then perhaps his children, who all followed in his footsteps, are. "I've got three major interests. One is theatrical, one is medical, one is art. My oldest daughter is the head of the art department in an advertising agency. My son is a nurse-practitioner. They all are in one field or another of what I have pursued. It's got to be genetic." At least one of his daughters, voice actor April Winchell, would probably agree—his ten-cent tuition for his ventriloquist's kit provided him and his family with a life far more interesting than medical school ever could have.

CREDITS

Adams of Eagle Lake (1975) TV Series .... Monty
Aristocats, The (1970) .... Chinese Cat
Banana Splits Adventure Hour, The (1968) TV Series .... Fleegle
Beverly Hillbillies, The (1962) TV Series .... Homer Winch (1962)
Bigelow Show, The (1948) TV Series .... Himself (regular performer)
Blue Aces Wild (1973)

Casper and the Angels (1979) TV Series
Clue Club (1976) TV Series . . . . Woofer
Dastardly and Muttley in Their Flying Machines (1969) TV Series . . . . Dick Dastardly/General
Dr. Seuss on the Loose (1973) TV . . . . White Dog in Hat (segment: "Green Eggs and Ham")
Everything's on Ice (1939) . . . . Voice of Dummy
Fox and the Hound, The (1981) . . . . Boomer
Fred Flintstone and Friends (1977) TV Series (voice)
Goober and the Ghost-Chasers (1973) TV Series . . . . Goober
Gummi Bears, The (1985) TV Series . . . . Zummi (1985–1989)
Heathcliff (1980) TV Series . . . . Marmaduke (1981–1982)
Help! It's the Hair Bear Bunch (1971) TV Series . . . . Bubi Bear
Jetsons, The (1962) TV Series . . . . Additional Voices
Killarney Blarney (1973)
Kingdom Chums: Little David's Adventure, The (1986) TV . . . . King Saul
Many Adventures of Winnie the Pooh, The (1977) . . . . Tigger
New Adventures of Winnie the Pooh, The (1988) TV Series . . . . Tigger (1988–1989)
Oddball Couple, The (1975) TV Series . . . . Fleabag
Paul Winchell and Jerry Mahoney Show, The (1950) TV Series . . . . Himself
Perils of Penelope Pitstop (1969) TV Series . . . . Clyde/Softy
Pooh's Grand Adventure: The Search for Christopher Robin (1997) Video . . . . Tigger
Skatebirds, The (1977) TV Series . . . . Moe Howard/Woofer
Smurfs, The (1981) TV Series . . . . Gargamel (1981–1989)/Baby Smurf/Nosey Smurf
Spider-Man (1981) TV Series (voice)
Stooge Snapshots (1984) TV (archive footage) . . . . Himself (in interview)
Tabitha and Adam and the Clown Family (1972) TV . . . . Ronk/Mr. McGurk/Haji/Ducks/Railroad
  Conductor
These Are the Days (1974) TV Series (voice)
Three Robonic Stooges, The (1977) TV Series . . . . Moe
Vernon's Volunteers (1969) TV . . . . Chief Vernon
Wacky Races (1968) TV Series . . . . Dick Dastardly/Clyde/Private Meekley
Wheelie and the Chopper Bunch (1974) TV Series . . . . Revs
Which Way to the Front? (1970) . . . . Schroeder
Winnie the Pooh: A Valentine for You (1998) TV . . . . Tigger
Winnie the Pooh: Imagine That, Christopher Robin (1999) Video . . . . Tigger
Winnie the Pooh: Seasons of Giving (1999) Video . . . . Tigger
Winnie the Pooh and Christmas Too (1991) TV . . . . Tigger
Winnie the Pooh and the Blustery Day (1968) . . . . Tigger
Winnie the Pooh and Tigger Too! (1974) . . . . Tigger
Winnie the Pooh Friendship: Clever Little Piglet (1999) Video . . . . Tigger
Winnie the Pooh Friendship: Pooh Wishes (1999) Video . . . . Tigger
Winnie the Pooh Friendship: Tigger-ific Tales (1988) Video . . . . Tigger
Winnie the Pooh Learning: Working Together (1999) Video . . . . Tigger
Winnie the Pooh Playtime: Cowboy Pooh (1997) Video . . . . Tigger
Winnie the Pooh Playtime: Detective Tigger (1997) Video . . . . Tigger
Winnie the Pooh Playtime: Fun 'n' Games (1998) Video . . . . Tigger
Winnie the Pooh Playtime: Happy Pooh Day (1998) Video . . . . Tigger
Winnie the Pooh Thanksgiving, A (1998) Video . . . . Tigger (speaking)
Yogi Bear and the Magical Flight of the Spruce Goose (1987) . . . . Dread Baron
Yogi's Treasure Hunt (1978) TV Series . . . . Dick Dastardly

SELECTED BIBLIOGRAPHY

Books

Blanc, Mel, and Philip Bashe. *That's Not All Folks! My Life in the Golden Age of Cartoons and Radio*. New York: Warner Books, 1998.

Blu, Susan, and Molly Ann Mullin. *Word of Mouth: A Guide to Commercial Voice-Over Excellence*. Los Angeles: Pomegranate Press, 1987.

Cabarga, Leslie. *The Fleischer Story*. New York: DaCapo Press, 1988.

Cartwright, Nancy. *My Life as a 10-Year Old Boy*. Bloomsbury Publishers, Ltd, 2000.

Cohen, Karl. *Forbidden Animation: Censored Cartoons and Blacklisted Animators in America*. Jefferson, N.C.: McFarland & Co., 1997.

Cox, Wally. *My Life as a Small Boy*. New York: Simon and Schuster, 1961.

Crafton, Donald. *Before Mickey: The Animated Film, 1898–1928*. Cambridge, Mass.: MIT Press, 1982.

Culhane, Shamus. *Talking Animals and Other People*. New York: St. Martin's Press, 1986.

Dunning, John. *Tune in Yesterday: The Ultimate Encyclopedia of Old-Time Radio*. Englewood Cliffs, N.J.: Prentice Hall, 1976.

Edgar, Kathleen, Senior Ed. *Contemporary Theatre, Film, and Television*. Detroit and London: Gale, 1998.

Erickson, Hal. *Television Cartoon Shows: An Illustrated Encyclopedia, 1949–1993*. Jefferson, N.C.: McFarland & Company, 1995.

Goldschmidt, Rick. *The Enchanted World of Rankin-Bass.* Chicago: Miser Bros. Press, 2001.

Grossman, Gary. *Saturday Morning TV.* New York: Dell Publishing, 1987.

Guralnick, Peter. *Careless Love: The Unmaking of Elvis Presley.* New York: Little, Brown and Company, 2000.

Johnston, Ollie, and Frank Thomas. *The Disney Villain.* New York: Hyperion, 1993.

Katz, Ephraim. *The Film Encyclopedia,* 2nd ed. New York: Facts on File, 1991.

Lenburg, Jeff. *The Encyclopedia of Animated Cartoons.* New York: Facts on File, 1991.

Maltin, Leonard. *Of Mice and Magic.* New York: McGraw-Hill, 1980; rev. ed. New York: Plume-N.A.L., 1987.

Morley Harvey, Rita. *Those Wonderful, Terrible Years: George Heller and the American Federation of Television and Radio Artists.* Carbondale: Southern Illinois University Press, 1996.

Neuwirth, Allan. *Makin' Toons.* New York: Allworth Press, 2003.

Palmer, Edward. *Television and America's Children: A Crisis of Neglect.* New York: Oxford University Press, 1988.

Scott, Keith. *The Moose That Roared.* New York: St. Martin's Press, 2000.

Solomon, Charles. *Enchanted Drawings: The History of Animation.* New York: Alfred A. Knopf, 1989.

Webb, Graham. *The Animated Film Encyclopedia: A Complete Guide to American Shorts, Features, and Sequences, 1900–1979.* Jefferson, N.C.: McFarland & Company, 2000.

Winchell, Paul. *God 2000.* Santa Monica, Calif.: April Enterprises, 1982.

Articles

AFTRA newsletter. "Jackson Beck Celebrates, Celebrated." *Stand by NY* 35, no. 3 (summer 2002).

Allstetter, Rob. "Billy West Laughs It up for Cartoon." *Chicago Sun-Times,* May 21, 1999. Online. LexisNexis Academic. October 21, 2002.

Allwine, Wayne, and Russi Taylor. "EMuck—Allwine/Taylor Invited Talk Transcript." Rich Koster Moderator. Online Posting. January 30, 1997, July 15, 2003, <http://www.emuck.com :3000/archive/allwine-taylor.html>.

Armour. "The Inc. Spot: Armour Hangs out with Homer Simpson." *Chicago Tribune,* August 19, 2001.

Brioux, Bill. "Ears to You, Walt; Memories of Disney's Legendary Patriarch." *Toronto Sun,* November 25, 2001. Online. LexisNexis Academic. July 15, 2003.

Collins, Glenn. "When Mia Meets Mama, It's Mae Questel." *New York Times,* February, 26, 1989. Online. LexisNexis Academic. November 10, 2002.

Elber, Lynn. "Billy West Is Heard and Not Seen in His Roles as Voice of Animation." *St. Louis Post Dispatch,* July 16, 1999. Online. LexisNexis Academic. December 27, 2000.

Fanning, Jim. "Sterling Holloway." *Persistence of Vision* 6–7, August 19, 2003. <http://disneypov.com/issue06-7/characters.html>.

Goodman, Martin. "Tell the Story! An Interview with John Kricfalusi." *Animation World Magazine,* January 23, 2003.

Goodwin, Christopher. "How Do You Doh?" *Sunday Times* (London), August 13, 2000. Online. LexisNexis Academic. September 12, 2002.

———— "Original Tigger Voice Bounced from 'Pooh.'" *USA Today,* November 25, 1998. Online. LexisNexis Academic. August 29, 2002.

"Jean Vander Pyl—The Wilma Within." The Cartoon Network Website. 1995.

Lederer, Andrew. "Mae Questel: A Reminiscence, History, and Perspective." Animation World News. *Animation World Magazine*. 2, no. 12 (March 1998, November 10, 2002). <http://www .awn.com/mag/issue2.12/2.12pages/ 2.12lentererquestel.ht ml>.

Mason, Dave. "Husband, Wife Team Make for Mousy Duo." *Chicago Sun-Times*, February 16, 2001. Online. LexisNexis Academic. July 15, 2003.

Miller, Bob. "Frank Welker: Master of Many Voices." *Animation World Magazine*. 5, no.1 (April 1, 2000, February 21, 2003). <http://www.awn.com/mag/issue5.01/5.01pages/ millerwelker02.php3>.

Olsen, Byran. "Tom Kenny." Standupcomic.com. Jananuary 6, 2003. <http://www.standupcomic .com/kenny.html>.

Pecchia, David. "He's All Talk—Voice Actor Moves between 'Pinky' and Jim Carrey." *Los Angeles Times Syndicate: Chicago Tribune*, January 18, 1998.

Roush, Matt. "'Ren & Stimpy' eez it//Animated Creator Is Ever Original." *USA Today*, August 11, 1992. Online. LexisNexis Academic. 27 December 2000.

Ryan, Will. "I Call on Charlie Adler." *Animation World Magazine*, February 1, 2001. November 10, 2002. http://mag.awn.com/index.php?ltype=search& sval=adler&article_no=65>.

Sibley, Celestine. "A Sterling Tribute to Cedartown's Favorite Son." *Atlanta Constitution*, May 2, 1999. Online. LexisNexis Academic. August 19, 2003.

Smallbridge, Justin. "Ren & Stimpy's Big Corporate Takeover." *Saturday Night*, April 1994.

Soucie, Kath. "And I Get Paid!?!: The Life of a Voice Actor." *Animation World Magazine*, March 1, 1998. <http://mag.awn.com/index.php?ltype=search& sval=soucie&article_no=96>.

Sterngold, James. "The Voice for Homer Simpson's 'Doh!" *New York Times*, July 16, 1997.

Wedman, Les. "Our First Lady of Acting." *Vancouver Courier*, July 29, 1987.

Television Sources

Judge, Mike. *The Late Show*. Interview with David Letterman. CBS Network, February 17, 1999.

Kunert, Arnold. *Daws Butler, Voice Magician*. Documentary. New York: Cinema Guild. Sabado Film Production, 1987.

Simpsons' Cast, The. *Inside the Actor's Studio*. Interview with James Lipton. Bravo Network, February 2003.

Internet Sources

awn.com (*Animation World Magazine*)
bcdb.com (Big Cartoon Database)
cartoonhistory.com (Animation historian Jerry Beck's web site)
Hollywood.com (Celebrity Biographies)
imdb.com (Internet Movie Database)
klaskycsupo.com (Official Klasky Csupo web site)
people.com (*People Magazine* web site)
povonline.com (Animation writer and expert Mark Evanier's web site)
museum.tv (Museum of Broadcast Communications, Chicago)

thesimpsons.com (*The Simpson*'s fan site)
tvguide.com (*TV Guide* online)
ultimatetv.com

Press Materials

Frees, Paul. Courtesy of Milton Kahn Associates. Public relations, 1984.
Holloway, Sterling, Courtesy of Kingsley Colton & Associates, Inc. November 1984.
Jay Ward Studios. Courtesy of Howard Brandy, Inc. November 24, 1961.
Kricfalusi, John. The SPUMCO Philosophy Press Release and assorted publicity materials courtesy of John Kricfalusi. 1995.
Reed, Alan. Courtesy of Hanna-Barbera. 1984.
Scott, Bill. Resume and other materials courtesy of Jay Ward Studios. 1984.
Vander Pyl, Jean. Courtesy of Hanna-Barbera. 1984.

Interviews

Adler, Charlie. Telephone interview. January 13, 1996.
Allen, Dayton. Telephone interview. October 2, 1984.
Andrade, Dino. Telephone interview. March 2003.
Barbera, Joe. Telephone interview. June 6, 1989.
Beals, Dick. Telephone interview. December 7, 1995.
Beck, Jackson. Telephone interview. February 20, 1995.
Bergman, Mary Kay. Telephone interview. May 18, 1995.
Blanc, Mel. Interview with Chuck Shaden, *Those Were the Days*, radio program, Chicago. 1978.
Butler, Charles. Telephone interview. 1999.
Butler, Daws. Remotely taped personal interview. June 18, 1984.
Cartwright, Nancy. Personal interview. March 23, 1995.
Caselotti, Adriana. Telephone interview. May 27, 1995.
Castellaneta, Dan. Telephone interview. April 6, 1995.
Clokey, Art. Telephone interview. April 20, 2000.
Coleman, Townsend. Telephone interview. December 30, 1995.
Covington, Tredwell. Telephone interview. November 15, 1989.
Cummings, Jim. Personal interview. April 19, 1996.
Daily, E.G. Telephone interview. December 14, 1995.
David, Nicole (Jaffe). Telephone interview. January 7, 2003.
Foray, June. Remotely taped personal interview. September 8, 1984.
Foray, June. Telephone interview. March 30, 2003.
Frees, Fred. Telephone interview. March 2003.
Frees, Paul. Telephone interview. July 28, 1984.
Gary, Linda. Telephone interview. April 30, 1995.
Guralnick, Peter. Telephone interview. March 2003.
Harris, Lee. Telephone interview. Febraury 24, 2004.
Hamlin, Bill. Personal interview. July 1999.
Judge, Mike. Telephone interview. April 2, 1996.

Kenny, Tom. "SpongeBob" lecture, Harper College, Palatine, Illinois. November 25, 2003.

Kricfalusi, John. Personal interview. March 23, 1995.

LaMarche, Maurice. Personal interview. March 23, 1996.

Macmillan, Norma. Telephone interview. April 29, 1989.

McFadden, Bob. Telephone interview. May 13, 1989.

Mercer, Virginia (Mrs. Jack). Telephone interview. April 10, 1995, and May 21, 1995.

Messick, Don. Remotely taped personal interview. July 7, 1984.

O'Hanlon, George. Telephone interview. July 19, 1984.

O'Hanlon, George, Jr. Telephone interview. September 24, 2002.

O'Hanlon, Laurie. Telephone interview. July 12, 1989, and September 23, 2002.

Paulsen, Rob. Telephone interview. May 4, 1995, and May 5, 1995.

Pope, Tony. Personal interview. March 25, 1995.

Rayle, Hal. Telephone interview. 1996.

Reed, Alan. Interview with Chuck Shaden, *Those Were the Days*, radio program, Chicago. February 17, 1975.

Sarandon, Chris. Personal interview. March 21, 1995.

Schreffler, Marilyn. Personal interview. October 14, 1984.

Seegar, Hal. Telephone interview. July 7, 1989.

Soucie, Kath. Personal interview. March 20, 1995.

Vander Pyl, Jean. Telephone interview. February 25, 1989.

Waldo, Janet. Telephone interview. July 1, 1989.

Welker, Frank. Internet email interview. April 2003.

Welker, Frank. Telephone interview. July 22, 1989.

West, Billy. Telephone interview. January 24, 1995.

Winchell, Paul. Telephone interview. October 24, 1984.

Young, Doug. Telephone interview. June 18, 1995.

INDEX

357